The Social Worker's Guide to the Internet

Rey C. Martinez
New Mexico Highlands University

Carol Lea Clark
University of Texas at El Paso

Allyn and Bacon
Boston • London • Toronto • Sydney • Tokyo • Singapore

Editor-in-Chief, Social Sciences: Karen Hanson
Series Editorial Assistant: Alyssa Pratt
Marketing Manager: Jackie Aaron
Production Editor: Christopher H. Rawlings
Editorial-Production Service: Omegatype Typography, Inc.
Composition and Prepress Buyer: Linda Cox
Manufacturing Manager: Julie McNeill
Cover Administrator: Brian Gogolin
Electronic Composition: Omegatype Typography, Inc.

Copyright © 2001 by Allyn & Bacon
A Pearson Education Company
160 Gould Street
Needham Heights, MA 02494

Internet: www.abacon.com

Between the time Website information is gathered and published, some sites may have closed. Also, the transcription of URLs can result in unintended typographical errors. The publisher would appreciate notification where these occur so that they may be corrected in subsequent editions. Thank you.

Many of the designations used by manufacturers and sellers to distinguish their products are claimed as trademarks. Where those designations appear in this book, and Allyn and Bacon was aware of a trademark claim, the designations have been printed with an initial capital. Designations within quotation marks represent hypothetical products.

Library of Congress Cataloging-in-Publication Data

Martinez, Rey C.
    The social worker's guide to the Internet / Rey C. Martinez, Carol Lea Clark.
        p.   cm.
    Includes index.
    ISBN 0-205-29735-8
        1. Social service—Computer network resources.   2. Social service—Computer network resources—Directories.   3. Internet (Computer network)—Directories.   I. Powell, Carol Clark.   II. Title.
HV29.2 .M37 2001
025.06'36132—dc21

                                                                00-038114

Printed in the United States of America
10 9 8 7 6 5 4 3 2 1   05 04 03 02 01 00

Credits

In memory of Michael John Gonzalez
—Colleague and Friend

Contents

Preface

The Internet has unleashed tremendous potential resources for social workers. Useful Web sites, discussion groups, and databases abound, but unless the social worker knows how to find them on the Internet and use them, they might as well not exist. This text was written to address the need for a comprehensive guide to Internet resources specific to social work. The purpose of this text, therefore, is twofold: (1) to serve as an academic textbook at accredited schools of social work and (2) to guide the licensed professional attempting to access the Internet to find resources in service to others.

An Academic Textbook

There is a national trend toward developing computer-related courses in social work baccalaureate degree programs. *The Social Worker's Guide to the Internet* is a text designed to introduce students to various Internet protocols and resources. Chapters in the book explain, for example, how to use E-mail, how to participate in a social work Listserv or Usenet newsgroup, and how to conduct research on the Web. In addition, one chapter is devoted to covering the basics in Web page construction, enabling social work students to construct personal Web pages or pages for community agencies as part of their course work. The text also discusses special precautions unique to social work, such as the confidentiality of client files that are transmitted electronically.

A Guide for Professionals

This textbook provides nontechnical instructions for professionals on how to access resources on the Internet. Human service professionals may be able to access a university computer network, but they may be unfamiliar with how a network functions. Such professionals who may not have used the World Wide Web will benefit from instruction on how to use Web browsers. Once they begin investigating Web sites, they will become interested in reviews of Web sites by social work colleagues in other parts of the country and will be able to obtain lists of specific locations of various resources.

The computer systems available to human service professionals in some social agencies are often less than state-of-the-art. They may not have the capacity to reproduce the graphics, sound, and video of the World Wide Web or may not be equipped with Netscape Navigator or Internet Explorer. This text explains how professionals can use text-based Internet protocols such as Lynx, a Web browser, and Gopher, a precursor to HTTP, with their existing systems.

Text Organization and Content

Taking a quick glance at the chapter headings, you will note that the book is organized first by type of Internet communication, such as E-mail, Usenet newsgroups, World Wide Web, and so on. Each chapter offers nontechnical, step-by-step instruction on how to use the Internet protocol focused on in that chapter. The details of the demonstrations are tailored to social work; for example, a social work Listserv is used to demonstrate how to subscribe to a Listserv. Each chapter includes valuable and carefully selected research sites specifically for social workers. Chapter 8, "Social Work Web Tour," is devoted to Web sites created especially for social workers.

You will also learn about real people in the text. Work-related scenarios and reviews of Web pages have been obtained from social work students and professionals from all over the country.

Level of Internet Expertise Required

The Social Worker's Guide to the Internet does not assume that the reader has any prior knowledge of the Internet. It includes basic information about getting connected to the Internet and how to use applications such as Netscape Navigator and Internet Explorer to browse Web sites. Of course, readers who are already frequent users of the Internet can move quickly to the parts of the text that are customized for social work, such as Chapter 8, "Social Work Web Tour," which features outstanding Web sites authored by social work educators, researchers, and practitioners across the United States.

The authors hope that this book enables you to employ your time and energy efficiently in making use of the wide variety of resources on the Internet, and that you find, as they have, that the ever-expanding world of the Internet is a rewarding part of your personal and professional lives.

Acknowledgments

We would like to thank our colleagues for reviewing our manuscript, which provided us with invaluable assistance in writing this text.

Mike Breghoef	Rose Rael
Jose Castrellon	Rhaelynne Scherer
Timothy Davey	Dick Schoeck
Adrian Delgado	Tobi Ann Shane
Andy Dieppa	Lynn Shelton
John Fahey	Linda Tippett
Michael Fife	Gerald Vest
Bart Grossman	Robert Villa
Anna Peralta Hines	Karen Watanabe
Henry Ingle	

chapter 1

What Is the Internet and How Is It Applicable to Social Work?

Logging On—Social Workers Online

George Roybal, LICSW, in Phoenix, Arizona, uses the Internet to download information from GrantsNet. This site is provided by the U.S. Department of Health and Human Services and can be found at http://www.hhs.gov/progorg/grantsnet. External funding would enable George's agency to expand its services.

James Kennigiser is interested in taking a computer course from the School of Social Work at the University of Texas at Arlington. James, however, lives in Biloxi, Mississippi—an incredible commute! Fortunately, this course is offered over the Internet. If James decides to enroll, he won't even have to leave his city limits!

Steven Johnson, a substance abuse counselor in Tacoma, Washington, participates in a nicotine recovery Listserv. He respects the support provided by its members and has helped subscribe clients whom he feels would benefit from it as an adjunct to treatment.

In the past few years, social workers have witnessed the rapid development of new information technologies. In the same manner that previous technologies—radio, telephone, and computers—made their way into the profession, the Internet is rapidly changing the way social workers locate resources, exchange information, and network with colleagues.

It has been suggested in other contexts that social work has a long history of technology avoidance. Ironically, social work and the development of new technology are uniquely interwoven. Our professional predecessors, a group of socially conscious individuals living in the nineteenth century, advocated for improved living conditions and safer working conditions, and they raised money to open the first settlement houses. Toynbee Hall, for example, was opened in London in 1884. The primary objective of the settlement house was to alleviate exploitation and improve working conditions attributed to the Industrial Revolution. The Neighborhood Guild established itself after the Toynbee model. In this country we trace our professional lineage to the establishment of Hull House in 1889, the archetype for subsequent community developments in the United States. Ultimately, the national effort to alleviate poverty and to improve the social functioning of individuals, groups, and families formed the basis of the social work profession. Currently, new information technology is being embraced by a growing number of professionals who recognize its potential for networking internationally and promoting the profession globally. Next, you will be provided with a brief historical sketch of respected social work entities and you will be introduced to Web-based technology.

Major Professional Social Work Associations and Activities

The National Association of Social Workers (NASW)

The American Association of Social Workers was established in 1921, later becoming the National Association of Social Workers (NASW). Several entities formed the National Association of Social Workers in 1950: (1) the American Association of Group Workers, (2) the American Association of Community Organization, (3) the American Association of Psychiatric Social Workers, (4) the Association for the Study of Community Organization, and (5) the Social Work Research Group. The National Association of Social Workers, now firmly established in both number and prestige, has a presence on the World Wide Web at http://www.naswdc.org. NASW uses its Web site to unify the profession by providing hypertext links to current information related to practice; to maintain and disseminate social work licensing and professional certification materials; and to promote the continuous development of the social work profession. Visitors to the Web site will find the standards of professional practice and Social Work Code of Ethics easily accessible on-line.

The Council on Social Work Education (CSWE)

In 1952, a merger of three organizations with related functions resulted in the establishment of the Council on Social Work Education (CSWE). Whereas NASW establishes professional standards concerning the delivery of licensed services, CSWE is the national accrediting body for social work education. It is an authorized agent of the U.S. Department of Education and the National Commission on Accreditation.

Fortunately, due to the widening interest in on-line information, CSWE is conveniently accessible on the Internet at http://www.cswe.org. The Web site offers information on accreditation standards, taking each item individually and providing interpretation. Among other things, you will find an updated list of current publications at this Web site and an easy-to-use directory of hypertext links to accredited social work programs arranged by state.

Social Work and Technology Working Group

One of the most significant contributions to the sanctioning and further development of Internet resources for social workers has been the Social Work Education and Practice Information Technology conference hosted by the University of South Carolina's College of Social Work. Cosponsored by NASW and CSWE, this conference draws both practitioners and academicians to discuss the manner in which the Internet and new information technologies are being used in professional service. At the second annual conference thirty-six Web site managers met to discuss the establishment of standards for social work content on the Internet. Dr. Martinez, coauthor of this book, is a member of the leadership committee. At present, the dialog among members continues though the use of designated Listserv and Internet chat conversations. Look for exciting new developments as social work makes a greater presence on the Web. For those wishing to stay updated, these two protocols will be discussed in Chapters 4 and 6, respectively.

Social Workers on the Internet: A Natural Extension of Generalist Practice

Historically, social workers have relied on elaborate networks to facilitate information exchange long before the first computer. Networks are commonly used to communicate information, to link clients to needed resources, or to solicit the cooperation of community leaders toward the design and implementation of a specific course of action.

A computer network is not much different from earlier networks. It consists of a group of computers that exchange information over a cable or phone lines and use language and a set of commands that are recognizable by all component parts. Your office computer, if hooked up to a printer, is a rudimentary example of a network. The computer communicates with the printer via cabling, sending it bits of recognizable information. Computer networks may vary in magnitude and even how they communicate, but are essentially just devices exchanging information over common links. Just as a group of people can make up a network, computer networks may be modest (two or three workstations on a single network sharing a printer), or may consist of several interconnected networks (the Internet) and connect thousands of computers across international boundaries.

Historical Development of the Internet

The Internet is an elaborate labyrinth of computer networks based on a shared communications platform known as *Transmission Control Protocol/Internet Protocol,* or simply *TCP/IP.* TCP/IP allows computers to exchange information although they are located at different agencies, in different states, or possibly on different continents. Just as social workers in different parts of the country share a common value base, speak a similar jargon, and adhere to an agreed code of professional standards, every computer hooked to the Internet utilizes a common language and set of protocols. This coding system, TCP/IP, allows computers at different locations and utilizing different platforms (Mac or PC) to send and receive data from each other.

The Internet had its origin in a U.S. Department of Defense program called ARPANET (Advanced Research Projects Agency Network) established in 1969. The objective of ARPANET was to allow researchers to share data and to collaborate on projects from distant locations. The original uses of the Internet were for electronic mail and the transfer of electronic files using file transfer protocol (FTP).

By the end of 1969, both UCLA and Stanford possessed the technology to successfully route data over ARPANET. Operations were expanded to involve additional government agencies and a host of other academic institutions. This resulted in the steady development of the Internet for uses other than Department of Defense research. Three years later the general public was allowed its first E-mail demonstration at the U.S. Internet Computer Conference. By 1977, the ability to connect to files remotely via the protocol Telnet was the most popular use of the Internet, followed by development of Usenet newsgroups in 1979.

The National Science Foundation officially took over responsibility for developing the Internet in 1990, when the U.S. government decommissioned ARPANET. Five years later the National Science Foundation withdrew from this responsibility, thus allowing a consortium of commercial providers to assume management. Presently, millions of computers throughout the world are Internet-connected, some via commercial providers such as such as MCI, Sprint, and America Online, others utilizing a university or "Freenet" interface. Various types of connections will be discussed in Chapter 2.

Clarification of Terms

Social workers often confuse the terms *World Wide Web* and *Internet.* The Internet, as mentioned previously, is an elaborate labyrinth of networks that allows for the exchange of information using TCP/IP protocols. The World Wide Web, however, did not make its appearance until 1989 and is actually a collection of interlinked documents written in hypertext markup language (HTML). HTML tells the Web browser how to display the page, its contents, and where to locate other hyperlinks embedded in the text. The Internet is the larger entity; the Web is a method of displaying information and is entirely dependent on that elaborate system of computer networks known as "the Internet." Chapter 7 will explain how HTML works, Chapter 8 will feature Web sites of significance to the profession, and Chapter 9 will explain how to develop a social work Web page.

In sum, the Internet (or information superhighway) is made up of series of "main lines" that are maintained by a consortium of education and research networks and commercial providers since they assumed this responsibility from the National Science Foundation in 1995. By connecting to each other, these networks create an electronic network that crisscrosses the nation and extends to the rest of the world. Consequently, social workers can use the Internet to locate resources for clients or to obtain government documents on any number of social welfare policies. We literally have the world at our fingertips.

What Can the Internet Offer Social Work?

The Internet offers the generalist practitioner an easy and inexpensive alternative to telephone communication, mail correspondence, and faxes. Network communication tools (e.g., E-mail programs, electronic discussion groups, electronic bulletin boards) also make interactive consultation concerning social policy or client needs possible.

In addition to housing information pertinent to practice located on the World Wide Web, the Internet allows many people to edit and contribute to joint projects. Consider a multidisciplinary grant proposal involving a community agency, a school system, and a group of medical social workers. Despite the fact that the proposal contains data from three distinct sources, software tools enable images and text to be merged together across the common network. The following section will summarize the benefits to individual practice and the use of the Internet for undergraduate and graduate students of social work.

Benefits to the Individual in Practice

In addition to the purposes just mentioned, some social workers in the practice sector use the Internet to expand their funding base. Internet search engines such as Infoseek, Excite, and Lycos provide convenient ways to conduct advanced keyword searches in pursuit of grant opportunities. Another useful exercise would be to visit the Substance Abuse and Mental Health Services Administration Web site at http://www.samhsa.gov to find employment opportunities, contact information, and grant opportunities.

Some executive directors of agencies—like Richard Sordecelli, LMSW, of Traveler's Aid Society—read both the *Boston Globe* (http://www.globe.com) and *New York*

Times (http://www.nyt.com) over the Internet on a regular basis. It allows them to track social problems and learn how other metropolitan areas are attempting to address these concerns.

Legislative decisions that affect the delivery of social services at regional, state, or national levels are accessible over the Internet. Maria Wilson, a social worker in South Texas, uses a resource known as "Thomas," located at http://thomas.loc.gov. Thomas, the Web site for the U.S. Congress, provides Ms. Wilson with summaries of bills that affect services along the Texas–Mexico border and allows her to track their status. Thomas also provides reports from special interest committees. Fortunately, most government officials, including the president of the United States, have designated E-mail addresses. A directory of addresses is provided by Thomas for engaging in what students at Boston College under the supervision of Dr. John McNutt refer to as "electronic advocacy."

One of the greatest benefits for practitioners is the ability to visit institutions that govern the profession without leaving the convenience of home or office. The national headquarters of the National Association of Social Workers (NASW) in Washington, D.C., is readily accessible via keyboard—no parking hassles. With the proper equipment (to be discussed in Chapter 2), the Council on Social Work Education, the Department of Health and Human Services (DHHS), and the Bureau of Indian Affairs (BIF) are only seconds away. In the meantime, readers will be provided with a Web tour and summary of these and other sites of significance to the profession.

Many nonprofit agencies and even private clinicians are creating Web pages and using the Internet to advertise their location, hours of operation, phone number, and services provided. Most of these pages are well designed and offer a visually aesthetic, interactive format. Other benefits for individuals include the growing practice of keeping in touch with colleagues using E-mail and arranging for clinical supervision or consultation on-line. A number of highly specialized discussion groups and chat groups are in existence for social work administrators, medical social workers, school social workers, substance abuse counselors, and academic program directors. Some social workers report using E-mail to send clients reminders or to reschedule appointments.

It is possible for the practicing social worker to pick up a refresher course in research methodology or community organization without having to commute to campus or stand in long lines to register. Some social work departments—including those at Michigan State University, the University of Texas at Arlington, and the University of Utah—are offering courses over the Internet. One can anticipate further development in this area. In fact, soon you will be able to obtain continuing education units (CEUs) or work toward an advanced degree in social work at an hour when it is convenient.

Benefit to Social Work Students

Research by Hooyman and colleagues (1987) indicates that field agencies consider computer proficiency an important factor when hiring for new positions. Students with

Internet experience are able to conduct library research at sites all over the world. The World Wide Web makes accessing social work journals and databases easy. Commonly, these on-line sources and more and more printed materials (e.g., textbooks) include the E-mail addresses of the authors. This could allow for personal dialog with leading scholars and practitioners in the social work field.

Another benefit for students is access to on-line communities specifically for social work students—for example, the Social Work Café located at http://www.geocities.com/Heartland/4862/swcafe.html. At this site members can search links leading to academic resources or share common interests in on-line chat sessions. Other benefits might include downloading free shareware for students from the School of Social Work at the University of Texas at Arlington or visiting accredited social work programs from the directory maintained by the Council on Social Work Education.

Summary

This chapter has described how the Internet is applicable to social work. Both clinical and administrative examples were provided. Networking in social work has happened historically and has paralleled the development of new technologies. In the same manner as the Industrial Revolution forever changed the provision of services, the Internet is rapidly changing the way in which social workers obtain information, locate resources, and assist clients. Just as Mary Richman encouraged turn-of-the-century social workers to incorporate the telephone as a tool in practice, this book is designed to help you make use of the Internet whether you are a seasoned professional or a practitioner in training. *The Social Worker's Guide to the Internet* begins with person-to-person communication by E-mail and then moves to person-to-group interaction in Listservs and Usenet newsgroups. Next is a chapter on real time communication, followed by chapters on protocols used to access information such as the World Wide Web, File Transfer Protocol (FTP), and Telnet. Chapter 9 explains how social workers can have a presence on the Internet by developing their own Web pages.

Discussion Questions

1. The Internet has been defined as a "worldwide network of networks." What does that mean?
2. What was the original use of the Internet?
3. Identify four ways in which the profession can benefit from using the Internet.
4. How is the term *networking* as it applies to computer connectivity analogous to what professional social workers do?
5. List at least five ways in which one can learn more about using the Internet in social work practice.

Works Cited

Engel, R. J., & McMurtry, S. L. (1987). Computer content in education for human services administration. *Computers in Human Services, 2,* 51–62.

Gingerich, W. J., & Green, R. K. (1996). Information technology: How social work is going digital. In P. R. Raffoul & C. A. McNeece (Eds.), *Future issues for social work practice* (pp. 19–28). Boston: Allyn & Bacon.

Hooyman, N., Nurius, P., & Nicoll, A. (1987). A study of computer utilization in social work settings: Pursuing a collaborative agenda between the field and the academy. *HUSITA, 1,* 19–21.

LaMendola, W. F. (1985). The future of human service information technology: An essay on the number 42. *Computers in Human Services, 1,* 18–23.

Nurius, P. S., Hooyman, N. R., & Nicoll, A. E. (1988). The changing face of computer utilization in social work settings. *Journal of Social Work Education, 24*(2), 186–197.

Quarterman, J. S. (1990). *The matrix: Computer networks.* Bedford, MA: Digital Press.

Randall, N. (1996). *World Wide Web.* Indianapolis, IN: Sams.net.

Weinman, L., & Pirouz, R. (1997). *Web communication design.* Indianapolis, IN: New Riders.

Yaffe, J. (1998). *Quick guide to the Internet for social work.* Boston: Allyn & Bacon.

chapter 2

Connections to the Internet

Logging On—Social Workers Online

Jose Castrellon, Director of Catholic Social Services in El Paso, Texas, serves on a number of community advisory committees and has been instrumental in interagency coordination of services. He was recently chosen as Social Worker of the Year by the West Texas chapter of NASW.

Mr. Castrellon also serves as a field instructor for the Social Work Program. As at many other universities around the country, the program in El Paso has plans to get Mr. Castrellon and all its agency field instructors on-line. This is accomplished by providing them with a dial-in connection, a guest account, individual instruction, and an inexpensive modem (if needed). The goal is to enhance communication among classroom teachers, field instructors, and practicum students. Here Mr. Castrellon comments on his experience.

"I was simultaneously nervous and excited about this new opportunity. I had heard so much about the Internet from my oldest son that I was eager to log on. Supervising students who know more about the Internet than me was not a problem. In fact, I think it helped them realize that learning is a two-way street.

"With help, I found it fairly easy to connect to the Internet. I was relatively familiar with how modems work since our quarterly reports are already sent to the diocese office over the phone line. Having access to the university mail server, however, makes me feel more a part of what the Social Work Program is trying to accomplish. It's helpful for me as a field instructor to know what's being taught in the classroom so that I can reinforce its application in the field. If all the program's field instructors were on-line, practicum students would benefit from greater continuity.

"The BSW interns that I supervise work at the agency only two days a week, but I've found that using the university's E-mail system is a good way to stay in contact. It enables me to follow up with them during the week. I gather my thoughts, quickly compose a message, and transmit it. Also, as field instructors we've agreed to provide a minimum of one hour a week of direct supervision. Thoughts, ideas, and learning opportunities, however, constantly surround me—not just on Tuesdays and Thursdays, and not only at an agreed-upon hour.

"Another benefit of the dial-in connection I've been provided with is the access to journal articles. As agency director, I do not have the luxury of spending hours at the library. This way I don't have to. I can access the university's card catalog from my desk. There's greater opportunity to stay current with the literature since I'm not required to leave the office for long periods of time or neglect any of my other responsibilities. Staying informed, along with my clinical and administrative experiences, I believe is a way to make good supervision even better."

As a social work professional or student, you may have a connection provided for you. Many social work agencies have a local area network (LAN) connected to the Internet, and most colleges offer free or low-cost access to their students. In both cases, however, systems provided may not be state-of-the-art. If that is the case, you may still find the connection is adequate for your needs, though it may require you to use a fairly unsophisticated E-mail program and a text-only World Wide Web browser. Or, you may find that you want to supplement this connection by purchasing a more modern connection to use from home. It is a good idea to become familiar with the different levels of Internet connectivity available, so that you can decide what is best for your needs.

Types of Connections

Network Connection

Your social work setting or college computer lab may provide computers connected to a LAN utilizing an Ethernet or Token Ring connected to the Internet through a gateway, making it a fast and efficient way to utilize Internet programs. You may find a Web browser such as Internet Explorer or Netscape Navigator already installed on your computer as well as E-mail and other useful programs. These programs may be accessed by clicking on an icon or using the Start menu.

Dial-in Network Connection

Serial Line Internet Protocol (SLIP) or Point-to-Point (PPP) connections allow sophisticated Internet programs to be installed on individual home or work-site computers. You then connect to your Internet service provider (ISP) via modem and run the programs as you need them. ISPs fall into several general types:

- *College or university connections.* As a student, your university may provide access to you free or at a low cost. If your university offers this type of connection, it will also provide instructions on how to install programs and access the system.
- *Free-nets.* Some geographic areas are served by free-nets, publicly funded networks that may offer access to individuals who register. They may also offer users a range of content such as on-line homework help and specialized discussion forums. In some cases, access is limited to short periods such as one hour per session.
- *Commercial providers.* America Online and other national providers offer Internet access along with additional content for their subscribers. These self-contained providers offer services maintained by the vendor and usually require installation of software they have developed to navigate their computer system. These providers charge a fee, either a flat monthly or a per-hour charge.
- *No-frills ISPs.* These local, regional, or national providers offer only the Internet connection without additional content. These are often lower cost than commercial providers.
- *Free ISPs.* In some areas ISPs offer free access to the Internet as part of a computer purchase package or in exchange for having part of your computer screen display advertisements.

Cable Connection

In some areas the cable company offers high-speed Internet access for a monthly fee. Most also offer some specialized content for their users similar to what America Online and other commercial providers offer. The service may be more expensive than modem-based services, but Internet use does not tie up your telephone line.

Terminal Access

A less sophisticated Internet access is offered though terminal access connected to a time-sharing system. These systems generally offer text-only access to the Internet and may have a shell system that provides menu access to programs. Or there may be a "naked prompt" that requires knowledge of commands to operate the system. In some settings, users are also able to access a time-sharing system when connecting off-site via modem.

Summary

The purpose of this chapter has been to discuss different types of Internet connections (e.g., network, dial-in, cable) as well as free-nets and no-frills ISPs. Bear in mind that most new computers come with sign-up programs for America Online (AOL) and other services. One of the major advantages of using sign-up programs (usually located on the desktop) is that they automatically take care of all communications configurations required in your computer. This can take away some of the frustration if you are a new user.

Discussion Questions

1. Explain two common ways for social work practitioners to connect to the Internet.
2. What are a dial-in network connection's potential advantages for social work field instructors?
3. Explain the significance of the term *SLIP.*
4. The electronic card catalog at your local library is an example of a "terminal access" connection. How does this differ from a point-to-point (PPP) connection?
5. Identify four commercial Internet providers in your community. What features would make one provider superior to another?

chapter 3

Electronic Mail

Logging On—Social Workers Online

Karen Watanabe, LMSW, lives in Honolulu, Hawaii. She works for a local mental health agency on Oahu, where she carries a caseload of twenty-two individuals and fifteen client families. Karen relies on E-mail for both consultation and a time-management tool.

"One of the first things I do before leaving the house for work is to check my E-mail messages. If staff meetings get rescheduled or other appointments are canceled, I suddenly have additional time for such tasks as record keeping, phone calls, or a follow-up home visit or two. I try to use my time as efficiently as possible.

"I'm currently using a local Internet service provider, and I highly recommend shopping around for the best deal. Find a service provider that offers good customer service. I found out the hard way how important that is! Some Internet providers even offer server space for their customers to develop a personal or professional Web page. I haven't pursued that option, but I do use E-mail regularly.

"At work I use my E-mail account for issues billing and referral. If I have a client who needs an evaluation, for example, I notify the billing office so that an appropriate referral can be made. Client status is constantly changing—some being closed and new referrals being added. I've found that E-mail is a good way to stay on top of it all, and that communication about individual cases can take place without violating client confidentiality. Best of all, I appreciate being able to send and receive messages from numerous individuals and being able to respond without having to retype my message. I've also made it my practice to print copies of client-related correspondence for the file before deleting sent mail.

"Correspondence also includes information from my colleagues on the mainland about upcoming social work conferences and peer consultation about resources not available in Hawaii."

Conceptually, electronic mail (E-mail) is not much different from regular mail; you need a message, an address, and, of course, a reliable carrier. The difference is that E-mail messages are broken down into small data called packets and each packet travels independently to the designated address. It's as if each page of a letter was mailed separately. Data packets weave their way through the Internet, each following a different route, passed from server to server, until they reach their established destination. It's not surprising that packets arrive out of order and often at different times. Once all packets have arrived, however, they are reassembled into their original form and are available for viewing. This procedure occurs quickly because very little bandwidth is required. Sometimes, however, an entire message can be held up because one data packet is still someplace in cyberspace. Usually, however, this entire process, traveling 3,000 miles or more, takes less than 60 seconds.

E-Mail Defined

Electronic mail allows one user to send a message to another over the Internet. This is an incredibly popular use of the Internet. Some people utilize it exclusively, never exploring any of the other uses of the worldwide computer network. In social work, individuals employ E-mail to network with colleagues in other cities. Students use it to ask instructors questions and to share information with each other. Another major use of E-mail is to send one message to a group of people. This can be accomplished by creating personal mailing lists in your E-mail program. Or you can subscribe to Listservs, on-line discussion groups discussed in Chapter 4.

An electronic mail message is similar to a letter or memo. You write a message, with the casualness or formality and length determined by your occasion for writing. As with a memo, you give your message a subject line, so your recipient can tell at a glance what is the purpose of your message. As with a letter, you designate a delivery address. Then you send your message. Instead of dropping it into an interoffice mailbox, however, you click on a **Send** button (or give a send command). Your message is sent from your computer to your Internet provider, then to the Internet, and finally to your recipient's Internet provider to wait until your recipient checks his or her mailbox.

You really don't need to understand how the worldwide E-mail system works in any detail. You need to understand only the anatomy of an E-mail address (which we shall discuss soon) and the workings of the particular E-mail program you are utilizing. It is helpful to understand that the individuals you communicate with may have different E-mail programs that may be either more or less sophisticated than yours. The sophistication of the programs may affect your ability to use features such as bold or italic type or to send images or other documents as attachments. If you have any type of E-mail program and an Internet connection, though, you can send messages to anyone else who has E-mail and an Internet connection. You need only that person's E-mail address.

Anatomy of an E-mail Address

A typical E-mail address has a log-in name (often a contracted version of the individual's real name or a nickname chosen by the person), followed by an @ symbol, standing for "at." Then comes the address for the E-mail system where the individual receives his or her E-mail. The address might look like this if you were John Smith who has an account with X university:

jsmith@xuniversity.edu

If the individual has an account on a commercial server rather than a university, the address might end in ".net" or ".com." An address might be longer or configured somewhat differently, but all have the log-in name (or sometimes numbers) first and the name of the system following the @ symbol.

Demonstrating Netscape Mail

Netscape Communicator has a built-in mail program that allows you to read and send mail without leaving your browser. From the Netscape main screen, go to the Communicator pull-down menu displayed in Figure 3.1, and select **Messenger** Mailbox. You will see a screen similar to the one in Figure 3.2.

Near the top of your screen are a series of buttons. Click on **Get Msg** to obtain your messages. You mail server may prompt you for a password, and then it will display a list of your incoming messages in the box below. To the left are listed the subject lines of the messages, then the sender, and finally the date and time the message was sent. Click on the subject of a message once to highlight it, and it will be displayed in the box at the bottom of the screen. In that box, the subject line, date, and sender are repeated, along with your E-mail address as recipient. Below this header appears the message.

If you would like to save your message, you can go to the **File** pull-down menu and select **New Folder.** You will be prompted to give the folder a name, and then the folder will be filed under **Inbox.** To save your message in this folder, go to the **File** pull-down menu and select the name of the folder. Later, if you want to access your

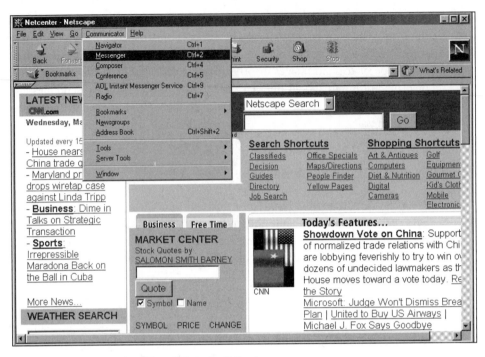

FIGURE 3.1   Accessing Netscape's Mail Feature

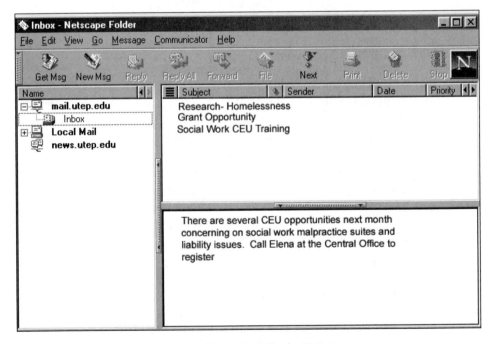

FIGURE 3.2   Obtaining Messages from the Inbox—Netscape

saved messages, you can select your folder name from the menu under **Inbox** in the small rectangular box just under the **Get Msg** button. From this same menu you can also select **Sent,** and you will see a list of your sent messages.

Creating Messages in Netscape Mail

To compose a message, click on New Msg or Reply, and you will receive a box (Figure 3.3) where you can write your text.

Enter your recipient's E-mail address on the To line and put your subject in the box provided. Your message goes in the large box at the bottom of the screen. You have options of changing your type size and making words bold or italic. If you do this, however, remember that your recipient must have a mail program that will display these features.

If you want to attach a file, just click on the **Attach** button, and you can browse for your file on your hard drive or floppy disk.

Demonstrating Internet Explorer Mail

Internet Explorer allows you to choose a mail client with which you can receive and send mail without leaving your browser. The programs, including Microsoft Exchange and Outlook Express, offer the same basic features. Access your mail client by clicking

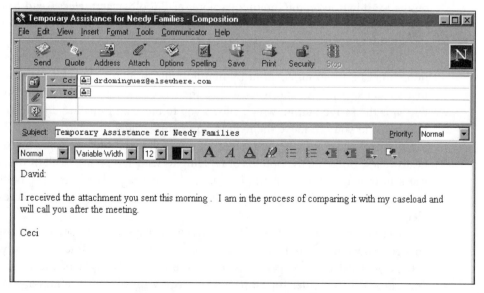

FIGURE 3.3   Composing a Message Using Netscape Mail

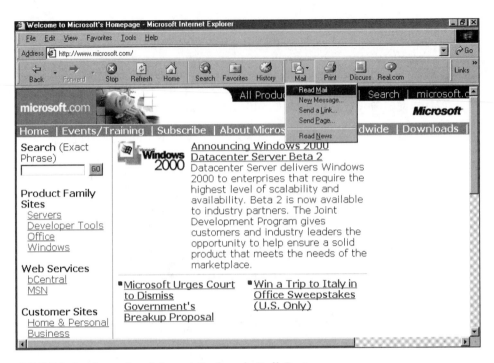

FIGURE 3.4   Accessing Internet Explorer's Mail Feature

on the **Mail** button on the Internet Explorer mail toolbar, and select **Read Mail.** (See Figure 3.4.) If you are using Microsoft Exchange, you will see a screen similar to the one in Figure 3.5.

Near the top of the screen is a menu bar of buttons that gives you a number of options. You can, for example, print by highlighting an item and clicking on the button that looks like a printer and is located to the left of the menu bar. Next to the **Print** button is the **Move** button, which allows you to move an E-mail to a folder. Click on this icon and you can move the item to an existing folder or create a folder. The button that looks like an X is the **Delete** button. Following that are three buttons with heads. These offer you the options of replying to sender, replying to all (if the message was sent to multiple people), and forwarding the message. The arrow key buttons enable you to move easily to the next or previous message. The last button accesses the Help screens.

The box on the left side of your screen displays your personal Microsoft Exchange folders. If **Inbox** is not already selected, click on that folder so that you will display your list of incoming messages in the box to the right of the screen. Later, you can select the folder for **Sent Items** if you want to review a message you have already mailed.

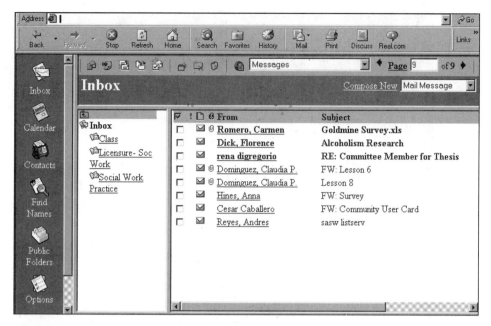

FIGURE 3.5   Viewing Microsoft's Inbox

The list of Inbox messages gives the name of the person sending the message, the subject line, and the date and time received. If you want to read a message, double click on it, and the text will be displayed in a box like the one in Figure 3.6. Microsoft Exchange lists the person the E-mail is from, the date and time sent, the addressee, and the subject line.

Creating and Sending Messages

If you want to send a message using Microsoft Exchange, you have several options. If you are reading a message or have highlighted a message, you can click on the **Reply** button (the one that looks like a head with an arrow pointing to the left) or go to the **Compose** pull-down menu and select **New Message.** If you are at the main screen for Microsoft Exchange, you can also click on a button that looks like an envelope. You will see a screen similar to the one in Figure 3.7 where you can enter the address of the person to receive the message, the subject, and addresses of others to receive copies of your message. The box below is for the main text of your message.

If you want to attach files to your message, place your cursor where you want to place the attached file. Then go to the **Insert** pull-down menu and select **File.** You will be provided a dialog box that enables you to browse your hard drive or floppy disk for the file.

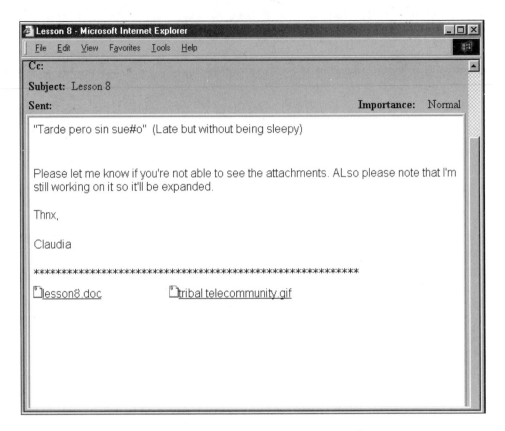

FIGURE 3.6   Viewing a Message Using Internet Explorer Mail

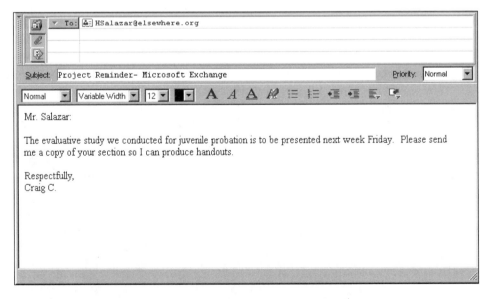

FIGURE 3.7   Composing a Message Using Microsoft Exchange

After you have completed your message, you can use the spell check included under **Tools** and then click on the **Envelope** button to send your message.

Demonstrating Pine E-Mail

Pine is the E-mail program used at many institutions or colleges that do not offer a PPP or SLIP connection. It is generally accessed from the institution's network or from home via a modem. Unlike Netscape or Internet Explorer mail programs, Pine does not offer many new features of E-mail such as variable type faces and sizes or images. You can attach files with Pine, however, so you can send documents or image files as attachments.

Take a look at the opening screen in Figure 3.8. Notice that Pine is menu-driven, with hot-key commands.

Use your arrow keys (not your mouse) to move the highlighting to the option you want to select such as **Help** or **Compose Message;** then press **Enter.** You can also use Pine's hot-key feature, which allows you, for example, to press **C** to select **Compose Message.**

Reading Mail in Pine

If you want to read your incoming mail, select **Folder List** and press **Enter.** You will see a screen where your folders appear. Until you have created folders, the only one

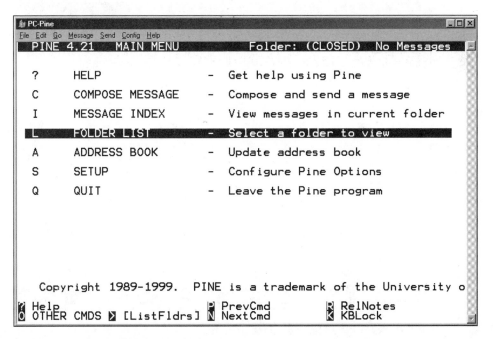

FIGURE 3.8   Pine Mail Main Page

listed will be **Inbox.** Select it, and you will see a list of your incoming E-mail messages. Using the arrow keys, highlight the one you want to read and press enter. You will see your E-mail message. If the message has a **+** sign in front, it is a personal message rather than one sent from a mailing list or Listserv discussion group.

The message header gives you the date and time it was sent, the address it was sent to, the person addressed, and the subject. Below the header is the message itself. Across the bottom of the page are hot-key commands (such as **R** for **Reply** or **M** for **Mail Menu**) that you can select.

Composing Messages in Pine

If you want to send a new message, select **Reply** (if you are reading a message). You can also choose **Compose Message** from Pine's opening menu, and you will see a screen similar to Figure 3.9 that displays a message ready to mail.

Note that Pine provides a memo-type header with places indicated to type your addressee's E-mail address, addresses of those to receive copies, and subject line. You can also send attachments by indicating the name and location of the file in the attachment line. The menu across the bottom of the screen gives commands that you activate by using the control key plus the hot-key symbol indicated. If you want to spell check, for example, the command is **Control-T.** Depending on where the cursor is in

FIGURE 3.9   Pine Mail Compose Screen

the page, the menus across the bottom of the screen change, offering you appropriate options.

Pine Folders

Pine allows you to set up a system of folders to organize your saved messages. If you are reading a message you want to save, simply press the **S** hot key. Pine will ask you the name of the folder, and you supply it. If the folder is not already created, Pine will prompt you to create it. Later, if you want to retrieve a saved message, just select the folder from your folder index (which you can reach from the main menu).

FREE E-MAIL RESOURCES ON THE INTERNET

A number of free Web-based E-mail resources are available on the Internet. Because messages are stored on the Web, they can be accessed from your office, a public library, a school computer lab, or any other site with a Web connection. This is an extremely helpful feature for workers whose job requires extensive travel or who don't own a personal computer. Here is a brief list of some of the top free mail service providers.

CollegeClub
Free E-mail for college students
http://www.collegeclub.com/members

EMUmail
Access to your current POP account
    from anywhere
http://emumail.net/emumail.fcgi

FiveStar Communications
Specializing in corporate intranet
    and Internet Services
http://www.5star.net/demos.html
Free E-mail, excellent features

FreeStamp
User friendly, reliable
http://www.freestamp.com

GeoCities
Free E-mail, guestbooks, counters
http://www.geocities.com/Heartland/
    Meadows/5674/email.html

LatinoLinkMail!
Free E-mail of interest to Latinos and Hispanics
http://mail.latino.com

Mail.EntrepreneurMag.Com
Free E-mail for small businesses
sponsored by Entrepreneur Mag.Com
http://mail.entrepreneurmag.com

MailCity
Free Web-based E-mail account
http://www.mailcity.com

Netaddress
http://mail.netaddress.com

RocketMail
Fast, intuitive, and popular
http://www.rocketmail.com

(continued)

continued

HotMail
Free Web-based E-mail from Microsoft
http://www.hotmail.com

Visto
Free E-mail, calendar, and file sharing
http://www.visto.com/welcome/zdnet.html

Jaydemail
Free, private, Web-based E-mail accounts
http://www.jaydemail.com

WebCentral
Free, easily accessible E-mail services
http://www.sonic.net/webcentral/email.html

Juno
Free E-mail service for anyone with
     access to a personal computer
     and a modem
http://www.juno.com

Yahoo! Mail
Free E-mail includes optional calendar
     reminders
http://mail.yahoo.com

To find additional providers not mentioned here, conduct a keyword search using the term *free E-mail* on the World Wide Web. For learning how to conduct searches on the Web, consult Chapter 7.

Summary

This chapter defines electronic mail and offers insight to the anatomy of messages. This chapter focuses on Netscape Mail, Internet Explorer Mail, and a popular text-only protocol, Pine. The manner in which messages are composed and the method of establishing an address book vary, but their principles are all the same. As stated in the vignette, one of the advantages of electronic mail is that it offers social workers the ability to send one message to several people simultaneously. Fortunately, there are several E-mail resources available for free over the Internet. A current listing has been provided.

Discussion Questions

1. List five ways that E-mail can be useful in social work practice.
2. E-mail not a perfect replacement for telephone calls because messages, especially playful sarcasm, might be misinterpreted. What can the person composing the message do to prevent this from happening?
3. Give five examples of domain names.
4. Briefly explain how Web-based mail programs differ from Pine.

chapter 4

Internet Discussion Groups

Logging On—Social Workers Online

Dr. Bart Grossman has served as the director of field education for the past twelve years at the School of Social Welfare at the University of California, Berkeley. As he and colleagues work to provide a quality field experience for graduate students, their goal is to help students integrate knowledge, skills, and social work values into professional practice. He subscribes to a Listserv for social workers on the Internet. Dr. Grossman describes how this tool has been of benefit to him professionally.

"I am amazed at the commonalities shared among social workers, especially those of us involved in field instruction. I subscribed to the Social Work Field Listserv a few years ago and really enjoy discussing topics that are so near and dear to my heart. A real sense of on-line community exists. Many of us know each other from social work conferences, but there are always new members—some social work students and others who are just curious about the subject.

"Here's how it works. When a member raises an issue, say, about field supervision, and it's something we've got a pretty good handle on here at Berkeley, I'm able to share that experience with the person. Others also subscribed can support what's been said, refute it, or simply submit a new topic to the group. However, just as often as I provide guidance, I'm the recipient of lots of good ideas and solutions proposed by other members. I like being able to stay connected to individuals with similar social work interests as mine. I especially like being able to get feedback on an idea or other people's opinions on policy issues that affect the field without having to wait to see them at a conference next year."

Countless social workers have discovered the Internet as an efficient way to distribute information to colleagues through the use of automatic mail lists. These are often referred to as *Listservs* although other automated programs such as Listproc rather than Listserv may be used. Listservs provide a means to communicate with individuals who share common interests through the exchange of electronic messages sent to the mailboxes of everyone who has subscribed. Before identifying specific Listservs for social workers and telling how to subscribe, first let's consider how Listservs differ from address books and from Usenet Newsgroups. Usenet Newsgroups are discussed in Chapter 5.

Address book. As discussed in Chapter 3, most E-mail programs offer a feature that allows the user to store the addresses of individuals with whom correspondence often occurs. Using this feature the user has an opportunity to use the person's first name, or perhaps a nickname, rather than having to remember long, cumbersome addresses such as dhaynes@mail.utexas.edu, cfigley@garnet.mail.fsu.edu, or rmartinez_5@hotmail.com. Another useful feature of address books (and something that gets them confused with a Listserv) is that a user can include the E-mail addresses of several individuals so that one message can be sent to an entire group of people. Because the recipients of the message have the option of replying to the person who originated the message or to all recipients, in this way the standard "address book feature" is similar to a Listserv. Listservs, however, are much more extensive.

Usenet newsgroup. Newsgroups (which are discussed in Chapter 5) provide a mechanism whereby mail messages may be "posted" to a particular site, thus allowing hundreds or thousands of people to view and respond. In contrast, Listservs are "subscribed to" by social workers and other individuals in that specific topic or issues (i.e., addiction counseling competencies, field supervision, social work curriculum development, child advocacy), and correspondence comes to your mailbox.

Finding the good fit between your social work interests and an existing Listserv is important. Once you've accomplished that, it is equally necessary to know the mechanics of how to properly subscribe, post messages, and reply to others. Knowing the acceptable standards of conduct is likewise essential. This chapter will address these issues among other salient topics concerning Listservs.

How to Subscribe

Whenever possible it's a good idea to get information about the Listserv before actually subscribing. In most cases this can be accomplished by sending the command **Info** to the administrative address of the Listserv. The administrative address to the Social

Workers of Colorado (SWCO) list, for example, is listserv@yuma.acns.colostate.edu. Sending a request for information will return the following description:

> The Social Workers of Colorado list (SWCO) is for practicing social workers, social work educators and researchers, social work students and other interested parties. Although this list has been primarily set up for those individuals in the state of Colorado, anybody is encouraged to subscribe. This list is an unmoderated list, and should provide a forum for discussions related to our field.

Not all Listserv groups provide this feature and those that do offer more detail than others. For example, the administrative address to the HIV–AIDS Social Work Education Canadian Network (SWEAIDS-NET) is LISTSERV@morgan.ucs.mun.ca. Sending a request for information will yield the following results:

> The SWEAIDS-NET mailing list is part of the HIV/AIDS Social Work Education Canadian Network, established to provide social work educators, field instructors, students and trainers a forum to share and exchange information concerning teaching/learning in social work and HIV/AIDS.
>
> The purpose of the list is to provide a forum for the professional discussion of all aspects of HIV/AIDS as it relates to Social Work Education, primarily within the Canadian context. This list is a place where social work educators, students, field instructors and trainers from different theoretical orientations and experiences can discuss all issues relevant to curriculum development and other aspects of social work education in the area of HIV/AIDS. The list also provides a network for the continuous sharing of ideas about research and demonstration projects and other issues related to HIV/AIDS in social work. The list is closed (subscription through list moderator) and unmoderated (messages sent to list will not be screened).
>
> If you have any questions about the HIV/AIDS Social Work Education Canadian Network or about the SWEAIDS-NET mailing list, you may email them to William Rowe D.S.W., sweaids@plato.ucs.mun.ca, School of Social Work, Memorial University of Newfoundland, St. John's, NF, A1C 5S7 (709)737–8165.

To subscribe, simply compose an E-mail message to the administrative address. Note that Listservs have two different addresses: the administrative address where you send automated commands such as **Subscribe** and another that you use to actually post messages. Be sure to leave the subject line of your message blank, unless instructed differently. Although syntaxes may differ slightly, most commands to subscribe are something like **subscribe listname [Yourfirst-name] [Yourlast-name].** This command should appear in the body of the message and be E-mailed to the designated address. On completion of this step, you will receive one of three types of messages.

■ *No list found.* Your system will send you this type of error message when the Listserv is no longer active or has changed its location, when you've made a typing error, or when your command syntax is incorrect. Check your source and try again.

■ *Subscription prohibited.* In some cases you may receive a message stating that you were not allowed to subscribe. Some social work Listservs carefully monitor whom they allow to participate in an attempt to ensure a high degree of professionalism. The Association of Oncology Social Workers (AOSW), for example, limits access to its new Listserv to members. A high degree of consultation and collaboration takes place on this Listserv, which necessarily restricts it from public access. Many other social work Listservs, however, will provide you with the name of a contact person. If it turns out that your request is professional rather than "recreational," you're likely to be added to the list.

■ *Welcome message.* Most of the time, you'll receive a message stating that your name was successfully added to the list. We advise that you save all information initially sent to you as a new member of the Listserv. The welcome message will contain a summary of this information including how to unsubscribe. Normally the same steps taken to subscribe to the Listserv are repeated with the exception of command **Unsubscribe** in place of **Subcribe** (e.g., **unsubscribe listname [Yourfirst-name] [Yourlast-name]**). If for some reason you inadvertently delete the welcome message, sending a message to the administrative address with the command **Help** will usually return a full list of recognized commands.

Avoid Clutter and Confusion

Active Listservs have the propensity to become overwhelming and may fill your inbox to its capacity. Make sure you know how to delete messages and how to organize file folders to retain those messages still desired. (See Chapter 3.) Bear in mind that the account you've been provided allows only limited disk space. Be sure you know how to unsubscribe if necessary. It's a good idea to unsubscribe or temporarily suspend incoming Listserv messages if you're going away for a long time. This can save tremendous headaches. See the welcome message for directions.

Where to Find Listservs

There are several excellent resources for looking up Listservs of interest to social workers. A popular mailing list directory such as Liszt (located at http://www.liszt.com) is a good place to start. Liszt maintains a directory of 90,095 mailing lists. This can be overwhelming. Narrowing your search by typing the keyword *social-work* yields fifty-seven possible entries. This is much more manageable.

Here is a list of popular Listserv directories like Liszt with their respective Universal Resource Locators (URLs):

COMMONLY USED LISTSERV SEARCH DIRECTORIES	
CataList Catalog of Listserv lists Over 10,000 public Listservs L-Soft International, Inc.	http://www.lsoft.com/lists/listref.html
L-Soft International Search engine for Listservs L-Soft International, Inc.	http://www.listserv.net/lists/list_q.html
Liszt The Liszt global directory of electronic lists	http://www.liszt.com/intro.html
Publicly Accessible Mailing Lists Over 63,000 mailing lists Stephanie and Peter da Silva	http://www.neosoft.com/internet/paml/
Search the List of Lists One of the largest directories on the Internet-Vivian Neou	http://catalog.com/vivian/ interest-group-search.html
Tile.net Global directory of electronic lists Tile.net, Inc.	http://tile.net/listserv/

Fortunately, there are several social work sites that have done the homework for you. The Association of Baccalaureate Social Work Program Directors (BPD) Web site maintained by Marshall Smith at the Rochester Institute of Technology is one such site that has collected numerous Listservs of interest to social workers. Go to http://www.rit.edu/~694www/lists.htm and scroll down until you find a Listserv topic that piques your interest. As you surf the Web you will undoubtedly find many others like the following examples.

SOCIAL WORK LISTSERV RESOURCES ON THE INTERNET	
Listserv Source and Administrator	**Listserv Address**
Allyn & Bacon Publishers Needham Heights, Massachusetts	http://www.abacon.com/popple/ list.html
Ashland University School of Social Work Ashland, Ohio	http://www.ashland.edu/~bweiss/ lsocwrk.html#list

(continued)

continued	
Listserv Source and Administrator	**Listserv Address**
Association of Baccalaureate Social Work Program Directors Rochester Institute of Technology Marshall Smith	http://www.rit.edu/~694www/lists.htm
Colorado State University Fort Collins, Colorado Linda Tippett	http://www.colostate.edu/Depts/ SocWork/lists.html
Social Work Access Network University of South Carolina College of Social Work Michael White	http://www.sc.edu/swan/cgi-bin/swan_ lists.shtml
Social Work Café Tobi Shane	http://www.geocities.com/Heartland/ 4862/maillist.html
University of Sydney New South Wales, Austrialia	http://www.library.usyd.edu.au/Guides/ SocialWork/#listservs
American Counseling Association Listservs for Counselors	http://www.counseling.org/resources/ listservs.htm

▊ Subscription Demonstrations

Since we've mentioned the BPD Listserv Resource, let's demonstrate how to subscribe using a standard Pine account and then retrace this procedure using a Web browser such as Netscape Navigator or Microsoft's Internet Explorer. By going to the Web address of the Association of Baccalaureate Social Work Program Directors just indicated, you will be connected to a screen that looks like Figure 4.1. Here you can find information about many interesting Listservs.

UNIX-BASED SUBSCRIPTION DEMONSTRATION.   Suppose I wanted to subscribe to the General Social Work List, SOCWORK, that I found listed on the BPD Web page. Following the instructions provided, I would send a message to the administrative address, in this case majordomo@uwrf.edu, a server located at the University of Wisconsin, River Falls. Before requesting to be added, however, I would familiarize myself with the Listserv by sending the command **Info** [name of listserv] to the administrative address. If I were using a Pine account, it would look like Figure 4.2.

Notice that nothing was put in the subject line. This is because the command **Info** is sent to a computer with preprogrammed instructions on how to process this and other commands. There isn't actually anyone sorting the messages and reading their contents. It is appropriate to leave the subject line blank under these circumstances.

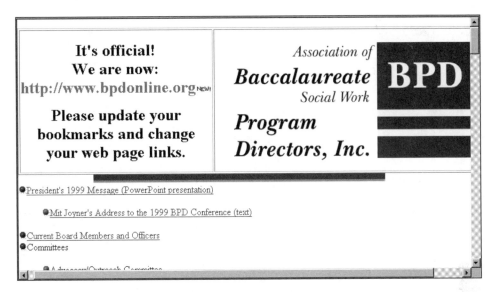

FIGURE 4.1 Association of Baccalaureate Social Work Program Directors Homepage

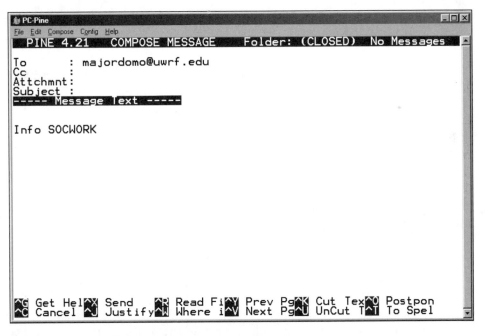

FIGURE 4.2 Using the Info Command in Pine

Executing the **Info** command will send information I need to determine whether the Listserv and my professional interests are a good fit. It turns out that SOCWORK is the oldest general social work discussion group for social workers, according to the information sent to me almost instantly. It is an open, unmoderated resource that will

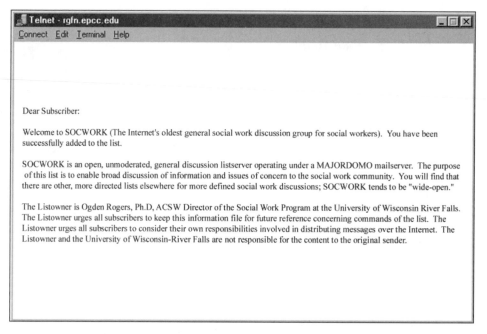

FIGURE 4.3   A Listserv's Welcome Message

enable me to dialog with others with similar interests. Its stated purpose, according to the information, is to "enable broad discussion of information and issues of concern to the social work community." Perfect! Now how do I subscribe?

All I must do to become a member of the SOCWORK Listserv is to send a message to the administrative address, majordomo@uwrf.edu, with the command **Subscribe SOCWORK Rey Martinez** in the body.

If all the steps are followed correctly, I should receive a message welcoming me as a new member of the Listserv. This presupposes that I did not make any typing errors and that the administrative address has not changed, which happens often on the Internet. (See Figure 4.3.)

WEB BROWSER SUBSCRIPTION DEMONSTRATION.   Let's repeat the same steps using a Web browser. You probably noticed that the BPD provides hot links to the administrative addresses for various discussion groups. That means I can simply click on the address and compose a message according to the instructions provided. Depending on where you are working from, it may be necessary to establish your identity before sending outgoing mail. Let's do that first. This can be accomplished by selecting Edit from the menu bar, scrolling down to the bottom, and selecting the item that says "Preferences." By clicking on **Preferences** I'll be taken to a screen that looks like Figure 4.4.

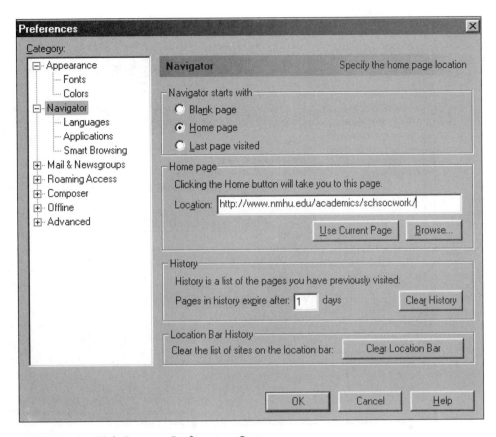

FIGURE 4.4　Web Browser Preferences Screen

From here, since you want to compose a message, select the Mail folder. You will find a number of suboptions in this folder. Right now, we're looking to establish our identity so that program will allow us to send outgoing mail. If you are using a home or office computer, you won't need to do this if you are using the browser as your mail processor. In other situations you may click on the Identity option to be provided with a dialog box that looks like Figure 4.5.

Enter your name and E-mail address in the spaces provided. Now we're ready to subscribe. Click on the hot link majordomo@uwrf.edu on the BPD Web page. It will take you to a dialog box where you can compose a message. In the body of the message I type the command **Subscribe** and my first and last names. Subscribing to the SOCWORK Listserv in this manner will look like Figure 4.6.

That's it! Unless you're using a home or office computer, it's probably a good idea to remove your name and E-mail address from the identity fields, especially if you're working in a computer lab or other setting in which many people use the same computer.

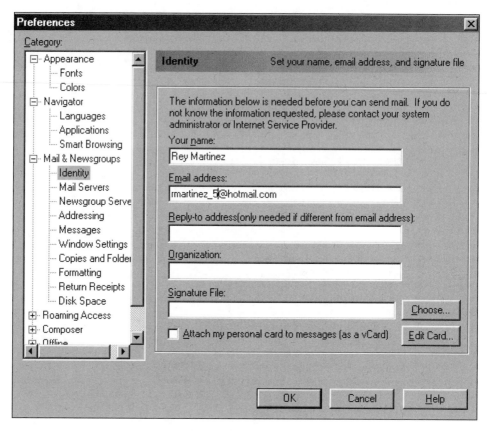

FIGURE 4.5   Web Browser Identity Dialog Box

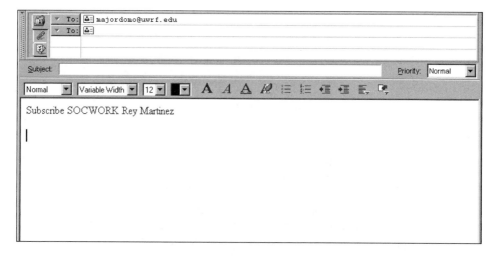

FIGURE 4.6   Subscribing to a Listserv

INTERVIEW WITH GERRY VEST

Gerry Vest is a social worker in private practice. Although recently retired from New Mexico State University (NMSU), he still serves as the SW Field Listserv Webmaster.

"A number of us involved in social work field instruction realized several years ago that we need each other. There are common issues that can be discovered, shared, and resolved. My first attempt was to design an electronic bulletin board. This addressed some of the needs initially, but was difficult to access and had many shortcomings. The current social work Listserv has been in existence for three years and is subscribed to by about 270 national and international participants. Most members are field coordinators or field instructors, but no one is screened out.

"As social workers we value networking. A lot of good ideas have been shared as a result of the Listserv and some of them have benefited the Social Work Department at NMSU directly. One time, for example, I was asked to devise a method of evaluating student field practicum outcomes. I put together a quick survey and sent it to the Listserv. In no time at all roughly forty schools had replied and it turned out that the majority of them had a successful approach already implemented. The consultation was invaluable. It also made it easier to justify our position when the administration required an explanation for the proposed changes."

If not, someone else could send E-mail messages to whomever they choose on your behalf. If necessary, take precautions by deleting your information from the mail preference page.

Listserv Summaries

To get you started, here's a brief summary of some of the Listservs you can expect to find at the site maintained by Linda Tippett in the Social Work Department at Colorado State University (http://www.colostate.edu/Dept/SocWork/lists.html). The following summaries are based on those she has compiled.

List: Child Abuse Research
List address: listproc@cornell.edu
Command: subscribe child-maltreatment-research [first-name] [last-name]

This Listserv is dedicated to discussing child abuse and related forms of child maltreatment from a research perspective. This includes sharing requests for proposals and occasional discussions of empirical studies recently published. From the nature of discussions it appears that professionals (e.g., agency administrators, program evaluators) and human service students needing guidance to complete an assignment are the most active participants. A social worker from Kansas recently raised the question, "How can I measure my own treatment outcomes?" A number of members provided consultation.

List: Child Welfare
List address: owner-childwelfare@ListService.net
Command: Subscribe

This Listerv is most appropriate for individuals who already possess a strong background in child welfare. Issues debated here are poignant and timely, ranging from the questionable benefit of court-appointed special advocates (CASAs) to discriminatory practices that may prevent qualified individuals from becoming foster parents. Entries submitted to this Listserv tend to be long and thorough and to possess a degree of vulnerability since so much thought, feeling, and effort usually go into composing a reply. Another way to subscribe to this Listserv is to visit http://www.childwelfare.ca/child-welfare.ca/. This site offers a WWW submission option. Simply enter your E-mail address in the space provided to be added to the list.

List: Computer Use in Social Services
List address: listserv@stat.com
Command: subscribe cussnet [first-name] [last-name]

This Listserv provides a general overview of the use of computers in social work and other human services. Subscribers share many interesting ideas and experiences not found in the hardcopy, published journal of the same name. Members of this Listserv are eager to pass along information ranging from virus protection to upcoming conference deadlines. This is a valuable resource.

List: Computers-in-Mental Health
List address: listserv@netcom.com
Command: subscribe computers-in-mental-health

The market offers many new software products designed specifically for use in human service. These include on-line diagnostic tools, modifiable database programs, and menu-driven applications for accounting and patient billing. Information about and evaluations of some of these new products are common topics of discussion among members of this Listserv. But that's not all. A recent conversation revealed the financial and ethical considerations of networking an entire social service agency to be able to share data and confidential client information. This conversation engaged many of the subscribers.

List: Computers in Social Work Education
List address: mailbase@mailbase.ac.uk
Command: join cti-soc-work-uk [first-name] [last-name]

This Listserv is ideal for individuals interested in baccalaureate and graduate-level curriculum ideas involving computers and the Internet. Announcements of social work projects available on the World Wide Web are commonly circulated. Members of this Listserv often discuss the role of computers in field placements and offer continuing-education–related suggestions for introducing seasoned professionals to new information technologies. Recently, a member from Texas posted a lengthy essay on how to guide students toward the successful completion of research projects. Each example in her essay included student use of computers to enter data and statistically analyze it.

List: Criminal Justice
List address: listserv@cunyvm.cuny.edu
Command: subscribe cjust-l [first-name] [last-name]

Social workers and other professionals who subscribe to this Listserv can benefit from the expertise of others by participating in on-line dialogs regarding immigration law, consumer rights, and legal advocacy. Whereas some conversations are more philosophic than others (e.g., an ongoing discussion of the underpinnings of the Western judicial system), the majority qualify as information and referral (I & R). Recently, a social worker inquiring about the efficacy of electronic monitoring was provided with the name and address of a contact person in Dallas who has conducted exhaustive research on that topic.

List: Employee Assistance Programs
List address: majordomo@utopia.pinsight.com
Command: subscribe eap

Social workers providing services through an employee assistance program have a valuable resource in this designated Listserv. Occasionally members submit clinical treatment issues, but most entries appear to be administrative in nature. Common issues discussed include billing, client confidentiality, client advocacy, and program evaluation.

List: Evaluation and Statistics
List address: listserv@sjuvm.stjohns.edu
Command: subscribe evalten [first-name] [last-name]

This Listserv is a good source of consultation. Questions and opinions about different commercial software are expressed openly by professionals in different disciplines all over the world. A researcher in Seattle recently sent members an Internet address for downloading a shareware program that helps to calculate effect size. Along with thorough instructions he provided examples of how he's using the program. Members who post information such as this often leave their personal E-mail address for others who may be interested in contacting them directly.

List: Feminist Social Work
Web address: http://tile.net/listserv/femswl.html
Instructions: Enter E-mail address in the space provided.

FEMISA list manager and co-moderator Gregory Kelson maintains an engaging site dedicated to discussing inequalities of all types from a social work perspective. This is a good place to post questions and request readings and other material for course syllabi, presentations, or personal growth. Many noted authors have subscribed and occasionally offer their perspectives. It's more than just a location to discuss feminist theory or gender studies. Job announcements and other information are also circulated. Visit the URL provided for a WWW submission option.

List: Healthcare Reform
List address: listserv@ukcc.uky.edu
Command: subscribe healthre [first-name] [last-name]

Initially a forum for like-minded individuals to speculate about the potential impact of reform, this Listserv has evolved to the site of lively conversation by individuals on both sides of the healthcare issue. Subscribers to this Listserv exchange E-mail addresses, gubernatorial information, and useful Web sites for tracking legislative policies related to healthcare.

List: Homelessness
Web address: http://tile.net/listserv/homeless.html
Instructions: Enter E-mail address in the space provided.

The Homeless List is maintained through Communications for Sustainable Future (CSF) at the University of Colorado at Boulder. Subscribers to this list represent a variety of backgrounds and use this Listserv as a forum to discuss a host of issues. Subscribers often exchange community-based solutions to the problems in their area. One member from Toronto recently shared a press release announcing Co-op Housing Day, a successful program geared toward single-parent families, low-income households, and others who have been excluded from the private rental market. Details for obtaining more information were also provided.

List: Human Services Information Technology Association
List address: list@cornell.edu
Command: subscribe husita-l [first-name] [last-name]

This Listserv is actually an international forum of human services professionals with special interest in new information technologies. Recently, much dialog has revolved around the association's annual conference and has generated tremendous enthusiasm. List members exchange conference tips, presentation highlights, and travel plans. Given the interdisciplinary nature of the projects described, one gets the impression that many of the collaborative relationships originate from active participation in this Listserv. Occasionally an E-mailed questionnaire is posted to members of the Listserv by who appear to be doctoral candidates conducting research.

List: International Social Work
List address: listserv@nisw.org.uk
Command: intsocwork [first-work] [last-name]

Members who subscribe to this Listserv send and receive messages from all around the world. Recently an individual from Australia started a dialog on "Spirituality and Social Work." Many subscribers replied from personal experience, while others simply offered suggestions on where to find reference material. Other social workers have used the Listserv to ask for information on the mentally ill and child abuse.

List: Intimate Violence
List address: listserv@uriacc.uri.edu
Command: subscribe ejintvio [first-name] [last-name]

This Listserv is a place on the Internet to share information and resources concerning the dark side of human relationships. When subscribing to a Listserv, it is appropriate to lurk several weeks before posting new information. This respectful practice holds especially true here. Many members have known each other for a long time, even if they've never met face to face. It's clear from their responses to each other that relationships have been established. To some, this Listserv is a valuable source of reliable information. Other members, however, describe it as their primary source of support.

List: Social Science Research Methods Instructors
List address: listserv@unmvma.unm.edu
Command: subscribe methods [first-name] [last-name]

Members of this Listserv tend to be community college and university professors who use the Listserv to obtain information, share teaching tips, or recommend textbooks.

Members seeking feedback on a proposed classroom assignment can anticipate several responses offering very different opinions. Despite the diversity of perspectives and geographic locations, it's noteworthy to see the similarity in methods used and commonality of approaches among individuals who previously did not know each other existed. It's not surprising that a sense of on-line camaraderie appears to exist among subscribers.

Summary

This chapter explains how Listservs can be a valuable source of information to practitioners. Instructions for subscribing and unsubscribing to Listservs of special interest to social workers were provided. In addition to Listserv summaries, this chapter offered suggestions for finding these and other Listservs.

Discussion Questions

1. There are two basic types of Listservs: unmoderated and moderated. Identify at least three ways in which they differ.
2. In your own words, briefly describe how to subscribe to a social work Listserv.
3. It has been suggested that retaining the initial copy of a welcome message is important. Why is this advisable?
4. Using the search feature described in this chapter, locate two Listservs of potential benefit to medical social workers.
5. Describe how an administrative address differs from a list address.

chapter 5

Newsgroups

Logging On—Social Workers Online

Mike Berghoef, LMSW, is an addictions counselor in Big Rapids, Michigan, and teaches a number of Web-based courses at Ferris State University. He writes of his experience using newsgroups.

"I've been in practice at the master's level for fifteen years, but I'm fairly new to Usenet newsgroups. Once I'd heard about this resource, I was eager to see how it worked. Once I finally located one, I was surprised how easy it is to use. Using a conventional Internet browser, the computer retrieved a directory of names of persons who had posted messages to the newsgroup. To read a message in its entirety, I clicked on the hotlink provided. Doing this not only displays the message but also allows the visitor to post a reply to the newsgroup or to send a personal E-mail message to the original author.

"In my estimation, the newsgroups that social workers are most likely to be interested in are very much like open-ended groups where people give and receive emotional support, except it's all on-line. I have observed interesting interactions at both ends of the continuum. Groups that appear productive are those that seem to be relating well to each other, very connected, and committed to sharing their knowledge. On the other hand, I've also come across groups that appeared to be promoting animosity. This second type would not be recommended for client referral.

"As a professional social worker, I may consider using newsgroups in combination with other things. There is good information, but one must be vigilant about its source. I have reservations about the credibility of many newsgroups and the advice that's being offered. Given

this caveat, I would direct clients only to newsgroups I'm familiar with. Clients and professionals need to recognize that information provided in these forums is not always credible and not a substitute for counseling.

"I'm very grateful for Web sites such as the SWAN hosted by the College of Social Work at the University of South Carolina. They've already assembled a directory of newsgroups of interest to social workers. I hope to see an expanded listing in the future."

Newsgroups, also called Usenet newsgroups, have a somewhat misleading title, which may lead to confusion about what they are, though the concept isn't complicated. The *news* in newsgroups doesn't mean *news* as in the news media. Newsgroups are a worldwide distributed discussion system. The system predates the World Wide Web and is separate from it, though you can access newsgroups through the Web. You can also access them through a news reader that is independent of the Web. Usenet newsgroups are a huge system, possibly the largest decentralized information entity in existence. There are about fifty thousand newsgroups spanning every topic imaginable from Apple computers to zoology.

To read newsgroup discussions, you connect to your news reader, be it a Web browser such as Netscape Communicator or Internet Explorer, or a program created specifically to read newsgroups. You then select a group from a list organized by topic and read what others have written. Unlike Listservs, where the messages come to you in your E-mail, you, in a sense, go to the newsgroups messages that remain on your server for you to browse. You can also post messages though your news reader. Usenet newsgroups are decentralized. There is no home office for the system. Rather, newsgroups are stored at numerous servers around the world. Your server won't subscribe to all fifty thousand groups but will rather offer a selection of groups that the administrators think will be popular. If your server does not offer a group listed in this book, you might contact the administrator and ask that it be added to the list. Usenet newsgroups generally have a casual atmosphere, much like a conversation. People are judged by their words rather than by appearance or qualifications. Remember, though, that newsgroups can be very powerful because your words can be read by a worldwide audience.

Moderated or Unmoderated Status

Newsgroups may be unmoderated, which means that anyone can access them to read and post messages. The only control over the content of these groups is through group pressure. If readers don't like what someone has posted, they can reply with a critical message. Extremely critical messages are called "flames" and are quite common in some groups. Moderated groups are controlled by a list owner who decides who may subscribe to the group and what postings appear. These groups may be local (such as a class newsgroup) with outsiders excluded. Others require certain characteristics to subscribe such as a certain profession or degree. All messages go to the list owner, who decides which ones will appear on the newsgroup. The advantage to having messages screened is that it can reduce the number of messages and eliminate ones that won't be of interest to the group. The disadvantage is that list owners control discussions and can exclude opinions they don't agree with.

How Newsgroups Are Organized

Newsgroups are organized by broad categories identified by a prefix before the group name. These are some common ones:

alt	Alternative groups on a wide variety of topics
biz	Business
comp	Computers and software
misc	Other
news	News about newsgroups
rec	Hobbies and recreation
sci	Research about science
soc	Social issues
talk	Debate

The prefix is followed by the specific name of the group. For example, one social work group name is soc.socialworkpractice.

Reading and Posting to Newsgroups

If you have a connection to the Internet that allows you to use a Web browser such as Netscape Communicator or Internet Explorer, you may want to take advantage of the news readers built into these browsers. If you have a text-only connection to the Internet, you will have to use a different news reader. Your service provider can tell you what readers are available and how they work. Most news reading software will organize newsgroup postings into topics, or "threads" as they are called in Usenet newsgroups. For example, soc.socialworkpractice may have ongoing discussions about child placement and alcohol abuse. Threads are indicated by subject lines, and postings related to particular subject lines are threaded together so you can move easily from one posting to the next, reading only those related to the topic that interests you.

Your browser display window will look something like the one in Figure 5.1. You'll notice similarities between this window and the one shown in Figure 3.2 for

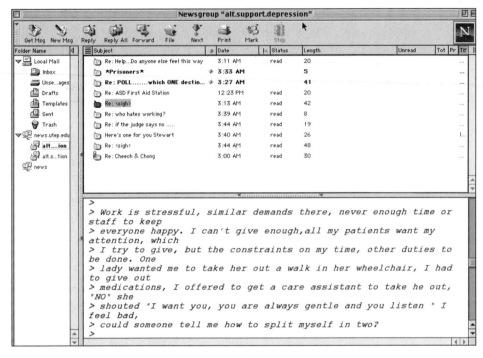

FIGURE 5.1   A News Window

reading E-mail messages. One advantage of using an integrated browser package such as Netscape Composer or Internet Explorer is the support for common functions such as E-mail and using newsgroups. In general, your News Window will have four distinct parts: (1) a series of control buttons at the top, (2) a list of newsgroups (i.e., alt.support.depression), (3) a list of posted items including subject, sender, and time, and (4) the actual message if a newsgroup has been selected from the list. Figure 5.1 shows an example.

Anyone who can read newsgroups can post messages. Your news reader should have a built-in text editor that allows you to compose a message. Posting messages or replying to a newsgroup is not difficult, since the process is very similar to sending E-mail. To reply to a message someone has posted, select the **Reply** option from the menu bar and determine which of the options would be most appropriate. Option one, **Post Reply,** is used to post a message to the newsgroup. Option two, **Post Reply and Mail,** is used to post the reply to the newsgroup but also sends a personal mail message to the person who posted the original message. Option three, **Mail Reply,** sends an E-mail message only to the individual who posted the original message, not the newsgroup. The best choice depends on the nature of correspondence you wish to have.

You can also create a news thread by designating a new subject line. It's important to have a subject line that is consistent with the content of your message because people generally decide whether to read a message based on the subject line. Remember not to compose your messages in all capital letters because this is considered discourteous in newsgroups.

Etiquette in Newsgroups

Newsgroup readers generally expect that new users will "lurk before posting," which means that you should read the group postings for several days before you post a message yourself. By doing so, you can indicate that you are aware of the conversation going on in the group, and you won't ask questions that would have been answered by just reading the group postings for a few days. It is also a good idea to read the group's FAQ (frequently asked questions) if they have one. If you are not courteous enough to read the group messages and FAQ before posting, you reduce your credibility in the group. Indeed, some groups will "flame" those who violate this principle, sending derogatory messages to the violator. In addition, if you disapprove of the content of a group, it's a good idea just to move on to other groups. Unless it is a group that invites debate, any efforts to change the tone or practice of a particular group are generally not appreciated.

To avoid flames of various temperatures reaching your mailbox, consider these additional guidelines.

1. Avoid spamming. That is, do not post annoying advertising material to the newsgroup. If you're trying to sell your car or wish to promote your spouse's Pampered Chef business, newsgroups are not the appropriate forum.
2. Be considerate to others when using quotes. Never quote a long entry only to add your brief response at the bottom. If you support the content of what's been said by a user, state that in an independent message.
3. Choose your newsgroup thoughtfully and post accordingly. Posting your position concerning the ethical responsibilities of social work practitioners to a newsgroup for network managers or one for sports enthusiasts is not a good idea.
4. Do not SHOUT. NOT ONLY IS TYPING IN UPPER-CASE LETTERS DIFFICULT TO READ, IT IS ALSO REGARDED AS SHOUTING.

New Users

If you haven't used newsgroups before, you might want to read some of the FAQs posted in newsgroups such as news.answers and news.announce.newusers. If you want to post questions about the nature of newsgroups, you can do so at news.newusers.questions. If you want to learn more about the characteristics of Usenet newsgroups, simply connect to a search engine such as Yahoo! (http://www.yahoo.com) and search for keywords *Usenet* or *newsgroups*.

Archives

If you want to peruse past postings of a newsgroup or do a general keyword search on a topic for all newsgroups, you can consult the computerized archives of newsgroup postings at DejaNews (http://www.dejanews.com). You can also use DejaNews as a resource for finding social-work–related newsgroups.

Where to Find Newsgroups for Social Work

There are literally thousands of newsgroups in existence. Finding newsgroups of relevance to the field doesn't need to be an overwhelming task if you begin at Tile.Net. Simply go to the URL http://tile.net and conduct a keyword search on the term *social-work*. Using the dialog boxes provided, indicate that you're interested in newsgroups by clicking in the appropriate box. At the time of this writing, 107 newsgroups match this request. One hundred and seven possibilities are manageable, but still time consuming. Fortunately a number of social work sites have compiled listings of newsgroups for you. Two popular examples are "The Social Worker Networker" found at http://www.spring-board.com/two/SocialWorkerNet/newsgrou.htm and the "Social Work Access Network (SWAN)" maintained by the University of South Carolina's College of Social Work.

Here is a list of some newsgroups accessible directly from the SWAN Web site at http://www.sc.edu/swan. If you are using a Web browser such as Netscape Communicator or Internet Explorer, you need only double click on the newsgroup of interest to execute the news reader application. If you have a text-only connection to the Internet, you will have to use a different news reader. In either case, your news reader program will enable you to reply and post messages to any of the following groups:

alt.child-support	alt.support.ex-cult
alt.psychology.help	alt.support.foster-parents
alt.society.mental-health	alt.support.grief
alt.support.abuse-partners	alt.support.learning-disab
alt.support.anxiety-panic	alt.support.mult-sclerosis
alt.support.attn-deficit	alt.support.musc-dystrophy
alt.support.cancer	alt.support.single-parents
alt.support.cancer.prostate	alt.support.sleep-disorder
alt.support.cerebral-palsy	alt.support.step-parents
alt.support.depression	alt.support.tourette
alt.support.depression.manic	misc.health.aids
alt.support.dissociation	misc.health.alternative
alt.support.divorce	misc.kids.health
alt.support.eating-disorder	talk.politics medicine
alt.support.epilepsy	talk.rape

Summary

In this chapter instructions were provided for reading and posting to newsgroups. In addition to a special section on Net-etiquette, this chapter offered suggestions for locating social work newsgroups.

Discussion Questions

1. Why does the notion of "a collection of electronic discussion groups" describe newsgroups?
2. Give two examples of how Usenet newsgroups could be beneficial in practice.
3. Describe how Usenet newsgroups differ from social work Listservs.
4. How can you access archived messages from a newsgroup to which you belong?
5. Define the term *thread* and explain its significance.

chapter 6

Real Time Communication

Logging On—Social Workers Online

Adrian Delgado is the editor of the newsletter and Web site of the Latino Social Workers Organization (LSWO) in Chicago. In addition to providing cutting-edge information through its Web site (http://www.lswo.org), LSWO raises awareness of social issues and policy decisions that impact the Latino community. LSWO has also developed a Mentor Program that works closely with established professionals affiliated with at least ten schools of social work throughout the nation. LSWO student members can request guidance as they prepare to enter the profession. Mentors can also help members already in practice make the transition to a different area of social work. Mr. Delgado describes a recent opportunity to provide LSWO assistance to a social worker "in transition."

"I was recently contacted by a social worker who had been surfing the Web for job openings and who came across our homepage. This person was working in Mexico and wanted to work in California or the Southwest. We communicated back and forth through a series of E-mail messages. This gave me an opportunity to tell her about LSWO and to learn how we could be of assistance. Fortunately we were able to agree on a time when we could meet live on the Internet. By visiting a designated chat room, she and I were able to discuss her professional interests and qualifications directly over the Internet. I could answer her questions and provide her with the information she sought. LSWO anticipates integrating more online messaging and video messaging systems to provide this type of consultation. Weeks later I was provided with an update. She received referrals and information that landed her a social work position in California."

As noted in Chapters 3 through 5, E-mail, Listservs, and newsgroups allow social workers to exchange information and discuss issues easily with individual or multiple people. The disadvantage of these methods, however, is that they require one person to send a message and then wait for a reply. Several types of real time communication exist on the Internet that enable individuals to communicate essentially real time.

Talk, MUSE (Multi-User Simulated Environment), and mIRC are examples of such programs found on the Internet. Talk is an older, less frequently used program that allowed limited real time communication. MUSEs (also sometimes called MUDs [Multi-User Domains] and MOOs [MUDs Object Oriented]) are text-based virtual reality settings sometimes used for educational purposes but also frequently employed by individuals playing multi-user games together. These often require special software to be installed on the local computer system and, therefore, are rarely utilized in social work. Internet Relay Chat (IRC), however, has replaced TALK and become very popular. Originally written by Jarkko Oikarinen of Finland (jto@tolsun.oulu.fi) in 1988, IRC gained international fame during the 1991 Persian Gulf War. Users who congregated at designated IRC "channels" found it a valuable method of sending and receiving updates from loved ones. In a similar manner, IRC users from Moscow provided the world with live reports during the coup against Boris Yeltsin in 1993; IRC users in Belgrade sent details of the crisis in Kosovo in 1999.

mIRC

mIRC is an easy-to-use shareware product developed by Khaled Mardan-Bey and mIRC Co., Ltd. It has the potential of enabling groups of social workers to converse with each other at a designated channel or via multiple channels. With mIRC, there is no restriction on the number of people, their geographic distance, or the number of channels that can be formed. This makes it a useful way for social workers in different states to communicate without running up expensive long-distance telephone charges for their agencies. mIRC can be downloaded for free at http://www.mirc.co.uk.

Once you have downloaded it from the Internet, you can participate in on-line chat sessions by simply launching it. To do this, double click on the icon and the main mIRC window will open. You will see a picture of the author and have the option of reading his bio. By clicking on the Introduction button, you'll be provided with a user-friendly Help screen that gives an excellent overview.

The first step will be to select an IRC server from the Setup menu. It's recommended that you try and connect to one that's geographically close. You can also choose the default option reading "Random US Undernet Server" from the pull-down menu. Next, enter your full name and E-mail address in the fields provided. The nickname that you enter is the name by which you will be known in the chat session. In Figure 6.1's example, the nickname is "Dr.M." You should also choose an alternative name in case your first choice is already in use. When you're ready, click on the button Connect to Server.

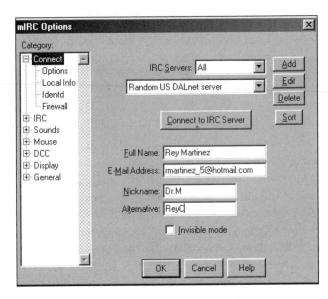

FIGURE 6.1 Connecting to a Server Using mIRC

The chat sessions are organized into channels. From the mIRC channels folder you will see a list of possible channels to join. (All channels will have the # symbol in front.) Scroll down until you find a channel of interest, and then click on the **Join** button. That's all that is required.

Depending on the popularity of the topic, however, you're likely to find yourself right in the middle of a conversation. Unless you're a frequent user of this channel, it's best just to observe for awhile. Respectfully listening before jumping in will give you an idea about what's being discussed. And don't be surprised if the channel name has very little to do with what participants are discussing. Simply leave the channel by typing the command **/part.**

For starting out, we recommend joining a channel on an IRC network specifically dedicated to new users such as #mIRCHelp or #newbieChat. These are good places to practice sending messages or asking questions. As shown in Figure 6.2, use the arrow keys to highlight the group #mIRCHelp (or an equivalent such channel) and click on the Join button. This will take you to a Channel Window that consists of three panels. Panel 1 (the largest window) will show all the messages typed by individuals using the channel. Panel 2 (the one-line box directly below) is the line in which you type your message to be sent to others in the channel. Panel 3 is the panel to the right of your screen. It will provide you with the nicknames of all the people currently in the channel. When you are ready to speak, just type in panel 2 and press the Return key. That's all there is to it! You will then see your message displayed among the others.

FIGURE 6.2   Joining an mIRC Chat Room

You will find that there are basically two kinds of things that you can do once you've joined a chat session: (1) type messages and (2) execute commands. The information you've typed in panel 2 will be displayed exactly as typed when pressing the Return key, along with your nickname. You can also execute basic commands that cause some action to be taken. In mIRC all commands are preceded by a forward slash (/). This enables the server to recognize them as a specific function you wish to be carried out rather than as part of your message. One of the first things to do, even in the Newbie's Channel, is to type the **/help** command and press the Return key. This will bring up a table of recognized commands (see Figure 6.3). When you choose to leave a channel, just type the **/part** command and press the Return key

Here are some of the commands you will often encounter.

MIRC NETWORK CHANNEL COMMANDS

Command	Designated Action
/help	Used to obtain help concerning these and other commands.
/away	If someone wants to stay connected to the channel but is required to be elsewhere temporarily, he or she may use the /away command. This will indicate to others that he or she has left the channel but expects to return.
/clear	Used to clear a screen that has become too cluttered.
/info	Used to obtain information about the author and copyright of the chat system. *(continued)*

continued

Command	Designated Action
/ignore	Used to ignore messages sent by another user.
/invite	Used to invite another user to join a certain channel. By typing "/invite nickname" the receiving user gets a message indicating that the sender has requested his or her participation in another chat room. The receiving user is free to ignore or accept the invitation.
/join	The command used to join a specific channel.
/list	Provides a list of active channels, the number of users of each, and the topics associated with each.
/nick	Used to change nickname. Command syntax is "/nick new-nickname." All users on one's channel will be advised of the change.
/signoff	Used to exit a chat.
/whois	Used to obtain information about individual users. By typing "/whois ReyC" you will receive log-in name and the name of the host from which he or she comes.
/who	Provides list of who is using chat. Users of public channels show up with their channel identified. Users of private channels appear, but they are specified as being on a private, unspecified channel.

Becoming a Channel Operator

While on-line you may notice that at least one nickname has an "@" symbol in front of it. This symbol designates who the "channel operator" is. The channel operator has special authority, such as determining who is invited to join. As mentioned previously, one enters a channel by using Join Channel in the Commands pull-down menu. If the channel #Swpolicy does not exist, for example, it will be created and you will be made its channel operator.

Potential Application to Social Work Practice

It is not difficult to think of potential social work applications for chat server usage. For example, you could organize a chat session for colleagues to meet at a designated night and channel to discuss bylaws and agency policy development or to converse with special guest speakers such as Adrian Delgado, director of the Latino Social Work Organization in Chicago.

WebChat

Social work professionals and students are also making use of WebChat. These are Web-based real time conferencelike chat systems that may be provided by commercial sites on

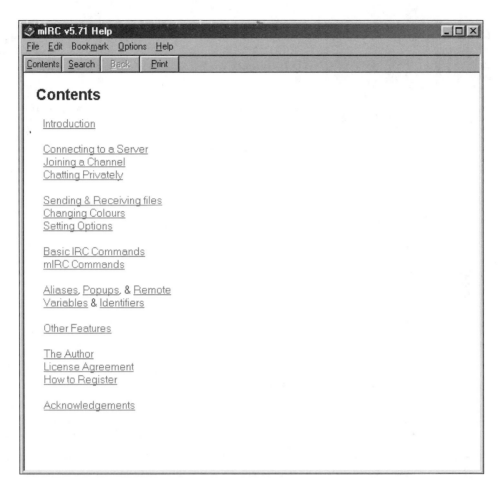

FIGURE 6.3   The mIRC Help Feature

the Internet and also by colleges and universities. At the time of this writing, social work students at the University of Texas at El Paso, for example, have a chat room connected to their Web site at http://www.utep.edu/socwork/sasw.htm. This feature allows members of the Student Association of Social Workers (SASW) to meet with the officers, discuss fund raising activities, or to network with invited guests, practitioners, or authors.

To participate in a WebChat forum or conference, you don't need to know special commands as you do with IRC, but you do need to know the address of the Web page host. The advantage of WebChat is that it is easy to use, requiring only point-and-click commands typical of the Web. The host page may ask you to register your nickname (or handle) and E-mail address before participating in discussions. Once you have accomplished this, the messages from participants will begin to appear in a box at the bottom of your browser screen. You will be able to join in the conversation by typing

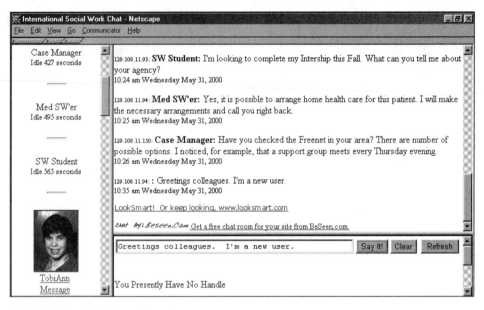

FIGURE 6.4   WebChat Example

a response and clicking **Say It.** If you are not familiar with using a Web browser, you may want to refer to Chapter 7 for an introduction.

Several other rooms exist specifically for social work practitioners and those in training. A fun and easily accessible example is the Social Work Café Chat Room located at http://geocities.com/Heartland/4862/swcchat.html. Typically, the screen is divided into two to three different sections. In the example in Figure 6.4, the left side of the screen lists the names or "handles" of individuals who are in the room. The second section, the large area in the middle of the page, displays the real time discussion taking place. The third section, typically at the bottom, is how the user participates. All that's needed here is to type in your sentence in the space provided and click on the **Say It** button.

Here is a list of other social work WebChat resources.

SOCIAL WORK WEBCHAT RESOURCES ON THE INTERNET

The New Social Worker's Careers Chat
http://www.socialworker.com

Michael McMurray's Chat listing
http://129.82.209.104/
chatrooms.htm

Tom Cleereman's Social Work Chat
http://sparknet.net/~tjcleer

The Social Work Café Chat Room
http://geocities.com/Heartland/4862/
swcchat.html.

Mental Health Net
Resource for psychiatry, psychology, and social work
http://www.cmhc.com/mhn.htm

Child Development Web Chat
Linda Chapman, social work professional
http://idealist.com/children/index.shtml

Healthlinks.net
Professional-level healthcare resource
http://www.healthlinks.net/

Human Services Support
University of Pennsylvania–School of Social Work
http://www.ssw.upenn.edu/Old/PennSupport/hschat.htm

WBS Support Chat (AOL subscription required)
Accessed through keyword *Social Work*
http://pages.wbs.net

Social Work Access Network
Comprehensive chat room listing
http://www.sc.edu/swan/chat.html

Summary

This chapter has described how social workers can dialog with colleagues at different locations using real time communication programs. When you're in a chat room, everything you type appears on the screen of everyone else participating. Two examples provided in this chapter were mIRC (a shareware product developed by Khaled Mardan-Bey) and WebChat (a Web-based, real time option growing in popularity due to its ease of use). Web chatting, as in the Social Work Café example, takes place within a Web page and is generally hosted as a discussion related to the Web page's topic. You will find that newer browsers such as Internet Explorer 4.0 have their own chat client (Microsoft Chat) fully ready for installation.

Discussion Questions

1. Give four potential benefits of real time communication programs for practice.
2. What do WebChat, mIRC, and programs like Netmeeting have in common?
3. When participating in a real time consultation, what sorts of precautions should a social worker take to protect client confidentiality?
4. What are the advantages and disadvantages of becoming a channel operator?

chapter 7

The World Wide Web

The World Wide Web is an interactive hypertext and hypermedia system that allows you to access documents stored in computers all over the world. The basic unit of the World Wide Web is the page, which is another word for a document displayed on your computer screen through a World Wide Web browser. A page is something like a page of a book, though it can be of any length, from a few inches to yards long. Though the document may look like a printed page, it is actually a computer file stored in hypertext markup language (HTML) format.

A primary advantage of HTML is that information can be organized and retrieved in a nonlinear fashion. Rather than forcing you to descend through lists of subdirectories, HTML allows you to jump from one place to the next through a series of embedded links. A link can connect a single word or phrase to information stored on a different computer halfway across the world. For example, someone viewing the directory of accredited social work programs maintained by the Council of Social Work Education (http://www.cswe.org) can be transported to those various geographic locations by simply using the mouse or a key command to connect. If you're interested in the graduate certificate program in social work and marriage and family therapy at the University of Arkansas at Little Rock, for example, double click on the initials for that state in the directory. Follow the set of embedded links to retrieve information housed in a server in Little Rock.

A single link may connect the user to a document, a graphic, or practically anything stored in an HTML-compatible format. Web pages are hypermedia documents, which means that the data displayed are not simply text. You will find photos, graphics, video, and sound displayed on Web pages. Web pages vary greatly in their sophistication, depending on the talents and budgets of their authors, but almost all are a definite improvement over the text-only files found on the Internet just a few years ago. Before we highlight the use of browsers for locating social work resources on the Web, we should consider the anatomy of Web addresses.

Web Addresses

Following the hot links from your Web browser is one way to explore the World Wide Web. However, you will likely need to connect to specific sites, so you need to understand Web addresses. A page on the Web is located by its uniform resource locator (URL). This, for example, is the URL or address of the job listings at the National Association of Social Work:

http://www.naswdc.org/JOB.HTM

To understand the address or URL, you need to understand its various components. Let's look at them from left to right. The **http** stands for hypertext protocol. This abbreviation, followed by **://**, tells your browser that the file to be displayed is in hypertext format. There are other formats that can also be displayed through browsers, but http documents are the most common. Next comes the **www.naswdc,** which is the domain name for the National Institute of Social Work's Web site. The domain name is a registered address, which is usually composed of an abbreviation of the organization's name, preceded by www and followed by a suffix that designates the Web page by type. This address has the suffix **.org,** which means that the site belongs to a nonprofit organization. Other common suffixes are **.com** for commercial, **.gov** for governmental, and **.edu** for educational. Many social work sites will have either .edu, .gov, or .org. Using the domain name will connect you to the homepage or main page of the organization. The last portion of the NASW address just mentioned is **JOB.HTM.** This is the file name of a specific page on the Internet. This particular one contains job listings for social workers. I could locate this page by connecting to the homepage, http://www.naswdc.org, and following the hot links to the job listings, or I could use the address, which includes the file name JOB.HTM, and go directly to that page.

Web Browsers

A Web browser is a program that allows you to access World Wide Web pages and display them. In this chapter you'll be introduced to two different kinds: text-only browsers and graphical browsers.

Text-Only Browsers

Lynx is the most common text-only browser that a social worker in the field is likely to encounter. To use Lynx it must be installed and accessible through your Internet host. Lynx is often found on menu-driven networks that provide access to the Internet. Another way to find out if it's accessible is to type the command **lynx** at your command prompt or ask your service provider.

Lynx is text-only, which means that you can't use it to see the colorful images and video on the Web, nor can you use it to hear sound files. You can, however, find much useful information for social work because many social work sites are heavily text-based.

For our demonstration we'll telnet to the social work site maintained by the National Association of Social Workers mentioned previously. In the top portion of the screen in Figure 7.1 you'll see the homepage of the institution or organization providing the computer network. At the bottom of your screen, as seen in the following example, you'll find a menu of commands recognized by the Lynx program.

Note the use of boldface type here. Every word or phase in bold type is actually a hypertext link. Using the prompts at the bottom of the page, we see that the up arrow and down arrow keys enable us to select (follow) or move back from a specific link.

We're at the top of the WWW Virtual page, which is a master index of jumping points to many areas of interest to social workers. From here you can go to various sites by using keyboard commands. Again, the highlighted command at the top left of the menu bar suggests that you can press the space bar to go to the next page of the Web page. Below that, it notes that you can use the up and down arrow keys to move about in the page. When you touch one of the arrow keys, it highlights a hot link on the page. Moving from one hot link to another, you can position the highlighting over the link you want to follow. Then you touch the right arrow key to fol-

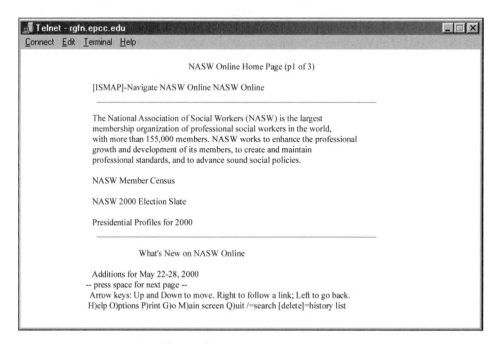

FIGURE 7.1   NASW Site Using Lynx

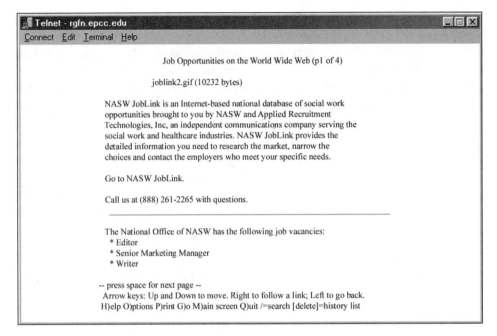

FIGURE 7.2   NASW JobLink Site Using Lynx

low the link and the left arrow to back up one link. If you want to connect to a specific Web page address, touch **G** for **Go,** and you will see a space where you can type in the Web page address. Other letter commands noted at the bottom of the screen are **H** for help, **O** for options (which gives you additional commands), **P** for print, **M** for main screen, and **Q** for quit.

Now, although Figure 7.2 may look like you're still at the NASW Web site, you are actually at the top of an Internet and telephone-based national database of social work opportunities. This site provides detailed information regarding the job market for social workers and necessary information to contact potential employers. You could continue indefinitely moving from site to site. Many Web pages of interest to social workers are primarily text, so a text-only connection may be all you need, though you will miss the color and sound of a full-graphical interface. Text-only browsers may not be visually aesthetic, but can be a powerful Internet tool for the human service professional using a system that does not support full hypermedia interface.

Graphical Browsers

The two most popular browsers are Netscape and Internet Explorer, both of which display the full hypermedia capabilities of the Web. To use these two browsers, however, you must have a connection that supports a full-graphical interface. (See Chapter 2.)

USING NETSCAPE NAVIGATOR.   Netscape is one of the most popular Web browsers and is often used in academic settings. It can be downloaded free from the Netscape site, http://home.netscape.com. If you already have it on your computer, you can generally access it from the Start button or an icon on your screen. Figure 7.3 shows the Netscape opening screen, displaying the homepage for the National Association of Social Workers, http://www.naswdc.org. Your opening screen will display a different Web page in the bottom portion, but you can easily go to one of the social work sites such as this one, once you understand the basics of the program.

Netscape, like all browsers, allows you to use the hypertext to move to other pages. With your computer mouse, move the cursor over the page displayed in the large box at the bottom of the screen. Whenever the cursor changes from an arrow to a hand, your cursor is positioned over a hot link. This can be either text or graphics. Double click and you will move to another page that is linked to the one you have been viewing. Then click on the **Back** button to the top left of your screen, and you will be returned to the previous page. Now try typing in the address of the NASW site, http://www.naswdc.org, in the box marked **Location.** Touch **Enter,** and you should see a screen similar to the one displayed in Figure 7.3. Now you can use the hypertext to explore the NASW site.

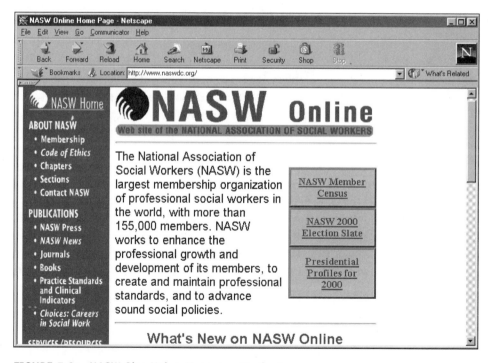

FIGURE 7.3   NASW Site Using Netscape Navigator

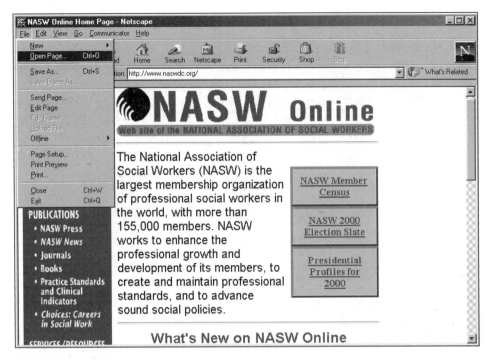

FIGURE 7.4   Using Netscape Navigator Pull-Down Menu Feature

Across the top of the Netscape screen are menus and buttons called toolbars. Their use is for the Netscape pull-down menus. (See Figure 7.4.)

The most important of these pull-down menus is the **File** menu, which accesses several useful functions such as **Open Page** (which will give you a dialog box where you can enter a specific Web address), **Print,** and **Save As** (which allows you to save a Web page on disk). The **Help** menu accesses the Netscape's help screens. The other pull-down menus are useful for checking mail and creating Web pages (both of which are discussed in other chapters).

Below the pull-down menus is a Navigation Toolbar which we see in Figure 7.5. The first two buttons, **Back** and **Forward,** allow you to move back and forward between previously viewed pages. The **Reload** button reloads the current page, which is useful if the page has not been transmitted properly. **Home** takes you to your default homepage. **Search** accesses Netscape's list of search engines, and **Guide** connects you to Netscape's guide to the Web. **Print** prints the page, and **Stop** will stop the loading of a page, which is useful if a page takes too long to appear.

These are the basics of Netscape's browser. If you want to know more, explore the Help screens accessed through the **Help** pull-down menu.

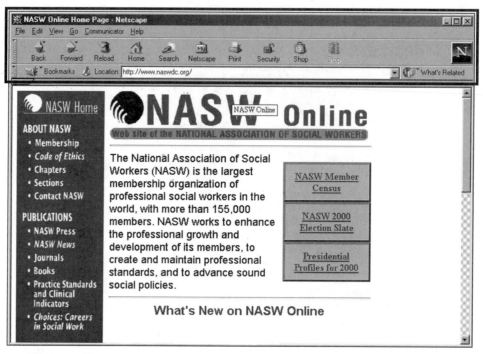

FIGURE 7.5 NASW Navigator Toolbar

Using Internet Explorer

Internet Explorer is the browser that comes preloaded on most PCs. You will generally access it through your **Start** menu or an icon on the opening screen of your computer, depending on the setup of your computer. If you are using an older computer, you can download the most recent version free from http://microsoft.com. Figure 7.6 shows the Internet Explorer opening screen displaying the homepage for the U.S. Department of Health and Human Services, http://www.hhs.gov. Your opening screen will display a different Web page in the bottom portion, but you can easily go to this or another social work site once you understand the basics of the program.

Internet Explorer, like Netscape and other browsers, allows you to use the hypertext to move to other pages. With your computer mouse, move the cursor over the page displayed in the large box at the bottom of the screen. Whenever the cursor changes from an arrow to a hand, your cursor is positioned over a hot link. This can be either text or graphics. Double click and you will move to another page that is linked to the one you have been viewing. Then click on the **Back** button on the top left of your screen, and you will be returned to the previous page. Now try typing in the address of the U.S. Department of Health and Human Services, http://www.hhs.gov, in the box

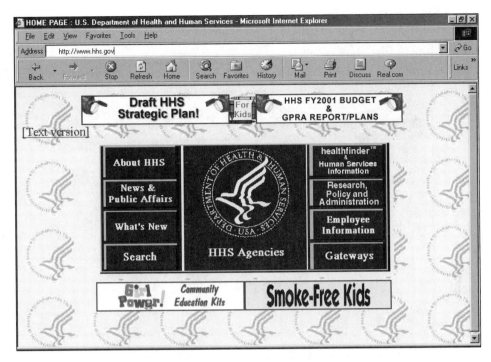

FIGURE 7.6   Department of Human Services Using Internet Explorer

marked **Address.** Touch **Enter,** and you should see a screen similar to the one displayed in Figure 7.6. Now you can use the hypertext to explore the HHS site.

Across the top of the Internet Explorer screen are menus and buttons called toolbars. Figure 7.7 shows the IE pull-down menus. The first of these pull-down menus is the **File** menu, which accesses several useful functions such as **Open** (which will give you a dialog box where you can enter a specific Web address), **Save As** (which allows you to save a Web page on disk), **Print,** and **Send** (which lets you send the page or link as E-mail). **Favorites** enables you to save links to favorite Web sites in a list you access through this pull-down menu, though this feature might be disabled in some institutional computers used by many different people. The **Help** menu accesses Internet Explorer's Help screens.

Below the pull-down menus is a Navigation Toolbar, which we see in Figure 7.8. The first two buttons, **Back** and **Forward,** allow you to move to move back and forward between previously viewed pages. The **Stop** button will stop the loading of a page, which is useful if a page is stuck and not loading properly. The **Refresh** button reloads the current page. **Home** takes you to your default homepage. **Search** accesses Internet Explorer's list of search engines. **Favorites** allows you to add Web sites to your shortcut list, which can be accessed from this button. **History** tells you what Web sites

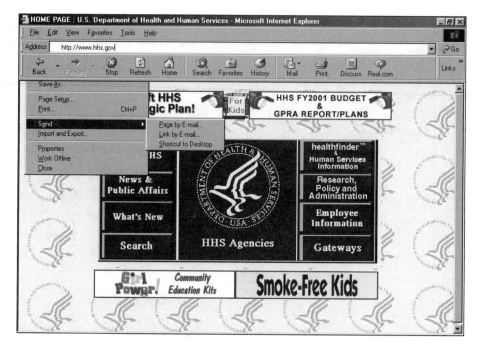

FIGURE 7.7   Using Internet Explorer Pull-Down Menus

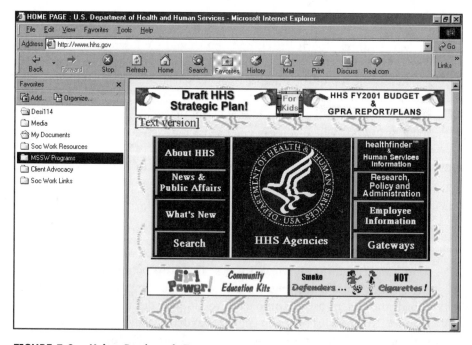

FIGURE 7.8   Using Bookmark Feature

you have viewed recently, and **Channels** connects you to Internet Explorer's guide to the Web.

These are the basics of Internet Explorer. If you want to know more, explore the Help screens accessed through the **Help** pull-down menu.

Summary

This chapter has been an overview of the World Wide Web and the manner in which HTML is used to retrieve on-line information through a series of embedded links. This chapter introduced the reader to two different types of Web browsers: text-only browsers and graphical browsers. Demonstrations featured both Netscape Navigator and Internet Explorer. In the next chapter you will be introduced to Web sites that social workers have found to be exemplary. Undoubtedly, you will find many other excellent resources for practice as you surf the Web!

Discussion Questions

1. Discuss the advantage of being able to retrieve information in a nonlinear fashion.
2. Make your own comparison between graphical browsers. Which features do you like best? Why?
3. Screen reading equipment is used by individuals who are visually impaired and do best using text-only connections to the World Wide Web. In what other situations would using Lynx be the most appropriate choice?
4. In addition to an E-mail link to the author and evidence that the Web site is updated frequently, what other criteria can help determine the credibility of a social work site?
5. Conduct a keyword search using the term *clinical social work* on different search engines (e.g., Yahoo!, Google, AltaVista, Hotbot). Was the information provided similar? Why or why not?

chapter 8

Social Work Web Tour

This chapter provides an overview of select Web sites of special interest to the profession. The summaries were submitted by the authors themselves, who, in many cases, are both social workers and Web Masters. Each briefly describes how these practitioners have used their sites as resources in social work service.

URL: http://www.cswf.org
Dean Allman
Web Master

deanallman@home.com

This site is for the membership and interested potential members of the Clinical Social Work Federation. It is used primarily to promote the organization and to act as a resource directory for members.

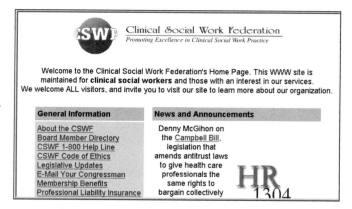

Clinical Social Work Federation
Promoting Excellence in Clinical Social Work Practice

Welcome to the Clinical Social Work Federation's Home Page. This WWW site is maintained for **clinical social workers** and those with an interest in our services. We welcome ALL visitors, and invite you to visit our site to learn more about our organization.

General Information	News and Announcements
About the CSWF	Denny McGihon on
Board Member Directory	the Campbell Bill,
CSWF 1-800 Help Line	legislation that
CSWF Code of Ethics	amends antitrust laws
Legislative Updates	to give health care
E-Mail Your Congressman	professionals the
Membership Benefits	same rights to
Professional Liability Insurance	bargain collectively

HR 1304

URL: http://www.nisw.org.uk
Mark Watson
Director of Information
mwatson@nisw.org.uk

NISW has been providing access to information for many years and is using the Internet to further exploit our resources and expertise. Our Web site contains several full-text reports, two dozen on-line briefings, an International Social Work Contents Page Service, newsletters, and other material. For those who have subscriber access, our 40,000-abstract caredata database is now available on the Web, as is the monthly caredata ABSTRACTS listing. Watch out for some more interesting developments!

URL: http://www.aosw.org
Neil O'Connor, ACSW, C-ICSW
AOSW Web Editor
njoconno@facstaff.wisc.edu

We started in 1996 as a source for Web links for oncology social workers. As our experience on the Web has progressed, we have changed the focus to organizational information and communication as well as oncology information for our membership and the general public. Our members have used the site for resource location, conference information, and access to the organization's leadership. I would also direct your attention to the Social Work Oncology Network (SWON), a Listserv operated by the AOSW. (Information is available from John Sharp, MSSA, at johnws@stratos.net.) SWON provides rapid communication among the members and has featured discussions of resources, techniques, and practice issues.

URL: http://www.aasswb.org
Troy Elliott
Communications Director
telliott@aasswb.org

The American Association of State Social Work Boards Web site contains information on social work regulation across the country. At the AASSWB site, social workers can learn about licensing examinations, access detailed information on licensure requirements in individual states, and download a copy of the association's model practice act. This site also contains information for social work consumers and members of state social work regulatory boards as well as links to other relevant sites.

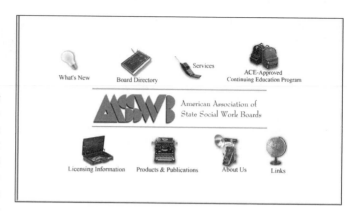

**URL: http://www.
socialworksearch.com**
Thomas Cleereman, MSW
webmaster@socialworksearch.com

This site features a search engine dedicated to social workers and other helping professionals using the Internet. Social Work Search offers an abundance of information about other Web sites for topics including licensing, therapy, managed care, and general practice as well as personal homepages and more.

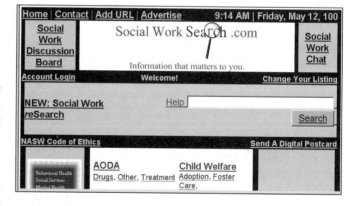

URL: http://www. socialworksearch.com/ email/index.cgi
Thomas Cleereman, MSW
webmaster@socialworksearch.com

This URL points to a Discussion Board for social workers. Social work students, social workers, or any other person who has an interest in social work can access this site to post and reply to messages left on the site. The program will automatically send you an E-mail when someone has replied to your message. Social workers are finding it a great way to communicate with each other from points all over the globe.

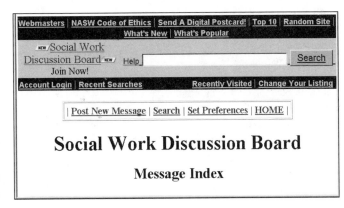

URL: http://www. healthfinder.gov
David Baker
Senior Publishing Advisor
(Internet)
dbaker@osophs.dhhs.gov

Healthfinder is an Internet gateway to reliable health and human services information from the U.S. government. The authors reviewed resources on over one thousand topics, from AIDS to Zidovudine. Many social workers use this site to obtain the latest information for their clients.

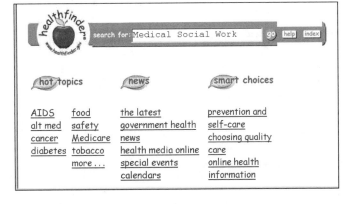

URL: http://iasw.eire.org
Heino Schonfeld
Head of Social Work
heino@connect.ie

Social workers practicing in Ireland use the site to inform themselves about their professional association and current issues of social work in Ireland. Practitioners abroad visit this site because they may want to work in Ireland or conduct comparative research. Journalists and members of the public visit the site for information and contacts. This site also features the two journals published by the IASW and provides subscription information.

URL: http://www.sc.edu/swan/gade/index.html
Ann Nichols-Casebolt, Ph.D.
GADE Chairperson
acasebol@saturn.vcu.edu
Web Master: Michael Wright

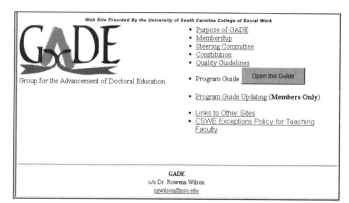

This site provides information about the Group for the Advancement of Doctoral Education in Social Work (GADE). A listing of U.S. social work doctoral programs and several international programs appears in the "Program Guide." Links of special interest to doctoral educators and students are periodically updated.

URL: tp://www.utexas.edu/ depts/sswork/cswr/index.html
John Trapp
Senior Systems Analyst
jtrapp@mail.utexas.edu

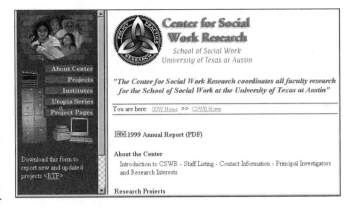

This site is used to profile the activities of the Center for Social Work Research (CSWR) at the School of Social Work, University of Texas at Austin. The CSWR coordinates all faculty research at the school. This site offers a listing of all faculty research from 1994 to the present, as well as conferences, the Utopian Lecture series, project pages, and related Web resources.

This site promotes social work research by providing a profile of faculty work, funding sources, and collaborative efforts. Future expansion will include the posting of research findings, reports, and data with project listings and a concentration on specialty areas such as domestic violence, cultural diversity, and welfare reform.

URL: http://www.samhsa.gov
Peggy Adams
Public Affairs Specialist
info@samhsa.gov

Web Master: Clay Hall

Click ☞ First-Time Study Describes Substance Abuse

The Substance Abuse and Mental Health Services Administration (SAMHSA) is the federal agency responsible for federal participation in the development of treatment and prevention programs for substance abuse and mental illnesses. In addition to information on SA/MH block grants to states, which bear directly on the programs that social workers administer, the SAMHSA site and its auxiliary pages provide information on topics such as children's mental health; homeless persons with mental illness; and substance abuse in women and in minority populations, youth, and criminal justice populations. Information on knowledge development and knowledge application grants, managed care implications for SA/MH treatment and prevention, and national statistics on substance abuse and treatment are also provided.

URL: http://www.handsnet.org
Michael Saunders
Executive Officer
msaunders@handsnet.org

Web Master: Erik Nelson

HandsNet aims to empower organizations to effectively integrate on-line communications strategies, improving programs and policies for children, families, and people in need. HandsNet with its new information service, WebClipper, allows social workers to effectively locate information on the WWW related to a range of human services issues.

MEMBERS ONLY
Log In to WebClipper or HandsNet Email.

BUILDING THE HUMAN SERVICES COMMUNITY ONLINE

HandsNet empowers organizations to integrate effective online communications strategies to strengthen their programs and policies for children, families and people in need.

WEBCLIPPER:
ONLINE NETWORKING

Like a personal clipping service,

click here
FREE TRIAL
MEMBERSHIP

TRAINING&
CAPACITY BUILDING

To help our community effectively integrate online technology, HandsNet offers a

URL: http://www.cswe.org
Todd Lennon
Manager, Information Systems
tlennon@cswe.org

The Council on Social Work Education (CSWE) Web site is used primarily by CSWE members as a resource for information regarding social work education. Most CSWE members are social work educators and programs, so the information is geared toward informing them about accreditation standards and processes, CSWE publications, projects, news, and other items of interest. A FAQ page on social work education and a directory of accredited programs are of interest to individuals considering the profession of social work.

COUNCIL ON SOCIAL WORK EDUCATION

WELCOME TO CSWE ONLINE

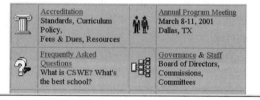

	Accreditation Standards, Curriculum Policy, Fees & Dues, Resources		Annual Program Meeting March 8-11, 2001 Dallas, TX
	Frequently Asked Questions What is CSWE? What's the best school?		Governance & Staff Board of Directors, Commissions, Committees

URL: http://www.seniornet.org
Marcie Schwarz
Senior Net Director of Education
marcie@seniornet.org

Web Master: Jeanne Blake

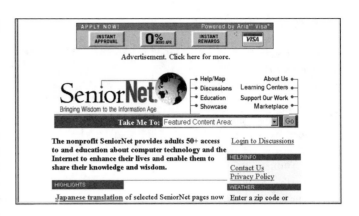

We have various RoundTable message boards that graduate students and professionals have used to gather data about older adults on topics such as computer technologies, health, and retirement. Some educators have brought their online classes in to ask questions.

URL: http://www.geocities. com/Heartland/4862/ swcafe.html
Tobi Ann Shane
bshane@hotmail.com

Web Master, Social Work Cafe

The Social Work Cafe was created as a vehicle for social work students, professionals, and educators to globally share and understand their common interests. Originally posting annotated E-mail listings by geographic location, in 1998 a movement began to further encourage the on-line exchange of ideas through various new interactive technologies (e.g., international chat areas, bulletin boards, and message centers).

Then in 1999, the Social Work Cafe merged with the Social Work Access Network's (SWAN's) advanced technology to create a more powerful directory of on-line social work students, professionals, educators, and affiliates. The combining of resources has led to the creation of "The Complete Social Worker" (CSW), an index of links to other on-line resources for social workers and their clients. CSW international leadership and research teams represent individuals and groups who stay abreast of issues facing the profession in the workplace (e.g., therapies, fund raising, advocacy, policy). Though in its infancy, the CSW shows great promise in bringing social work professionals together to discuss, evaluate, and create new resources on the Web.

URL: http://www.nacsw.org
Rick Chamiec-Case
Executive Director
NACSW@aol.com

Web Master: Michael Wright

The North American Association of Christians in Social Work (NACSW) launched its Web page in early 1998, primarily to assist Christians in social work to integrate their faith and practice. Since then, we have received a great deal of feedback that it has made NACSW much more visible and accessible to its members as well as to those who are interested in finding out more about our organization.

Ways social workers can use our Web site include (1) learning about the mission, history, and benefits of NACSW, receiving current organizational information and announcements, and becoming a member on-line; (2) shopping for and purchasing materials published by NACSW; (3) learning about NACSW's upcoming annual conventions and registering on-line; (4) participating in chat room discussions; (5) finding information about NACSW's local chapters; (6) discovering links to other resources and organizations of special interest to Christians in social work.

URL: http://cassw-acess.ca
Crystal Hache
Administrative Coordinator
cassw@cassw-acess.ca

This Web site provides information about schools of social work in Canada. This site is bilingual (English–French). You will find information about the Canadian Association of Schools of Social Work including its board of directors, constitution, and membership. There is information about accredited schools of social work, including their locations, deans, and directors, plus a brief description of their programs. Also you will find subjects such as current projects the association is involved with, its accreditation manual, and upcoming meetings.

**URL: http://www.tcada.
state.tx.us**
Amy T. Carr
Research Editor
research@tcada.state.tx.us

The mission of the Texas Commission on Alcohol and Drug Abuse is to provide the leadership and resources needed to prevent our children from using drugs, to help persons who are addicted recover, and to protect our families and communities from the dangers of drug abuse.

Social workers can find state and county-level statistics and other information on substance use, misuse, and gambling behavior among a variety of Texas populations including youth, adults, and criminal justice populations. The latest substance abuse trends and epidemiology data are available. This Web site also provides information on prevention initiatives, training opportunities, and the Texas Addiction Technology Transfer Center (TATTC).

URL: http://www.health.org
Tina Sweep
Web Site Developer
tsweep@health.org

The National Clearinghouse for Alcohol and Drug Information (NCADI) is the information service of the Center for Substance Abuse Prevention of the Substance Abuse and Mental Health Services Administration in the U.S. Department of Health and Human Services.

NCADI is the world's largest resource for current information and materials concerning substance abuse prevention and treatment. NCADI's Web site, PREVLINE, is located at http://www.health.org. PREVLINE is a full-service Web site—the biggest alcohol, tobacco, and other drug (ATOD) prevention-and-treatment-information–related Web site in the country. PREVLINE offers rapid access to documents available on-line; an electronic catalog (free materials and publications); on-line databases; research and statistics; campaigns/initiatives; a daily news room; research briefs; a conference calendar; and funding opportunities/grant announcements.

URL: http://www.nyu.edu/ socialwork/wwwrsw
Gary Holden
Associate Professor
gary.holden@nyu.edu

The World Wide Web Resources for Social Workers site (WWWRSW) has been under development since 1993. Our goal is to improve information access for social workers throughout the world, from BSW students to faculty in DSW/PhD programs. WWWRSW contains over 6,800 links, many of which are to full-text documents of potential utility to social workers. The site averages 850 hits per day. WWWRSW is sponsored by New York University's Ehrenkranz School of Social Work and the Mount Sinai–NYU Medical Center and Health System. Dr. Gary Holden is the site director. Dr. Thomas Meenaghan and Dr. Gary Rosenberg comprise the Editorial Advisory Board.

www.nyu.edu/socialwork/wwwrsw

World Wide Web Resources for Social Workers

Search:

[   ] Go!

Browse by Category

· Government
· Higher Education
· Journals and Newsletters
· Professional Associations

· Reference
· Search and General Indexes
· Social Work
· Telehealth

URL: http://www.epfo.org
Guillermo Mendoza, M. D.
Project Officer, Partnerships for a Healthy Border
vph@usmbha.org
Web Master: Jimmy Devenport

Social workers use this Web site to learn more about bi-border public health. They visit the epidemiology section to know about the health status of the communities of both sides of the U.S.–Mexican border,

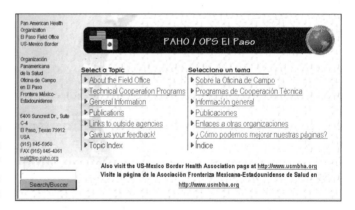

to know about the public-health–related meetings organized along the border, and to easily access the Web sites of other health-related agencies, be they local, borderwide, national, or international agencies. They also visit our Web site to get information about the U.S.–Mexico Border Health Association, its members, and its activities.

URL: http://alz.org
Rory Dick
Specialist
rory.dick@alz.org
Web Master: Michelle Turner

Social workers can use the Alzheimer's Association Web page to gain the most current information on Alzheimer's disease, links to our chapter network, and data on upcoming conferences and events.

URL: http://www.sc.edu/ swan/index.html
Michael Wright
Graduate Assistant/Web Master
michaelw@cosw.cosw.sc.edu

The Social Work Access Network (SWAN) has always been a data depository for social work information on the Web. Listservs, Web links, newsgroups, schools, professionals, and more continue to be a part of the site. Yet, SWAN has a

distributed data model that transforms the site from a depository into a dynamic data warehouse. Members of SWAN can now update all its resources in real time. In addition, SWAN supports free advertising of social work resources, conferences, and chat events.

The most popular areas of the site are the Social Work Schools and Conference Listing pages. Many visitors use SWAN as a jump station for other social work resources as evidenced by the popularity of the Topics page. With strategic partnership with the Social Work Cafe and Grassroots: Social Science Search, SWAN has solidified its commitment to networking and on-line research, respectively.

**URL: http://dominic.barry.
edu/~kelly/aaswg/aaswg.html**
Tim Kelly
Web Master
tkelly@mail.barry.edu

The Association for the Advancement of Social Work with Groups
(AASWG) Web site is used for networking and information dissemi-
nation. There are links to AASWG
chapters and other organizational
resources plus links for syllabi and
other group work-related resources.

**URL: http://www.
ClinicalSocialWork.com**
Patricia D. McClendon, MSSW, CSW
Social Worker
Pat@ClinicalSocialWork.com

Social workers have used this Web
site to locate resources involving
professional organizations; professional mailing lists and news
groups; hard-to-find articles; on-
line journals; treatment centers;
links of interest to the social work

profession; and so on. They also use it to network with other therapists on a one-on-one basis. By joining the database of therapists at the Web site, they are making themselves available to new clients as well
as to other mental health professionals for peer-to-peer consultation.

This Web site has a large variety of resources about abuse, the Internet, dissociation, ego state therapy (including articles by John and Helen Watkins), gender, health, the law school, social work, therapists, treatment modalities/approaches, and violence. This Web site has resources for therapists, clients,
and the general public, but emphasis is placed on trauma-related symptoms and therapy. It also contains
a growing database of therapists and treatment centers.

URL: http://www.rit.edu/ ~694www/bpd
Marshall L. Smith
Web Manager
docsmith@mail.rit.edu

The Association of Baccealaureate Social Work Program Directors, Inc. (BPD) Web site is a primary source for baccalaureate social work educators, students, and graduates. It is a resource for information on the nine areas of the BSW curriculum.

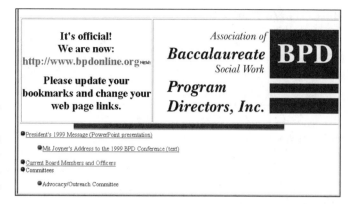

URL: http://www.nattc.org
Jennifer Tate Giles
Project Manager
tatej@nattc.org
Web Master: Gene Tucker

Social workers use the Addiction Technology Transfer Centers' national Web site to obtain instant access and links to the latest information on addiction treatment and prevention including training opportunities and free or low-cost

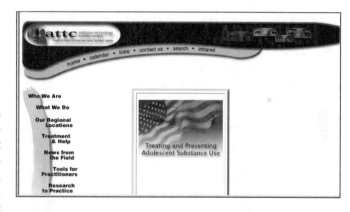

curricula and education products. One of the products of great interest to social workers is *Addiction Counseling Competencies: The Knowledge, Skills, and Attitudes of Professional Practice* (Tap 21) in the Substance Abuse and Mental Health Services Administration, Center for Substance Abuse Treatment Technical Assistance Publication Series. This document presents the knowledge, skills, and attitudes needed for achieving and practicing competence in addictions. This document provides guidelines not only for addiction counselors, but for all professionals who have an opportunity to intervene in the lives of addicted people. This document is available for viewing or downloading from our site.

URL: http://www.naswtx.org
Andrew T. Marks, LMSW
Program and Membership
Coordinator/Web Master
naswtex@realtime.net

This is the host site for the Texas
chapter of the National Association
of Social Workers. The Texas chapter represents 6,400 social workers
in Texas. Our site offers information to both members and non-
members; however, some sections
are available only to members. You

can find information about the association and social work in various parts of Texas as well as resources
on social work across the Internet. We also have one section dedicated to the Texas legislature and social work issues during the legislative sessions.

URL: http://www.omhrc.gov
LaJoy Y. Mosby
Deputy Director
info@omhrc.gov
Web Master: Ida Miggins

Our site is used by social workers
seeking information on cultural
competency and consumer information in various languages. We list
resources that provide multilingual
materials for consumers. We also list
national minority organizations as

well as programs, documents, and articles on various aspects of minority health. To our knowledge, we are
the nation's largest repository of information on minority health. We also provide data on grants and current legislation affecting minorities. We make additions to our "What's New" section several times weekly.

URL: http://www.tiac. net/users/swes
Stephen Antler
Director
swes@tiac.net

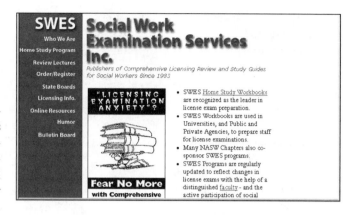

The Social Work Examination Services, (SWES) Web site provides information about licensing requirements and procedures. Visitors can request a free sample and can purchase SWES workbooks for all levels of social work licensing. A schedule of SWES review courses is also provided. Courses are offered in New York, Connecticut, and Massachusetts for all levels of AASSWB license exams.

URL: http://www3.nf. sympatico.ca/nlasw
Bruce Cooper, MSW, RSW
Executive Director and Registrar
nlasw@nf.sympatico.ca
Web Master: Ed Kennedy

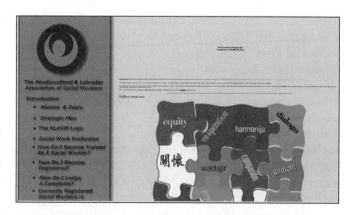

Members of the Newfoundland & Labrador Association of Social Workers (NLASW) can use the Web site to access the roster of all registered social workers in the province, information about continuing professional education, information about current projects and initiatives being undertaken by the NLASW, links to other social work sites, and tools to assist members in job searches across the country. We are also developing a listing of volunteer positions available within the NLASW and we are examining the notion of having on-line renewal of social work licenses and on-line continuing professional education delivery.

**URL: http://www.bc.edu/
bc_org/avp/gssw/
ea_resources.html**
John McNutt
Social Work Professor,
Boston College
mcnutt@bc.edu

This site contains information about using technology for advocacy in social work practice. The site includes a bibliography and links to valuable sources of information.

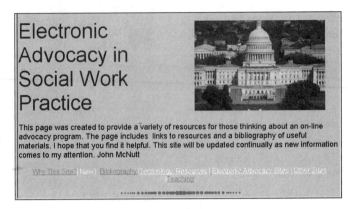

**URL: http://www.
socialworker.com**
Linda M. Grobman, ACSW, LSW
Editor/Publisher
linda.grobman@paonline.com

The New Social Worker Online was started in 1995 as a companion Web site to the national print magazine for social work students and recent graduates, *The New Social Worker*. Like the print publication, the Web site places strong

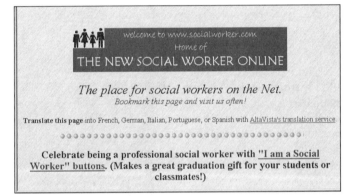

emphasis on career development for new professionals. Major features include sample full-text articles from the magazine, an Online Career Center with career- and job-related links, current job listings, and a page of links to social work–related sites. Over time, the site has grown into a full-fledged on-line social work community with interactive features such as a chat room and a message board.

At the center of this on-line community is the Discussion Forum (http://www.socialworker.com/discus/board.html), an on-line message board where social workers from the United States, Canada, and elsewhere exchange ideas and information. Here you will find ongoing discussions of social work schools, ethical issues, careers, and much more. Chats with guest speakers leading real time discussions of topics such as social work ethics, job search techniques, and current events as they relate to social work are periodically featured.

URL: http://socwork.uindy. edu/index.html
Dawn O'Shea
Graduate Assistant
osheade@uindy.edu

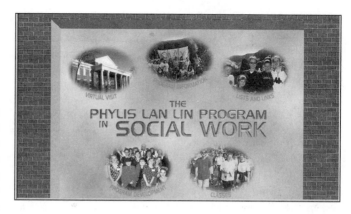

This URL listed is the social work homepage. This particular page is designed in five parts used partially for recruitment purposes but primarily for students working on a BSW. This page can be used by anybody who is interested in professional social work, for recruitment, and for administrators.

The other pages that contain links to other social work programs' pages and search engines are http://socwork.uindy.edu/links/meta1.htm and http://socwork.uindy.edu/links/search1.htm. The first is a list of links to other programs and other meta-lists. The second is a guide to using search engines on the Internet for social workers.

URL: http://www.uindy. edu/~kml/resources/ socialwork/index.html
Shirley Bigna
Assistant Director
bigna@uindy.edu

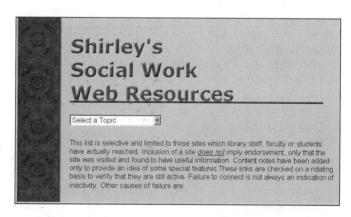

This award-winning site was recognized in the March 1998 issue of *College & Research Libraries News.* It contains over seven hundred annotated sites for social work professionals, students, and faculty. More than fifty subject areas are covered. The homepage receives over 150 hits a day from around the world. This site has been used for research and classroom instruction, and E-mail communication can extend the research arena. The site is updated every four months. The site has been compiled and maintained by Shirley Bigna and Kim Wenning.

URL: http://www.lakefield. net/~tjcleer/ring.htm

Thomas Cleereman, MSW
Social Worker
Webmaster@socialworksearch.com

This is the popular Social Work Web Ring. Other social work Web masters can submit their sites to the ring for free. Once in the ring, they will have the HTML code at their site, which allows their visitors to click through the ring to see the different social work Web sites. There are currently over eighty members. Statistics show there are thousands of people moving through the ring each day.

Tom Cleereman's Social Work Web Ring Setup

To add your site to the "Social Work Web Ring" please follow steps 1-3 below. After you have completed the steps and added the appropriate HTML code to your page you will be added to the "Ring" as soon as I have a chance to review your site for inclusion.

Step #1: Read the following license before moving to step #2. (Following through on step #2 means you agree to these terms).

The Social Work Web Ring is a free service to social workers and other professionals who have web pages on the internet. If your site contains adult material that offends others or is not suitable for the Social Work Web Ring it will NOT be added to this web ring service. If you ever romove the web ring from your site I ask that you notify me at tjcleer@lakefield.net and I will delete it from the web ring service. The web ring must be placed at the URL you describe in "Step #2". Your site will not be added immediately to the web ring until after I have accepted it for inclusion (1 to 2 days). I hope this service brings more traffic to your site and I am interested in any feedback regarding the web ring that you may have.

Step #2: Fill out the information and click "Add To Queue". Make sure your password is atleast 4 characters long with no white spaces.

URL: http://www.lakefield. net/~tjcleer

Thomas Cleereman, MSW
Social Worker
webmaster@socialworksearch.com

The homepage of Thomas Cleereman, this site contains lots of interesting information about social-work–related topics. It features information about criminal thinking, has a social work E-mail list, and a jokes page.

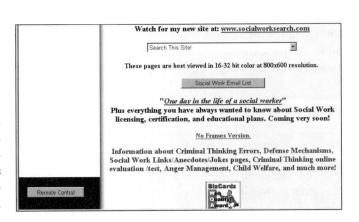

chapter 9

Authoring Web Pages

Logging On—Social Workers Online

Michael Fife has worked in oncology for thirty years and was a charter member of the Association of Oncology Social Work (AOSW) back in 1984. As president of AOSW she has seen a growing use of the Internet among social workers. In response, AOSW established its own presence on the World Wide Web a few years ago.

"One of the things we're seeing is some of the younger persons new to social work don't have the same apprehensions about using the computer as older people do. They also have a good idea about what can be accomplished with the technology. Our goal is to meet practice needs by sharing information, providing network opportunities, and identifying resources for social workers. This is especially critical for individuals who are the only oncology social worker in their geographic area, or other professionals who do not have the expertise one acquires working in oncology day after day. Many times we're separated from those in need of specialized information by great geographic distances. Using the Internet makes it possible to share information concerning patient advocacy or financial resources for families.

"We have designed our Web site to be an electronic gateway to a host of social work information. Laying out our Web site and updating its contents is definitely a collaborative effort. We meet as a group to decide how our pages should look and what they should say. The ideas you see on our Web site are a collective product. Normally the chairs of subcommittees assume responsibility for getting material to the board to review for accuracy. Once material is approved, that individual forwards the information to our Web master either via

E-mail or as a diskette. Thanks go to Greg Jesemski, John Sharpe, and Neil O'Connell, who provide much of the technical assistance. Once received, our Web master posts the information on the World Wide Web. It's very exciting to think that what we come up with can be viewed all over the world."

The World Wide Web offers unprecedented opportunities to social work professionals and students. Your social agency is now able to offer information to the public without printing or postage costs. You may also reach a clientele who would not otherwise be aware of your services. As a social work student, you are able to create personal Web pages containing a resume and academic papers. This can be useful when you're applying for jobs or graduate school.

You can begin by understanding HTML (hypertext markup language). HTML is the tag language used to create Web pages. You can learn the intricacies of HTML and write your own code for your pages. Alternatively, you can use a Web page editor, either a free-standing program or the ones built in other programs such as Netscape Communicator and Microsoft Word. Even if you use an editor program, you should know a little about HTML so that you will know how to correct problems when they occur in constructing pages.

Authoring World Wide Web Pages

HTML uses tags, or commands in brackets < >, to give instructions to a browser program about how to display a Web page. For example, if you wanted to display the title of a book in italics, you would type <I>A Social Work Guide to the Internet </I>. The <I> before the title tells the browser to start displaying italics, and the </I> tells the program to stop displaying italics.

A Basic Web Page

The most basic Web page would begin with the tag <html> and end with </html>. This page could be displayed in a Web browser, but it would simply be a blank page. Just add a few more tags and some wording, and you would have a test page. Try this:

<html>

<head>

<title> Test Page </title>

</head>

<body>

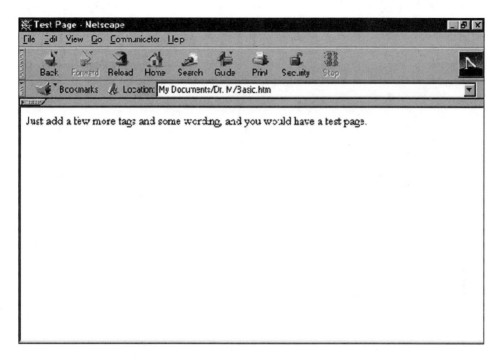

FIGURE 9.1   Test Page Example

Just add a few more tags and some wording, and you would have a test page.

</body>

</html>

If you displayed this page in Netscape, it would look like Figure 9.1. The <head> and <title> tags instruct the browser program to place the title of the page, Test Page, at the top of the browser screen. The <body> tag indicates the beginning of the body of the actual page, and </body> indicates the end.

Learning HTML Tags

You don't need to know every HTML tag to construct a Web page. Just a few basic tags will get you started, and then you can add to your repertoire of tags as you construct your pages. Numerous handbooks available on-line will instruct you in more advanced tags; just search for keywords such as *World Wide Web* and *Web Authoring* in your search engine. Many HTML tags are toggle tags, which means that you turn them on with an initial command and turn them off with a second command preceded by a forward slash **(/).** For example, <body> and </body> is one toggle tag set. Other

---

ESSENTIAL HTML TAGS

Toggle tags:

<body> </body>	Begins and ends page
	Centers text
<font size=+1> </font size=+1>	Enlarges text (+2 is even larger, etc.)

Nontoggle tags:

 	Line break
<p>	Paragraph (adds a blank line)
<hr>	Horizontal rule

---

tags such as <br> for line break are not toggle tags. The "Essential HTML Tags" box shows the basic HTML tags. HTML tags, unlike Web addresses, are not case sensitive, so <html> and <HTML> are the same tag.

Hypertext Links

In order to link one Web page to another, you need to use the tags for a hypertext link. Use the <a href="location"> for the opening tag and </a> for the closing tag. HREF stands for hypertext reference and "location" is the Web address for the linked page. Whatever comes between <a href="location"> and </a> is highlighted as a hot link. For example, if you wanted to establish a link on your Web page to the American Cancer Society site, it would look like this:

<a href="http://www.cancer.org"> American Cancer Society </a>

If the linked page is to be within your own collection of Web pages, you don't need to include the complete address, just the name of the file.

Images

The tag for an image is <img src="location">, with location being the address of the image file. Images on the Web generally are in .gif or .jpg format, so a typical image source code for a Web page might look like this:

<img src="photo1.gif">

You place the source code where the image is to go. If the image is to be centered, you add the toggle tags for centering:

** <img src="photo1.gif"> **

Backgrounds

To add a color or image as a background for your page, you modify the <body> tag. Background colors are made up of six-digit HEX numbers (1234567890ABCDEF). If you wanted a black background, for example, you would use this body tag:

<body bgcolor="#000000">

To locate codes for colors to use for backgrounds or text, consult Web pages that index colors in hexadecimal numbers. These include http://www.lynda.com/hex.html, http://www.visibone.com/colorlab, and http://www.hidaho.com/colorcenter, or search for *background colors* in your search engine. If you want to use an image as a background, you would need this tag to specify the location of your background image:

<body background="image.gif">

You can also find many background images to use for your Web pages on the Web itself. Just search for the term *backgrounds* in your search engine.

Text Color and Size

If you want to modify your text color, you can use the same color codes as are used for backgrounds and change your <font> tag. White text, for example, would have the code **<font color="ffffff">.** To enlarge the size of your type slightly, use the tag **<font size="+1">;** use +2 for larger and so on. To turn off the type size or color you have specified, use the tag **</font>.**

E-Mail Address

Include a link to your E-mail address near the bottom of your home page. If you use this tag, clicking on the hot link created will generate a form where the user can send you an E-mail message.

<a href="mailto:yourlogin@e-mailserver"> your E-mail address </a>

Viewing Pages in a Browser

You can test your Web pages before you load them on your server by going to the File menu of your browser and selecting Open File. You will see a dialog box where you can indicate the HTML page you want to view.

Loading Pages onto a Server

Use your FTP program to load your Web pages and image files on your server so that they are made public. The next chapter will demonstrate how to use common FTP programs.

Practice Example

Using the instructions provided, practice page source code for a Web page might look like this:

```
<HTML>
<HEAD>
<TITLE> Social Work Faculty: Rey Martinez </TITLE>
</HEAD>
<BODY BGCOLOR="#FFFFFF" LINK="#003366">
<IMG SRC="world2.gif">

<CENTER><B><FONT SIZE=+1>New Mexico Highlands University
Social Work Faculty</FONT><</B>
<P>

<FONT SIZE=+2>Rey C. Martinez</FONT>
<BR>Associate Professor of Social Work
<BR><I>B.A. University of Hawaii; MSW Boston University;
Ph.D. Florida State University</I><P>

Send email to <A HREF="mailto:rmartinez_5@hotmail.com">
rmartinez_5@hotmail.com</A>
<BR>or call (505) 454-3307</CENTER>

<P>

<H2>Professional Interests:</H2>
<UL>
Marriage & Family Therapy <P>

Multicultural Social Work Practice

Group Work Intervention <A HREF="http://www.utep.edu/
socwork/guide.htm">(Study Guide)</A><P>
</UL>
</BODY>
</HTML>
```

This source code when viewed in a browser would look like the Web page in Figure 9.2.

New Mexico Highlands University

Rey C. Martinez

Associate Professor of Social Work

B.A. University of Hawaii; MSW Boston University; Ph.D. Florida State University

Send email to rmartinez_5@hotmail.com

or call (505) 454-3307

Professional Interests:

- Marriage & Family Therapy
- Multicultural Social Work Practice
- Group Work Intervention (Study Guide)

FIGURE 9.2   Basic Web Page Example

Using Netscape's Built-In Editor to Create a Web Page

There are a number of HTML editors that you can use to construct a Web page without learning the HTML tag codes. Netscape Navigator has one called Composer included in its browser program. To begin using the editor, go to the Netscape Navigator File menu and select **New** and then **Blank Page.** (See Figure 9.3.)

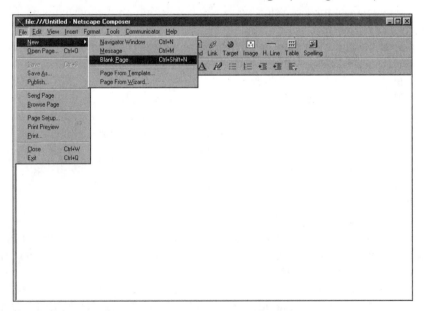

FIGURE 9.3   Accessing Netscape Composer Page

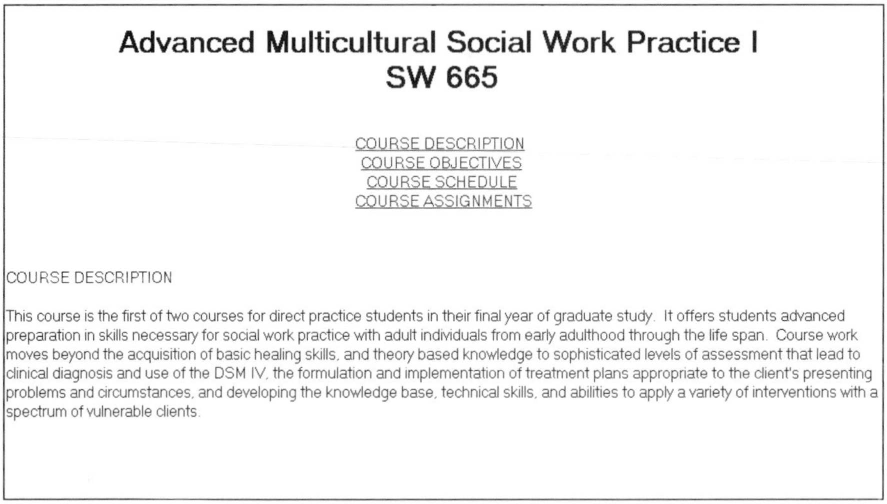

Advanced Multicultural Social Work Practice I
SW 665

COURSE DESCRIPTION
COURSE OBJECTIVES
COURSE SCHEDULE
COURSE ASSIGNMENTS

COURSE DESCRIPTION

This course is the first of two courses for direct practice students in their final year of graduate study. It offers students advanced preparation in skills necessary for social work practice with adult individuals from early adulthood through the life span. Course work moves beyond the acquisition of basic healing skills, and theory based knowledge to sophisticated levels of assessment that lead to clinical diagnosis and use of the DSM IV, the formulation and implementation of treatment plans appropriate to the client's presenting problems and circumstances, and developing the knowledge base, technical skills, and abilities to apply a variety of interventions with a spectrum of vulnerable clients.

FIGURE 9.4   Example Using Netscape Editor

You will see the Composer screen with a blank space where you can create your Web page. The text in Figure 9.4 was created by selecting the typeface, size, and color of type from the pull-down menus on the Composer screen.

The first menu on the left allows you to select heading size if you want. Or, you can just choose a type size in the third menu from the left. Choose a typeface in the second menu from the left. Select type color by clicking on the fourth menu and choosing a color. If you like, select normal type, italics, bold, or underlined type by clicking on one of these. Center your text by clicking the alignment button and selecting centered text. Next, you can select a background image by going to the **Format** menu and selecting **Page Colors** and **Properties.** You will see this dialog box where you can input the name of your image file or search for it by clicking on **Choose File.** When you have selected your background image, click on **OK.** (See Figure 9.5.)

If you want to include a photograph (such as the one maintained by Kathy Schmeling at Ruether Library), position your cursor where you want the photo to go, and click on the **Image** icon. You will see an **Image Properties** dialog box similar to the following one. Click on **Choose File** to select an image from your hard drive or disk. Once you have selected one, click on **OK,** and it will appear in your Composer screen window. (See Figure 9.6.)

To create a hypertext link, highlight text that you want to be the hot link, and then click on the **Link** icon. You will see a dialog box that allows you to enter the Web address to be linked to. After typing the URL, click on **OK.**

To create a link to your E-mail address, highlight the text you want as a link and insert the MAILTO command instead of a Web page address. The MAILTO command looks like this:

mailto:*login@server.address*

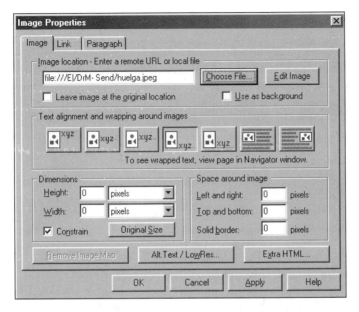

FIGURE 9.5   Using the Image Properties Feature to Insert a Picture

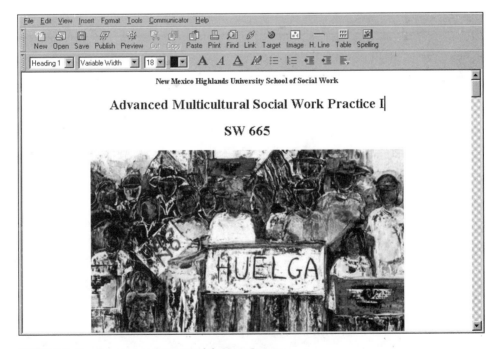

FIGURE 9.6   Composer Screen with New Image

Ruether Library Collections, Wayne State University. Artist: Norma Mendoza. Used with permission.

Summary

This chapter has been a guide to basic HTML commands for constructing Web pages. Part of learning them requires being able to differentiate toggle from nontoggle tags. This chapter demonstrated how to establish hypertext links and insert images using both HTML and the composer option provided by your Web browser. As discussed in the vignette, more and more social work agencies are establishing a Web presence to make their information available on-line.

Discussion Questions

1. What are some advantages and disadvantages of using raw hypertext markup language (HTML) over a conventional Web authoring program?
2. The Communicator suite offers a program entitled Page Composer. How easy is it to use? Which features do you like most? Which features do you like least?
3. Internet Explorer includes a program entitled Frontpage Express. It too is a WYSIWYG (what you see is what you get) Web authoring tool. How easy is it to use? Which features do you like most? Which features do you like least?
4. Newer versions of popular word processing programs (e.g., Word, Word Perfect) offer the ability to save your work in an HTML format. Discuss and compare the advantages of developing a personal page using a word processing program.

chapter 10

File Transfer Protocol

Logging On—Social Workers Online

Tim Davey, clinician and researcher, has devoted much of his professional effort to providing services and advocating for the homeless. He strives to impart his passion and personal commitment to the underserved to his classes at the Virginia Commonwealth University, where he's a member of the social work faculty. Here Dr. Davey describes his use of File Transfer Protocol (FTP).

"I recently collaborated on a project with another social worker that involves our working on two separate documents and then bringing them together as a single manuscript. My areas of expertise are clinical and program evaluation; his are administration and budget. Using the Internet we were able to combine our areas of strength to write a proposal to bring more resources to serve the homeless in our region. Although we live in the same city, my schedule does not allow us to meet regularly. However, the fact that we could communicate via E-mail and send copies of our respective documents for review as attachments made a face-to-face meeting not necessary. My colleague wrote the budget narrative whereas I designed the intervention. Using FTP, our two separate pieces came together as a single document in time for the deadline.

"FTP is an Internet tool that allows me to move a file from one place to another. If you're using Netscape mail or Eudora or have a hotmail account, you can simply compose a message, click on the Attach Document button (sometimes shown as a paper clip), identify the appropriate file, and then send your message. I use FTP primarily to send Word Documents, but the "file" could be a digital image, a PowerPoint presentation, or even a video with sound. In fact, anything that can be saved on a computer can be transferred.

"Many social workers aren't aware that there are several FTP sites of specific interest to the profession. These sites allow visitors to log on as anonymous users and retrieve files that have been stored there for the purpose of sharing. For example, I recently downloaded a free copy of the *Stress Inventory Test,* version 5.2, designed by Dr. Robert Hillman from the FTP site maintained by the School of Social Work at the University of Texas at Arlington. Visit this site for a review of new software products and access to resources for both classroom and practice."

Developed in the 1970s by ARPAnet users, File Transfer Protocol is an old protocol on the Internet. It was created so that people could send files between computers. For many years, it was one of the most popular uses of the Internet. Even today, though E-mail and the World Wide Web are the most commonly used protocols, FTP is still very much employed because it is a straightforward way to transfer files, especially when you know exactly where the desired file is located. With FTP, you can transfer your own files to a social work colleague at a different site, or you can access millions of files available in the public domain.

To use FTP you must have client software that establishes a connection with a remote computer that is running server software. Once established, this connection enables you to explore the file directories on the remote computer. Old FTP programs such as Unix-based FTP client programs are less friendly, but knowledge of a few basic commands will allow you to find the files you need. Unix-based FTP will be demonstrated in this chapter because of the probability of workers encountering it in the field. Newer programs such as WS-FTP and FETCH are much more user friendly and don't require you to know commands not indicated on the screen with form boxes and buttons. Instructions for using these are likewise provided.

Full-Service versus Guest FTP

With full-service FTP you need a password as well as an FTP address. The password will enable you to add files to the remote computer in addition to downloading files. This is important if you are establishing a Web site, for example, because you need to place your HTML and image files on a remote server that will house your Web site. Guest FTP, on the other hand, allows you to access a remote FTP archive site, log in as "guest," and download files. You cannot upload any files to the site. In social work, these FTP sites contain "shareware" and "freeware" programs you can use in your practice, most of the time for free.

What Is an FTP Address?

The addressing scheme used to explain other Internet Protocols is applicable to FTP as well. This means that each location has a discrete address that resembles an E-mail address, except without the username prefix and @ symbol. Here are sample FTP addresses of interest to social work:

Address	Location to Visit
ftp.uta.edu/cussn	/ssw/cussn
ftp.stolaf.edu	/pub/archives/social-work-dept
ftp.cc.utexas.edu	/depts/admissions/tccn/1998-00/ social-work.html
ftp.mssm.edu	/pub/Find-Levy-Library-Resources/ Social-Workers-Guide Social-Workers-Guide

All those just listed use "ftp" as part of their address; some others do not. In fact, there's no standard way of naming an FTP site. Sometimes you'll see an FTP site name that's just a string of numbers separated with periods, like this:

129.107.56.183

This also is an FTP site's IP address on the Internet. If the site manager does not register a domain name for his or her computer's IP address, the site will be referred to as "129, dot 107 dot, 56 dot, 183." Or, you could also say, "ftp.uta.edu/cussnet," which is the address given at the top of the preceding list.

INTERVIEW WITH SOCIAL WORK EDUCATOR DICK SCHOECK, PhD

Dick Schoeck is an associate professor at the University of Texas at Arlington.

"Originally, it all started when I agreed to provide reviews of various software programs from a social worker's perspective and to disseminate freeware programs for use in the field. This was an extremely valuable service. Anyone needing a disk copied could bring it by; I had developed a system that allowed me to do the work quickly and efficiently. Not much later the requests were too numerous to keep up with.

"The FTP site featured in this chapter came on-line in 1997. Now interested social workers are able to access the site at their convenience from anywhere in the world. The site requires some maintenance but it's worth the effort for providing software reviews, shareware, and demo commercial programs for temporary use. Whether using Unix or a full-graphical browser, you can go to http://www.uta.edu/cussn."

Using File Transfer Protocol

If you are using a type-sharing system such as Unix, VAX/VMS, or IBM/VM, you may have an FTP client accessible either at the command prompt or from a menu listing. After you have accessed your FTP program, you will have a dialog box or system prompt where you can give the address of the remote computer and specify the directory where your file is located. If you don't know the location of a specific file, you can specify "pub." This is where most publicly accessible files are located.

Guest FTP

When connecting to a recognized site, you should be able to log in with the username **anonymous.** Your password, however, will be your personal E-mail address. Here's an example:

open ftp://ftp.uta.edu/cussn
login: **anonymous**
Password: **rmartinez_5@hotmail.com** (Note: Your password will not be shown.)

Although Unix is an elaborate programming language, there are only a handful of commands you'll need to use FTP. These commands will instruct the host computer (remote site) what to do, rather than being executed on your own terminal.

Essential Unix-Based FTP Commands

Here are commands you will be using if logged into a social work FTP site using a conventional Unix-based system:

ascii	Indicates that items to be transferred are ASCII text files only
cd..	Command used to move up one directory
cd *directoryname*	Command used to move to a specific directory on the server
dir	Displays the content of the current directory
get	Command used to download a file from the server to one's account or terminal
help	Displays commands recognized by the host computer
ls	Lists content of the current directory without specific information about each file
open *hostname*	Command used to connect to the host computer located at the specified address
put *filename*	Command used to upload a file from one's account or terminal to the server
quit	Ends an FTP session

Unix FTP Demonstration

Let's walk through a typical FTP session using the site maintained by Dick Schoeck at the University of Texas at Arlington's School of Social Work (ftp://ftp.uta.edu/cussn) and download a free computerized Stress Inventory Test (Hillman, 1993) to administer to clients. It can be found in a directory entitled **cussn** (Computer Use in Social Service Networks) as part the filename **tests1.zip.** When using Unix, the first step will be to type the command "**ftp**" at the system's prompt. This will retrieve the FTP software necessary to download the file of interest. Once the software is running, the **Open Hostname** command will connect the users to a prompt where they can log on as "anonymous" and use their E-mail addresses as passwords.

ftp> open ftp://ftp.uta.edu/cussn

Once you're connected, a welcome message will appear on your screen. Do not be concerned about all the numerals "230" that precede each line. This is a common Unix method of displaying a system message such as the one in the screen capture in Figure 10.1. But pay close attention to the text. As stated, all commands and transfers are logged by the system. People who are uncomfortable with having their transactions monitored, in accordance with policy, are advised to log out. This policy is actually to the user's advantage. The system reduces the probability that viruses or corrupt files transferred inadvertently (or maliciously) end up on your computer or diskettes. The Welcome screen also offers useful tips for users who are new to the site.

As seen in Figure 10.1, one of the first commands is to move the school of social work directory. This is accomplished by using the **cd** command followed by the name of the directory—in this case, **cd ssw.** As mentioned previously, the **dir** command

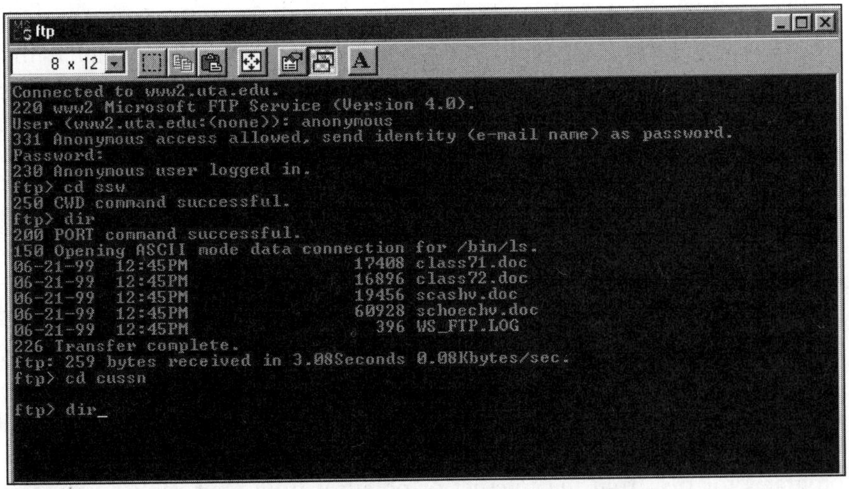

FIGURE 10.1   Using Unix to Access an Anonymous FTP Site

FIGURE 10.2   Using the "get" Command to Download Files

displays the content of the current directory. The next step, therefore, is to change directories again, this time to the CUSSN directory where the desired file has been archived. As seen in Figure 10.1, this is accomplished by typing the appropriate command and touching enter: **cd cussn.** Again, the command **dir** displays file names found in the directory. This time, as shown in the screen capture in Figure 10.2, the file name we're looking for, "tests1.zip," is among those listed. The last step is to instruct the computer to retrieve the file and transfer it to our machine or diskette so it can be used.

As shown in Figure 10.2, the command used to download a file from the server to one's account or terminal is "**get.**" Since Hillman's computerized Stress Inventory Test (1993) is stored as "tests1.zip," the command to download it is as follows: **get tests1.zip.** That's all there is to it.

Don't be alarmed if after many attempts you still feel awkward using a Unix-based file transfer protocol. Admittedly, it requires a lot of practice and resembles the old disk operating system (DOS). In the same manner that DOS systems still exist in many nonprofits (despite being considered obsolete by other professions), Unix-based FTP is still the method of choice. For others, WIN-FTP or FETCH (for use on Macintosh computers) will be used primarily.

Using FTP Windows

If you are using a computer lab, your computer may already have an FTP program such as WS-FTP. You may be able to access the program by an icon on the desktop or from the computer's Start menu. If your computer is not preloaded with an FTP client but you have a PPP or SLIP connection to the Internet, you can download one of these programs for free from the Internet or obtain it from your service provider. Consult your service provider for the best way to obtain an FTP client.

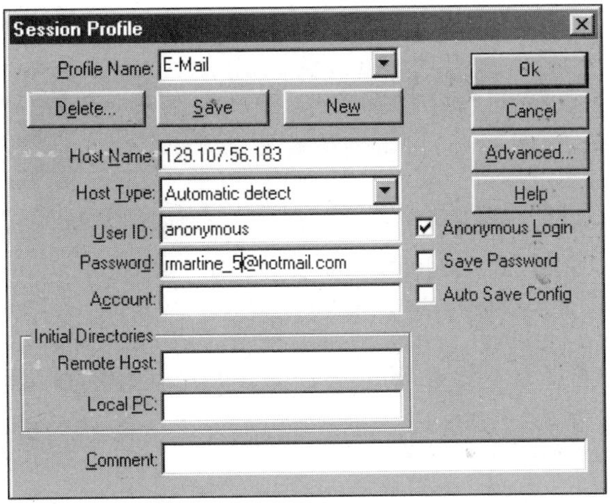

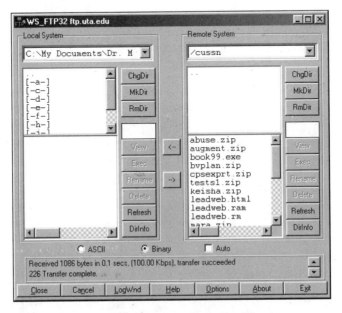

FIGURE 10.3   Logging onto WS-FTP

Figure 10.3 portrays a typical session profile dialog box. The numbers 129.107.56.183 represent the host name. As with most anonymous FTP sites, the User ID is simply "anonymous" and your E-mail address serves as the password. In the next dialog box where you will encounter using WS-FTP, the left side of the screen represents the local system, in this case the hard drive of the computer you're using. As demonstrated in Figure 10.4, the right side of the dialog box represents the remote system. In this case, it represents the server located at the University of Texas at Arlington.

FIGURE 10.4   Using WS-FTP to Transfer Files

Using this program, files are easily transferred to the specified directory simply by selecting the appropriate arrow.

Summary

This chapter has explained the rationale and use of File Transfer Protocol. To publish your Web page, for example, you will need space on a designated Web server. This chapter has focused on moving information, whether text file or source code, from one location to another. Both Unix-based and Windows-based examples have been provided. An FTP site for sending and downloading programs of relevance to social work has also been featured.

Discussion Questions

1. What does the term *client/server program* mean in reference to File Transfer Protocol (FTP)?
2. Identify four possible uses of FTP in social work practice.
3. Describe how Unix-based FTP differs from WIN-FTP.
4. Give working examples of two social workers needing to exchange materials of various file types (e.g., text, video, graphics).

Works Cited

Hillman, J. (1993). Computerized stress inventory test. (Accessed 1999, November 23) [Online]. Available FTP: ftp.uta.edu/cussn.

chapter 11

Telnet

Logging On—Social Workers Online

Rhaelynne Scherer is a medical social worker at Brigham Women's and Children's Hospital in Boston, Massachusetts.

"Telnet is a program I use regularly on my job. It allows me to check my E-mail and stay informed on patient needs and status when I'm away from the hospital. Most Windows operating systems have a Run option in the bottom left-hand corner that appears when you click on the Start button. I type in the command **Telnet** followed by the server address in the field provided and I am immediately connected to the mail server at work. I can do this from home, professional conferences, airport, or anywhere else where there's a computer with access to the Internet.

"But there is a special use of Telnet that I've only recently discovered. It's called Freenet. A Freenet is a type of local community computer system that's linked to the Internet. Most cities, I've discovered, have a Freenet system. Freenets are an excellent way to obtain information on cities throughout the United States and all over the world. If you're interested in health clinics in the Miami area, not a problem. If you need information about Dayton, Ohio, or Tallahassee, Florida, it's all at your fingertips. I am able to incorporate the use of community Freenets as part of my discharge planning whenever appropriate."

Telnet is a tool that enables social work practitioners to browse journals and other on-line material at libraries all over the world. Telnet predates the World Wide Web and is still used by libraries and many other institutions to make information available to those who may not have a Web graphical connection. If you use Telnet to access a remote library catalog, for example, you can maneuver it as if you were standing in the reference room using one of the library's own computerized catalogs. Many libraries now have World Wide Web pages that provide an entry point for their catalogs, but sometimes the Web page leads to a Telnet session.

"Guest" versus "Full-Service" Telnet

Using a remote library catalog is referred to as "guest Telnet." This is because you are a guest in the system and do not have a password of your own. In contrast, Telnet can also be used to connect to older E-mail systems, college systems, or Freenets (which we discuss later). This is known as "full-service Telnet" because you are provided with a password that gives you privileges in the system such as being able to send and receive E-mail. Another advantage of this type of system is that it enables you to check your E-mail from a remote location if you are able to get access to Telnet.

Using Telnet

To use Telnet, you must access Telnet software. How you accomplish this depends on the type of connection you are using. There are two typical ways to access Telnet:

1. If you have a full-graphical connection to the Internet, one that allows you to use a Web browser, you can simply access the Telnet software that is preloaded on most PCs. If you are working in a computer lab, the staff may have conveniently provided you with a Telnet icon or connected Telnet to the Start menu. If you don't already know where that software is located, use the Find feature from your Start button and search for Telnet. Your computer will locate the application for you. Double click on it and you will see a screen with a menu bar across the top. Choose the **Connect** pull-down menu and select **Remote System.** You will see a dialog box that allows you to enter the address of the Telnet site. Click on **Connect** and your computer will contact the remote site.
2. If you are using a network system (such as a Unix system) that gives you a command prompt, try typing "Telnet" and touch Enter. You will then need to type "open" and the address of the site.

Telnet Addresses

A Telnet address, like all Internet addresses, is typically a group of numbers separated by dots, such as **208.136.234.19,** or two or more collections of letters separated by dots, such as **rgfn.epcc.edu.** As far as the computer is concerned, these addresses are exactly the same. For us, however, it's usually easier to remember the latter.

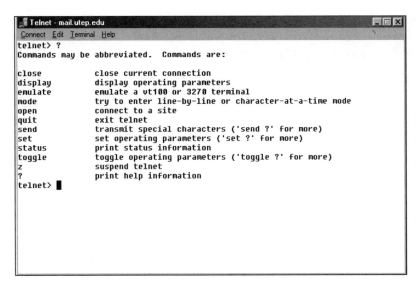

FIGURE 11.1   Telnet Commands

Telnet Commands

Unlike most Internet protocols, Telnet has no one set of commands that work at all sites. When you connect to a site, it will generally give you some basic information, and most have links to Help screens. If you're using a network system (i.e., Unix), type "Telnet" at the command prompt and press **Enter.** Doing so will enter you into Telnet's command mode. The command prompt will change to "Telnet" as it waits for you to enter your next command. From here you can type a question mark (?) to display a list of commands recognized by the system. Typically, **Close** and/or **Quit** will end your Telnet session. (See Figure 11.1.)

Telnet Demonstration Session

Host computers on the Internet operate differently but with enough similarity that connecting with one will provide you with the necessary experience to work with others. Fortunately, most publicly accessible Telnet computers offer a "shell" design (a special type of user interface) that makes navigating easy. When visiting a new site, spend time familiarizing yourself with the commands at the bottom of the screen or accessing the on-line Help screens.

For a practice Telnet session, we'll Telnet to the University of Texas Library in Austin and conduct a MEDLINE search. As we just saw, you use the Open command to initiate a connection to a Telnet address you wish to access. (See Figure 11.2.)

telnet> open medline.lib.utsystem.edu

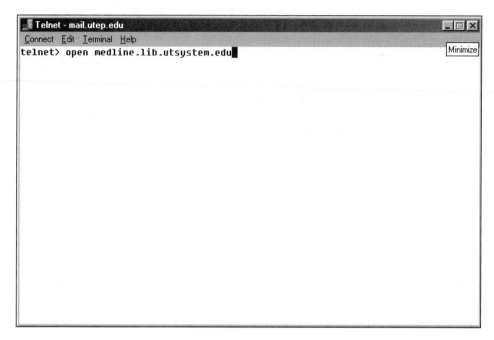

FIGURE 11.2   Using Telnet to Access Remote Library

Typically the host computer will display important information such as who's eligible to use the system and where to report problems. Now that you are successfully logged in, all commands to navigate the computer will be determined by the remote computer. Watch for menu items that lead you to Help screens and the key commands to use if you get stuck and need to get out. As indicated on the screen, before conducting your first search it is necessary to select a database. Use the arrow keys to highlight the desired database; then press **Enter.** (See Figure 11.3.)

To conduct a keyword search on the term *social work,* press **U** for **Subject.** (See Figure 11.4.) Continue this procedure until all the keywords have been entered. Now we're ready to combine terms.

By pressing the letter **O,** we're instructing the remote computer to **combine** the terms *social-work* and *diabetes* and to search the database. It turns out that these two terms show up twenty-nine times. The next step is to view the abstracts and to determine which ones to obtain. This is accomplished by pressing the letter **V** for **View.**

For the social work practitioner or administrator writing a grant proposal to increase the agency's healthcare services to ethnically diverse populations, this abstract from the Telnet site looks extremely useful. (See Figure 11.5.)

It would be helpful to receive a copy. To do this, pick the **S** for Save option. At this point you'll enter your E-mail address and the abstract will be forwarded to you electronically. You'll still need to obtain the entire article from your library to cite it

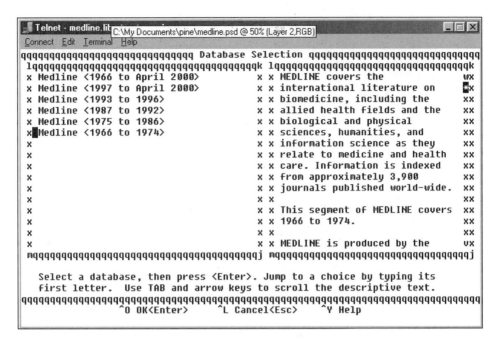

FIGURE 11.3   Selecting a Medline Database During a Telnet Session

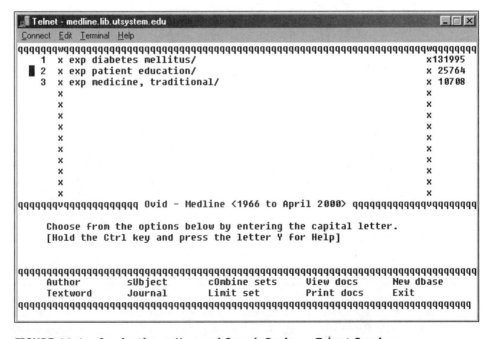

FIGURE 11.4   Conducting a Keyword Search During a Telnet Session

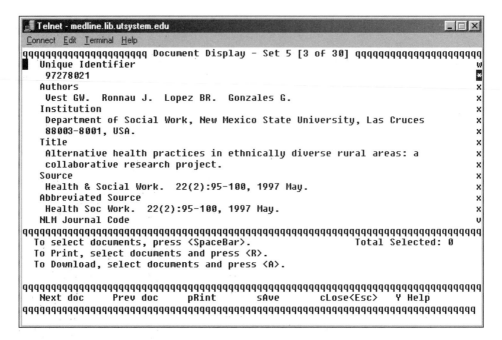

FIGURE 11.5   Identifying Journal Articles via Telnet

properly, but the abstract includes all the necessary information to help you locate it: the journal title, name of the article, volume number, page number, and year published. (See Figure 11.6.)

Terminal Emulation

Sometimes when Telnetting to different sites you'll be asked to specify your "Terminal Type." This is because the remote computer needs to know what keys you're pressing. If you're connected to the Internet via modem from your agency, your telecommunications software settings determine what kind of computer you're emulating. If you're working at a university lab, you'll need to ask your system administrator for the appropriate response. Conventionally, the remote computer either will ask you if VT100 is all right (default) or give you a list of terminal types to choose from. If this happens, it usually works to select VT100.

Introduction to tn3270

Some IBM mainframe computers have a different interface than other "command line" computers. If the IBM computer you're logging into does not provide its own version of 3270 emulation, you will need to log in using a Telnet tool called "tn3270." To us, that simply means it may be necessary to slightly modify the commands used to con-

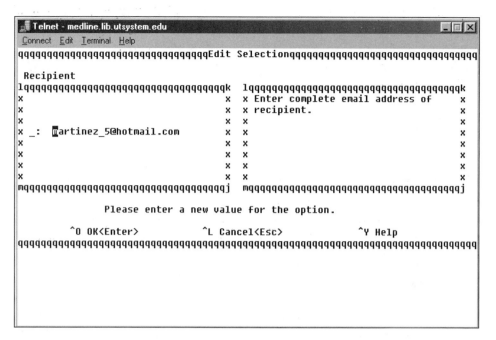

FIGURE 11.6   Using the Telnet Mail Feature to Obtain a Full Citation by E-mail

nect to the remote computer. For example, instead of typing "open rgfn.epcc.edu" to access the Rio Grande Freenet, it may be necessary to type "**tn3270 rgfn.epcc.edu**."

Freenet: A Special Type of Telnet Session

Freenet first came into existence in 1984 as a research project at Case Western Reserve University. The objective of the project was to establish a means for citizens to ask health-related questions to local experts using an electronic bulletin board. This practice grew in popularity. Freenets are now associated with local governments. Most provide announcements of city council meetings, discussions of zoning issues, and relevant information concerning community social services. Most Freenets will allow you to log on as a guest, but some restrictions apply unless you establish an account. Freenets provide an easy way for social workers to access community information for their clients pertaining to housing, healthcare, educational resources, and job opportunities.

For practice, let's pretend we're working with a client family who will be relocating to Seattle, Washington. In preparation for the session, we'll use Telnet to reach the Seattle Community Network to see if we can identify any on-line resources before they leave. We use the same protocol identified as before, and the Unix command at the systems prompt looks like

telnet open scn.org

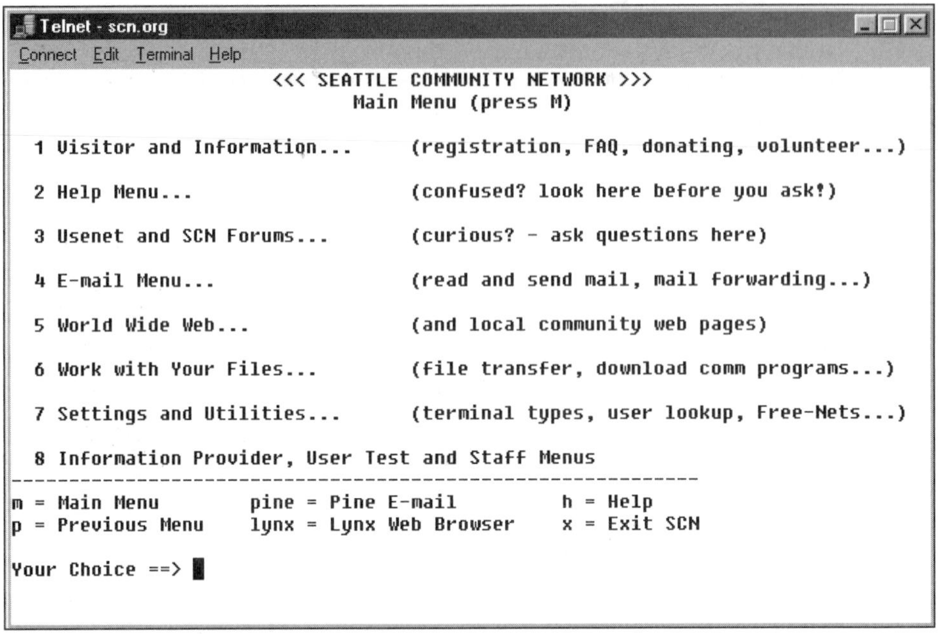

```
 _____
|  Telnet - scn.org                                [_][□][×] |
|  Connect  Edit  Terminal  Help                            |
|              <<< SEATTLE COMMUNITY NETWORK >>>            |
|                    Main Menu (press M)                   |
|                                                          |
|    1 Visitor and Information...    (registration, FAQ, donating, volunteer...) |
|                                                          |
|    2 Help Menu...                  (confused? look here before you ask!) |
|                                                          |
|    3 Usenet and SCN Forums...      (curious? - ask questions here) |
|                                                          |
|    4 E-mail Menu...                (read and send mail, mail forwarding...) |
|                                                          |
|    5 World Wide Web...             (and local community web pages) |
|                                                          |
|    6 Work with Your Files...       (file transfer, download comm programs...) |
|                                                          |
|    7 Settings and Utilities...     (terminal types, user lookup, Free-Nets...) |
|                                                          |
|    8 Information Provider, User Test and Staff Menus     |
| --------------------------------------------------------- |
| m = Main Menu       pine = Pine E-mail       h = Help    |
| p = Previous Menu   lynx = Lynx Web Browser  x = Exit SCN |
|                                                          |
| Your Choice ==> ▌                                        |
|_____|
```

FIGURE 11.7   An Example of a Popular Freenet

As soon as we've connected to the remote computer, we're provided with instructions on how to log in. In this case, we're instructed to type "guest" (lower case) and then press the Return key. (See Figure 11.7.)

We'll be provided with a welcome screen. We will also be given a statement concerning the privileges we have as a guest to the system. (Expect limited access unless you become a registered member.) By following the prompts at the bottom of the screen, we'll eventually find our way to the main page. Read the welcome segment. It will explain what you can and cannot do while at this site. Most Freenets will also explain what fee is required to become a registered user. By following the prompts at the bottom of the screen, you will be able to navigate through the various screens until you reach the Social Services option. Typically, this section will provide the visitor with an overview of services available to individuals and families. Most commonly these include veteran's information services, local support groups, vocational counseling, and telephone directories for area healthcare centers and educational institutes.

One of the best sites to obtain information is from Freenet, a public service Web site developed by Peter Scott of Northern Lights Internet Solutions, Inc., in Canada. This site is easy to use and can be accessed at http://www.lights.com/freenet/. (See Figure 11.8.)

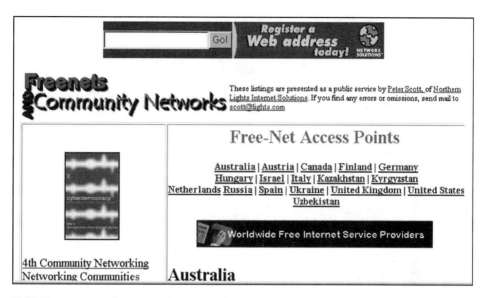

FIGURE 11.8   Web-Based Directory of Freenets

© Peter Scott, 1993

Summary

This chapter described use of Telnet in social work practice. It differentiated guest from full-service Telnets and offered a text-based example of a MEDLINE search. This file section was dedicated to obtaining information from Community Freenets. Both text-based and Web-based examples were discussed.

Discussion Questions

1. Telnet is a protocol that allows remote access to a distant computer. How would this be helpful in social work practice?
2. Use Telnet to check your E-mail messages from a remote site. How easy is it to use?
3. Visit a community in a neighboring state via Freenet. Discuss the steps you took. What was the predicted weather? What kinds of job openings are available?
4. Explain how the Freenet system might be used by school social workers.

Appendix

World Wide Web Resources for Social Workers

Diversity

Professional social work education is committed to preparing students to understand and appreciate human diversity. Programs must provide curriculum content about differences and similarities in the experiences, needs, and beliefs of people. The curriculum must include content about differential assessment and intervention skills that will enable practitioners to serve diverse populations. Each program is required to include content about population groups that are particularly relevant to the program's mission. These include, but are not limited to, groups distinguished by race, ethnicity, culture, class, gender, sexual orientation, religion, physical or mental disability, age, and national origin (CSWE, 2000).

http://www.jamardaresources.com/home.htm

"Celebrating the beauty and the challenge of diversity," is Jamarda Resources' motto. Its main goal is to expand healthcare workers' knowledge of different cultures, ethnic groups, and religions. It plans to increase this knowledge by various types of workshops, training, and consulting. Healthcare workers are "ethically obligated" to provide the best care possible to their clients, and in order to provide such care healthcare workers must first be open-minded and willing to help others. This site consists of eight links such as About Jamarda Resources, Lectures, and Cultural Manuals. The frame in the upper right-hand corner that features a diverse group of people is an attractive feature.

http://familyeducation.com/topic/front/0,1156,1–3374,00.html

This is a fun site to visit, with lots of life and color. This Web site is by the Family Education Network, and its topic is diversity in schools. It gives up-to-date articles about the news, a poll, exploring diversity, and expert advice. This site gives you the option of choosing the particular group of children on whom you wish to find information. Whether your clients or your children are in preschool, elementary school, middle school, or high school and beyond, it gives you a variety of topics that can be discussed by each age group. Each area has a heading that reads "Browse Our Topics." Here you can look up topics such as Health & Safety, Activities, and Homework Help. This site is useful not only for healthcare workers but also for parents who have questions or simply want to learn about what's going on in their child's school.

http://www.emc.maricopa.edu/diversity/populate.html

The topic of this site is "Diversity in Our Population." Maricopa Community College is "an institution dedicated to serving the educational needs of its communities." This site has five topics (four out of the five are links) and each area has a brief summary of what that area is all about. The five areas are ethnic minorities, women, older students, disabled persons, and gays and lesbians. This encompasses some of the major diversities in our society, and each link that can be connected to has a great deal of information. For example, the topic of gays and lesbians links you to the Gay & Lesbian Human Rights Association of the Maricopa Community College District. Statistical charts are available for writing research proposals or seeking demographic data.

http://www.hrpress-diversity.com

This Web site offers products for workshops and training for cultural diversity. There are videos, games, surveys, calendars, and other training tools that can be ordered.

http://weber.u.washington.edu/~diverse/index.html

The Community and Environmental Planning Diversity Committee monitors diverse learning environments. Its Web site discusses how to support and encourage activities that promote diversity.

http://www.inform.umd.edu/DiversityWeb/Priorities/MDN.html

Visit this site for news on diversity. The commitment to diversity on campuses is clearly evident. Additional resources available at this site include a diversity database and "Diversity Connections."

http://www.diversityforum.com

This site has many links related to diversity. It offers links to Private Diversity Resources, Non-Profit Diversity Resources, Public Diversity Resources, Other Diversity Websites, Good Faith Effort, Diversity Information, and Diversity Events Calendar. Each site contains links to many different organizations related to either ethnicity or gender by task.

http://www.socialworkonline.com/socservices.htm#activism

This page was designed for general social work resources and organizations. Its directory includes Resources to Non-Profit Services and Foundations; Child Welfare; Political and Government Resources; Social Activism; Social Services; and Social Services–Regional. This site will connect you to any number of topics of interest to social workers. There is also a brief subtitle to each topic to narrow the search process.

http://www.earthsystems.org/ways

This site features a hyperbook on how to work, understand, and advocate for the homeless. Each of the hyperbook's sections provides information relevant to the chapter. Well designed, it's very useful regardless of your geographic location.

http://www.ssa.gov/SSA_Home.html

This page provides program information and an explanation of the various benefits provided by Social Security. This site allows social workers to research eligibility requirements for various programs available to their clients regardless of age, race, income, or gender. This site offers information on disability services, youth questions, and much more.

http://www.pathfinder.com/altculture/aentries/g/gayxmarria.html

This Web site covers laws, moral rights, anti–gay rights, and other information about gay marriages. Gay marriages are portrayed as yet another legitimate attempt to normalize gays and lesbians. Such information is helpful to all social workers whether or not they are working with a gay population.

http://www.religioustolerance.org/hom_umc.htm

This page looks at the role of homosexuality and religion as well as the Methodist Church. Anyone interested in reconciling congregations, transforming congregations, or reviewing decisions made at United Methodist conferences will find this site outstanding.

http://now.org/issues/diverse/index.html

This site of the National Organization for Women focuses on ending discrimination by taking action to stop racism. Some actions involve Women of Color and Allies Summit and the People of the Seneca Nation. There are viewpoints from millions of women of different races and cultural backgrounds. This site also interviews those who have faced discrimination and discusses how it has affected their lives. It also emphasizes issues that surround women and offers information needed to join support groups.

http://www.diversitymetrics.com

This site is designed to aid organizations in meeting the goals of managing diversity through designing studies, collecting data, performing analyses, and generating reports to maximize the ability of all employees to contribute to organizational goals that focus on group identities such as gender, race, nationality, age, or sexual orientation.

http://diversity.diversitylink.com

Diversity Link connects females, minorities, and other diversity professionals with proactive employers offering career opportunities. Employers and search firms wishing to affirm their commitment to diversity in the workplace are invited to leave their information on the Diversity Link, as are women and ethnic minorities seeking employment.

http://www.introspecinc.com/index.htm

This Web page is for those seeking to understand and address diversity issues, personal motivation, and conflict resolutions through consulting and training provided by Introspec.

http://www.empowermentworks.com/symp.html

This URL will connect you to the "Corporate Revolution and Making Diversity Work in Business" Web site. It offers suggestions on empowerment workshops with regard to leadership development and cultural sensitivity in the workplace.

http://www.antiracism.com/film.html

This Web site offers useful information with respect to films and other multimedia products. It describes educational programs for public and private schools committed to the development of self-awareness, diversity, and group identity.

http://www.cs.org

This Web page has a description of Cultural Survival, a nonprofit organization founded in 1972. The group's intentions were to defend the human rights and cultures of indigenous peoples and oppressed ethnic minorities. Through research and publications, this organization focuses attention on violations of those rights and advocates alternative policies that avoid ethnic conflict and the destruction of other peoples' ways of life. Cultural Survival also develops educational materials that promote tolerance and understanding of other cultures as well as respect for indigenous peoples. The site offers other links such as Education & Outreach, Links to Related Sites, and Active Voices: CS's Online Activist Forum. Its Info Center is very informative.

http://hanksville.phast.umass.edu/defs/independent/ ElecPath/elecpath.html

The site contains the organization mission of Electronic Pathways, a national nonprofit organization. Its primary mission is to ensure that underrepresented and underserved individuals, schools, and communities have equal access and opportunity to fully participate in the advantages of today's technology in the Information Age. It has a particular emphasis on mathematics and science educational reform as well as career development. It provides informative links such as Primary Programs and Tasks, Environmental Science Careers for Women, Community–School Alliance Initiative, and Careers Communications Network for Women and Girls.

http://www.nclr.org

This is a major Web page site that describes the National Council of La Raza (NCLR), a private, nonprofit, nonpartisan, tax-exempt organization established in 1968 to reduce poverty and discrimination and to improve life opportunities for Hispanic Americans. NCLR's goal is to provide organizational assistance in management, governance, program operations, and resource development to Hispanic community-based organizations in urban and rural areas nationwide, especially organizations that serve low-income and disadvantaged Hispanics. Its links include Job Announcements and Mission Statement.

http://www.indians.org

The Native American Adventure Web site maintains a directory for the National Assembly of State Arts Agencies. The Indigenous People's Literature page is well designed and useful.

http://www.worldcitizen.org/syntegrity/cultdivr.html

Visit the World Citizen Web site for an encouraging breath of fresh air. It contains articles designed to promote respect among all people. Let's celebrate diversity.

http://www.diversitydtg.com

This organization provides diversity training, mentoring, and consultation regarding multidiversity marketing. Visitors to this Web site are provided with an extensive bookstore that features the latest diversity support materials and the ability to participate in a Discussion Room to obtain answers to diversity questions. Although this is not a social work site, it's still a valuable resource.

http://www.aimd.org

An Atlanta, Georgia-based nonprofit organization founded in 1984, the American Institute for Managing Diversity was created to expand human consciousness on diversity and to advance the field of diversity. This site is useful to social workers because the organization predicts direct trends that affect policy development. The commitment to education and research is apparent as it seeks to understand issues of diversity and its inherent benefit.

http://www.elderhostel.org/EHORG/Diverse.htm

Elderhostel is a diversity outreach program that is strongly committed to serving a racially and ethnically diverse population of older adults. It is currently working on developing several new and exciting programs that reflect the diversity of its participants. A number of its programs offer an opportunity to study different cultures and histories.

http://www.ameasite.org/books.html

The Association of Multiethnic Americans (AMEA) homepage contains many interesting facets. Feature of the Week covers multiethnic issues currently being discussed in the news; it also allows you full text access to articles. The site offers multiethnic educational resources such as books. It contains many links to other sites that feature multiethnic and racial issues. You can access the United Nations homepage from here as well.

http://www.lib.umich.edu/libhome/rrs/classes/multicul-as-lat-nat.html

This multicultural resource Web site contains selected resources on Latino, Asian, and Native American cultures. For example, you can access MOLIS (Minority On-Line Information Service), which promotes education, research, and diversity. The Latino link covers issues of importance to the Latino culture.

http://www.andrews.edu/SOWK/grassroots.htm

This Grassroots social science search Web site indexes WWW resources of interest to social work professionals. This Web site searches for and contains links to social work content areas. The links cover diverse populations and issues. It's a very useful Web site for social workers.

http://www.skmainc.com

This Web site belongs to S. K. Morgan Associates, Inc., which focuses on raising diversity awareness in a professional environment. Its program focuses on five critical elements of diversity awareness and has a series of three workshops on gender aware-ness, cultural awareness, and sexual orientation in the professional environment.

http://weber.u.washington.edu/~diverse/index.html

This Web site is about an organization called the Community and Environmental Plan-ning Diversity Committee, "a task group dedicated to promoting and supporting a di-verse learning environment in the CEP major." They "act as a forum for CEP members and others to engage in discussion of topics not found in the core CEP curriculum." They also "support and encourage activities such as proposal writing and joining other groups dedicated to diversity."

http://www.vix.com/men/index.html

This informative Web site contains articles and resources pertaining to topics of spe-cial need in the areas of fathering and fatherlessness, false accusations, single dads, child support, custody, visitation, and battered men. Links to men's organizations in the United States and Canada are also provided. This site sends reviews of one hundred books covering men's issues. If interaction is desired, this Web site provides mailing lists, bulletin boards, and chat and forum rooms as well as telephone hotlines. This site is highly recommended for social workers and any other professional who requires in-formation on these subjects that are not often discussed.

http://www.inform.umd.edu/EdRes/Topic/Diversity

This Diversity Database is provided by the University of Maryland. A vast amount of information can be obtained from searching this site. Its area with definitions of words, phrases, and policy relating to multicultural and diversity issues should be useful to any professional dealing with diversity. Another area that handles specific issues contains links to valuable resources on age, class, disability, gender, national origin, race and eth-nicity, religion, and sexual orientation. The News Bureau contains news releases per-taining to all areas of diversity from 1995 to the present. This site contains a keyword search to all of the data in its directory to assist the visitor.

Promotion of Social and Economic Justice

Programs of social work education must provide an understanding of the dynamics and consequences of social and economic injustice, including all forms of human op-pression and discrimination. They must provide students with the skills to promote social change and to implement a wide range of interventions that advance the achievement of individual and collective social and economic justice. Theoretical and practice content must be provided about strategies of intervention for achieving social and economic justice and for combating the causes and effects of institutionalized forms of oppression.

http://www.lawlink.nsw.gov.au/adb.nsf/pages/harassment

Inform yourself and learn how to protect yourself from harassment and discrimination. Know your rights. By definition, harassment occurs when one person (or a group of people) use power inappropriately over another person or group of people. If you have clients who have been discriminated against because of age, race, marital status, or disability, this site tells you their rights. Be informed; don't be a victim.

http://www.youth-guard.org/dayofsilence

The Day of Silence, as explained at this Web site, is to draw attention to those who have been silenced by hatred, oppression, and prejudice. This site offers a behind-the-scenes look at organizational efforts to coordinate youth participation in a visible silent protest with follow-up educational events. Public service announcements and press releases are also available.

http://www.ssc.msu.edu/~sw/advocacy.html#labor

This resource is provided by the Michigan State University School of Social Work. Here you will find topics such as African Issues, Blindness/Low-Vision Issues, Children's Issues, Deaf Community Issues, Domestic/Family/Sexual Violence, Economic Justice Issues, HIV/AIDS Issues, Human Rights and Peace Issues, Latino/Hispanic Issues, Lesbian/Gay/Bisexual/Transgender Issues, Michigan Issues, Native American/Indigenous Peoples Issues, and Women's Issues as well as Government Links. An understanding of these issues is essential to all social workers.

http://www.azstarnet.com/~afscaz/borderlands.html

The Borderlands subcommittee works for social and economic justice on the Arizona–Mexico border. If you plan to work in this area, this site is a must. It contains information on border issues that will help you understand what is happening in this area and what is being done in promoting social and economic justice. You will also find links to border issues and justice in the global economy.

http://www.accessatlanta.com/community/groups/chre/index.html

This URL is the Web address of the Center for Human Rights Education in Atlanta, a new national training and resource center for social justice activists. Its goal is to promote progressive social change in the United States based on shared learning and instruction in teaching methods about human rights education. There are several links to Government/Politics, Education, and Service Organizations. You will find information on different community groups and can post your own information for others to read.

http://www.hud.gov

This Web site is sponsored by the U.S. Department of Housing and Urban Development (HUD). This site offers easy access to a vast amount of data that social workers will find relevant to economic justice and social intervention. Topics in the area of housing include money for a down payment, HUD homes for sale, and local housing assistance. There is access to a housing hotline and information on household dangers. You will find information on community planning and free software to assist in community organization. The wealth of information and guidance a social worker can receive from visiting this site is phenomenal.

http://www.usda.gov/fcs/fcs.htm

The U.S. Department of Agriculture (DOA) does an excellent job in providing information on food and nutrition services through this Web site. Eligibility qualifications and benefits are detailed for the Food Stamp Program, Child Nutrition Programs, and other programs controlled by DOA. In addition, information, contacts, and other sources are available concerning ways to get food into the mouths of the hungry and out of the mouths of the dumpster through the Food Recovery program. Social workers who feel a calling for this particular intervention in their community will find this Web site beneficial.

http://www.aoa.dhhs.gov

The Web site provided by the Administration on Aging includes information designed for older Americans and their families about services available to enrich the lives of older persons and support their independence. Along with program descriptions, this site offers news, updates, budget reports, statistical data, and local resource information for social workers and other professionals. This includes the Eldercare Locator, a nationwide directory assistance service. This service can connect social workers to referral networks operated by state and local agencies on aging. This Web site also offers links to other Internet sources on general aging issues and federal programs for the aged.

http://www.columbia.edu/~ljw17/jfrej/#Who

In May 1990, a small group of communal leaders, rabbis, educators, writers, and activists, upset by the growing amount of racial and ethnic tension, violence, and economic injustice in New York City, founded Jews for Racial and Economic Justice (JFREJ). JFREJ has brought together Jewish support to improve economic justice for many groups within the city. Be inspired by their persistence and creativity by visiting the Web address provided.

http://www.wola.org/home.htm

The Washington Office on Latin America (WOLA) encourages economic justice in Latin America and the Caribbean. Concerned social workers can track the progress of programs that WOLA initiates between government and nongovernment entities. Visit this site to learn about WOLA's reporting, education, and advocacy efforts.

http://www.afsc.org/pdesc/pd175.htm

The Economic Justice and Empowerment Program in Akron, Ohio, is a good example of a group effort to promote economic justice. This is a good resource for the profession, particularly agency directors, field instructors, and community organizers.

http://www2.csbsju.edu/library/internet/socijust.html

If you're looking for Internet links on social justice, this Web page is a good place to start. The directory includes links to the Children's House, the Hunger Web, and National Coalition for the Homeless. This Web site was developed by Honors Symposium students at the College of St. Benedict and St. John's University.

http://www.wowwomen.com/win/cawa/economic.html

An economic task force of California's leading women is featured at this Web site. Its stated objective is to advocate for gender equity in the workplace by calling for women and persons of color to voice their needs and expectations. Recommendations leading to social and economic justice are provided.

http://www.vera.org

The Vera Institute designs and implements programs that encourage just practices in public services and improve the quality of urban life. The Vera Institute has been in existence for 35 years and is using the World Wide Web to call attention to the need for economic justice and related research projects.

http://www.shareintl.org/spej.html

This Web site offers a directory of topics relevant to social, political, and economic justice. Topics discussed include the faces of poverty, hunger, ensuring healthcare as a human right, women's issues, and "World Peace: Only through Sharing?" This Web page provides information that social workers can use in writing proposals and handling daily work situations.

http://earthops.org/socialserv.html

This Web page is provided by the Administration for Children and Families in the U.S. Department of Health and Human Services. Its mission is to "promote the economic and social well-being of families, children, individuals and communities." It provides information and assistance to homeless persons, prostitutes, victims of violent crime, and children. This Web page can help social workers find local and national resources for their clients.

http://www.economicjustice.org

This site is for those who are interested in the economic policies being made and who would also like to become involved in promoting economic justice for all. Economic Justice Now (EJN) focuses on issues of economic justice with an intention to promote egalitarian alternatives. EJN works with community-based groups primarily in the San Francisco Bay area, but membership is available to anyone with a similar passion. Visit this site to learn about events, campaigns, and the organization's background.

http://www.igc.apc.org/cfj/econjustice.html

If you believe that all people have a right to the basic needs in life (food, shelter, clothing, employment, education, and healthcare), you may want to join the Economic Justice Campaign. This campaign is in part conducted by the California for Justice Education Fund, which is dedicated to build power in communities that have been pushed to the margins of the political process. The California for Justice Education Fund raises issues of economic justice for all whose rights have been denied.

http://www.mnsj.org/index.html

Social workers interested in promoting social and economic justice for residents in the Metro Toronto area are encouraged to visit the Metro Network for Social Justice (MNSJ) Web site. This organization is a nonprofit network with a mission to develop and organize toward political, social, cultural, and economic alternatives that will create justice, equity, and sustainable communities. MNSJ provides education on economic and political literacy to help members become better informed about issues that affect them.

http://www.shareintl.org/e-injust.html

Research by Share International suggests that there are over one hundred million people living in absolute poverty. A good reference source, this site offers an overview of major problems our civilization faces and how we can unite to correct our faulty economic and political structures.

http://www.afscpdx.org

The American Friends Service Committee is a Quaker organization including people of various faiths who are committed to social justice, peace, and humanitarian services. It is based on the Quaker belief in the worth of every person and faith in the power of love to overcome violence and injustice. The site covers news items, events, and volunteer opportunities. You will also find information about "Visionaries," a nonprofit television production dedicated to innovative programming to create positive social change throughout the world.

http://harvestinstitute.org

The Harvest Institute is a proactive public policy research organization founded on social, economic, and political concepts. The Harvest Institute advocates "powernomics" as a self-empowerment plan for African Americans focused on economic and political development. It maintains links to other sites and offers recommended reading material.

http://www.familiesusa.org

This on-line source created by Families USA advocates high-quality affordable health and long-term care for all Americans. This well-organized site has numerous articles and reports on Medicare, Medicaid, managed care, and consumer protection issues relating to healthcare. There are plenty of healthcare-related links. If you are interested in healthcare issues, visit the Health Policy Links page. You won't be disappointed.

http://www.ed.gov/prog_info/SFA/StudentGuide

This site lists resources available from the U.S. Department of Education and demystifies the basics of obtaining financial aid. You will find good articles on job search strategies and other useful tips. This site is of special interest to college students.

http://epn.org/epi.html

This is an excellent site on the Economic Policy Institute, a nonprofit organization that seeks to widen the public debate about strategies to achieve a prosperous and fair economy. This site provides a complete text on-line of reports published by the institute. Resources are arranged by category: economics and politics; required living standards; and budgetary items.

Field Practicum

The field practicum is an integral component of the curriculum in social work education. It engages the student in supervised social work practice and provides opportunities to apply classroom learning in the field setting.

Each educational program must establish standards for field practicum settings that define their social work services and practices, field instructor assignments and activities, and student learning expectations and responsibilities. Individual programs may organize their practice in different ways but must ensure educationally directed, coordinated, and monitored practicum experiences for all students (CSWE, 2000).

http://www.mun.ca/sweaids/links2.html

Here are select links that will lead you to Internet sites with social-work–related content. You will find links to a number of indexes including the National Institute for Social Work, the New Social Worker On-Line, and the Home Page for Social Workers.

http://www-unix.umbc.edu/~gmitchel/manual.htm

University of Maryland–Baltimore County (UMBC) offers a directory of placement agencies affiliated with the UMBC program. This manual is published to help students and field instructors deal with questions that are frequently asked by social work students and instructors. The site goes into further detail by describing the curriculum to prospective students. The field instruction page offers a close look at eligibility requirements. At its conclusion this field page reads, "Field placement is often the most meaningful part of the social work curriculum for students. It is challenging because it represents a real test of skill, commitment, and knowledge. It is the time when students first assume professional responsibility for intervening in other people's lives. It will provide direction, confidence, and a great increase in skill. It may be a lot of things, but one thing it is unlikely to be is irrelevant."

http://www.nmsu.edu/Academic_Progs/Colleges/Health_and_Social/ socwork/public_html/fieldfac.html

The Department of Social Work at New Mexico State University wants to ensure that all students have a quality educational experience in practicum settings. Its Field Instructor–Supervisor Training Program has been designed to provide professional continuing education leading to certification of its graduate and undergraduate field instructors and supervisors. The Department of Social Work is interested in updating and advancing its program to meet the needs of students and to support the field faculty through continuing professional education. At least four workshops, conferences, and/or symposiums are held annually. These programs fulfill the basic training that field faculty members are required to attend if they wish to obtain certification as New Mexico State University field instructors/supervisors. There is a link that can be accessed in order to receive a complete description of the field requirements.

http://www.umanitoba.ca/SocialWork/degrees/
bsw_policy/field_at_employer.html

This particular Web site of the Social Work Program at the University of Manitoba offers links to its program description and its BSW table of contents. The purpose of field instruction is carefully outlined: (1) to provide opportunities for the student to use knowledge, (2) to provide opportunities for the student to use self, (3) to provide real practice situations for the student to carry responsibility as a professional social worker in ways appropriate to expected learning, and (4) to provide instruction and help to the student.

http://www.uwf.edu/~socwork/field.htm

The BSW program at the University of West Florida uses its Web site to outline its field instruction expectations, student support, and academic requirements for entry into the field. This site is very well organized and maintains links to other useful resources.

http://www.orst.edu/Dept/hdfs/hdfs410/part1.htm

Oregon State University has posted its *Field Instruction Handbook* on the Web. This site discusses eligibility requirements, offers an on-line application, and has a directory of placement sites.

http://www.uakron.edu/faa/schools/socialwork.html

The social work program at the University of Akron prepares students for beginning and professional social work practice. The field practicum is an extensive and vital part of a social work student's education; here students are placed in social service agencies to become familiar with the field study and become able to apply these skills in the social work field. This program also focuses on a variety of social systems, theories, and practice to prepare students for their social work careers. This site gives you additional information needed regarding the university's departments, programs, and registration.

http://www.tulane.edu/~tssw/Journal/maintaining_quality.htm

This site is for those interested in social work education from a distance. This page contains a report made by Paul P. Freddolino that raises issues in delivering quality in distance education for all students. Students involved in a social work program aimed to improve electronic instruction share their experiences, concerns, and overall evaluations. This site gives in-depth information on the notion of quality in distance education programs in social work, methodology, results, technology problems, and more for those who are interested in education from afar.

http://www.research.umbc.edu/~blais

This site is for social work students interested in the mental health field in Maryland. The Social Work Department at Springfield Hospital Center provides field instruction opportunities. Students are given the opportunity to work in settings such as admissions, intermediate care, geriatrics, and deaf services to help the students gain hands-on experience with patients in diverse diagnostic and cultural backgrounds. This site gives you information about the Social Work Department at the Springfield Hospital Center, UMBC, and additional subjects.

http://www.miseri.edu/academic/departs/socwork/Curriculum.html

This Web site states that College Misericordia's Social Work Program's Curriculum Policy Statement "is organized around the Program's primary goal of preparing competent baccalaureate-level generalist practitioners. It evolved institutionally from the Religious Sisters of Mercy's own call to compassionate service through the ministries of teaching and healing and developed according to required knowledge and skills identified by the Undergraduate Social Work Curriculum Project and mandates for curricular content established by the Council on Social Work Education."

http://www.carfax.co.uk/jsw-ad.htm

This is the *Journal of Social Work Practice* homepage. This journal is published twice a year and contains articles from psychodynamic and systematic perspectives. The articles cover issues from education and training to social work practice. The journal strives to have an avenue for professionals to gain insight on current applications of social work practice, from the individual to the community. It contains Listservs for specified areas of interest. You can subscribe to the journal from here and locate previous issues.

http://psychcentral.com

The Psychcentral Web site contains information related to psychology, support, mental health issues, people on the Net, and resources. It offers live interactive chats every week, which is great for feedback. You can access mailing lists, book reviews, and Newsgroups who share the same interests. The site allows you to link to other relevant Web sites, such as ISMHO (International Society for Mental Health Online), promoting on-line communication for the mental health community. The suicide Help-line is also available for suicide resources on the Net.

http://www.health.org

The National Clearinghouse for Alcohol and Drug Information prevention on-line. You can access resources and referrals, research, statistics, publications, and alcohol and drug facts. This is a useful tool for social workers with clients dealing with these issues. It contains many relevant and informative links.

http://www.niagara.edu/socialwork/field.html

This Web page has information about the field practicum of the Niagara University BSW program. Students begin their field work in their senior year. Once they have completed most of the courses required and they are ready for beginning social work practice, they are given the opportunity to work as professionals, under close supervision, with clients. Each student is given quality opportunities as well as supervision.

http://www.indiana.edu/~caps/trainingmanual/practica.html

This Web page gives information on psychology and social work practica. It gives a summary table of both psychology and social work activities (experience, hours per week). Counseling and Psychological Services (CaPS) accepts a limited number of social work practicum students each year. Specific task assignments may be supervised by social work and psychology staff members or by predoctoral psychology interns.

http://www.colm.u-net.com

This Web page is about the help offered to people who have been sexually abused. The organization entitled "One in Four" uses its Web site as a clearinghouse to connect people to women's groups, men's groups, lesbians' groups, gay men's groups, and mixed groups. Visit this site, read the vision statement, or visit the poetry pages.

http://www.colostate.edu/Dept/SocWork/field_agencies.html

This Web site identifies a variety of field agencies in which students can be placed while they are in school trying to attain a bachelor's degree in social work. These field placement agencies and programs are essential in social work education.

http://www.usnews.com/usnews/edu/beyond/gradrank/gbsocwrk.htm

This Web site offers the rankings of the top graduate schools in social work. The ranking system uses a five-point scale to rate schools based on scholarship, curriculum, and the quality of the program's faculty and graduate students. Schools rated distinguished received five points; strong, four; good, three; adequate, two; and marginal, one.

http://www.uvm.edu/~socwork/field.html

This site is a product of the MSW program at the University of Vermont (UVM). The program is structured to provide continuity between classroom instruction and field experience. Its field practicum is described and goals of the Office of Field Education are outlined. Visit this site for UVM's undergraduate and graduate manuals and an explanation of the field planning process. Information includes getting ready for field experience, field expectations, field instructor seminars, and much more.

http://www.socialworksearch.com

This site takes you to all kinds of links: Disability, Unemployment, Direct Practice, Entertainment, Human Services, Licensing and Credentials, Magazines and Journals, Mental Health, Research and Statistics, Violence, Sexual Minorities, Education, Child Welfare, Computer and Internet, and miscellaneous resources. In addition, the site has a chat room and a discussion board. You can also get What's Cool and What's Not!!!

http://www.arts.unimelb.edu.au/Dept/SocialWork

The University of Melbourne's Social Work School offers courses toward a Bachelor of Social Work as well as study at the higher degree level, including postgraduate diploma, various master's programs, and a PhD program. The site includes information on research units such as Aging and Long-Term Care Policy and Practice Research Unit, Children's, Families and Young Person's Practice Research Unit, Health Services Research Unit, Mental Health Practice Research Unit, and Women's Studies Unit.

http://www.bls.gov/oco/ocos060.htm

The *1998–99 Occupational Handbook* is an excellent resource for students as they contemplate social work as a career. This Web site offers information on the nature of social work, various settings that a social worker can practice in, average working conditions, and required and optional qualifications. This site also discusses the job outlook for social workers. It gives insight into what particular areas of social work will be growing and explains the reasons for this interpretation. Average salaries for social workers are provided. The *1998–99 Occupational Handbook* also identifies additional resources that the visitor can contact in writing.

http://www.idealist.org

This site is a data bank of opportunities for possible internships in nonprofit organizations, with information provided by 15,000 organizations in 130 countries. A visitor can conduct a search by geographic location and/or mission. Although opportunity searching is the major focus of this site, it includes other areas of interest such as information about computing and the Internet, fundraising, accounting and management, legal issues, and nonprofit support organizations.

http://www.project.org

This Web site is sponsored by Project America, an organization founded in 1993 by three college students. This organization strives to connect volunteers to areas of need in their local communities. At the site you can find valuable information pertaining to all aspects of volunteerism. Areas include news articles about specific projects, books related to volunteering, and an on-line search for opportunities or organizations in specific areas. Here a visitor can find a guide to community service projects as well. It offers ideas on how to deal with building a team and developing a service project; managing volunteers; forming committees; budgeting and fundraising; publicizing a project; and legal issues. This Web site is an excellent source for people interested in helping their community to prosper.

http://www.isw.org

This site welcomes participation in the creation of a program titled International Social Work Field Instruction. It concentrates on development of practica outside the United States for baccalaureate and graduate students enrolled in degree programs accredited by the Council on Social Work Education.

http://www.hecua.org

This site offers study programs for undergraduates based in Latin America, Scandinavia, and the United States. It utilizes experiential learning and connect theory with real-life issues of inequality and social change. It will connect you to other Web sites as well as news and publications. The Higher Education Consortium for Urban Affairs (HECUA) is a group of midwestern colleges and universities that have come together to offer high-quality programs in field practice.

http://www.ssc.msu.edu/'sw/field/sswfld.html

This Web page is from the Michigan State University Social Work Program. It gives the various programs for undergraduates and graduates who are interested in field instruction. It gives the class schedule for spring, fall, and summer courses. It also gives the field instruction program fact sheet, which tells what field instruction is.

http://www.nyu.edu/socialwork/fieldinstruct.html

New York University has a list of social service agencies in New York City, Connecticut, New Jersey, Long Island, and New York counties that are affiliated with the university as teaching centers. At the centers future social workers are trained and helped with any questions about field instruction. Throughout the years these centers have represented a wide range of services in many fields of practice. The list is seven pages long and contains agencies from A to Z.

http://blues.fd1.uc.edu/www/socialwork/bfield.htm

The School of Social Work at the University of Cincinnati provides a section related to its field instruction for those in the BSW program. There is a partial list of agencies and instructors in the local area who provide field experience. Information can also be obtained on the college itself as well as other sites related to social work.

http://www2.uta.edu/ssw/field.htm

This page begins with the words "Field is the heart of social work education." It is a Web site from part of the University of Texas at Arlington's School of Social Work. Included is information on first (foundation) placement as well as second (advanced) placement for those pursuing an MSSW. For those interested in a BSW, field courses are also put on this page. Links are provided to help people learn a little about the university and decide whether they would be interested in attending and even take part in field instruction in the area.

http://www.csw.ohio-state.edu/field.htm

This Web page presents history of the origins of field work for the social worker, how and why social workers are required to obtain field experience, and how field instructors evaluate field work. Information is based on the Ohio State University standards.

http://www.jmc.msu.edu/jm07002.htm

You should see field experience as a four-step process. First, investigate yourself and opportunities available. Second, focus on your goals. Third, conduct an internship. Fourth, reflect on your experience utilizing academic requirements. Field experience is a central part of the curriculum at James Madison College. Students apply classroom exercises to circumstances of the work, build professional relationships, and understand their career goals and build career experience.

http://itech.fgcu.edu/Cps/MSW/courses.htm

This Web page describes course requirements, required courses, elective courses, and internship schedules at the Florida Gulf Coast University. The Master of Social Work program teaches people to become social work professionals and to provide services to oppressed and diverse populations. Admission requirements are past academic performance, letters of recommendation, previous professional experience in social work, a biographical sketch, personal interview with program faculty, and scores on the Graduate Record Examination (GRE). In addition, students who have completed a BSW within the past five years may apply for exemptions from foundation course work for up to 15 semester hours.

http://www.usc.edu/dept/publications/9698sowkbul/acadpro/index.html

At the University of Southern California, field practicum provides students the opportunity to apply and use what has been taught in the curriculum. Selected agencies, organizations, and centers are visited in the Los Angeles area. This Web page has links to learn more about the master's program in social work, the curriculum, the core courses, field practicum, and admission to the program.

http://www.ollusa.edu/academic/worden/worden.htm

This is the Web site for the BSW and MSW programs at Our Lady of the Lake University. The site has information on the school itself and describes some faculty and staff. It has a link to the Association of Latino Social Work Educators' Web site. The school is designed to prepare students to practice general social work, to work toward economic and social justice, and to be sensitive to differences of culture, ethnicity, and at-risk populations.

http://www.arts.su.edu.au/Arts/departs/social/home.html

This is the Web site for Department of Social Work, Social Policy and Sociology at the University of Sydney in Australia. It has an overview of program goals. There is information on the BSW courses and field instruction courses. Students begin the field courses in their third year. This site also has information on admissions to the program and a description of the program by each year (freshman year, sophomore year, etc.). There is also a link to get a brief description of the staff.

http://www.ssc.msu.edu/~sw

This site is the Michigan State University social work site. The site's various links include domestic, family, and sexual violence, African issues, blindness issues, children's issues, deaf community issues, economic justice issues, government links, HIV/AIDS issues, human rights and peace issues, Latino/Hispanic issues, lesbian/gay/bisexual/transgender issues, Michigan issues, Native American/indigenous peoples issues, and women's issues sites. The site also has information about scholarships offered to social work students. There is information on local, national, and international social work issues. The MSW programs at the school are described. There is a link to the field instruction manual. It goes into detail about the policies and guidelines, the placement procedures, the evaluations, and the curriculum. It also has links to the class schedule for fall and spring and it has links to read about the administration, faculty and committees, and the university.

Social Work Practice

At the baccalaureate level, professional social work education prepares students for generalist practice with systems of all sizes. Practice content emphasizes professional relationships that are characterized by mutuality, collaboration, and respect for the client. Content in practice assessment focuses on the examination of client strengths and problems in the interactions among individuals and the well-being of people as well as on helping to ameliorate the environmental conditions that affect people adversely. Practice content must include the following skills: defining issues; collecting and assessing data; planning and contracting; identifying alternative interventions; selecting and implementing appropriate courses of action; using appropriate research to monitor and evaluate outcomes; applying appropriate research-based knowledge and technological advances; and termination. Practice content also includes approaches to and skills for practice with clients from differing social, cultural, racial, religious, spiritual, and class backgrounds, as well as practice with systems of all sizes (CSWE, 2000).

http://Web.syr.edu/~thechp/womprt1.htm

Women with disabilities face two problems in their fight for equality. They face discrimination because of their disability along with discrimination due to their gender. This Web site offers a good review of materials and links for working with disabled clients.

http://www.mercycorps.org

This Web site offers an overview of Mercy Corps, a nonprofit organization dedicated to alleviating poverty, suffering, and oppression. Mercy Corps provides shelter, food, healthcare, and economic opportunities for individuals and families in crisis. It provides assistance in over fifty countries.

http://eric-Web.tc.columbia.edu/families/refugees/iccb_mission.html

This is the Web site of the International Catholic Child Bureau, which is dedicated to serving children around the world. The bureau supports projects that promote the well-being of families and children. These projects aim to help children facing poverty, neglect, violence, drugs, and disabilities. Training seminars, pilot projects, and educational materials are available.

http://www.clinicalsocialwork.com/incest.html

"Incest/Sexual Abuse of Children" is the subject of this Web page by Patricia D. McClendon, MSSW. It contains useful information concerning the impact of divorce and sexual abuse from a clinical perspective. This page offers vital information, statistics, and reference material for social workers in clinical practice.

http://www.private-eyes.com/Violence.htm

This Web site offers guidelines for working with women who are victims of abuse. This useful site offers reference information and assessment tools for identifying domestic abuse or abuse in other relationships. It offers a safety list for men and women to follow in different environments.

http://www.homehealthsocialwork.org

This Web site is for a professional association, American Network, that is organized to benefit social workers employed in home healthcare settings. This association describes its purpose and mission on its Web site and welcomes those who agree with its bylaws to become members.

http://www.fz.hse.nl/causa/swbib/sw_r1008.html

This Web site is based on a paper written about the daily practice of social work and how it is impacted by the use of computers and other information technology. The author notes that despite a great deal of optimism about the use of computers, the development of the software in this area has not kept pace with other high tech advances.

http://Weber.strath.ac.uk/www/dipswx.htm

This Web site describes the Diploma in Social Work, a two-year course of study that is accredited by the Central Council on Education and Training in Social Work (CCETSW). The curriculum is designed to equip students for social work practice in a wide variety of settings in the United Kingdom and Ireland.

http://www.socialworkonline.com/psychbooks.htm

This Web site directs the viewer to clinical social work books available at an on-line bookstore. These books are written by practitioners in the field.

http://www.naswnyc.org/practice.html

This Web site covers the National Association of Social Workers (NASW) chapter in New York City. Its 9,600 members are employed in every area of social, educational, and health services. This chapter's Web site contains a wide variety of information that will be helpful to all.

http://www.library.ohiou.edu/subjects/indexes/socwork.htm

This Web site contains the Alden Library Reference Desk at Ohio University. It speaks of two separate databases: (1) Social Work Abstracts containing more than 450 journals in all areas of social work including theory and practice, areas of service, social issues, and social problems and (2) the Register of Clinical Social Workers, a directory of clinical social workers in the United States.

http://www.scotland.gov.uk/news/releas98_1/pr0932.htm

This Web site contains quotes from the Scottish Social Work Minister on the role, purpose, and value of social workers in Scotland.

http://www.carfax.co.uk/jsw-ad.htm

Here is the Web site of a social work journal published twice a year. This journal welcomes submissions concerning social work practice (e.g., counseling, social care planning, education and training, research, institutional life, management, organization, policy making). It provides the visitor with a membership application on the Web, or the application can be mailed to Peter Pearson, 120 Church Road, Hanwell, London W7 3BE, UK.

http://www.rld.com/abuse/html/personal.html

This is an example of a personal Web page from Jacquie De Petris, clinical social worker. In it she describes her professional background and clinical interests. There are numerous interesting links and a page that describes what social workers do.

http://www.columbia.edu/cu/csswp/centerde.html

This is the Web site for the Center for the Study of Social Work Practice at the Columbia University School of Social Work. Research conducted at the center is based on practice realities and is guided by social work theory. Featured topics include suicide among pre-adolescents, group interventions for grandparents raising their grandchildren, and child abuse prevention. Detailed information is provided for those interested in attending center events.

http://www.ncpg.com/dstorrs.html

This is an example of how a professional Web site can look. It describes clinical social worker Dee Storrs' areas of expertise—in this case, stress management, adolescent transitions, grief and loss treatment, and women's growth and career issues. It also describes her work in the community. Questions and comments may be sent to her E-mail address, which is conveniently located.

http://www.linkcare.org/index.html

Here's the Web site of the Link Care Center, which is dedicated to holistic health (psychological, emotional, intellectual, familial, cultural, and spiritual). Services include a broad range of testing and assessment, with specializations in child, adolescent, adult, marital, and geriatric psychology and group and family therapy. The Link Center offers counseling for pastors and missionaries.

http://www.libertynet.org/iwg/other.html

This site refers to pages that offer a starting point for learning about gay rights, reproductive freedom, and the diversity of religious opinion. It offers regularly updated articles from different points of view on issues such as religion and sexual orientation; reproductive freedom; and organizations advocating equal treatment of gay and lesbian persons.

http://www.sc.edu/cosw/center/center.html

The Center for Child and Family Studies provides training and support to agencies in the areas of child and adult protective services, adoption, foster care, parenting skills, victim assistance, family independence (via TANF, the Temporary Assistance for Needy Families program), and substance abuse. This Web site describes the center's range of activities, publications, and products.

http://www.open.gov.uk/cre/faq.htm

This site is dedicated to addressing racism. Racism is the belief that people from some races are innately inferior to others because of things like the color of their skin, their ethnic origin, or the country that they come from. Prejudice is knowing next to nothing about people but prejudging them anyway on the basis of stereotypes. Visit this site for interesting and useful information.

http://www.familysupport.org

The mission outline in this Web site is to prevent child abuse and neglect by promoting positive parenting, healthy families, and homes where children are valued and loved. Visit this site to learn about free support services for parents. Programming is also provided for the children of group participants. Public education and community-building activities are also under way to end violence.

http://www.bc.edu/bc_org/avp/gssw/tech.htm

Available through the Boston College Graduate School of Social Work, this Web site is designed for those interested in the changes that are taking place within social work practice. One section contains links to resources for students, faculty, or practitioners who are creating new forms of practice so that they can be more in step with the future. In addition, a section is provided with links for those wanting to initiate new ideas in social work education.

http://www.vanhosp.bc.ca/rehab/social.html

If you're interested in learning about social work practice in settings outside the United States, this site is a good place to visit. This is a page from BC Rehab, a provider of rehabilitation services for people with physical disabilities in the province of British Columbia, Canada. Most patients are seen by a social worker who helps them in adjusting emotionally and socially. One link shows specific programs and services provided, such as the residential program and drug/alcohol intervention. Another link discusses the practicum opportunities at BC Rehab and the criteria that a student must meet.

http://www.rit.edu/~694www/bpd/prac-new.htm

The Association of Baccalaureate Social Work Program Directors provides educational resources on this Web page. It begins with a statement on social work practice from the CSWE curriculum policy. Based on that, there are other links of significance available. For example, there are links to see issues from NASW on-line, links on licensure, and much more. This is an excellent resource.

http://www.cmrg.com

This Web site is an absolute necessity for social workers in practice. It contains a free, searchable database of over 110,000 specialty healthcare services, facilities, businesses, and organizations. Social workers can search for a facility by category, region, or keyword. Information and resources for disease management can also be located through this Web site. Health organizations, self-help groups, federal government agencies, and other resources are categorized by topic. Many of these national organizations and agencies can refer you to their local chapters and provide information and/or financial support. In addition to this wealth of information, this Web site offers continuing education credits for case managers through the Commission for Case Manager Certification and links to companies that provide software specific to case management.

http://www.tiac.net/users/swes/index.htm

This Web site offers lecture programs and home study courses for recent graduates and experienced practitioners taking any level of Social Work Licensing Examinations in any state. Within the site, areas can be viewed pertaining to different aspects of social work licensing. Some helpful areas for practitioners as well as students are sample examination questions, general information about licensing, comments from colleagues, and continuing education requirements. This Web site provides quick access to required information so visitors can keep current in a social work career.

http://www.jobcorps.org/main.htm

This Web site is maintained by the Job Corps, a division of the U.S. Department of Labor. The Job Corps is the nation's largest and most comprehensive residential education and job training program for at-risk youth, ages 16 through 24. This site contains vital information about the organization and programs that it offers. Links are provided for nationwide center locations, training possibilities, and support groups within the organization. Eligibility and enrollment procedures are also available for review. Social workers considering this particular intervention for a client would benefit from visiting this site.

http://www.vnis.com/index.html

This Web site contains information pertaining to veterans. Any social worker who has clients who are veterans or active-duty military should visit this site. This site will keep practicing social workers updated with current issues related to this particular lifestyle. A social worker can locate support groups specifically oriented to veterans, join in chat sessions with veterans, and access links related to other military issues. Social workers can also assist their clients with finding employment by utilizing the provided veteran job search link.

http://www.virtualcity.com/youthsuicide/ethnic.htm

This site is a chapter from the Gay, Lesbian, and Bisexual Factor in the Youth Suicide Problem. Gay, lesbian, and bisexual people of color may experience abuse in the form of racism. You will also find links to additional information related to racism in North American gay, lesbian, and bisexual communities.

http://gwbWeb.wustl.edu/Websites.html

This site is of the George Warren Brown School of Social Work. In this page you will find information and many links to other social work and social services sites. Check it out!

http://naswca.org/clinical.html

NASW has taken appropriate responsibility for establishing standards of practice for all clinical social workers. This site maintained by the California chapter is very well done.

http://www.abacon.com/socwk/swhome.html

This site is especially designed as a social work Web site. Allyn & Bacon is constantly revising this site and it is always being updated with the most recent social work books. Each book is a link that will take you directly to a homepage about the book, such as the book's author, a review of the table of contents, and details on how to order it. This particular Web site has many useful books not only for social work students, but also for professionals. This site features eight recent books dealing in particular with social work practice.

http://www.naswdc.org/practice.htm

This useful Web site offers the most recent links to issues concerning social work practice and a directory of NASW chapters with Web sites. There are over sixty up-to-date links in such areas as HIV; problems with Medicare; health insurance; welfare; managed care; and violence and abuse.

http://www.socialservice.com

This Web page provides links to search for a social service job. You could search using the state where you would like to find employment. Even if there are no jobs available on this page, there are links available to agencies with job opportunities. Some links are the *Los Angeles Times* Employment Classifieds, Job Openings with the Texas Youth Commission, and the Mental Health Net–Job Openings in Texas. This Web page is of use to every social worker seeking employment.

http://www.umanitoba.ca/student/counselling/spotlights/socialwk.html

This Web site in Manitoba, Canada, offers information on the job market for social workers. You can even compare salaries for different social work positions. This is a very informative Web site with many links for social workers.

http://www.naswpress.org/publications/books/health/settings.html

The purpose of this Web page is to provide information on a book for social workers about how to survive in a rapidly changing healthcare system. It emphasizes the role of the social worker in a variety of healthcare settings (e.g., psychiatric, hospice, rehabilitation, administrative).

http://www.naswnyc.org/practice.html

This exceptionally good Web site provides social workers with recommendations for improving their work environment. There's even a page entitled "Truth, Lies, and Social Work Practice." Other practice topics are addressed at this site as well.

http://www.ssw.pdx.edu

This is the site of the Graduate School of Social Work at Portland State University. Its stated goal is to prepare students for agency-based direct social work practice with individuals and families in their environment. The proposed practice gained from this program is designed to help students understand the range of theories and modalities, and be able to assume multiple roles with different people and systems. A list of requirements to enter this program is available at this site.

http://www.csw.utk.edu

Here's the Web address to the University of Tennessee College of Social Work. The college's stated mission is to educate and train students for professional practice and to prepare them to use their skills and knowledge effectively in their future professions. This site provides information on the university, the School of Social Work, and its curriculum.

http://www.basw.demon.co.uk

This Web site contains information, news, and publications of the British Association of Social Workers. You will find its code of ethics and professional principles of practice as well as other background information on this association.

http://www.nmcop.org

This is the Web page of the National Membership Committee on Psychoanalysis in Clinical Social Work, Inc. Its stated purpose is to represent and protect psychoanalytic social work practitioners and educators by providing a strong organizational identity for practitioners. This Web page states its objective of establishing the highest standards of practice and quality care for the public.

Research

The research curriculum must provide an understanding and appreciation of a scientific, analytic approach to building knowledge for practice and to evaluating service delivery in all areas of practice. Ethical standards of scientific inquiry must be included in the research content. The research content must include quantitative and qualitative research methodologies; analysis of data, including statistical procedures; systematic evaluation of practice; analysis and evaluation of theoretical bases, research questions, methodologies, statistical procedures, and conclusions of research reports; and relevant technological advances (CSWE, 2000).

http://www.radcliffe.edu/murray/overview/index.htm

This site contains information from the Murray Research Center at Radcliffe College. Its focus is on women's topics such as work, education, family, aging, and, especially, mental health. The center provides assistance and its resources to all researchers. On this page it is also possible to find out when conferences and events are coming up as well as information on programs, grants, and publications. People interested in employment at Murray or just planning to visit can also look at this site.

http://www.icsi.net/~intresch

International Research has provided psychosocial action research for corporations, organizations, and agencies for over a decade. Its services include public opinion surveys, focus groups, training, and research projects done by a professional staff.

http://www.naswpress.org

This Web site provides articles from *NASW News,* which is published monthly. There is a section of resources as well, such as tools for authors and advertising for the association's publications. More importantly the site is very useful in finding information on other scholarly journals, books, and reference sources in the social sciences. Practitioners, agencies, and social work researchers can benefit from this site.

http://www.wcu.edu/library/research/social/socialwork/index.htm

This site is actually a section from the Hunter Library at Western Carolina University. It gives the names and locations of bibliographies, encyclopedias, dictionaries, and indexes to journal articles in the library. This site can be useful for someone searching for information on the Internet. It also has many links to other Web sites in the area of social work.

http://www.lessonplanspage.com/apa.htm

This Web site is an excellent research writing tool for social workers. A summary of the rules for writing in the American Psychological Association (APA) style is presented here with examples. The rules are explained in layperson terms to make understanding easy. The rules are arranged in topical order and correspond with the arrangement of the APA publication manual. Although this Web site is of great assistance, it should not be used as a substitute for the actual manual.

http://www.uwsp.edu/acad/psych/apa4b.htm#intro

This hypertext guide is an attempt to make the style of writing used in the field of social work clear to you. It summarizes a lot of the material available in the *Publication Manual of the American Psychological Association* (fourth edition, 1995) and is oriented toward undergraduate students. Emphasis is on common errors made by students. This Web site contains links to other areas that would be useful in understanding the APA rules for writing research documents.

http://trochim.human.cornell.edu

This Web site is for people involved in applied social research and evaluation. This site contains many useful areas for researchers. Some areas include detailed examples of current research projects, useful tools for researchers (such as a guide to selecting a statistical analysis), an extensive on-line textbook, a bulletin board for discussions, and more. The Research Pointers page is connected to other resources that will aid in research of various kinds. The World Wide Web Resource Center will point to resources to help you learn to use the Web as a research tool and to write simple Web pages. This Web site is a must-see for all social workers involved in research of any type.

http://www.colostate.edu/Dept/SocWork/lists.html

This Web site provides a lengthy list of Listservs appropriate for social workers. Listservs are electronic discussion groups for people with similar interests. There are quite a few that are specifically related to social work research. The Web site resources area contains many links to useful sites for social workers on the Internet. The vast choice of topics available makes this site a necessity for all social workers.

http://www.cpa.ca/guide6L.html

This site gives you a guide to conduct nonsexist research. The "Guidelines for Nonsexist Research Prepared by a Task Force of Division 35 (Psychology of Women) of the American Psychological Association (APA)" gives you a psychological point of view. This site has information useful to any person who is interested in doing research free of biases.

http://www.hscsyr.edu

This site is for the State University of New York Health Science Center at Syracuse. Click on Research to be in the Research Development Office homepage. Here you will find information on many topics related to doing research. This site provides information on how the university provides support to its Health Science Center faculty in their research and also information about grant applications. It's a useful site for persons interested in research. You will find very interesting material on the following topics: HSC research policy and procedures, electronic forms, and WWW agencies and resources. Click on them and find out.

http://www.unc.edu/depts/irss

This site is under the University of North Carolina, Chapel Hill. You will find information on social science funding and research resources, a guide to social science research services, statistics, Institute for Research in Social Sciences (IRSS) publications, and short courses. This is a very interesting and informative site.

http://www.founders.howard.edu/SWL/SWLHOME.htm

From here, you can access Howard University's School of Social Work homepage and library. The library's resources and services support the School of Social Work's

MSW and PhD curricula, research, and services for the students and faculty. The library is a professional collection on the history and philosophy of social work/social welfare, social welfare policies and services, micro and macro practice, social research, and statistical methods. The collections are also developed to support the following fields of practice/areas of specialization: criminal justice, displaced populations (refugees, immigrants, disaster victims, homeless, etc.), family and child welfare, social gerontology, social work in healthcare settings, and social work in mental health settings.

http://www.uea.ac.uk/menu/acad_depts/hsw/swk/Teaching/mares.htm

This site is for the School of Social Work (SWK) Teaching and Courses/SWK Home of UEA Norwich School of Social Work. The school offers a two-year part-time research degree for people working in the field of human service. It is a part-time master's program that begins each year in October. In this site you will find information about the course, how to apply, and more. You can also visit the SWK homepage and take a look research, teaching, publications, and other links useful in social sciences.

http://www.socialworker.com/csw.htm

This Web site offers a directory of empirical studies recently completed. Topics include aging, social service review, child psychiatry, and adolescent psychiatry.

http://cwis.unimelb.edu.au/research.report/current/196.html

The Web page is from the University of Melbourne Office of Research and Graduate Studies. It lists research in progress of interest to social workers. Examples include alcohol and drug dependency; children and family welfare; family group interventions; and juvenile justice. A list of published work by social workers is provided, as is a listing of grants that have been awarded.

http://mrx.psoc.ox.ac.uk/sdrgdocs/current.htm

This is the Web page of the Socially Disadvantaged Research Group. It gives lists of current members and research that has been done. This group was founded by the Joseph Rowntee Foundation. The use of geographical information systems in the strategic planning of health and social services in rural areas was pioneered by this research group.

http:/www.columbia.edu/cu/ssw/projects

This Web site identifies research efforts and training activities affiliated with Columbia University's School of Social Work. This site contains papers, bibliographies, and links to research sites of relevance to social work.

http://www.arts.unimelb.edu.au/Dept/SocialWork

Research conducted at the School of Social Work in Melbourne, Australia, is featured at this Web site. This program is operated mainly through five practice research units. The most extensive is the Children's, Families and Young Person's Research Unit established in 1994. This program serves families and covers such areas as child protection and juvenile justice to aid the needy. To learn more about evaluation, visit this Web site.

http://snipe.ukc.ac.uk/PSSRU

Run by the University of Kent at Canterbury in England, this site gives a review of care management arrangements in community and long-term care in various countries, showing how they reflect system contexts and client needs, and describing leading programs and evaluation evidence about their impact on equity and efficiency. Research programs are listed in the Web page.

http://www.iwpr.org

The Institute for Women's Policy Research is a nonprofit, independent organization that evaluates social programs and disseminates its findings. Visit this site and learn about current projects in the areas of healthcare, social security, labor force participation, and pay equity.

http://www.ssw.umich.edu/trapped/collab.html

This Web site identifies research on welfare, work, and domestic violence conducted by the University of Michigan's School of Social Work. This Web page explains how to start social research and tells where, when, and how reliable research should be conducted.

http://www.csulb.edu/~libWeb/subj/swork.html

This address will take you to the Cal State University at Long Beach Library, where you can access electronic and printed resources for research in many areas of study. A summary of the social work program and how to apply for admission is provided.

http://www.mental-health-matters.com/mhealth/research.html

The Mental Health Matters site provides a wide variety of links into research of all types in the social work field. There are sites for clinical research, searchable databases, statistics, and other Internet resources.

http://www.anglia.ac.uk/sphs/piasp/home.htm

The Participatory Inquiry and Action in Social Practice Network maintains this site in association with the Collaborative Action Research Network. As explained in the Web site, the importance of a dynamic relationship between research, practice, and policy should be ever present. The aim of this project is to establish a database of social work professionals interested in action research as a method of inquiry and development.

http://www.ccsd.ca

The Canadian Council on Social Development (CCSD) is a national, self-sustaining, not-for-profit organization. Its work focuses on research and analysis of social and economic trends and their effect on social programs and policies that serve the community. The council also has experienced staff who offer services such as research design and management, primary and secondary data collection, quantitative analysis, report writing, graphic design, and creation of Internet homepages.

http://cfrcwww.social.uiuc.edu

The Children and Family Research Center (CFRC) is part of an initiative by the School of Social Work at the University of Illinois at Urbana-Champaign and is designed to coordinate public service and outreach efforts for the state. The CFRC was created to maintain a research program that would contribute to scientific knowledge about child safety, permanency, and child and family well-being.

http://www.sprc.unsw.edu.au

The research center featured here operates as an independent unit of the University of New South Wales. The center undertakes research in a wide range of social policy issues. The findings of this research are made available to specialist audiences and the general public through publications, seminars, and conference presentations. Emphasis is given to the study of changes in society that affect future needs for social services and the capacity of the community to finance them.

http://trochim.human.cornell.edu

The Bill Trochim Center for Social Research Methods is a World Wide Web Learning Lab containing many useful features. It contains a search engine, links to a beginners guide to HTML, and much more. By clicking on the Selecting Statistics option, you will be guided through a series of questions that will help you determine what statistical techniques are appropriate for your data. In addition, this site contains published and unpublished research papers. This is an excellent social work/social science resource.

http://www.indiana.edu/~ssdc/eric_chess.htm

The ERIC (Educational Resources Information Center Clearinghouse for Social Studies/Social Science Education) contains access to sixteen subject-oriented clearinghouse centers across the nation. Each clearinghouse specializes in a subject area related to education, such as application of theory and research/development projects. ERIC is one of the largest databases of educational information, with access to teaching guides, articles, research reports, books, and other materials. ERIC also provides many other useful services.

Social Welfare Policy and Services

Social welfare policy and services content must include the history, mission, and philosophy of the social work profession. Content must be presented about the history and current patterns of provision of social welfare services, the role of social policy in helping or deterring people in maintaining or achieving optimal health and well-being, and the effect of policy on social work practice. Students must be taught to analyze current social policy within the context of historical and contemporary factors that shape policy. Content must be presented about the political and organizational processes used to influence policy, the process of policy formulation, and the frameworks for analyzing social policies in light of the principles of social and economic justice (CSWE, 2000).

http://www.naswtx.org//leg.html

This site sponsored by the Texas chapter of NASW offers a directory that includes information on welfare reform, healthcare, human rights, youth issues, managed care, professional issues, and health and human services funding. You'll also find a historical outlook on the NASW/Texas and its legislative activities. The legislative advocacy activities are coordinated by the director of governmental affairs in Austin.

http://www.igc.apc.org/dgap/imfsteve.html

Although the International Monetary Fund (IMF) was established with the specific mandate to help stabilize currencies for the purpose of facilitating international trade, it has assumed over time the ever-expanding role of dictating overall national economic programs around the globe, particularly in the countries of South and Central Europe. This Web site explains how the IMF has impacted small business and how this affects social policy.

http://www.sc.edu/swan

The Social Work Access Network (SWAN) was acquired in 1995 from its creator, Peter Thomas. It is now maintained and operated by the College of Social Work at the University of South Carolina under the leadership of Michael White. The SWAN site offers a directory that can help social workers stay informed of issues that affect public policy. Other topics of interest include publications, schools, policy, and government information.

http://www.york.ac.uk/services/library/subjects/spswint.htm

This site provides a series of links (in alphabetical order) of full-text electronic journals, departments, and organizations. It's an excellent source of policy and legislative information.

http://comet.summit1.com/jcpr_old/resources.html

The Joint Center for Poverty Research Web site contains government information and publications on welfare reform, health policy, and related research. You will find a specific focus on poverty research and policy-related issues.

http://www.neconasc.org/welfare.htm

Are you looking for a subject related to welfare and policy? At this site you are able to locate the information needed, whether it is about organizations and associations, periodical resources, legal resources, statistical resources, or related topics. This Web page offers you in-depth information plus additional information related to your topic.

http://www.upenn.edu/gse/ncoff/fatherlink/research/recent/9804nccp.htm

The National Center for Children in Poverty (NCCP) site is intended for those interested in NCCP publications, such as "Children and Welfare Reform" and the "Child Poverty Fact Sheet." The Web page also contains further documents on father- and family-related policies.

http://www.jcpr.org/additional.html

"How much does additional income help children?" This site will provide you with facts, debates, and policy implications of Joint Center for Poverty research about the different measures of children's well-being and parents' income.

http://hs.plym.ac.uk/spsw/spsw.html

The Department of Social Policy and Social Work at the University of Plymouth UK provides a curriculum leading to an advanced degree in social work. Curriculum areas include policy, practice, social life, housing, health education, crime, youth, aging, poverty, social exclusion, and inequality.

http://epn.org/idea/health.html

This article discusses problems faced by families who are not insured. Families USA analyzes options for parents that do not have health insurance. CHIP, a form of health insurance, aims to help those who are uninsured.

http://cnn.com/US/9706/26/medicare.vote.react/index.htmlMeMedicar

The current administration allows senior citizens to choose from a menu of new health plans beyond the old Medicare program. Retirees can open a medical savings accounts using Medicare benefits. This can lead to tax-exempt savings accounts for the elderly, but not everybody supports the measure. Visit this site to read about current efforts to save Medicare from bankruptcy.

http://www.clasp.org

The Center for Law and Social Policy (CLASP) submits this article concerning laws and policies affecting the poor. This article focuses on the economic conditions of low-income families. The organization also provides videos, tapes, books, and other resources to help low-income families.

http://www.opendoor.com/hfh/journal.html

The Journal of Children and Poverty Web site contains information about the Institute for Children and Poverty and its research objectives. It offers a summary of empirical findings and policy initiatives in the areas of education, social services, and welfare reform as they affect children, youth, and families. This site also contains an informative directory of links under the heading "Challenge and Opportunity."

http://ccp.ucla.edu/archive.htm

The University of California at Los Angeles's Center for Communication Policy page was created by Jim Reynolds and Sherif El Dabe and is regularly updated. It contains information on the center, which offers a forum for discussing the development of policy alternatives, issues concerning the media, and the limitations of communications policy.

http://157.142.136.54/cm/cmhome.htm

This site introduces several links with the following information: Child Maltreatment's mission, the Child Maltreatment editorial board, Child Maltreatment's format, and related resources on the Internet. They are all very informative in relation to child abuse and neglect. The organization's diverse membership is comprised of psychologists, social workers, physicians, attorneys, judges, law enforcement professionals, nurses, public child protection staff, researchers, prevention specialists, and others.

http://www.ncswt.or.th/The_National_Council1.htm

This site provides information on Thailand's National Council. The council provides social welfare services to the needy, the disabled, and the disadvantaged. The council has provided assistance in counseling, legal advice, financial support, rehabilitation for the disabled, and educational funds for poor children.

http://www.wa.gov/fpc

The Washington State Council is composed of the five state agencies dealing with children and family services, four members of the legislature, and a representative from the governor's office. It also provides informative links such as Community Public Health and Safety Networks, Legal and Policy Information, and Links to Other National Sites.

http://www.policy.com/community/univ.html

This is the policy news and information service Web site. It contains access to policy centers, institutes, universities, and research groups that evaluate and study policy issues at local, state, and federal levels. For example, the Web site allows you access to the Center for Policy Research at Syracuse University, which conducts a broad range of interdisciplinary research and related activities in areas such as aging, disabilities, and income security. Many of the sites offer links to other relevant Web sites and information. The Web site contains a content search, glossary, and organization-by-issue sections. The Web site also allows you to reach your representatives by offering congressional and state legislatures directories.

http://povertycenter.cwru.edu

This Web site is put together by the Center on Urban Poverty and Social Change. The center's goal is to understand how social and economic changes affect low-income communities. The center also addresses how living in these communities affects their residents. The center would like to bring about change through community strategies and reform the way institutions and service organizations respond to the needs of community residents. The research is done by a multidisciplinary team consisting of social welfare experts, economists, and demographers who also perform research using approaches of other disciplines and professions. Although the research done by the center covers a specific community, the research offers valuable insight that can be used in application and reference to similar communities.

http://glrain.cic.net/icwa.htm

This Web page is dedicated to the Indian Child Welfare Act and provides a historical summary of the act. It defines who is protected under this umbrella legislation from the reign of terror imposed by adoption agencies and their constituents. This will be of use to social workers needing information on policies that affect Native Americans.

http://www.law.umich.edu/childlaw/index.html

This Web page is an overview of the Michigan Child Welfare Law Resource Center. Clicking on Child Welfare Law Program gives you access to its mission statement. In it you will find another link to its history and its areas of research. The research directory offers an alphabetical listing of resources.

http://www.cwla.org/cwla/sitenews/new52098.html

The Child Welfare League of America Web page can be of use to social workers needing information. You'll also find brief histories on the Black Administrators in Child Welfare and of the Council of Latino Executives.

http://ajax.abacon.com/books/ab_0023205822.html

This Web page features books on welfare policy in the Allyn & Bacon catalog. Text books are available on social problem analysis, dimensions of social welfare policy, and theoretical framework for the analysis of social welfare policy.

http://nch.ari.net

This Web site is of interest to all concerned about homelessness. Here you will find facts about homelessness, legislation and policy alerts, and a calendar of events. This site is hosted by the National Coalition for the Homeless, a national advocacy network of homeless persons, activists, and service providers seeking to end this problem.

http://members.amaonline.com/nrogers/ada.htm

This Web page can be used by social workers looking for resources relating to the Americans with Disability Act (ADA). You can also find resources on other disability issues such as the Rehabilitation Act. It gives pamphlets and articles about ADA concerning diversity, disabilities, and many other topics.

http://www.welfarewatch.org/county/wlc.html

The Center on Social Welfare Policy and Law helps poor people get the basic subsistence, justice, and fairness to which they are entitled. The Center on Social Welfare Policy and Law has worked on behalf of poor people to ensure that adequate income support (public funding provided on the basis of need) is available whenever and to the extent necessary to meet basic needs and foster healthy human and family development. The center serves as counsel or co-counsel in welfare litigation across the country, works with and represents organizations of low-income persons, and leads advocacy efforts (through litigation and other means) regarding the formulation and implementation of state and federal income support programs for needy families.

http://www.ozemail.com.au/~acswc3

The Australian Catholic Social Welfare Commission is an organization of the Australian Catholic Bishops' Conference and is dedicated to advise the Catholic bishops on matters pertaining to national social welfare issues. It develops, advocates, coordinates, supports, researches, and advises on social welfare issues. The commission strives to achieve social justice, especially for those who are disadvantaged, devalued, or distressed. It carries this out by interacting with governments, churches, and people to develop social welfare policies, strategies, and programs that will enhance the well-being of our communities.

http://www.welfarewatch.org/county/wlc.html

A directory of organizations working on welfare issues in California is available at this Web address. This Web page gives addresses and phone numbers for client referral. The Center aims to help low-income families obtain basic requirements and works to ensure fairness for all. The Center specializes in cash-income support programs to promote the creation, maintenance, strengthening, and fair administration of the programs.

http://www.idbsu.edu/SOCWORK/DHUFF/history/central/core.htm

This site, designed by Professor Dan Huff, is an excellent resource for acquiring information and pictures about the history of social work. A visitor can step back into any time period in history on this page. Past years are grouped into eras and each can be entered separately. As visitors travel throughout history, they discover illustrations that depict life in that era and important historical events of that time period along with interesting social events.

http://cnn.com/ALLPOLITICS/1997/gen/resources/infocus/ welfare/intro.html

This Web site sponsored by CNN is an up-to-date information center for all types of social policy. This particular area deals with welfare reform. A timeline is provided with the history of all of the welfare policies that have been enacted in the United States. This site contains photos of the presidents who are relevant to social welfare issues and a background of their involvement. Changes in welfare law are also explained, and links provide specific sites for more in-depth study. Lists of waivers, block grants for each state, and a timeline of important events that affect social welfare policy are available at this site. In addition to this valuable information, a visitor can obtain and read news articles pertaining to welfare reform from *Time* magazine.

http://epn.org/idea/welfare.html

This Web site is a collection of information on various topics that pertain to welfare and families. Covered areas include welfare in transition, welfare rights of new residents, jailing kids, social security reform, and child protection and support. Links can be found to other issues, articles, statistics, and Web sites within each of these specific areas. This site is updated regularly; bookmarking it for future reference would be a benefit to the visitor. Articles and areas of interest are archived by topic for easier research. Additionally, this Web site offers an area to sign up on a mailing list. This list is devoted to encouraging a discussion of policies and programs that supplement income and wages in order to help families escape poverty.

http://www.brynmawr.edu/Adm/SWSR/MLSP.html

This site is from Bryn Mawr College in Bryn Mawr, Pennsylvania. The school offers a post–master's degree program for professionals in social work, in other human service professions, or in public administration and policy analysis related to social welfare. "Law and Social Policy Programs in Social Work" is the name of the program and the MLSP degree is awarded upon successful completion of all requirements. It consists of eight courses, field instruction, and basic skills of legal analysis, legal research, advocacy, and mediation.

http://www.urban.org

This site is of a nonpartisan economic and social policy research organization, the Urban Institute. It investigates social and economic problems, government policies, and public and private programs. Much of its research is available to the public. The institute's objective is to increase citizens' awareness of important public choices.

http://www.aphsa.org

This is the site of the American Public Human Services Association, a nonprofit, bipartisan organization of individuals and agencies concerned with human services. It educates members of Congress, the media, and the broader public on what is happening in the states concerning welfare, child welfare, healthcare reform, and other issues involving families and the elderly. In this site you will find links to the news on human services, state and local news, press releases, and welfare reform news. You can also link to affiliates and related organizations such as American Association of Food Stamp Directors (AAFSD), American Association of Public Welfare Attorneys (AAPWA), American Public Human Services Association–Information Systems Management (APHSA–ISM), Association of Administrators of the Interstate Compact on Adoption and Medical Assistance (ICAMA), and Association of Administrators of the Interstate Compact on the Placement of Children (ICPC).

http://www.york.ac.uk/services/library/subjects/spswint.htm

This Web page provides social workers with a number of Internet options for finding information on social welfare policy. This is a valuable library resource.

http://www.gnofn.org/~jill/swhistory/

This is a very useful Web site. It is a timeline from the year 1869 to the current year. There are over sixty links ranging from Jane Addams and Hull House to Columbia University School of Social Work openings to the NASW (National Association of Social Workers) revision of its Code of Ethics. As stated by Web master Jill Murray, "This page will be revised regularly, so come back again."

http://www.advocatehealth.com/mvphil.html

This Web site has everything that you would want to know about Advocate Health Care. It gives links about its mission, values, philosophy, and history. Each link gives a brief summary of its area. For example, under Values it gives a breakdown of subjects that the group feels are important to follow, such as equality, compassion, excellence, partnership, and stewardship. It's a good site to visit for both pleasure and education.

http://www.sc.edu/swan/politic.html

The social work profession requires one to remain informed of policies and legislation that affect clients. At this Web site you will find helpful links offering reliable information on issues that impact professional practice. Headings include education, alcohol, drugs, and requests for proposals. The section reviewing current court decisions is frequently updated.

Populations at Risk

Programs of social work education must present theoretical and practice content about patterns, dynamics, and consequences of discrimination, economic deprivation, and oppression. The curriculum must provide content about people of color, women, and gay and lesbian persons. Such content must emphasize the impact of discrimination, economic deprivation, and oppression on these groups. Each program must include content about populations at risk who are particularly relevant to its mission. In addition to those populations, such groups include, but are not limited to, those distinguished by age, ethnicity, culture, class, religion, and physical or mental disability (CSWE, 2000).

http://inet.ed.gov/offices/OCR/ocrage.html

The Age Discrimination Act of 1975 prohibits discrimination against students on the basis of age in education programs or activities that receive federal financial assistance. However, there are exceptions under certain circumstances that one must be aware of. Learn for yourself at this interesting Web site.

http://www.csnp.ohio-state.edu/csnp/CSNPADM.htm

This Web page gives an overview of the Center for Special Needs Populations at Ohio State University. The center was established to provide interdisciplinary support for national, regional, state, and local projects related to special-needs or at-risk populations.

http://www.lambdalegal.org

The Lambda Legal Defense and Education Fund is the nation's oldest and largest legal association working for the civil rights of lesbians, gays, and people with HIV/AIDS. This Web site gives you the latest news on U.S. Supreme Court decisions, updates on homosexual issues, and data about this organization and its members.

http://www.lungusa.org/pub/states/map.html

This site examines and targets areas in the United States with risk factors such as pollution and air quality and the effects on all individuals.

http://www.rit.edu/~694www/bpd/par-new.htm

This site brought to you by the Rochester Institute of Technology describes theoretical perspectives and consequences of discrimination, economic deprivation, and oppression.

http://www.webtest.state.oh.us

This site reviews health risks to the general public. Its goal is to identify hazards and to recommend appropriate interventions. The section on nicotine and alcohol consumption is particularly revealing.

http://www.aracnet.com/~libcoll/index.html

Liberation Collective is a nonprofit organization whose goal is to link social justice movements to end all oppression. Liberation Collective would like to change negative public mindsets through positive educational experience and nonviolence. This site contains numerous links to other liberation organizations.

http://eric-web.tc.columbia.edu/development

This Web site contains annotated bibliographies and reviews of publications related to helping urban/minority students. Some of the topics covered are school dropouts and intervention, youth needs, and educational needs. The review pages offer links to other sources and reference materials.

http://users.bournemouth-net.co.uk/~lloyd/index.html

A Jewish contribution to eliminating discrimination, this Web site houses links to topics such as racism and gender discrimination. Visitors are also provided with an opportunity to submit their own assessment of the topic.

http://www.usc.edu/isd/archives/ethnicstudies/race_discrim_main.html

This Web site at the University of Southern California offers information on racial discrimination and prejudice. It contains topics such as the history of racial discrimination in the United States and includes links that enable the viewer to locate books, video recordings, and newspaper articles.

http://www.cdcnac.org/geneva98/trends/trends_4.htm

This site provides information about high-risk populations. "Trends in HIV Diagnoses," "Historical Trends Prevention," "Evaluating the Impact," and "A Closer Look at Trends" are examples of hypertext links.

http://people.unt.edu/~mperez/latinos.html

The Hispanic/Latino Health and Culture site provides an introductory description of the Hispanic/Latino population in the United States. It offers insight to cultural values, Mexican Americans, and folk beliefs that are important to consider when working with Latinos.

http://people.unt.edu/~mperez/migrant.html

This is the place to go for information regarding migrant health, one of the largest concerns of migrant and seasonal farm workers in the United States. Links include access to the U.S. Department of Agriculture, U.S. Department of Education, U.S. Department of Health and Human Services, the National Center for Farm Workers, the Rural Health Association, and Rural Information Center Health Services.

http://www.caps.ucsf.edu/capsweb/toolbox/Riskhome.html

This site has extensive information about what puts families at risk of becoming homeless. It explains that homelessness often occurs due to a combination of substance abuse and chronic mental illness. It also contains a survey and a directory of links pertaining to HIV.

http://www.nida.nih.gov/NIDA-Notes/NNVol12N3/DirrepVol12N3.html

Visit this site for a look at factors that put youth at risk. Prevention programs and research on effective family-, school-, and community-based prevention programs are described for use in your community.

http://flag.blackened.net/revolt/ppapers/lgb.html

The article found at this site focuses on the spread of AIDS among the gay and lesbian community and how they have been subject to discrimination and prejudice worldwide. It compares oppression of gays and lesbians to that of women and ethnic minorities. This is one of the many articles published in *The Workers Solidarity Movement Newspaper.* This organization produces three regular publications, which generally appear on the Web approximately one month after publication.

http://www.randomhouse.com/tid/files/TID/D01963/F00374.htm

The Global Diversity Forum is a discussion list for individuals engaged in human resource management, education, or social work, as well as training consultants and anyone else in a group-leading managerial capacity. The main purpose of the Global Diversity Forum is to provide a platform of cross-disciplinary communication on a global level with a focus on aspects of human relations in business, education, and social work. In addition to the global dialog, the mailing list serves as a resource for up-to-date information on conferences, books in print, professional publications, and reviews of articles and research papers that deal with a variety of issues. It covers issues from diversity to treatment among special populations.

http://www.hrc.org/issues/aids/aidsprev.html

The Human Rights Campaign talks about AIDS prevention. It states that even though "new treatments" have helped reduce the number of AIDS deaths, CDC data show that new HIV infections remain essentially the same. Women, people of color, and young people are particularly at risk of becoming infected. This is an informative site.

http://www.educ.washington.edu/coe/centers/StudentsAtRisk.htm

This Web site is about the Center for Students At-Risk (C-STARS) that was "established to foster inter-professional projects to encourage students to stay in school." This "Center collaborates with city, state, and private service agencies and advances inter-professional interagency collaboration through research, professional development of current practitioners, and facilitation of cooperative efforts for common and client populations of students and families." This Web site is beneficial to all interested in working with at-risk students and their families.

http://www.thearc.org

Welcome to the homepage of the Association for Retarded Citizens (ARC), the largest national nonprofit organization dealing with mental retardation. Its history is provided as well as information on its services and efforts to end discrimination. Visit this site for links to resources for mentally retarded citizens.

http://www.nsclc.org

The National Senior Citizens Law Center (NSCLC) was established to help older individuals live their lives free from poverty. NSCLC attorneys help in legal issues and practice areas that affect the welfare of those of limited income. Information is given on the available services as well as other areas such as Medicare, Social Security, nursing homes, and pensions.

http://www.hud.gov/fhe/fheact.html

This Web site discusses HUD (the U.S. Department of Housing and Urban Development), which promotes equal housing opportunity. The Fair Housing Act prohibits discrimination because of race, color, sex, marital status, or handicap. Information is given on actions prohibited against people based on these areas. There are also details on how to receive help from HUD and the steps that can be taken if rights have been violated. More importantly, at the beginning of this site, there is a way to find out about the department itself, to see where local offices are, and even to search the Web for documents on HUD.

http://www.health.org/pubs/primer/glb.htm

The research suggests that gays, lesbians, and bisexual Americans are at special risk for alcohol and other drug problems. Prevention requires understanding of the risk factors. Visit this site to learn about prevention strategies for gay, lesbian, and bisexual clients. Numerous links are also included.

http://www.geocities.com/Heartland/Acres/8796/index2.html

This Web site is a collection of links containing information related to foster care and child welfare. For quick and easy access, topics are categorized into different subject matters. Areas include foster parent resources, journals and legislation, and child abuse prevention. Visitors can search for resources by region as well. Each category contains an excellent variety of links that will enable a social worker, counselor, or other professional to find answers to many questions or concerns pertaining to children at risk. In addition to informational resources, this Web site offers the opportunity for dialogs about child welfare issues in a special forum.

http://www.at-risk.com

This Web site is sponsored by the Bureau for At-Risk Youth. This organization provides resources to help today's youth cope with the issues that they face today. At this Web site, a visitor can request a free catalog that describes hundreds of videos, publications, posters, programs, and other educational resources. A listing of worldwide ongoing events featuring youth-oriented activities is also available at this site. An informative area of this Web site is the "reality clock." This area provides shocking statistics on issues that young people face in society today. Topics include the number of people 18 years old and under who are killed by handguns, and the number of babies born to unwed teenage girls. In addition to the statistical data and useful resources, this site provides a forum for teachers, parents, students, and others to connect, discuss, help, and learn about issues that are prevalent among today's youth.

http://www.virtualcity.com/youthsuicide/index.htm

This Web site is a plethora of research papers pertaining to all aspects of youth suicide. These papers have been submitted from authors worldwide authors and cover various topics. For each paper, a brief abstract is provided to avoid unnecessary reading. The papers are topically arranged for quick access. In addition to research papers, this Web site contains PhD and master's theses. Any social worker in need of data, statistics, or general information regarding youth suicide will benefit from this site.

http://www.health.org/pubs/primer/toc.htm

This site is of the National Clearinghouse for Alcohol and Drug Information. It is the Prevention Primer site. An excellent reference tool for prevention practitioners, it incorporates the principles of a public health approach to preventing alcohol, tobacco, and other drug problems in its summaries of issues and strategies. It gives you topics in alphabetical order. Go to H and click on Hispanic/Latino to find important information about this group.

http://www.discriminationattorney.com

This site is a guide for nonlawyers and lawyers alike in the growing field of employment law and other areas of civil rights law. The Web site has sections on nearly every area of employment law, including sexual harassment, whistleblowing, and age, race, and disability discrimination. By being informed, social workers can better help their clients, especially those in populations at risk.

http://www.nolo.com/chunkEMP/emp3.html

Many individuals fortunate enough to be healthy in mind and body and to be employed lament the difficulties a workplace can impose. But for those with physical or mental disabilities, many workplaces can be truly daunting. The Americans with Disabilities Act (ADA) prohibits employment discrimination on the basis of workers' disabilities. This site gives information on exactly whom the ADA protects. How can I tell if a particular accommodation offered by my employer is reasonable? When can an employer legally claim that a particular accommodation is simply not feasible?

http://www.gov.nb.ca/ael/rights/e1defini.htm

This guide is published by the New Brunswick Human Rights Commission as a source of information on human rights in New Brunswick, Canada. It is not a legal interpretation. It gives information on defined terms such as *culture, sex, racism, prejudice,* and *physical disability.*

http://www.naswdc.org/Prac/hivaids.htm

This site discusses how the National Association of Social Workers is aiming to give social workers the education and training needed to provide assistance to the population suffering from HIV/AIDS. The site discusses the development of the center, how it started, its committee of social workers, and advisory trainers who instruct its workshops.

http://home.glassla.org/glass

The GLASS (Gay and Lesbian Adolescent Social Services) Web site consists of nine main links: (1) What Is GLASS?, (2) Become a Foster Parent!!, (3) GLASS Success Stories, (4) GLASS Services, (5) Job Openings!, (6) How Can I Help?, (7) Books for Sale, (8) About Our President, and (9) Related Links. The Related Links page is divided into two main areas: "Links to Relevant Sites," and "Other Related Resources." It's a valuable resource for social workers.

http://www.plannedparenthood.org/Library/externallinks/sexuality.html

This site sponsored by Planned Parenthood consists of six main areas of concentration: (1) Gay, Lesbian, and Bisexual Issues, (2) Safer Sex, (3) Sexuality Education, (4) Sexuality and Disability, (5) Sexuality and Religion, and (6) Transgender and Transvestite Issues. A gateway to useful information for social workers is found here.

http://www.igc.apc.org/wri/wr-98-99/malnutri.htm

Malnutrition is a serious condition. This Web site explores the root cause of this growing problem in the United States. Families are at risk when they lack the economic, environmental, and social resources to purchase or grow enough food.

http://www.glnh.org

Accessible nationwide, the Gay and Lesbian National Hotline is a resource that provides peer counseling, information, and referrals. All calls are toll-free and confidential. This Web site summarizes a list of services available and maintains links to gay and lesbian Web pages.

http://www.virtualcity.com/youthsuicide/ethnic.htm

This Web site suggests that minority groups who are gay and lesbian suffer double discrimination. White gay and lesbian youths only have to deal with discrimination due to their sexual orientation. Minority youths not only have to deal with the discrimination from white society, but they also lack support from their own families.

http://www.shareintl.org/spej.html

This Web site provides a long directory of topics related to social and political economics. Topics include the faces of poverty, healthcare, and gender equity. This Web page provides information that can be referenced when writing proposals.

http://add.miningco.com/msubrisk.htm

This Web page provides information on at-risk youth in the school systems in terms of (1) Linking At-Risk Students and Schools to Integrated Services, (2) Preventing Antisocial Behavior in Disabled and At-Risk Students, (3) Providing Effective Schooling for Students at Risk, (4) Rethinking Learning for Students at Risk, and (5) Who Are the "At-Risk" Students? Each topic provides information about issues that affect students such as family responsibilities, poverty, and work status.

http://www.health.org/pubs/primer/hispanic.htm

This Web page reviews alcohol and tobacco use data among populations at risk—namely, Mexican Americans, Puerto Ricans, Central/South Americans, and Cubans. Authors of this Web site urge that prevention programs consider the knowledge, attitudes, and practices of Hispanic/Latino users.

http://www.coloradohealthnet.org/diabetes/
diabetesQnA/dm_her

Dedicated to the treatment of diabetes, this Web page follows a question-and-answer format. Visit this site to learn about the role heredity and diet play among ethnic minority patients.

http://www.mercycorps.org

Mercy Corps' goal is to alleviate suffering, oppression, and poverty. It helps more than fifty countries around the world. It provides healthcare, food, economic opportunity, and shelter to people in developing countries.

Social Work Values and Ethics

Programs of social work education must provide specific knowledge about social work values and their ethical implications and must provide opportunities for students to demonstrate their application in professional practice. Students must be assisted to develop an awareness of their personal values and to clarify conflicting values and ethical dilemmas. Among the values and principles that must be infused throughout every social work curriculum are the following (CSWE, 2000):

Professional relationships are built on regard for individual worth and dignity, and advance by mutual participation, acceptance, confidentiality, honesty, and responsible handling of conflict.

Social workers respect individuals' rights to make independent decisions and to participate actively in the helping process.

Social workers are committed to assisting client systems to obtain needed resources.

Social workers strive to make social institutions more humane and responsive to human needs.

Social workers demonstrate respect for and acceptance of the unique characteristics of diverse populations.

Social workers are responsible for their own ethical conduct, for the quality of their practice, and for seeking continuous growth in the knowledge and skills of their profession.

http://www.csw.utk.edu/ethics/codeofet.htm

This site outlines the National Association of Social Workers Code of Ethics, its purpose, and ethical standards. These standards include (1) social workers' ethical responsibilities to clients, (2) social workers' ethical responsibilities to colleagues, (3) social workers' ethical responsibilities in practice settings, (4) social workers' ethical responsibilities as professionals, (5) social workers' ethical responsibilities to the profession, and (6) social workers' ethical responsibilities to the broader society. This is an excellent source for classroom use or agency reference.

http://www.demon.co.uk/via

This Web site is sponsored by Values into Action (VIA), a nonprofit organization that works for the rights of people with mental disabilities. VIA believes that people with learning difficulties have the same rights as other citizens: mainstream schooling, employment, housing, and health services. Although this organization is based in the United Kingdom, membership is offered internationally. Members will receive a newsletter covering upcoming events, projects, and other information pertaining to advocacy for the mentally ill.

http://www.naswdc.org/CODE.htm

The NASW Code of Ethics is intended to serve as a guide to the everyday professional conduct of social workers. This Web site contains an overview of this code. A summary of each section is provided to help social workers gain a complete understanding of the ethics and values that they are obligated to uphold. The entire document is available for downloading as a Word document.

http://www.fsu.edu/~spap/orgs/ethics/papers.html

The National Symposium on Ethics and Values in the Public Administration Academy provides papers written by professors and students from universities across the United States. These papers are arranged by topic and provide the address of the author for readers seeking further information on the subject. The topics cover a wide range of areas concerning ethics and values in various situations. Many of the papers are available for downloading into Wordperfect, Word, and ASCII.

http://www.socialworker.com/index.shtml

This Web site contains valuable information for social workers. An interesting and informative area is the "On Your Mind" survey. Current and previous years' questions and answers are provided. The topics covered in the survey consist of situations and dilemmas involving social work values and ethics. Another area of this Web site contains information regarding *The Social Worker's Internet Handbook,* a manual pertaining to the use of the Internet to enhance your social work practice. This area also provides information on which Web sites can best benefit you and your clients. In addition, links to Web sites on subjects related to social work values, ethics, and organizations are available here.

http://english.ttu.edu/STC/ethics.htm

This Web site features ethical guidelines in professional activities in areas other than social work practice. Topics include legality, honesty, confidentiality, quality, fairness, and professionalism.

http://www.naswnyc.org

When you visit this Web site, click on Ethics & Professional Liability. You will find articles and much more information, including "Limits of Confidentiality."

http://www.amia.org/wg39.html

This site of the American Medical Informatics Association aims to raise awareness of ethical, legal, and social issues (ELSI) in health informatics.

http://www.act.acs.org.au/index.html

This is the homepage of the Australian Computer Society. By clicking on the link that reads "ACS Submissions and Position Papers," you will find a code of ethics very similar to that of social work. A review of the duties owed to the community is inspiring.

http://www.nohse.com/index.html

Welcome to the homepage of the National Organization for Human Service Education. This organization unites educators, students, practitioners, and clients in a conversation about preparation of effective human service workers. Click on Ethical Standards for Human Service Workers to see the responsibilities adhered to by other helping professionals.

http://www.naswdc.org/PIECES.htm

Check out NASW happenings, recent press releases, NASW news stories, and much more! Click on the link Sanctions Imposed in Ethics Cases to learn from real examples.

http://www.pbs.org/adventures/PTMenu/honesty.htm

This site is very colorful with animated adventures from the Book of Virtues. The stories in this episode help teach some of the values of being honest as well as the consequences of being dishonest. The site also includes stories about courage, compassion, honesty, and other virtues.

http://www.ed.gov/pubs/parents/Behavior/pt2.html

Here's an educational site devoted to parenting. It reminds us that a responsible character is formed over time and is made up of daily habits, feelings, thoughts, and actions. This site offers insight to appropriate behavior in a variety of settings. It also maintains interesting links on self-control, self-respect, and compassion for others.

http://www.basw.co.uk/pages/info/ethics.htm

Visit this site for an overview of the professional social worker in the United Kingdom. The Code of Ethics is available on-line to review and compare. The stated objective is to make these principles clear in order to protect clients and members of society.

http://www.ifsw.org/publications/4.4.pub.html

Knowledge of ethics is an essential part of professional social work practice. Visit this Web site brought to you by the International Federation of Social Workers (IFSW) in Berne, Switzerland, for an excellent overview.

http://www.und.ac.za/und/socialw/moral.html

Mel Gray provides a summary of ethical principles in social work. You'll enjoy reading this article entitled "The Role of Moral Rules and Principles."

http://www.ohio.gov/csw/ethics.htm

The State of Ohio Counselor and Social Work Board offers an overview of ethical principles in professional practice at the Web address provided.

http://weber.u.washington.edu/~sswWeb/nasw.html

This Web page housed at the University of Washington specifically addresses social work ethical responsibilities to clients, colleagues, and employees. You can follow the links to learn more about the school of social work at U.W.

http://www.goshen.edu//sswa/sowkiii.htm

This Web page from the Social Work Education Program at Goshen College summarizes values and ethical principles as outlined by the National Association of Social Workers Code of Ethics, and the Council of Social Work Education's Curriculum Policy Statement. The site lays out the material in an easy-to-follow format. Each value is followed by an ethical principle. One can use the links to learn more about the Social Work Education Program at Goshen College in Goshen, Indiana.

http://www.umanitoba.ca/SocialWork/degrees/code_ethics/ethics_definitions.html

This Web site is sponsored by the Canadian Association of Social Workers. It contains a complete listing of ethics for social workers in Canada. It has ten specific items and each item is linked to a chapter containing detailed information. This is a well-organized and valuable resource for learning about the code of ethics in Canada.

http://www.abacon.com/socwk/quiz/index.html

The Social Work Career Quiz found at this site consists of twelve sections. The quiz on social work characteristics and ethics consists of seventeen questions. This is a fun way of evaluating what you know about the profession. Don't worry, it's not graded but does offer an explanation for each answer.

http://www.scu.edu/Ethics/practicing/decision/approach.shtml

The Ethics Connection is brought to you by the Markkula Center for Applied Ethics. This Web site contains many interesting features regarding ethics, such as different ethical approaches. It has the latest news and publications in the field of ethics. You can use the internal search engine to refine your search.

http://www.ethics.ubc.ca

The University of British Columbia's Centre for Applied Ethics has created this good Web site for locating books and journals related to ethics. It contains details on ethics information from different professions. There is also a page available for finding resources on the World Wide Web.

http://www.socialworker.com

The New Social Worker Online is for social work students and recent graduates. It's a good source of information regarding issues of importance and enables users to subscribe to its journal. Informative articles deal with topics such as ethical dilemmas with special populations and boundary issues for practicing social workers. You can order back issues as well. The site also contains a message board, chat rooms, and social work links.

http://www.wrame.amedd.army.mil/patientinfo/ethicssocial.htm

Well worth visiting, this Web site gives the summary of the major beliefs. It summarizes a social worker's conduct, competency, and ethical responsibility to clients, colleagues, employers, and employing organizations, the social work profession, and society.

http://www.state.il.us/dcfs/ethics.htm

Use this Web address to visit the Illinois Department of Children and Family Services Code of Ethics. This comprehensive site gives the entire Code of Ethics for Child Welfare Professionals in the State of Illinois.

http://www.ethics.ubc.ca/resources

This address will take you to a directory of World Wide Web sites such as Health Care Ethics, Environmental Ethics, Animal Welfare and the Ethics of Animal Use, Business Ethics, Moral/Ethical Decision Making, Professional Ethics, and Computers and Information-Technology Ethics. These topics may be of interest to social workers participating on interdisciplinary teams.

http://www.ssc.msu.edu/~sw/oldeth.html

This site is a must for all social work students. This site presents the entire NASW Code of Ethics. The code is intended as a guide to the everyday conduct of members of the social work profession. This site is provided by Michigan State University's School of Social Work.

http://www.west.asu.edu/humansvcs/socwork/naswcode.htm

This Web page features the NASW Code of Ethics. It explains major principles that social workers need to abide by in professional practice. Arizona State University–West maintains this useful site.

http://www.naswca.org/sindex.html

This site reminds social workers of the obligation to uphold the highest principles in conduct towards clients, colleagues, and employers. This Web site also contains links to practice standards with adolescents, child protection issues, and much more. Clinical indicators are available for acute psychiatric hospitals, acute medical care hospitals, and nursing homes.

http://www.tmn.com/odn/credo.html

This Web site explains the position of the Human System Development Organization, a nonprofit group committed to upholding values and ethics among professionals working in human service.

http://www.unisa.edu.au/library/internet/pathfind/sw_ethic.htm

Are you ready for ethics training? This site contains information on an educational videotape developed by the NASW. It is recommended for in-service training and staff development. Topics include protection of the client, boundary issues, and risk management.

http://www.naswpress.org/publications/books/practice/profchoices.html

This site contains information on Internet resources for social workers and human service workers in terms of following codes of ethics. This page provides the codes of ethics of the Australian Association of Social Workers, British Association of Social Workers, and International Federation of Social Workers, and additional information available on the Internet.

http://www.scu.edu/SCU/Centers/Ethics/practicing

This Web page was designed to provide you with a resource for ethical decision making. As you click on the various headings, it will provide you with information, articles, and an electronic bulletin board. Topics include ethics in the workplace, ethics in health systems, and business law. Santa Clara University hosts this useful and detailed Web page that will assist social workers in any area of the field.

http://re-xs.ucsm.ac.uk/ethics

This site features "Social Ethics," an academic discipline taught at the University College of St. Martin in Lancaster, England. Its stated purpose is to study a range of questions about values in society, probing such social issues as criminal justice, discrimination, drugs, poverty, third world debt, and animal rights. These topics are categorized by headings that visitors will find interesting.

http://www.ethicsusa.com

The Bureau of Essential Ethics Education provides a newsletter, information on seminars, and a list of schools using values in action on this Website. Essential values are given for adults, but they are presented in ways for kids to easily remember. In addition, there is a directory of links for children and their families.

http://cavern.uark.edu/plscinfo/pub/ethics/guide.html

This page provides questions that are meant to stimulate thinking about ethical decision making. Links are provided that lead to content on ethics in public policy and practice. Additional links lead to case studies that exemplify value clarification.

http://www.aasw.asn.au/pgm/ethics/pgm_eth.htm

This Web site belongs to the Australian Association of Social Workers, which is currently drafting its Codes of Ethics for Consultation. This Web page is interesting because it gives us an opportunity to consider how professional ethics interface with social work practice and policy.

http://www.ssc.msu.edu/~sw/nasweth.html

This site features the Social Work Code of Ethics and its application to everyday professional practice. This site includes four sections: Preamble, Purpose, Ethical Principles, and Ethical Standards. Each is explained in detail.

http://www.curtin.edu.au/curtin/dept/sw/whoweare/staff/fcrawford/ETHICS.html

This address leads to a lecture posted on the Internet that deals with ethical issues of relevance to social work. If offers examples of social workers working through professional dilemmas.

http://isassw.org.il/ethics.htm

Visit this site for a trustworthy guide to professional practice, the NASW Code of Ethics. As outlined here, responsibilities include ethical behavior toward clients, colleagues, employers, and the profession. This is a good site to familiarize yourself with before being confronted with ethical dilemmas.

Human Behavior and the Social Environment

Programs of social work education must present theoretical and practice content about patterns, dynamics, and consequences of discrimination, economic deprivation, and oppression. The curriculum must provide content about people of color, women, and gay and lesbian persons. Such content must emphasize the impact of discrimination, economic deprivation, and oppression upon these groups. Each program must include content about populations at risk that are particularly relevant to its mission. In addition to those just mandated, such groups include, but are not limited to, those distinguished by age, ethnicity, culture, class, religion, and physical or mental disability (CSWE, 2000).

http://www.unicef.org/voy

Children's work is hazardous when it is harmful to their health and development, when there are limited opportunities to play, when the work affects their participation in school, or when it causes physical or emotional stress. This UNICEF site discusses the need for healthy development. It contains excellent pictures and links to children's sites.

http://www.ahrd.org

This site provides information about the Academy of Human Resource Development and its purpose (to study human resource developmental theories). Its overall mission is to disseminate its findings. Links include Career Planning, Membership Services, and The Virtual Forum.

http://www.childbirth.org/

This Web site offers links to information on prenatal care and other educational material on healthy birth and delivery. Birth stories, an interactive birth plan, and links regarding travel and pregnancy are provided.

http://www.mirror-mirror.org/eatdis.htm

Eating disorders affect thousands of people. This site can help social workers and clients recognize the signs and symptoms and it tells where to find help. If you need to approach someone, are interested in relapse prevention, or wish to chat on-line, this site is for you.

http://www.envmed.rochester.edu/wwwrap/behavior/jaba/jabahome.htm

This Web address is to the Journal of Applied Behavior Analysis, which is dedicated to the study of behavior problems and their social importance. On-line subscriptions to this human development resource are available.

http://www.womens-health.org.nz

This is the homepage of the Women's Health Action based in New Zealand (a charitable trust that aims to provide women with reliable information and education services to help them make informed choices about their health and healthcare). The focus is purposefully holistic as opposed to a narrow medical perspective.

http://psychologymatters.com

The purpose of this site is to make available professionally written articles covering a wide variety of psychology areas for professional therapists. Articles from the on-line library are free to download. The authors welcome submissions of professionally written manuscripts for consideration.

http://kramer.ume.maine.edu/~jmb/welcome.html

The *Journal of Mind and Behavior (JMB)* is dedicated to interdisciplinary research conducted by helping professionals. *JMB* calls for the exploration of the interrelationship between the mind and human behavior in the social environment.

http://www.jiwh.org

This Web site offers the latest publications published by the Jacobs Institute. Topics include the status of women's health in all fifty states and the District of Columbia. The Institute offers other material related to family income, risk factors for illness, healthcare coverage, and use of preventive services. This is a useful resource.

http://www.healthnetconnect.net

This Web address is for an on-line library of healthcare information called "Health Net Connection." It is sponsored by Blue Cross & Blue Shield United of Wisconsin. This site offers healthcare information for patients, providers, and government policy makers.

http://157.242.64.83/hbes.htm

This Web site explains how modern evolutionary theory can be used to understand human behavior. The Human Behavior and Evolution Society (HBES) is an interdisciplinary, international society of researchers from the social and biological sciences who use evolutionary theory to discover human nature including evolved cognitive, behavioral, emotional, and sexual adaptations. The society was formed to promote the exchange of ideas and research findings using evolutionary theory, including studies of animal behavior, to better understand human nature. Scholars from a number of fields (psychology, social work, anthropology, psychiatry, economics, medicine, law, philosophy, literature, biology, sociology, business, artificial intelligence, political science, and art) participate in this interdisciplinary society.

http://www.pbs.org/wgbh/aso/thenandnow/humbeh.html

Many people suffer from stress in an industrial, urbanizing society. They may experience a variety of nervous disorders, such as insomnia, headaches, anxiety, and exhaustion. Some doctors think this is a disease they call "neurasthenia," and there are many patent medicines claiming to be cures. Some people think that you are born with a temperament prone to this condition, as are those who succumb to serious mental illness and are confined to asylums for the insane. A few doctors look for a way to treat the mind, rather than the body, to cure these conditions. The site looks at a variety of theorists and their theories about behavior and the human mind. It also allows you to get an overview of the books that these people wrote about their different theories. Theories from Freud, Binet, Pavlov, Piaget, and many more are displayed along with their discoveries, which make us understand that our mental condition is part of a complex interplay between our biology and our environment.

http://www.solbaram.org/articles/family.html

This report examines the etiology of major social problems and offers recommendations for addressing basic needs. This Web site provides an overview of sexual relations and family roles and how these influence behavior.

http://www.isdd.indiana.edu/capdd.html

The Center for Aging Persons with Developmental Disabilities (CAPDD) is one of seven centers supported by the Institute for the Study of Developmental Disabilities (ISDD) at Indiana University, Bloomington. The ISDD is dedicated to the promotion and maintenance of a seamless system of inclusionary services for all individuals with disabilities and their families across the life span. CAPDD focuses on the needs of individuals who present bio-psycho-social changes that are associated with the aging process.

http://www.abacon.com/list/sw0105.html

This site offers a variety of book titles pertaining to human behavior and the social environment. These books can assist social work students and professionals considering issues of race, class, and gender in their work with clients.

http://www.ecdgroup.com/cdt.html

This educational site is dedicated to exploring the developmental needs of children at different stages. The site also maintains a list of sites relevant to various theories.

http://www.ceousa.org

The Center for Equal Opportunity (CEOUSA) is an organization dedicated to countering the negative impacts of race-determined policies. Categories addressed by the center include immigration, assimilation, and multicultural education. This site offers links to journals, news sources, and other related issues. It also contains a link for viewers interested in buying publications related to these issues.

http://www.valdosta.edu/~whuitt/psy702/sysmdlhb.html

The systems model of human behavior is given on this Web page hosted by Valdosta State University. Although the site is used primarily as a psychology resource, most of the information provided is relevant to social workers as well. The mind and body are discussed, as are environmental factors that affect development. An image map of the model is shown, making it more understandable. Terms included in the picture, such as *culture, family,* and *school,* can be clicked on retrieve an explanation of each. This is a very scholarly, well organized resource.

http://www.loshorcones.org.mx/personalrel.html

Los Horcones, a community in northwestern Mexico, was founded due to the interest in the prevention and solution of personal and social problems. Holding the view that we learn to behave as we do by interacting with our environment, one of its organizational areas deals with relationships among both children and adults. This page discusses human behavior in the community. An index is also provided to get to the community's main Web site, which contains a history, images, work organization, and a great deal of other information describing Los Horcones in English and Spanish.

http://www.jstor.org/journals/00959006.html

This Web site provides access to the *Journal of Health and Human Behavior.* There is a way to do a basic search by subject, author, or title in this particular journal as well as in other types of journals. An individual may just decide to browse the seven volumes that are available though; each shows its issues that can be retrieved, including whole articles. On this page, there is also a link to the *Journal of Health and Social Behavior* that provides the same options.

http://www.dnai.com/~children

This Web page serves as a voice for children. Children Now uses research and mass communications to make the well-being of children a top priority across the nation.

This organization helps parents talk to their kids about tough issues such as sex, AIDS, violence, drugs, and alcohol. It addresses the growing health crisis among our nation's children through creative public education strategies, outreach, and policy analysis. It also examines the social and government structures to see how well they support or fail to support children and families (particularly those who are low income), with links for each of these issues. Figures cover, for example, child support in California.

http://nch.ari.net/wwwhome.html

The National Coalition for the Homeless (NCH) is a national advocacy network of homeless persons, activists, service providers, and others committed to ending homelessness through public education, policy advocacy, grassroots organizing, and technical assistance. This page covers facts about homelessness, legislation and policy, NCH projects, and calendar of events.

http://www.childrennow.org/media/mc98/DiffWorld.html

Is behavior influenced by what children see on television? Research conducted by Children NOW suggests that child viewers relate more commonly with mainstream Anglo characters than with ethnic minority persons on television. Visit this site to learn more about children's perceptions of race and class in media. Follow the links to access reports, action guides, and much more. This site offers articles from the press.

http://gopher.vt.edu:10021/H/hwy/simple

A person's temperament is formed by many things: our experiences, how we are taught to act and react, even some intangible inner qualities that we are born with. But what we think of ourselves and our self-esteem are fashioned in large by what we think other people think of us. Our self-worth depends on our notion of how worthy we are to others and on how we were taught by others to view ourselves. From nowhere but the relationships we have with others can come pride, love, honor, shame, trust, envy, or hate. This site offers chapters on how to survive, means to survive, living together, settling differences, groups and rules, behavior and religion, and basic instincts and beyond.

http://www.parentsplace.com

This is an excellent Web site for studying human behavior. "Parents Place" covers issues dealing with all ages of children and parents. Health concerns, educational choices and problems, emotional stresses, and employment situations are among the areas discussed at this Web site, which can be tailored to the viewer's needs and concerns at a click of the mouse. Special tools for parents are available as well. One example is the personal pregnancy calendar, a day-by-day customized calendar detailing the development of a baby from before conception to birth. Other tools include a personal immunization chart, a body mass index, and a personal health report. In addition to information, resources, and tools, this site provides chat rooms, bulletin boards, and an area to ask questions of professionals.

http://www.circleofinclusion.org

This Web site offers information on inclusive educational programs for young children. It can serve as an excellent resource for families of young children with disabilities as well as service providers. Social workers can greatly benefit from the information offered at this site. On-line discussion groups and special forums are available for communication with other professionals, parents, and Circle of Inclusion staff. Portable Document Format (PDF) files pertaining to early education, checklists for evaluating inclusion programs, and general information on the World Wide Web are available for downloading at this site. In addition, active links are provided to other areas pertaining to early childhood education and inclusion.

http://www.cmhc.com/guide/pro22.htm

This Web site is a valuable resource for social workers with clients on medication. Medications are listed by generic name as well as brand name. They are conveniently listed in alphabetical order for easy reference. With the click of the mouse a visitor can check any of several drug resources to find details on a particular drug. Possible areas of interest and use are description of the drug, indications and usage, warnings and precautions, and drug interactions. This site also provides direct links to several drug references and databases that contain valuable information and press releases pertaining to pharmaceutical issues.

http://www.siue.edu/SOCIOLOGY/sociology.htm

Southern Illinois University at Edwardsville offers an excellent overview of theories studied by social work students. This Sociology page can help social workers take a systematic approach to working with client families and lead to a greater understanding of the relationship between human behavior and social groups. Visit this site if you want to know more about human behavior.

http://www.isc.rit.edu/~694www/hbse.htm#top

This Web site hosted by the Rochester Institute of Technology Social Work Department offers information on the National Forum on Family Security, a Complete Guide to Sites Related to Psychology, Gerontology Resources, Alzheimer's Disease, and Children Now. It's an excellent resource for both students and practitioners.

http://www.utexas.edu/world/lecture/sw

This page was designed and is maintained by the University of Texas Austin Web Team. It contains links to pages created by faculty worldwide who are using the Web to deliver class materials. Examples are Co-dependency: A Paradigm Shift, Computer Supported Practice, Holistic Family Practice, Homelessness: Issues and Action, and Human Behavior and Social Environment I. These classes are delivered entirely over the Internet.

http://www.gl.umbc.edu/~acasta1

This site provides a list of agencies social workers can use in their work with sexual minority clients. There are a number of useful links: Stop AIDS; The Gay, Lesbian & Bisexual Factor in the Youth Suicide Problem; and After Dark Bookstore. Visit GLSTN (the Gay, Lesbian and Straight Teachers Network) for a listing of community resources.

http://www.gfn.com

This site is constantly being updated to offer a list of the week's top articles from magazines such as the *Wall Street Journal, Gay Financial News Weekly,* and *Your Money, Your Rights.* Each article has a brief summary telling the author, date, and what magazine it is from. This site also consists of various sections, which are links as well, such as Corporate Gay Policies and Business Referral Network.

http://www.d.umn.edu/~dfalk/hbse.html

This page provides links relevant to Human Behavior in the Social Environment (HBSE) classes in the Social Work Department at the University of Minnesota at Duluth. It's maintained by its creator, Dennis Falk, who teaches the HBSE classes at the university.

http://www.health.gov.au/hfs/pubs/menthlth/access.htm

The objectives of the National Mental Health Strategy for preventing intentional or unintentional discrimination against people with mental or physical disabilities are outlined here. Visit this site to familiarize yourself with client rights.

http://www.blacknet.co.uk/youthara/section1.htm

Anti-Racist Alliance is a Black-led organization that campaigns against the rising tide of racism, anti-Semitism, and hate crimes. Visit this site to learn about awareness events and media conferences. The Anti-Racist Alliance (ARA) was established in November 1991.

http://www.ssc.msu.edu/~sw/webcrse/intcrse.html

The Michigan State University Social Work Web page offers several courses students may take via the Internet. The program is designed to prepare students for entry-level practice in human behavior and the social environment, research, and a practicum experience. There are two courses currently offered over the Internet. For more information, visit this site.

http://www.socialworkonline.com/resource.htm

This Web page provides a wide range of information about various types of resources that the social worker can obtain through the Internet. The focus is on social work and mental health sites. Though it is geared toward the clinical social worker, it offers current information to anyone concerned with mental health and therapy issues. A social worker can obtain information as to how and why clients behave in a particular environment and how their behavior is affected by society as well. This page helps the social worker to obtain books that can be a resource or research tool in all areas of social work.

http://www.pathfinder.com/altculture/aentries/g/gayxmarria.html

This Web page provides various points of view about gay marriages. This site covers laws, moral rights, anti–gay rights, and other issues in gay relationships. This information is important to a social worker working with a gay population.

Works Cited

Council on Social Work Education (CSWE). (2000). Curriculum policy statement. [Online]. Available http://www.cswe.org/bswcps.htm.

Index

mirror mirror

on the wall ...
you are the fairest of them all

an identity handbook for life

dianne wilson

HarperCollins*Publishers*

HarperCollins*Publishers*

First published in Australia in 2005
by HarperCollins*Publishers* Australia Pty Limited
ABN 36 009 913 517
A member of HarperCollins*Publishers* (Australia) Pty Limited Group
www.harpercollins.com.au

HarperCollins*Publishers*
25 Ryde Road, Pymble, Sydney, NSW 2073, Australia
31 View Road, Glenfield, Auckland 10, New Zealand

National Library of Australia Cataloguing-in-Publication data:

Wilson, Dianne.
    Mirror, mirror: an identity handbook for life.
    ISBN 0 7322 7444 3.
    1. Self-esteem in women. I. Title.
158.1082

Cover design by Ellie Exarchos
Cover photograph: Getty Images
Typeset in 10.5 on 14 pt Gill Sans Light by Kirby Jones
Printed and bound in Australia by Griffin Press on 79gsm Bulky Paperback

8 7 6 5 4 3   05 06 07 08

This book is dedicated to the memory of Richard,
a young man downtrodden by life,
who eventually saw the Truth.
He is now living the happily ever after life in Heaven.
His life was not in vain.

Thank you

Thank you my husband for always
treating me like a queen.
Thank you Mum and Dad for always
treating me like a princess.
Thank you Father in Heaven for always
treating me like a royal daughter.
Thank you for believing in me.

Be You

Dare to be yourself.
Dream, imagine, explore. Take initiative.
Don't be afraid to face your fears.
Always seek the Truth.
Value your identity.
Celebrate life — take hold of the adventure.
Never settle for less than what you can have
and what you can give.
Love never fails so hang onto love with all that you are.
Be strong yet soft.
Spend every moment of your life living —
don't waste a moment.
You are royalty with a purpose
greater than yourself.
It doesn't matter what life has dealt you —
what's happened to you so far.
Your future is in your hands.
Believe in the Almighty —
the Creator of all things beautiful.
Rest in His presence.
Be beautiful — be bold.
Be You.

DIANNE WILSON

Contents

Mirror, Mirror

an identity handbook for life

Who am I? Discover the Mirror of Truth that reveals your true identity, and a life of true freedom. You were not born to live a small and contained existence, always wishing that life could be different. You were born to live an expansive and fulfilling life. You were born to realise your true value, and you were born to make a difference.

**The two most important days in a person's life are the day they are born and …
the day they find out why.**

Mirror, Mirror *will touch the life of anyone who has ever felt at any time — unattractive, left out, self-conscious, confused, misunderstood, outcast, abused, useless, worthless or forgotten. This book is full of practical keys to help you unlock the potential of your future. When you know the Truth, the Truth will set you free.*

Dianne Wilson

Dianne is a bestselling author and spokesperson on the issues of body+soul+spirit, healthy living, healthy body image, value and identity. A wife and busy mother of four, her entrepreneurial approach to life and her passionate message of freedom have created a strong platform for her to help many people. Her incredible insight and commitment have resulted in many understanding their true value. Dianne has devoted her life to this cause — seeing people live in freedom and released into all that they were created to be, body+soul+spirit.

Other books by Dianne Wilson

Back in Shape After Baby
Fat Free Forever!
Fat Free Forever Cookbook
Fat Free Forever 101 Tips
Easy Exercise for Everybody

Foreword

Mirror Mirror provides a unique and powerful means of focusing on many of the critical life and death issues people face today, such as insecurity, prejudice, rejection, abuse of all kinds, hatred, jealousy, addictions, social pressure, eating disorders, adoption and family dysfunction.

By applying a new twist to some well-known and loved fairy-tales and stories, Dianne Wilson masterfully writes to capture the attention of those most affected by poor or unhealthy self-esteem and consequent destructive behavioural patterns. She confronts the unrealistic and unattainable fantasies and the ugly realities of life. Yet in so doing, she manages to raise genuine hope that true happiness is not just a fairy story, and that no matter what has happened in the past, by addressing critical attitudes and beliefs in the present, the 'happily ever after life' is not an impossible dream. Instead, it is indeed something that can become reality for those courageous enough to continue to dream, to commit and to work to change their current circumstances and belief patterns.

Dianne has used some of her own experiences as proof that change and healing are possible, and that each and every person has been created with a divine destiny — if they are prepared to seek it. She has provided relevant information and resources concerning critical issues that can be used effectively for individual personal development, research or in school curriculum and personal development programs.

A great book and resource — highly recommended.

Vivienne C Riches
Psychologist
BA, Dip Ed., MA(Hons), PhD, MAPS
Clinical Senior Lecturer, The University of Sydney

Body image is what our eyes see when we look in the mirror.
Self-esteem is how we feel about what we see when we look in the mirror.

Introduction

The Mirror of Truth

Perception is powerful.
What you see is what you believe.
But is what you see who you really are?
Discover the Mirror of Truth.
Find the true you.
Be free.

a perfect reflection gives a three dimensional view:
body soul spirit

The Emperor's New Clothes

Once upon a time there was an emperor who was obsessed with himself, his appearance and his achievements. The emperor was anxious to become the most popular emperor who ever lived. He wanted to win popularity at any cost.

One day, two dodgy fashion designers came to the palace, claiming to make the most beautiful range of clothing imaginable.

The emperor was excited about the beautiful clothing, so he sent one of his trusty servants to inspect the designers' work.

'Good lord,' thought the servant, 'I can't see a thing.' The dodgy designers begged him to step closer to see the quality and workmanship of the special fabric. The poor man stared long and hard but could see nothing. He thought to himself that he must be a fool and, fearing the emperor's volatile response, he left, deciding not to say anything about the invisible fabric. He told the emperor that the clothing was magnificent, so the emperor commissioned a new outfit for the spring royal procession.

The emperor's ever-faithful yet disloyal entourage continued to mutter platitudes such as, 'What style! What imagination!' People around the emperor had learned to tell him what he wanted to hear, rather than the truth.

The emperor finally came to see the garments for himself. He stood in shock, as he could see nothing. He said to himself, 'Am I a fool, that I cannot see? If I don't wear this outfit, everyone will know that I can't see it. Oh no, nothing could be worse than that!'

Desperately worrying about what people might think, the emperor, in complete denial, said, 'The fabric is stupendous. Nothing could be finer!'

The day of the royal procession was drawing near and the emperor was presented with his new clothes. The crooked designers pointed out all the wonderful detail. All the members of the royal court smiled and agreed. Meanwhile, the emperor was secretly feeling like a complete fool, but the need to protect his image consumed him.

Standing in front of the royal mirror, he pretended to look impressed. 'A perfect fit!' he said firmly.

Not wanting to be seen as fools themselves, the servants stooped down and pretended to lift the royal cloak from the ground. Everyone went along with it, further fuelling the denial in which the emperor was living.

The procession began and the emperor stepped out in his new clothes. Suddenly a voice called out from the crowd, shouting, 'He's got nothing on! The emperor is naked!'

The people started to whisper and murmur and it wasn't long before the emperor heard what everybody was saying. The emperor blushed deeply, realising it was true. But pride and fear overtook him, and he insisted that the procession go on. In royal fashion he walked on, completely naked, with his servants holding up his invisible cloak.

Just then, a young boy spoke up above the crowd.

'Your Royal Emperor, sir, I thought that I must come and tell you that everyone is laughing at you. Can't you see what's wrong?'

The emperor's heart sank at the boy's honesty. He couldn't hide behind his pretence any longer — there was something compelling about this young boy's honesty that demanded the emperor face the truth. The next day, the royal court cheered with gladness and relief as the emperor had dressed himself for the first time in a long time. In his new-found freedom, the emperor and his subjects were able to live free and happily ever after.

The End

Pillars of Self-Esteem

Value
> To think highly of; to hold in high esteem;
> to hold in respect and estimation;
> to appreciate; to prize.

Worth
> Being very highly valued or desirable;
> high quality;
> deserving of admiration or respect.

Esteem
> High estimation or value;
> great regard;
> favourable opinion, founded on supposed worth.

Truth
> The quality of being true, genuine or factual:
> something that is true:
> a proven or verified fact; principle.

Hope
> To trust or believe;
> a feeling or desire for something, usually with confidence
> in the possibility of its fulfilment.

Freedom
> The state of being free;
> liberation from slavery;
> the right or privilege of unrestricted access;
> the power to order one's own actions and life.

Mirror, mirror on the wall, who is the fairest of them all?

You are, of course! You were not born to live a small and contained life, always wishing that life could be different. You were born to live an expansive and fulfilled life. You were born to make a difference. You were born to know your value, worth and esteem, and to live in truth, hope and freedom, all of which are the foundational pillars of this book. When you live with a correct concept of how truly valuable you are, you will be able to experience the powerful and life-changing dynamic of a positive and healthy identity — body, soul and spirit.

Regardless of what life may have dealt you, you are as valuable as the day you were born because your value cannot increase or decrease. Think about a one hundred dollar note. It was made crisp, fresh, unwrinkled and unstained, not yet used or abused. Then, after a few years of wear and tear, trading and mislaying, it starts to look less pristine than it did the day it was made. Yet regardless of the wear and tear factor, that hundred dollar note is still as valuable as the day it was created. Each one of us was born with our self-esteem intact, and it wasn't until life's blows came along and knocked us about that our self-esteem began to suffer. It is your perspective or opinion that can change and it's my desire that through this book you will see yourself in a new light, discover your true value and begin to esteem yourself in a wonderful new way.

The term *self-esteem* comes from a Greek word meaning reverence for self. *Self* means who we are, body, soul and spirit, including the values, beliefs and attitudes that we have about ourselves. *Esteem* means the value and worth that we give ourselves. A healthy self-esteem means that we have a healthy regard for, or opinion of, who we are. This means not considering ourselves more highly or more lowly than we should. A healthy self-esteem is found in the balance.

Self-esteem is an attitude that we have about ourselves, either positive or negative. It is the product of what we see reflected in our mirror under the influence of our culture, society, family and relationships.

The development of self-esteem is a dynamic process stemming from two main types of sources — internal and external. Internal sources involve the way we see ourselves; external factors depend on affirmation from others. Both sources of self-esteem are shaped by internal and external factors and are therefore open to improvement — which is good news!

Henry Ford once said, 'If you think you can or you can't, you're right.' How true this statement is, because it highlights the power of thinking to shape our lives.

Motivational author Napoleon Hill once said, 'A positive mental attitude is an irresistible force that knows no such thing as an immovable body.' As we think, so will we be.

Your mirror may be broken, blurred, magnified, compact and inadequate, or you may have put it away so you don't have to face it. This book is designed to be a mirror of truth. It is designed to be a wide-angled lens and to help you to see yourself the way you really are, improve your self-esteem and sense of identity, and show you that you have the potential to live in freedom.

All truth is confronting but it is truth that brings the conviction necessary for change. When you need to face the truth and make some changes, *not* changing will be destructive to your life. Whatever you fail to change in life you are destined to repeat. At a conference I attended Dr AR Bernard explained this concept, which I have made into a flow chart for you to follow.

The Chain of Change
Truth
➔ Confrontation
➔ Courage
➔ Decision
➔ Dedication
➔ Action
➔ Change

The journey to truth and freedom, if travelled well, will bring healing and skills to your life so that you will be able to experience:

▶ **H**appily: joy no matter what
▶ **E**ver   :   forever and not temporarily
▶ **A**fter :   after all you've been through
▶ **L**ife   :   Heaven on earth.

Remember that settling for *good* rather than *the best* is an enemy to your self-esteem. In his book *Self Matters*, Dr Phillip C McGraw (also known as 'Dr Phil') talks about the influence of society, family, marketers and friends on us, to be a certain way. He encourages the true YOU to fight to win every time there is an opportunity for you to feel like you need to become someone else.

It's time to take control of you and your identity!

There are many reasons for a person having a poor sense of identity. Whatever the reasons, poor self-esteem results in a distorted view, image or reflection of life. When we grow a healthy self-esteem, we see both ourselves and our world more clearly, and we can live life much more effectively.

This book has been written to help you see the truth about you and your identity. This book has been created to present the mirror of truth. The mirror of truth isn't just any ordinary mirror. The mirror of truth is a reflection of what is real rather than just the perception of an ideal.

Objects that reflect or admit light can be looked at in many different ways. A window can either be looked through or looked at, and the same is true of a mirror. Sometimes all we see is the dirt on the window, instead of the expansive view. The same is true of the mirror of truth: you can either look at the shallow smudges on the mirror that detract from your true image, or you can look through the smudges and see the true, deep, clear reflection of who is really there. If you choose to look deep into the mirror of truth, beyond the smudges and the things that you don't like about yourself or your life, you will see and discover many wonderful things about yourself.

It comes down to perception and what you choose to look at and see. You may not be exactly who you want to be right now, but as long as you have breath in your lungs, are grateful for your life, and believe you can get to where you want to be. You are well on your way. You can choose to look into a magnifying glass, which magnifies all your faults and imperfections, or you can look into the mirror of truth, which shows your incredible potential for a life of genuine freedom.

Freedom is not just a final destination; it's a journey. If we don't build healthy self-esteem into our lives when we're young, we will have unhealthy self-esteem and identity issues when we are older. We know that problems don't disappear with age and the reality is that they tend to grow as the years tick along unless we choose to deal with them. That's why it's not too difficult to find women and men in mid-life going through a crisis that could have been prevented if it had been addressed in earlier years.

If we are going to navigate this journey of life successfully, we need to have a proper understanding of our value. Value is not what you do, the title you hold or the way you look. Value is who you are as a person, and that is priceless (remember the hundred dollar note story). Your value is so high that it is impossible to increase; you just need to acknowledge and believe it. Without that real sense of value, healthy self-esteem will always seem elusive.

We have all been created body, soul and spirit, and we need to nurture each of these three areas of our lives if we want to have a healthy self-esteem and realise our true identity. Focusing on just one or two aspects will cause imbalance in your life, so it's important to understand that you are a *tripartite* being:

Physical/body — body image
    — *External*
Emotional/soul — confidence
    — *Internal*
Spiritual/spirit — destiny
    — *Eternal*

The soul consists of our mind, will and emotions, and it is a key area in determining the outcomes of our life. I like to think of the soul as the steering wheel of life, which can lead us into great health or poor health, great self-esteem or poor self-esteem.

The spirit relates to that eternal component of us. It connects us from the here and now (the temporal) to the eternal and is not limited by time or space. I believe the spirit in us yearns to find that eternal significance, whereas the soul yearns much more for temporal gratification and significance. Our soul is much more connected to the temporal, the here and now, and is affected by it; our spirits are much more connected to the spiritual and affected by that. Soul has a goal — that is, wanting to go somewhere, beyond the here and now, and getting there on your own. Spirit has a destiny — knowing that you are meant to go somewhere beyond the here and now, and it implies assistance and involvement from something bigger than yourself; for me that is God.

Just as we can communicate verbally body to body, we can also communicate spiritually, spirit to spirit. This is often done through prayer. The best way to do it is to find a quiet time and place where you won't be interrupted, sit comfortably, and start speaking to God about what is on your heart and mind and the changes you long for in your life. Speak aloud if you can — it may seem strange at first, but it's a good way to make the conversation more real and to stop your mind from wandering. Take the time to listen, too — you may find that you hear a clear response in your mind, or you might get a wonderful sense of God being there with you. Try it — you have nothing to lose and everything to gain!

Just as the body needs nourishment, so does the spirit. If we are not doing things like praying, I believe that we are neglecting a part of us that needs to be nourished. This can explain why people who are physically well and have healthy souls still find that there is something missing from their lives. I would suggest that they are neglecting their spirit.

In order to help you nurture all of these areas and create balance, I encourage you to start a journal, to track your progress.

From this you can establish how far you have grown during the course of reading this book. At the end of this book, the action plan section includes an outline for a 21-day journal to help you break unhealthy self-esteem cycles that may be present in your life. Below is a guide to help you start tracking your self-esteem from an external, internal and eternal perspective.

body soul spirit

Body/External *(physical being/appearance)*
▶ List what you don't like about your appearance.
▶ List what you do like about your appearance.
▶ List what you eat in a day on average.
▶ List how much exercise you do in a week.
▶ Write a plan to improve your eating and exercise habits.

Soul/Internal *(mind/will/emotions)*
▶ What are your greatest frustrations in life?
▶ What thought patterns do you need to change?
▶ Challenge the challenges in your life. List what they are.
▶ Who do you think understands you best and why?
▶ If you could do anything, and you couldn't fail,
  what would it be?

Spirit/Eternal *(heart/life force)*
▶ What is your eternal perspective?
▶ What difference might spiritual balance make in your life?
▶ Do you have peace in your heart and mind?
▶ List some tragedies that have led to good outcomes
▶ Try praying when you need guidance or when you face
  difficult situations

Each area of our life affects our identity, either positively or negatively. Regardless of your appearance, job, social class or education, everyone is susceptible to low self-esteem. For some people it may be a constant struggle, shaped by deeply ingrained beliefs and unrealistic relational and social expectations.

Self-esteem, or how well you regard yourself, is important to your wellbeing. People with poor self-esteem usually judge and reject certain aspects of themselves and other people. Sometimes this may be a way of avoiding issues that are too painful to deal with. If you have low self-esteem, you may find it difficult to make friends, go for a job interview or persevere with a long-term goal.

Poor self-esteem can often lead to other problems such as eating disorders, depression, alcoholism and substance abuse, child abuse and domestic violence. All of these can come from a feeling of low self worth. Then there are other traits such as blaming yourself when things go wrong, and setting standards of perfection that are impossible to attain.

Perhaps you compare your skills and achievements with everyone around you while exaggerating your weaknesses, and you criticise yourself for the smallest and most insignificant mistakes. Maybe you constantly remind yourself of past failures or perhaps you label yourself with words such as stupid, ugly, fat or inadequate. You may even feel that other people are easily bored or ashamed of you. You may also simply lack motivation, be introverted, shy, lacking in confidence and fearful.

I wonder if you've ever met people who suffer from a very poor self-esteem and observed their behaviour? A person may be feeling bad about who they are, their identity may be unstable and they may not be able to feel a sense of self worth. When people feel like that, there are usually a couple of outcomes. They can either feel terrible about themselves and act like victims, or they can take the opposite track and behave with very challenging, in-your-face behaviour. Victims tend to keep quiet, look down, not express their feelings outwardly, procrastinate and often act out their feelings of anger by sabotaging important relationships, while aggressive persecutors put others down so that they can feel better about themselves. These types of people not only have poor self-esteem, but they also have poor coping and communication skills!

If you can relate to any of these traits, your self-esteem could do with a boost. Cheer up — help is on the way!

Once you have established that your self-esteem needs improving, the next thing to do is to look at why you feel the way you do. In the following chapters I have addressed many reasons why our identity suffers and how we can work on improving it. You may see yourself in one or all of the chapters and you may identify with the fairy-tale or story at the beginning of each chapter, or the personal story relating to self-esteem at the end of each chapter.

These chapters have been designed to shed light on issues that may have been brushed over or buried deep down in your life. I have personally found through writing this book that I have grown in strength as I have explored the subject of self-esteem and identity and discovered new truths about myself and other people in my life. Truth is a powerful force if used in a positive and constructive way.

I have come to realise more than ever that it is our choices which determine the strength and condition of our identity.

On the following pages are listed Seven Deadly Sins and Seven Heavenly Virtues. For every negative and selfish thought or emotion we need to create positive thoughts and energy, in order to build our identity and build our lives. When our lives are built with these Seven Heavenly Virtues rather than the Seven Deadly Sins, our lives will change for the better and our self-esteem will grow, and that's a goal we all need to work towards in the journey of life.

seven deadly sins

1. **Pride**
   Excessive belief in one's own abilities. It has been called the sin from which all others arise. Pride is also known as vanity.

2. **Envy**
   The desire for another person's traits, status, abilities or situation.

3. **Gluttony**
   An inordinate desire to consume more than one requires.

4. **Lust**
   An insatiable craving for the pleasures of the body.

5. **Anger**
   Manifested in the individual who spurns love and opts instead for fury. It is also known as wrath.

6. **Greed**
   The desire for material wealth or gain at any cost, also known as covetousness.

7. **Sloth**
   The avoidance of work, also known as laziness.

seven heavenly virtues

1. **Humility**
   Freedom from pride and arrogance and a modest (but balanced) estimate of one's own worth.
2. **Kindness**
   The quality of being warm-hearted, considerate, humane, sympathetic, kind and forgiving.
3. **Love**
   A feeling of strong devotion and affection induced by that which delights or commands admiration.
4. **Faith**
   Confident belief in the truth, value or trustworthiness of a person, idea or thing. Belief that does not rest on logical proof or material evidence.
5. **Hope**
   To wish or desire for something with confident expectation, trusting in its fulfilment.
6. **Charity**
   Whatever is given freely to the needy or suffering for their relief; alms; any act of kindness.
7. **Grace**
   The exercise of love, kindness, mercy, favour; a disposition to benefit or serve another.

Life is a process and we're all working through different challenges at different stages, at different times of our lives. Some of these are:

▶ *Stage 1: The prisoner or monster within*
We need to realise and understand that there are things that we need to deal with that are holding us back from being all that we were made to be. It's time to get help.

▶ *Stage 2: The princess or prince within*
We need to realise and understand who we really are and how valuable we really are. See yourself with a crown on your head. It's time to realise.

▶ *Stage 3: The wonderwoman or superman within*
We need to realise and understand that each of our lives has an assignment or purpose attached to it, that we can make life count for something greater than just us. It's time to trade in the crown for a cape!

Whatever the stage, it's time to face the truth.

My version of *The Emperor's New Clothes* at the start of this introduction is a story about self-deception, or denial. Before being able to successfully deal with any issues relating to building healthy self-esteem, facing the facts means that you can no longer live in denial about your problems. However, facing the facts doesn't mean a life sentence to them. When you determine the truth about what can be changed and what can't, you can move forward into a life of freedom. When we deal with the issues of self that keep us contained, we can begin to build a strong foundation for a healthy identity and we can start to know a life of freedom.

Throughout history, various cultures have used myth, parable and story to give a sense of identification, value and meaning. I have chosen to re-tell well-known fairy-tales, stories and parables to help you to identify or see yourself, and to pinpoint the issues that you may need to deal with in order to begin to build a healthy self-esteem.

A parable is described as 'the placing of one thing beside another with a view to comparison', or 'a narrative drawn from human circumstances; the object of which is to teach a lesson'. A parable is basically a short story that uses familiar situations to illustrate a point. The parables here are true to life for all people who struggle to gain a sense of worth and value in terms of their self-esteem.

It's important to remember that in many of the fairy-tales, physical beauty is a metaphor for inner worth. The message is not that beautiful people are better, but that we can all strive for inner beauty, which is made up of the seven heavenly virtues (humility, kindness, love, faith, hope, charity and grace).

I hope that you will read between the lines contained in the chapters that follow and as you do, allow yourself to be changed from within. Each of the chapters begins with a fairy-tale or story which highlights key issues that contribute to or detract from a healthy and positive self-esteem. Some examples of potential issues are listed below.

▶ Cinderella: self-pity
▶ The Ugly Duckling: self-preservation
▶ The Little Mermaid: self-possession
▶ Pinocchio: self-absorption
▶ Goldilocks: self-destruction
▶ Little Red Riding Hood: self-determination
▶ Beauty and the Beast: self-consciousness
▶ The Three Little Pigs: self-indulgence
▶ Sleeping Beauty: self-defence
▶ Snow White: self-sufficiency
▶ Joseph the Dreamer: self-expression
▶ The Slave Trader: self-righteousness

Each chapter follows a clear pattern, which will help you apply this book as a life manual to gaining a healthy self-esteem and sense of identity. The outcome of a healthier self-esteem is clear, and this is how you will reach your goal:

▶ Identify the problem areas in your own life.
▶ Be informed about issues you may have to deal with or work through.

▶ Acknowledge you are not alone in your problems.
▶ Follow the keys to freedom.
▶ Continually assess your progress and success.

I am confident that if you follow the principles contained within the pages of this book, you will be able to see the following changes in your life:

1. You will be able to accept yourself.
2. You will not desperately wish you look different.
3. You will think more about your successes than your failures.
4. You won't worry about people not liking you.
5. You will be confident around confident people.
6. You won't be afraid to take risks.
7. You will be comfortable around attractive and successful people.
8. You won't be afraid to make mistakes.
9. You will know your significance and effectiveness.
10. You will know your true value.

In my experience as a personal trainer, pastor, speaker and life coach (not to mention wife and mother), I have learned a great deal about people and why they feel the way that they do about themselves. It is these great people, full of potential, who have inspired me and are my motivation for writing this book.

I hope that these pages and the thoughts and stories that are found within will be like a mirror of truth to you, so you will be able to see yourself the way you really are. I want to encourage you to stop, shine some light, take a good look and see yourself in the mirror of truth, and allow what you see to change your life, from the inside out.

It is my desire to help you honour and value who you and others really are. As you read, you may experience tears, laughter, anger and pain along the way, but be determined to allow yourself to be challenged and changed.

Remember the Truth: you are worth it!

Mirror, Mirror

Mirror, mirror on the wall,
Who's the fairest of them all?
You are, of course!
Why can't you see?
Just be the best that you can be.
Discover the truth inside my frame,
And see your worth and value named.
Hope, truth, grace and freedom bound
The true you is set at last to be found.

Chapter 1

Step to Stepping Stone

freedom from dysfunctional family life

'TRUTH breaks the cycle of dysfunction.'

Cinderella

Once upon a time, a wealthy gentleman lost his beloved wife. Grief-stricken he remarried, but the woman he chose was very cruel and she hated his lovely daughter, Cinderella. Sadly, soon after Cinderella's father wed this hardhearted woman, he died from a broken heart.

Cinderella's stepmother ordered her to live in the cellar and work with the servants. She felt so small and insignificant; she was unloved and told time and again how useless she was. Cinderella began to lose her identity as her soul became buried beneath the torment of her life.

One day, everyone was invited to a royal ball. Cinderella's two stepsisters made a great fuss of putting on their finest clothes. After they left, Cinderella sat in a corner and wept. Suddenly, Cinderella's godmother arrived and found her precious goddaughter in a terrible state.

'I wish I could go to the ball,' sobbed Cinderella.

'You shall,' her godmother said, and produced the most magnificent gown, woven in the finest silk and gold, with a beautiful pair of glass slippers. Cinderella put on the gorgeous gown and slippers and stood nervously in front of the mirror. She couldn't believe her eyes. The mirror reflected her inner beauty, love, kindness, gentleness and self-control. She saw her true self, an image she had not seen for a very long time.

Blooming with newfound confidence, it was Cinderella's turn to be a princess. There was just one condition: she had to return home before midnight, when the magnificent gown would disappear, leaving her in her familiar rags.

When Cinderella arrived at the ball, the prince was immediately drawn to this mysterious young woman and invited her to dance. They danced and danced until suddenly the clock struck twelve. Cinderella fled without even saying goodbye, and in her haste she dropped one of the glass slippers.

When Cinderella arrived home, her godmother was waiting for her. She led Cinderella back to the mirror, but Cinderella was too afraid to look — she couldn't bear to see herself in filthy rags again. When she finally opened her eyes, Cinderella saw that she was as beautiful as she had been just hours before. The mirror had captured her true reflection.

After the ball, the prince could not rest. He proclaimed he would search the kingdom and marry the woman whose foot fitted the glass slipper. When his messengers arrived at Cinderella's home the next morning, the stepsisters tried to squeeze their feet into the slipper, but it was impossible for them. Right then, Cinderella knew she had a choice. She could keep her ragged shoes on and remain the servant, or she could dare to step into the glass slipper and into her future.

Trembling, she said, 'Sir, please let me try the slipper.'

Her stepsisters and stepmother burst out laughing and mocked Cinderella, saying, 'This slipper belongs to a princess.' But their mockery was soon silenced as the messenger slid the slipper onto her foot and it fit her perfectly. Exchanging her rags for riches, the beautiful young woman held her head high as she walked towards her future with the handsome prince, and they lived together happily ever after.

The End

Fact

One in two marriages are ending in divorce.

Truth

Divorce doesn't have to mean dysfunction.

Mirror, mirror on the wall, why is my family the most dysfunctional of them all?

I am proud to be an optimist, and I am optimistic enough to believe that we have the power to change our lives, regardless of our circumstances. One of the circumstances affecting today's families and young people more than any other generation in history is the breakdown of the traditional family unit. In a nation and a world where this is escalating, it's important to face the facts about what can be done to help beat the statistics. Living in denial does nothing to help change our present or our future. Once we face the facts, we can then search for the truth and find a solution that will bring freedom to our lives.

Family Breakdown

The facts are that an Australian marriage has a 46 per cent chance of ending in divorce and that, out of Australia's 4.6 million children aged under eighteen, 1.1 million children live with only one of their natural parents.

Today we are surrounded by so many people who have experienced divorce that when we come across people who have been married for forty-five years, like my parents (who are still madly in love), it's both a pleasant surprise and a rare find.

Any breakdown in marriage affects many more people than just the adults in the marriage. If there are children involved, they are obviously affected, along with other relatives, friends and onlookers. The ripple effect is usually far and wide-reaching, and there's often a questioning of one's value and place in life in the midst of any family crisis.

Although these facts represent the lives of many people, they do not necessarily define whether or not a family is functional or dysfunctional. The reality is, functional people make functional families and dysfunctional people make dysfunctional families.

In their book *The Fresh Start Divorce Recovery Workbook*, Bob Burns and Tom Whiteman say, 'A family is like a mobile. If one part is moved, all other parts are set in motion as well. They are individual units, but they're tightly connected.'

You may have found yourself 'in motion' as part of a non-traditional family, but it doesn't mean that you are necessarily part of a dysfunctional family. And if there are elements of your family that seem like they don't work or are dysfunctional, you can break the cycle by taking responsibility for and focusing on the truth of your life and making it functional.

Our family should be those who we can rely on, gain security from, and make happy memories with. Sadly, however, because of life's tragedies some have found themselves battling to gain happy and peaceable ground in their family situations. This can destroy, or at the very least disturb, one's sense of personal value and self-esteem. Whether yours is a single parent, step, widowed, foster or seemingly perfect family (no one's really perfect …), I believe you have the ability to rise above your circumstances and become all that you were created to be, regardless of how dysfunctional your family life may be.

Cinderella

Cinderella is a story known to us all. It's the original rags to riches, Prince Charming to the rescue fairy-tale. She was a beautiful young woman downtrodden by her family dysfunction and the oppression of a nasty stepmother and stepsisters. In order to break the cycle, she had to be brave enough to step out of the mould and to see herself as the beautiful young woman she was, and she had to be willing to begin a new family life. In this instance, her godmother kindly stood her in front of a mirror to show her how truly beautiful she was — inside and out.

Cinderella chose to listen; she chose to listen to her godmother and to believe what she saw in the mirror. This empowered her to ignore the voices of the past: the negativity, criticism, ridicule and all the harsh words of her stepmother and stepsisters. She proved herself able to rise above her circumstances by turning her 'stepfamily life' into 'stepping stones' to her future.

In a perfect world there wouldn't be marriage break-up and family breakdown, but we are not living in a perfect world. Instead many of us contend with stepfamily or single parent life, either good or bad. Each of us should be able to enjoy the security that a happy family brings. We should be able to feel safe in who we are as people. Instead when relationships go through challenges, uncertainty, comparisons, jealousy and sibling rivalry are just some of the negative results.

In the story, Cinderella faced almost insurmountable obstacles every single day. Instead of complete love and security, Cinderella's life was one of insecurity and obscurity. I can just about imagine her crying out in desperation for SPACE from the turmoil!

When our family situation brings a sense of hopelessness, we need to replace it with hopefulness. When we are feeling a sense of worthlessness, we need to take action to produce a sense of being worth something.

When you lose a mother, father, husband, wife, son or daughter, there is a desperate sense of wanting something that you cannot have. The tendency is to remain focused on the loss and not on the future. I know what it is to experience the loss of a marriage. All I ever wanted was the 'white picket fence' family; after all, that's what I had grown up with and it was all I knew.

Cinderella had lost her mother and became part of a blended family as a stepchild, with a stepmother and stepsisters. She then lost her father and, in his absence, she was subjected to emotional and physical abuse. She was told that she was unattractive and useless. Cinderella's self-esteem was at an all-time low. She experienced insecurity and uncertainty because she was deprived of the love and concern of a caring family. In her new family she was given no sense of purpose, future or hope. Many people can relate to the story of Cinderella.

When you are told continually that you are worthless, that you don't have value, that you are ugly or stupid and that you will never be good for anything, you start to believe it, especially when it is your family saying these things. I have lost count of the number of people I've met who have told me about hurtful things family members or people have said to them over and over again and eventually they began to believe what they had been told. The bad stuff is always easier to believe.

Negative emotional attacks are soul-destroying, and so too is being completely ignored. It may be that you haven't been consistently insulted, but maybe you are hardly ever noticed, spoken to or considered. Perhaps you feel as though you are so unimportant that no one would notice if you weren't around any more. That is just not true! That is a lie that has entered your life in order to destroy it. Please believe the truth that you are valuable, important and that you have hope and a future.

The story of Cinderella represents people today who have a number of issues to deal with, both in their family situation and personally, which affects their self-esteem, among other things. We need to find out who we really are and why on earth we were born.

Function vs Dysfunction

You probably know plenty of married people and traditional families who are completely dysfunctional, who live with unhealthy silences, family secrets, infighting and sibling rivalry. One thing is for sure: dysfunction does not discriminate between traditional and blended families.

When it comes to blended family life, I speak from experience. It is something that I have had to come to terms living with. In fact, my family now is not considered just blended, it is regarded as 'highly blended' because of the complexities of the relationships of some of the people involved. Even so, I am very grateful to be able to say that my immediate family unit is very loving and very functional. In our home there are no *steps*, only people. We choose to put the emphasis on the *father* or the *mother*, the *sister* or the *brother*, not on the *step*.

I believe that we reach a certain age or level of maturity that requires us no longer to blame our parents or ex-spouse for the mess that we may find our family life in. Blame casting only keeps us bound in dysfunction and misery. In order to break the cycle, we need to recognise the dysfunction around us and then take responsibility for our own lives. That's how we discover the truth and break the cycle.

Many blended or stepfamilies are anything but dysfunctional. They may have had to work at making it great, but so does any healthy family. I can testify that I have a wonderful, functional (highly blended) family life.

Grief

Stepfamilies exist as a result of some sort of loss. The loss may be the death of a spouse or parent, or the break-up of a marriage or relationship. Adjusting to loss and change is a difficult and complex process, and it involves experiencing grief. Both adults and children grieve.

Adults grieve the loss of a partner and the loss of a marriage or relationship. They also grieve the loss of dreams about the way they thought life would be. They may need to come to terms with the fact that they are not 'the first' for their new partner.

Children also grieve. In his book *Counselling Families After Divorce*,

Dr Gary R Collins says, 'Adolescents live and die by self-esteem. The perception teenagers have of themselves controls virtually every aspect of their development.' He then goes on to say, in relation to family breakdown, 'Self-esteem losses are strongly influenced by parent absence.'

You may be able to relate to the loss of a parent living under the same roof, or even the initial loss of stability at home. Some also suffer the loss or lessened availability of a parent or parents who decide to remarry. There are a number of unsettling issues arising from divorce or death, including a new place to live, new school, loss of friends, having to make new friends, loss of identity, formation of a new identity or name. There is no doubt that the loss of a person's ideal of family — the way they want it to be — affects their sense of self-worth greatly.

The adjustments are enormous when two worlds collide. For most, it's a big adjustment getting married the first time, but for those of us who have been married for the second time, it can be rugged. The odds are stacked against us and often we have to fight for our marriages and our families in order to maintain a healthy home life.

It's important to realise that it is difficult for some children to adjust. It may be difficult for them to adjust from being the youngest to the middle child, or from being the eldest and most responsible to being the third child down the ladder. They may feel displaced, so maintaining a healthy sense of self-worth can be challenging for them.

Following are some classic comments from children who have gone through family breakdown.

▶ 'I want my old family back. I miss things the way they were — even though Mum and Dad fought.'

▶ 'Nobody has enough time for me.'

▶ 'I'm sad when Mum's sad, and I'm sad when Dad's sad, and they are both sad too much.'

▶ 'I don't know what they want from me.'

▶ 'I'm angry and I don't know why.'

▶ 'Dad is busy with his new family.'

▶ 'It's boring over at Dad's house.'

▶ 'It's great at Dad's house. I wish I could live with Dad.'

▶ 'I miss my father.'

▶ 'Dad and I have a great time, except for *her*.'

▶ 'He gives more to her kids and to her than us.'

▶ 'He never thought about us when he moved.'

▶ 'Dad left Mum, but he really left me.'

▶ 'There must be something wrong with me.'

▶ 'Mum is wonderful, but that friend of hers is awful. She's always paying attention to him and not us. She lets him tell us what to do.'

▶ 'They go away together and leave us alone.'

▶ 'She has always done things for me, and now he says she spoils me.'

▶ 'She lets him say awful things about me.'

▶ 'I don't want to say hello to him.'

▶ 'I wish he wasn't here.'

▶ 'We've been doing just fine without him. Why do we need him now?'

▶ 'I don't know where I belong.'

▶ 'Mum doesn't have enough money. I wish I could help her out.'

▶ 'Dad doesn't know how hard it is at home without him.'

▶ 'My stepmother is NOT my mother, OR the boss in this house!'

▶ 'It's not fair ... !'

Myths vs Truth

Seeing the truth about the potential of your own future will enable you to rise above your family situation. After all, there are myths surrounding what stepfamily life is like, and it's important to distinguish myths from the truth.

Myth #1: 'I love my new partner, so my children will too.'
We all know that affection takes time and effort to grow, as not everyone wants to 'come on board' and change. Reduce your expectations and you should start to see them exceeded in time. Always respect those around you and watch the changes that will occur.

Myth #2: 'Children of divorce and remarriage are damaged forever.'
It is true that children go through a painful period of adjustment after a divorce or remarriage. Feelings of guilt overwhelm parents and children as they come to terms with pain. Some feel as though they need to make amends for the rest of their lives. However, the good news is that research indicates that although it takes some time, children can recover emotional stability when issues are addressed. Down the track, they can be found to be no different from children in first marriage families in many significant ways.

Myth #3: 'Stepmothers are wicked.'
This myth always makes me laugh because I am a stepmother. Stepmothers and stepfathers are often at a disadvantage when they take on their new role because, as research shows, it is the hardest to fulfil in a stepfamily situation. They are often up against resentment, grief and anger, both from their partner's children and from their partner's relatives, colleagues and friends. Be patient and positive, avoid slanging matches and let your own light shine through. Change will come over time.

Myth #4: 'Adjustment to stepfamily life occurs quickly.'
People are optimistic and hopeful when they remarry. They want life to settle down and to get on with being happy. Because stepfamilies can be complicated, it can take years for people to get to know each other, create positive relationships and develop some meaningful family history. Time is a great healer.

Myth #5: 'Children adjust to divorce and remarriage more easily if biological fathers (or mothers) withdraw.'

The truth is, children will always have two biological parents, and will generally adjust better if they can access both. Sometimes visits can be painful for the non-resident parent, but they are very important to the child's adjustment and emotional health, except in instances of parental abuse or neglect. It helps if the resident parent and step-parent can work towards making access by the non-resident parent an important part of the child's development. This means not viewing the visitations your child has with the non-resident parent as 'time out' of your child's life, an inconvenience and not important to the child. You may be disconnected from your former partner, but the child should never be. They should know that this time is seen as valuable and essential by both parents and it should be meaningful and purposeful. That perhaps means, firstly, changing your attitude and your own schedule. It may also mean sharing things with the other parent that you would rather keep to yourself: photographs, school work, concerts, sporting events. It may also mean offering to arrange or allowing special outings for your child and former partner to attend, things such as camping, going to the zoo, visiting the museum, having a shopping day or a day at the beach. You need to value what the other can bring to your child's life and not keep competing. Sometimes this can't happen right away, but it can be something to work towards. Remember, regardless of who's spending the most time with your child or the most money, your child will still love YOU.

Myth #6: 'Stepfamilies formed after a parent dies are easier.'

People need time to grieve the loss of a loved one, and a remarriage may 'reactivate' unfinished grieving. These emotional issues may be played out in the new relationship with detrimental results. It can also be difficult to think realistically about the person who has died. He or she exists in memory, not in reality, and is sometimes elevated to perfection, which makes bonding with the child difficult for the step-parent.

Myth #7: *'There is only one kind of family.'*

This is the myth that says the only kind of family is the biological family. Anything different is said to be dysfunctional. Today there are many different kinds of families: first marriage, single parent, foster and step, to name a few, and each of these present different characteristics and challenges. There are many biological families who live in utter chaos. Dysfunction does not discriminate between biological and blended families and some blended families are very successful. As I have said before, functional families are simply made up of functional people.

Shattered Dreams

Tragically, my white picket fence fell down when my first husband decided that he didn't want to be a family man any more. This meant tragedy for me, and tragedy for our children. In order to get on with our future, we had to learn to focus on the future and not the loss we had experienced. It is absolutely normal and important to grieve when you lose someone either through death or divorce, but eventually you have to change focus to the future. This is not only for your sake, but for your loved ones' sakes also.

Our identity is challenged and rocked by going through situations that we don't think we can bear. This kind of experience takes its toll. It's then we start to compare our life with others' and sometimes even question our existence. I have felt like nothing on earth. I can remember feeling like I was living a discarded existence inside a garbage bin with the lid down tight and a sign out the front saying, 'Do not disturb'. I was in so much pain that I felt I couldn't bear it. The last thing I was thinking about at the time was that I was valuable or worth anything at all.

I can remember how incredibly vulnerable I felt when I had to fill out an application form for the first time after my divorce. One set of boxes said 'married', 'single', 'separated', 'divorced'. When I ticked the 'divorced' box, I had to make a decision then and there that this form was not going to frame my life and my future.

New Beginnings

I believe that the happily ever after life of freedom is available to all, regardless of the family situation you may find yourself in. We all need someone to help us see ourselves as we really are. Just as Cinderella stood in front of a mirror and finally saw the truth, we sometimes need a mirror, such as this book, to reflect the truth about our potential, not just the facts about the problems we may be facing.

Problems don't just disappear, they need to be worked through and solved. The key to a life of freedom and a brighter future is to recognise what you cannot change, and learn to live a great life by changing what you can.

Many people who have had a traditional family life, only to lose it and begin again, have to face some immense obstacles. In order to conquer these obstacles they can't afford to feel sorry for themselves or take on the woe-is-me-bitter-forever syndrome.

The power of forgiveness plays a significant part in the healing and growing process. We have to release the power of forgiveness over our family (yes, those who have caused us grief), in order to move on. This requires us to forgive them regardless of their response. Forgiving others is the catalyst that sets us free. Forgiving others not only releases others of their debt to us, but it releases us from holding onto resentment or hatred that hurts us and damages our identity. You can make whatever you want of your life if you allow forgiveness and healing to take place. In Chapter 9, you will find some keys on how to forgive others who have hurt you.

Please don't allow labels or any other 'boxes' to trap you into a life of containment, a life boxed in your past. You are not defined by your marital, parental or family status. You are defined by who you are as a human being. If I had to rely on marriage for my identity and self-esteem, I would still be living a sad and broken life, because my first marriage ended and I wouldn't be in any healthy state to build another marriage, second time around.

Some of us need the fairy story. Without it, we might believe that life will inevitably be lived in the cellar. We can have the fairy story when we allow the reality in our lives to be overlaid by the happily ever after life story. Have faith for the story to become your reality.

Just as the author of the original *Cinderella* penned the ending to be happily ever after, you have the opportunity to write your own ending to your life story. It's up to you. I was brought up to believe that I am someone special. You are someone very special too, regardless of whether you are a step-parent or a stepchild. You too can turn the *step* in your life into stepping stones to your future.

This is not the end of the story. One door may have closed in your life, but you can be sure, as you search, another door will be opened.

Remember the Truth: divorce doesn't have to mean dysfunction.

Faith
*Faith is being sure of what we hope for
and certain of what we do not yet see.*

HEBREWS 11:1, THE BIBLE

Sarah's Story

Before I was born, I was unwanted. My mother wanted a career and a life of her own, but I was born on 23 July 1964, about two and a half months early, weighing only a few pounds.

My parents had two more children shortly after my birth and Mum struggled raising our family. She struggled so much that she left us when we were young. I think I was about four years old. My dad tried to raise us alone with the help of his friends while still working at his job in the factory. But the authorities discovered our situation and we were placed in a children's home. I was separated from my brothers and I was sent to another place to live without my family for about six months. Dad visited on the weekends.

Finally Dad persuaded Mum to come back home as he didn't want the family to be separated any more. He wanted his children at home, so we all returned. Mum came back but not of her own free will and suddenly, after a long period of freedom, she had the renewed responsibility of three children she didn't want.

Mum really struggled to relate to me. She did not like the attention I received from my father and, because I got in the way of her career in nursing, I had ruined her plans and she couldn't love me. So I lived in a whirl of constant emotional, physical and verbal abuse. Even the fact that I am left-handed was a curse to her.

My role at home was to look after the house and help raise the children. So that is what I did. I did not do well at school but my younger siblings did just fine; they did not have to work in the house.

Mum loved my youngest brother. I was so hungry and desperate for love from my mother that I would try anything to get an ounce of acknowledgment from her, but nothing worked. I didn't know what I had done wrong. I thought if I was a boy my mum might start to like me, so I refused to wear skirts and wore my dad's clothes, and I became the biggest tomboy.

I always felt ugly; in fact I was frequently told that I was ugly. Mum always made derogatory remarks about the size of my nose. She didn't care who was around at the time. At the rare times we had visitors in the house, she would call me names in front of them to belittle me even more.

So many nights I spent crying on my bed, not knowing what I had done wrong. Not knowing how I could make her happy. Why was life so painful? I didn't ask to be born. I used to tell God that these were not my parents. They couldn't be; I was so different, and they didn't even want me. Everything was my fault.

I needed to leave home. I wanted to study. I needed to study, so I enrolled in a diploma course in Mathematics, Statistics and Computing. Finally I left home and started to experience freedom. No longer was I the shy and timid, introverted girl who left home, I was becoming the life and soul of any party. Not only that, I did so well in my first-year exams that the lecturers asked me to move up to a degree class. I laughed and told them they had the wrong girl. I did not believe them and asked to see my exam papers. It was true ... I had finally proven that I was not stupid after all.

I graduated from university with a 2:1 degree in Applied Statistics; it was incredible considering my background. Yet despite all these outward changes and signs of success, my self-esteem was poor. I still wore men's shirts and grew a long fringe to hide my face. I still lacked something.

I loved my job, I had set up my own company, had my own company car and earnt lots of money but I realised I was still frustrated with life, so I decided to leave England and work overseas in Australia.

In Australia I had a life encounter that has changed me forever. A friend gave me a tape series by an international speaker called Joyce Meyer, entitled 'Battlefield of the Mind'. My whole life I had believed that I was nothing, deserved nothing and even though I didn't want to stay hidden I believed it was the best place for me. That way I couldn't hurt anyone and no one could hurt me.

My poor thinking about myself, low self-esteem and lack of confidence kept me locked in a negative cycle of thinking, and I wanted desperately to get off the treadmill! This tape series showed me who I really am and my true value. I'd never heard words like these before and they connected deep within my heart and enabled me to believe for the first time that I was special and worth something.

I now understood something: I was different. I knew I had value and worth, I had gifts and talents but most importantly for me, I knew that I had purpose. I am significant not because of what I do, but because of who I am.

I had been a POW [prisoner of war] in the region of my mind. Through listening to this tape series I was able to see the truth about my own life. I was only living at my own level of thinking, which at that time was pathetic. My potential was a whole lot bigger than that, so the solution was to grow my mind and my thought processes to a capacity which enabled me to live a free and fulfilled life, which I can say today I am.

I did this by allowing my beliefs about myself to be challenged by my friends, by focusing on positive aspects of my personality and by refusing to settle for second-best thoughts about my life. I also had to deal with the mirror. I now like the true reflection I can see.

Overcoming my poor self-esteem created a genuine desire to help others, so I decided to go back to study. As I stood at the college graduation ball before my friends and my parents, clothed in a gown fit for a princess, I knew that this gown now fitted me perfectly because of the life-changing revelation of who I was inside.

I am now working with an incredible overseas organisation that helps young women who have been through similar life experiences to me. If I hadn't welcomed change in my own life, I wouldn't have been much help to anyone else. It is great to be able to stand in front of a mirror now and not despise what I see and who I am.

10 Keys to Freedom

from dysfunctional family life

Unlike the fairy stories, there is no magic wand that you can wave to make change easy. You may find some of these keys enormously challenging, even frightening. It may take time for you to see how they can be applied in your life. Even if they seem too scary or crazy to tackle, give them a try — it's only by breaking out of your box that you can be free. Every positive step you take is one closer to FREEDOM.

1. Resolve to see your life differently and positively from now on — don't be boxed or labelled by words. Refuse to hear the negative and speak to yourself positively.
2. Don't feel sorry for yourself, as self-pity will keep you trapped.
3. Forgive everyone who has hurt you, and forgive yourself — not always easy, but essential.
4. Be honest and open with how you feel. This means wisely choosing who you talk to. Find someone who will listen, but also someone who is mature and will help you move on.
5. Try to see the bright side of your life — there is one. You have a choice to laugh. It may not and probably will not be easy, but make an effort to bring joy to your family and yourself.
6. Don't dwell on that which you cannot change.
7. Seek professional help if needed — everyone needs someone they can talk to.
8. Be patient — building new relationships takes time. Be prepared to wait.
9. Stop thinking about all the things in life you don't have and be grateful for the family, friends, work and home you do have.
10. Believe that you can have a great future, great marriage and great kids, regardless of your past.

body soul spirit

ACTION PLAN

body
Your home is your castle, so try to make it as warm and cosy as you possibly can. Looking after your surroundings will help you look after yourself.

soul
Be a positive contributor to the atmosphere at home. Encourage family members with whom you may not get on and they will eventually respond positively. You can make a difference.

spirit
Pray for the family life you desire. Ask for help to become the person you have been born to be. Ask for help to love the difficult people in your life.

My goal is freedom
FROM DYSFUNCTIONAL FAMILY LIFE

Chapter 2

Celebrate Your Uniqueness

freedom from rejection

*'I cannot always change how people see me,
but I can change how I see me.'*

The Ugly Duckling

Once upon a time, deep in the forest, a mother duck sat on her nest waiting for her eggs to hatch. All but one burst open and the little baby ducklings poked their heads through the shells. The last egg was a large one. The mother duck waited and waited, and became agitated — she was tired of this little duckling even before it was born.

At last, the big egg burst open and the duckling crept out. Not only was he very large and ugly, he sounded different from the others too.

The mother duck thought he must have been a turkey because of his size, so she pushed him into the water to see what would happen. Much to her surprise, he swam instantly.

The poor ugly duckling was bitten, pushed and jeered at by the other ducks. Even his brothers and sisters hated him and wished that a cat would pounce on him. He was an outcast. Rejection became part of his life and survival his sole priority. He needed somewhere to belong and someone to belong to.

Seasons changed. The leaves in the forest turned golden and brown and the clouds came in low with heavy snow. It grew cold and the poor little duckling had nowhere to go.

One day he saw a flock of dazzlingly white, graceful swans. He didn't know the name of the beautiful birds, and he didn't know where they were flying to, but he would have loved to have joined them.

Winter made way for spring and sunshine crept through the reeds. The duckling discovered he could flap his wings. He flew all the way over to a lovely garden.

Out of a thicket came three glorious white swans. The duckling remembered the beautiful creatures, but he felt saddened by their presence. Because of his ugliness he felt he could never be part of their group.

One swan, the leader, was extraordinarily handsome and

statuesque; he held himself with grace and authority. The other swans called him the prince. He noticed that the young bird wasn't acting the way in which he was created to act.

The swan prince flew down towards the young outcast, causing him to bend towards the ground in shame. As the little bird bent down, he saw his own image reflected in a crystal-clear pond. He was now a beautiful swan! He saw that he was no longer clumsy, ugly and hateful to look at.

The swan prince's perfection had made the young swan see his own flaws, until he looked into the mirror that reflected the truth of his own beauty and saw his own lovely reflection. The other swans swam around him and stroked him with their beaks. For the first time he was welcomed into a family. For the first time he felt as though he truly belonged.

The sun shone warmly on his wings as they rustled. He lifted his graceful neck and cried happily from the depths of his heart. He had never dreamed of such happiness.

In appreciation for his rescue, the handsome young swan shared his experience with other young swans, encouraging them by telling them that one day they would evolve into the most magnificent of all birds. Together they lived happily ever after.

The End

Fact
Everyone faces rejection.

Truth
You don't have to live in rejection.

Mirror, mirror on the wall, why do I feel like the biggest reject of them all?

One of the greatest fears faced by people today is the fear of being rejected. It's right up there with the fear of flying, public speaking, spiders and death! At the core of everyone is a desire to be accepted and to belong, and this is natural. Although there is nothing intrinsically wrong with this natural desire, there are times in our lives when it can cause us grief. Each one of us at some time in our lives will face the challenge of what to do when we are not accepted by others, and how that makes us feel about ourselves.

We all want to be endorsed, accepted, affirmed, encouraged and welcomed and we all want to belong, but all of us have faced rejection to some degree or other and know the pain that is experienced through being rejected. Rejection is experienced when someone ignores us, puts us aside, declines to be in our presence, excludes us, withholds from us, refuses us, denies or discards us. Rejection is usually expressed in any combination of the following three behaviours: cold and unaffectionate, hostile and aggressive, indifferent and neglecting. When any of these occur, our natural inclination is to shut down, withdraw and escape — internally, externally or both. No one likes being rejected.

Rejection

There are many reasons why people are rejected, such as:
- Not fitting in with the crowd
- Looking different or being different

- A parent leaving home
- Relationship breakdown
- Speech impediment, such as a lisp or stutter
- Family background
- Wrong school
- Poor housing area
- Education (either too much or too little)
- Race
- Religion
- Beliefs, opinion and convictions
- Disability
- Self-consciousness
- Shyness
- Fear of being rejected
- No reason at all!

If we look at race for example, Australia is a melting pot of many different nationalities and cultures, with over 160 nationalities represented. Racial prejudice thirty years ago was much more pronounced than it is today. Fortunately it is now illegal to discriminate against someone based on their nationality. Australia prides itself on moral values such as respect for difference, tolerance and a common commitment to freedom.

Uniqueness, individuality and that wonderful difference in each one of us is what makes the world, especially Australia, such a fantastically diverse place to live in. Being born a different shape, size or colour should not make any difference, but sadly, often it does.

It's usually a series of circumstances that keeps people trapped by rejection and loneliness. Many are rejected before they are even born. Rejection from birth can be the most difficult to deal with. It can cause people, even those with great potential, to live with that potential unrealised. It's as though they were forced to give up on life before it even started. It's when we finally get a glimpse of who we really are, that we can reject rejection and live our lives above the opinion of others.

All too often, we allow our world to be shaped by other people's opinions. With age, maturity and wisdom, other people's opinions should matter less and less. I can remember times in my earlier years where I felt absolutely crippled by what people thought about me and by not knowing how I could change their opinion of me. I learned that I couldn't change them, but I could change me, and I have grown in my own thinking of who I am and where I belong, so my self-esteem has increased and stabilised, and my identity is secure.

It doesn't seem to matter where we turn, people will always feel free to comment about how we look, what we do and what we believe in. Sometimes we can feel as though we are never going to fit in anywhere. Sometimes people make all kinds of judgments and decide that we're ugly just because we don't look exactly the same as them. What a boring world it would be if we all looked the same. Different isn't ugly, it's just different.

The Ugly Duckling

Growing up, one of my favourite stories was The Ugly Duckling, mainly I guess because I felt as though I could truly identify with what the little duckling went through (and I really loved the part about him becoming the most beautiful one of them all, as a blossoming swan).

In a perfect world we would all be loved and accepted just the way we are. We would be treated kindly and nurtured to become beautiful, happy and confident people. With this unconditional love and acceptance, we could live in genuine freedom. Our identity would be healthy and we would esteem others because of how we feel about ourselves. Imagine how wonderful it would be if this were true for everyone. It is true for some, but unfortunately it is not a reality for all.

In the story of the ugly duckling, the moment the prince swan extended his unconditional love and acceptance to the young swan, who then caught a glimpse of himself in the mirror of the water, the young swan's eyes were finally opened to see the truth. The truth became his hope. It is only when we experience unconditional love and acceptance that we can catch a glimpse of our true selves, and live free from our pain.

The mirror of who we really are and who we are created to be is available to us, we just need to find it and look into it. Freedom is there for us, but it's up to us to be awakened by the truth.

The beautiful young swan could have had negative thoughts when he saw himself as a swan — that he still looked different, or that he still felt like a duck and so spend the rest of his life wishing he was one. But he didn't. The beautiful swan in you is waiting to be awakened and realised.

After suffering rejection in his youth, the beautiful swan finally found himself in the midst of a family who loved and accepted him. He finally belonged.

We can all feel awkward and left out, but when we find our rightful place in life, a sense of true belonging overtakes us, making us strong and secure.

The inner beauty of the young swan made him even more attractive and that caused his peers to bow in his presence. He could have lived his life with a chip on his shoulder, saying that the world owed him a favour, but instead he chose to celebrate his new-found existence as the creature he was always destined to be.

Being brought up in a family of ducks when you are a swan really isn't the problem; many people are brought up in a family that isn't their biological family through adoption or fostering (see Chapter 1). It was loneliness and the lack of unconditional love that destroyed the young swan's sense of identity — and it was the power of the true reflection he saw in the mirror that brought freedom to his life, forever.

Feeling lonely and alienated from others can be a symptom of low self-esteem. If you consider yourself a bit of a loner and you avoid pursuing or actively engaging in relationships, or if you like working in a job that allows you to work in solitude, not just because you enjoy your own company, but because you are afraid of relationships, then this may be you.

Relationships

The real story is that deep down, most people do crave relationships and can suffer from feelings of deep soul pain because they believe that they don't have the capacity to be accepted.

Many people believe that they will be rejected because it seems as though everyone else can win at relationships except for them. You may have told yourself, over many years in an internal dialogue, that you are inferior to others: not as smart, good looking or capable. You dread being rejected, insulted or put down by others and so you just forgo the desired friendship and companionship to avoid the anticipated pain. You may have even brought rejection upon yourself in order to get the rejection over with. You may doubt that someone could really like you so you test them to prove their affection for you. On a subconscious level you are saying, 'If they really care for me they will still like me even if I provoke them.' You may precipitate rejection by saying things you know you shouldn't or by acting foolishly ... and then you say to yourself, 'You see, I told you I was a loser ... everyone else thinks so too. Why am I so lonely ... I feel like I am alone against the world. I guess it's my destiny. It's just who I am and what I deserve.'

It's very hard to build relationships if you continually anticipate and rehearse rejection. Rejection may start small, as a seed that is planted in our lives through different things that happen to us, but if we don't deal with its negative effects, it will develop roots and it will eventually become a tree with lots of branches.

If you are rooted in acceptance and love, then you will develop good things in your life like self-control, faithfulness, goodness, kindness, patience, peace, joy and love. If, however, you absorb rejection easily, every rejection will further depress your self-esteem and will reinforce the feelings you may have that you'll never get out of this cycle of loneliness and alienation.

In order to identify rejection in your life, see if you recognise the following characteristics in yourself:

▶ Do you have a difficult time loving others and receiving love from others?

▶ Are you critical of others?

▶ Do you feel inferior or inadequate?

▶ Are you an angry person?

▶ Are you a perfectionist (arrogance and pride are feelings which try to mask genuine insecurity)?

▶ Are you easily hurt?

▶ Are you suspicious of others' actions?

▶ Do you live your life in isolation to avoid pain?

▶ Do you suffer from depression because you failed your own expectations?

The Power of Rejection

The power of rejection is so real that it can cause us to be blind to what is beautiful about ourselves. Sometimes just looking at the people you want to be accepted by can cause immense pain. Also, we can sometimes be unable to walk in acceptance and freedom because we see ourselves as unacceptable.

Not only will others' opinions keep us from being all that we were created to be, our own unaccepting opinion of ourselves will keep us in a state of isolation and loneliness. We were never created to be lonely. We were born to be embraced and free and we need to realise that this true freedom starts from within us. External freedom can't break down an internal prison of fear and low self-esteem, only truly finding oneself can do that.

Living with the pain of rejection is a fact of life for so many people, and this pain is not limited to the young. In cases of complete despair, rejection can cause some people to lose the will to live.

Feelings of rejection and isolation have been found to be significant contributing factors in youth suicide in Australia, which has one of the highest suicide rates of young males in Western countries.

Suicide is not only a tragedy for the victim and his or her family, it is also devastating for entire communities. It is incredibly tragic that increasing numbers of young people are feeling so desperately unhappy, pressured, rejected and overburdened that they are prepared to take their own lives. Alarmingly, more people die in Australia by suicide than by motor vehicle accidents.

▶ The ratio of male to female suicides is approximately 4:1. Although the number of completed suicides is higher for males, the number of attempted suicides is higher for females. The Australian Bureau of Statistics states that 'although the completed suicide rate is lower for females, suicide attempts are more common among females than males. Much of the difference in the death rate is attributed to the relative effectiveness of the methods of suicide employed by males and females'.

▶ It is estimated that for every actual suicide, 20 to 100 suicide attempts are made.

▶ The number of attempts each year is equivalent to approximately 1 per cent of the population.

Suicide is a complex issue and although there appears to be no single reason for the increase in youth suicides, a common thread of rejection is found. People today face a combination of pressures and demands that arise in the form of homelessness (family rejection), physical and/or sexual abuse, sexuality, substance abuse, school, family or interpersonal conflicts (relational rejection) or unemployment (job rejection).

The good news is that rejection can be turned around to be a catalyst for positive change. Rejection produces perseverance in some people, and destructive behaviour in others. This destructive behaviour can include drug-taking and sexual promiscuity to find acceptance and significance, and generally succumbing to negative peer pressure; these things are often a cry for love and attention.

Alienation

I have known the pain of rejection well. I can remember thirty years ago being subjected to racial prejudice because I looked European. I am a fourth-generation Australian, but I have very dark hair and eyes, and in a household and suburb of blond Australians with blue or green eyes, I continually felt rejected and left out simply because of the way I looked.

In my primary years I was teased, pushed aside and alienated. I was called 'wog' on a daily basis and thought I would never know what it was like to feel accepted and beautiful. My family loved me and told me I was beautiful, but I could only hear loud voices of prejudice booming in my ears telling me how horrible I was. My self-esteem was incredibly low and my identity was uncertain.

It took years and years for me to shake this rejection and I recognise that it always has the potential to return, if I am not keenly aware of my own sense of identity and security. The key thing that all those years of rejection has done for me is that it has given me grace and understanding for people who also suffer with a sense of rejection.

It has become obvious to me over the years that those who inflict pain on others by rejecting them, often themselves have issues of rejection to deal with. Somewhere, sometime, someone rejected them, and they are now projecting that rejection onto others. The cycle starts with rejection, then self-protection, then projection, and continues on again and again. It's a sad reality that hurt people hurt people (I will be talking more about that in Chapter 12). The fact is, rejection will always come, but you don't need to accept it and you certainly don't need to project it onto others.

Rejecting Rejection

We have all suffered rejection, so it's good to remember that you are not alone. People suffer from rejection for all kinds of reasons, and there are many who have suffered rejection for simply 'having a go' in life.

There are lessons to be learned from those whose brilliance often allowed others to reject them and mislabel them as failures. When you think of Elle Macpherson or Dawn Fraser, you don't exactly think of rejection or failure. They are just two of the many famous people who have had to deal with knock-backs and rejection and who have become brilliant successes. There are so many renowned people like that with personal failures and rejection experiences so vast that it is amazing that they managed to succeed at all.

People are often rejected and told that they are failures many times before they reach their goal. It is through their determination and self-confidence that they prove their critics wrong. The following people have overcome some form of rejection or failure in their lives, to go on to be very successful.

- Henry Lawson became profoundly deaf at fourteen years of age. He didn't receive a proper education and his marriage broke down. But he went on to become one of Australia's greatest poets and authors.
- Dr Victor Chang, Australia's most renowned heart surgeon, emigrated to Australia from China in 1951 after losing his mother to cancer when he was just twelve years of age.
- Albert Namatjira, Australia's most famous Aboriginal artist, was rejected by his biological parents and adopted into a new family. He was the first Aborigine to be granted full citizenship in 1955, and it was a further ten years before the rest of the Aboriginal population were granted the same rights.
- JK Rowling, a single mum and school teacher, had her novel *Harry Potter and the Philosopher's Stone* rejected by numerous publishers. Millions of copies later, those same publishers are probably now kicking themselves!

- Michael Jordan was rejected from his high school's basketball team, but went on to become basketball's most celebrated player.
- Elle Macpherson, Australia's most famous supermodel, struggled early on in her career. She often had trouble landing modelling jobs because of her curves, for which she is now world famous.
- Dawn Fraser, Australian swimming champion, suffered with severe asthma and found that joining in activities with friends was a problem. Dawn knew what it was to be left out. To help her condition she began swimming. Eventually she went on to win eight Olympic and eight Commonwealth medals.
- Dame Joan Sutherland is one of the world's greatest opera singers, a true diva. However, when Joan auditioned to sing in the school choir she was told her voice was too loud.
- Beethoven was physically beaten by his father, and his music teacher said that as a composer, he was hopeless. He went on to become one of the world's greatest ever composers.
- Thomas Edison, the famous inventor, was told as a boy by his teacher that he was too stupid to learn anything. Thomas went on to invent many things, including the light bulb.
- FW Woolworth got a job in a dry goods store when he was twenty-one, but his employer would not let him wait on customers because he was told that he didn't have enough sense. He went on to build the super-successful Woolworth chain of stores, famous for customer service.
- Walt Disney was fired by a newspaper editor because, he was told, he had no good ideas. Walt didn't give up and went on to build the Disney empire including theme parks, movies and merchandise worth several billion dollars.
- Steven Spielberg dropped out of high school. He was persuaded to come back and placed in a learning-disabled class. He lasted a month and dropped out of school forever, but has become one of the world's most highly acclaimed feature film directors.

▶ Clark Gable became known as the King in Hollywood, but not before he was rejected for having big ears. Yet in his day, he was known as a romantic screen hero and every woman's dream.

▶ Albert Einstein was thought to be mentally retarded at school because he took so long to answer questions in class. His grades were so poor that a teacher asked him to quit, saying that he would never amount to anything. Albert Einstein is regarded as one of history's greatest geniuses.

▶ Jesus Christ was rejected and murdered by the religious leaders of the day because of his radical approach to religion. He made a comeback and became Saviour of the world.

If all these people could turn their rejection into a fantastic future, then I believe that we can too — providing we deal with our feelings instead of just using them as a stepladder to achievement and success.

In her book *The Root of Rejection*, author Joyce Meyer writes about noted physician and counsellor Dr Tournier's observations on emotional deprivation. He relates the startling fact that a large number of the world's well-known leaders had one thing in common: they were orphans. Some of these super achievers had been victims of abuse and some were severely mistreated. 'This is confirmed in numerous studies of high performers,' writes Dr Tournier. He reported that as many as three-quarters of those who become celebrated achievers are estimated to have suffered serious emotional deprivation or hardship in childhood. In extreme cases, because they feel so worthless inside, they work themselves practically to death trying to have some value. As a result of that, many of them become successful.

This kind of success is not healthy and is unsustainable. That's why we need to work on our hearts and our motives. Our ultimate goal is to be healthy on the inside, before we start using our past experiences as a stepladder to our future.

Lesson Learned

Once you have identified the feelings of rejection, you can reject the feelings by refusing them entry into your heart and mind. It's important to recite truthful, positive affirmations about yourself such as 'I am highly valuable' and 'I am wonderfully made' and begin to accept yourself.

It's important that you realise that you are loved. If you don't think anyone loves you, be sure that God does, and I'm sure that there is at least one person out there who loves you too; perhaps they have just had difficulty expressing that love to you in a way you can recognise and receive. Your rejection has not been about you but about other people's inability to accept you as you are, so you can refuse to accept rejection.

I have suffered rejection because of my religion, and I know I am not alone. It takes courage to stand up for what you believe in, and although I have had people snub and misunderstand me at times, I simply won't walk away from my convictions. Because I am a person of conviction, I understand that rejection can sometimes come with the territory because not everyone is going to agree with what I believe.

When we look at how to deal with and benefit from rejection, it is important to realise that it will take confidence to rebuild your life. We also need to take responsibility for our reactions and to realise that rejection is part of learning. Ask yourself the question, 'Am I going to let this ruin my life?'

Understanding what is behind someone's rejection of you is a powerful key to the healing process. If you can see clearly that there are issues involved that don't relate to you, it is far easier to reject the rejection coming your way.

Learning from rejection also requires us to look at our own lives to see whether we are doing anything to cause others to reject us. Often we blame other people because they don't want to have anything to do with us, when it actually could be our fault. Many people who live their lives in a hurtful and selfish manner bring rejection and alienation on themselves, and then cry, 'no one loves me'.

I wholeheartedly believe that we should love and accept people and not judge them. However, it would be naive to think that all the behaviour of all human beings is acceptable, and that's where it's important to draw the line. We must be accepting of people but learn to decipher and reject those aspects of their lives that cause us pain. You don't have to accept a person's actions, nor do they have to accept yours, but I do believe that we simply need to accept each other as human beings. Our humanity is a great equaliser. This is a vital key to establishing boundaries and learning to reject rejection.

Rejecting rejection is about refusing to take on board another person's negative stereotypes. To do that one must have a totally integrated, positive identity and acceptance of oneself. We need to understand our incredible value as human beings, regardless of what anyone says, thinks or does against us.

The truth is that your negative feelings about yourself are undeserved and unfair. You may have had some tough knocks and some ups and downs in relationships so you have convinced yourself in your heart, mind and soul that you are just not a social and likeable person. Begin to say, 'I am liked because I am likeable.'

List all the things you do like about yourself — body, soul and spirit — and work on the things you don't, until your positive list outgrows the negative.

Give yourself time to understand and discover the beauty of your true reflection. Take time to develop the sight of your own eyes, which will see deeper than the eyes of those who do not know or understand. Take the time to find grace for who you are and why you were made.

Remember the Truth: you don't have to live rejected.

Acceptance
Accept one another,
just as Jesus Christ has accepted you.

ROMANS 15:7, THE BIBLE

Alistair's Story

Memories of my childhood are not pleasant. I was born with large ears that stuck out, so I was consistently teased and called names at school. Some of the favourites were 'Wing Nut', 'Milk Jug Head' and 'Dumbo'. They said that my head looked like the front of a car with its doors open. My reaction? I laughed with them of course and then walked away, unable to think of a quick comeback or a smart reply. I longed to be accepted by the 'cool' crowd. I was overwhelmed by anger and helplessness when others ridiculed me. Every time I was teased, it felt as though a part of me died.

Occasionally I would come home from school crying and depressed because of the names people called me. When I told my parents what was happening, their response was, 'But darling, your ears don't stick out. You're very handsome.' My parents loved me, but their words were like putting a band-aid on a broken leg. They didn't know it, but I felt like they were denying my pain and my feelings. I felt completely alone and helpless; they couldn't see things the way I did, the way I lived every day. No one seemed to understand.

In my mind there was no way out of the embarrassing cycle that I was trapped in. Society has a standard of beauty and I did not measure up to that standard. I hated the way I looked. I wanted to be handsome and charming, not skinny with ears that made people laugh at me. I wanted to be James Bond, but I was Mr Bean.

By the end of school I had learned to shut people out. I wanted to protect myself from any more ridicule, yet I was also desperate for attention. I became distant, withdrawn and constantly depressed. Often, I loaded the gun we kept in our house, placed the barrel in my mouth and then took it out, cursing myself because I didn't have the courage to pull the trigger. I felt worthless, ugly and totally alone with my pain and embarrassment.

I never told anyone how I was feeling. I got along with a group of people at my youth group — I thought it was because of my sense of humour. But I tried not to be seen and not to be heard, I wanted to have as little to do with people as possible. I was afraid of them. I was so preoccupied with my own inferiority that I felt socially inadequate and there was a side to me that nobody knew, a side that was less friendly. It was dark, obsessive, solitary and totally absorbed with self-hatred.

From an early age I had developed an unhealthy interest in death and weapons, particularly knives. I constantly fantasised about killing and injuring the people who teased me. In these fantasies no one could hurt me. I was in control.

When I moved out from my parents' house at the age of seventeen, I started to rent hard-core horror movies on a weekly basis. I soaked in the filthy mutilation that those films offered while drinking myself to sleep. I bought camping knives and cut my face so that I would bleed. The adrenaline rush that I felt when I did this was the only thing that made me feel good. I enjoyed hurting myself, plus it made people feel sorry for me when they saw the wounds on my face the next day. I had found a way to get the attention I was craving and I told lies to cover up what I was doing.

I turned nineteen and the hatred I felt for myself, combined with an obsession with horror, was so intense that I now wanted to do something more than cut my face. One night I walked down to the local mall and bought a pair of scissors at the newsagent. I went into the public toilets in the mall and stood in front of the mirror. I saw what I hated and I cut off my right ear. I got such a rush. I was getting revenge or some kind of justice for the way I looked. The pain felt good. I flushed my ear down the toilet and got into a taxi and went to the emergency ward at the hospital.

I didn't tell anyone what had happened; nobody would understand the way I felt, so I invented a story to cover up what I had done. I consequently had two plastic surgery operations in an attempt to restore my ear to a normal shape.

About four months after this incident I began counselling and my life was changed. For the first time someone understood my confusion and the way I was feeling. But greater then this, I began to realise how valuable I was. Others did understand, love and accept me. Once I realised this, I cried for hours. The most healing part of my counselling was when I verbally forgave everyone who had ever made fun of me and I forgave myself for all the injury that I had inflicted on myself over the years.

I remember waking up the morning after and having a feeling of being fully alive, like I had been reinvented and given another chance. Learning to love myself was a process and it took time. I needed to unlearn the lies that I had lived with all my life.

It's easy to describe how I feel now. Life is so rich and full of meaning and possibility. I love the person I was created to be. My heart breaks for those people who can't appreciate the uniqueness and beauty of who they are.

My life continues to unfold and the challenges that I have faced in my past still continue to surface but I do try to remain resolute. I have experienced true freedom and it's that kind of freedom that I believe is worth fighting for over and over again.

10 Keys to Freedom

from rejection

To reject rejection, learn to look clearly at other people's motivations for criticising and dismissing you. Get an opinion from someone you know and trust. Your FREEDOM will come as you take a stand, tell yourself that you are worth it and then make for the finish line! All of these keys are aimed at building you up rather than letting you be knocked down.

1. Look beyond your faults and see your positive attributes. They may not be easy to identify initially, but start with one thing you think might be a positive, or ask a trusted friend.

2. Don't listen to unkind criticism. Surround yourself with good people who will say positive and helpful things.

3. Choose not to react to other people's prejudiced behaviour. This is where it helps to have great friends, or trusted others who we can talk to.

4. Remember that life always has the potential to get better.

5. Enjoy the uniqueness of how you have been created.

6. Work on your internal beauty more than your external beauty. The inward shines further than anything outward!

7. Celebrate the differences in other people. Appreciate them as you would like to be appreciated.

8. The feeling of rejection should always help you remember how not to treat others.

9. Don't allow rejection to rock your sense of personal value. You ARE valued and beyond value: TRUTH!

10. Find out what you were designed and created to achieve with your life, and do it with all of your heart. A little effort will go a long way.

body soul spirit

ACTION PLAN

body
Maximise your uniqueness. Be creative with how you present yourself, and make the most of what sets you apart from everyone else. Dress like YOU, talk like YOU, walk like YOU. Create like YOU. Give yourself permission to do this and it will help others in your life to do it too.

soul
Celebrate your individuality. Research your background and family culture, spend time with like-minded people, and help educate your less-informed friends about your culture and interests.

spirit
Thank God for making you different and pray for the ability and wisdom to help others who struggle with alienation and rejection. Use your experience to befriend and include others who feel that they are alone.

My goal is freedom
FROM REJECTION

Chapter 3

Your Grass is Always Greener

freedom from body discontentment

*'One person's faults are
another person's fantasy.'*

The Little Mermaid

Once upon a time, a young mermaid lived in a majestic ocean. She was very beautiful; her skin was clear and delicate, her eyes sapphire blue and her body ended in a curvaceous tail. Unlike her sisters who adored the sea, the young mermaid craved freedom from the watery depths.

One day she rose up out of the sea and swam towards the cabin window of a large ship, where she looked inside. She saw a handsome young prince with large dark eyes and the little mermaid instantly fell in love. Suddenly a dreadful storm broke, engulfing the ship with crashing waves. As the ship began to sink, the prince swam through a broken window, deep into the dark sea. The little mermaid swam after him and she held his head above the water and brought him ashore. When a group of humans arrived, the sea-princess quickly swam away.

Longing for a life with the prince, she wished to know everything about the lands above the sea. 'Why am I different?' she asked her mother. The little mermaid looked in her large shell mirror and sighed, looking mournfully at her curvaceous tail, wishing she could exchange it for legs so that the prince might fall in love with her.

The next day, on her way back to the surface, she came across a dreadful sea witch. This monster had the power to give her exactly what she wanted, but the cost would be her soul — if the prince married another, the little mermaid would die, her soul claimed by the witch. But not seeing the value of her soul, the mermaid traded it in exchange for the legs and life she thought she wanted.

The spell was cast and the sea delivered her to the shore, but when she met the prince, he did not recognise her. The young woman he loved had a curvaceous tail and lovely personality, but he had not seen her since the night of his rescue. The sea-princess now realised the terrible price she had paid for what she *thought* she really wanted. As the days passed she fell more deeply in love with the prince, yet he saw her only as a friend. His heart belonged elsewhere. He had fallen in love with the little mermaid as she was. He no longer recognised her.

Soon it was announced that the prince must marry, and that the daughter of a neighbouring king would be his wife. The little mermaid felt as if her heart was breaking in two. She thought her human form would cause the prince to love her more, but alas, he didn't even recognise her now.

The wedding ceremony began and the little mermaid heard noises behind the rocks on the shore. It was her sisters, who had come to rescue her. 'Quickly!' they said. 'Come with us! If you come back to the sea before the prince marries, your life will be saved. We gave our precious jewels to the sea monster in exchange for your life.' The little mermaid was rescued just in time.

The little mermaid returned to the sea and her family. She stood before her shell mirror once again and now saw her true magnificence. She was grateful for a second chance under the sea, where she belonged.

And the little mermaid lived a contented life happily ever after.

The End

Fact

Most people are discontent with their body.

Truth

Contentment starts from within.

Mirror, mirror on the wall, why don't I like what I see at all?

If you can relate to this question, you are not alone. Thousands of women and an increasing number of men look in the mirror every day and dislike or even despise what they see.

When you look in the mirror, what do you see? When you walk past a shop window and catch a glimpse of your body, what do you notice first? Do you see something you like, something you are proud of, something you were born with and live with happily? Or do you criticise and pick apart how you look in your mind: I'm too fat, I'm too puny, my breasts aren't the right size, I'm too short? And if this is the case, do you wonder why you think this? What about your naked body in front of a mirror — do you avoid mirrors when having a shower?

However, one person's faults are another person's fantasy. Sometimes we get caught up on facts, like our feet being too wide or our nose being too big or our lips being too thin and our hips too wide, when we should be looking at the truth, which says that we are all beautiful in our own way.

Sometimes we are simply never satisfied with what we have and how we have been made, and we are too busy focusing on all of our faults, instead of celebrating or appreciating our strengths. My personal observation has shown me that it doesn't matter how beautiful someone is, there's always something about the way that they look or sound that they don't like.

One thing is certain: for every body part you are dissatisfied with, there will be another person wanting to swap with you!

In a world that judges men and women alike on the way that they look, it's important to discover for yourself what your life priorities are. Brawn, brains and beauty may be an attractive combination, but vanity is not. Are your looks more important to you than your character, or is your character all that matters so you neglect your looks? How about a balance of both? Living a balanced life opens you up to great opportunities and a life of freedom.

Body Discontentment

Let's take a look at some examples of certain aspects of our bodies that we sometimes wish we could change. See if you can identify with any one or more of these:

▶ height
▶ weight
▶ hair
▶ eyes
▶ skin
▶ body type
▶ facial features
▶ bone structure
▶ voice.

The list could go on.

While understanding that what we think is beautiful may actually be different through someone else's eyes, it is also important for us to appreciate different kinds of beauty that may not necessarily be to our taste. We need to appreciate what we have and the life we've been given.

Here are some facts and figures released by the Department of Health and Ageing in Australia relating to body image dissatisfaction:

▶ Adolescent girls are consistently more dissatisfied with their bodies than adolescent boys. In a survey of high school students, 70 per cent of adolescent girls wanted to be thinner, compared to 34 per cent of boys. Only 7 per cent of girls reported wanting to be larger, in comparison to 35 per cent of the boys surveyed.

▶ A study involving 869 girls aged fourteen to sixteen found that more than one-third (36 per cent) of the girls reported using at least one extreme dieting method in the past month (crash dieting, fasting, slimming tablets, diuretics, laxatives or cigarettes). In addition, 77 per cent of the girls said they wanted to lose weight.

▶ The Australian Longitudinal Study of Women's Health found that of 13 003 women between the ages of eighteen and twenty-two, 74 per cent reported wanting to weigh less, with only 25 per cent of women in the 'healthy weight' category being happy with their weight.

One way to measure how you feel about different aspects of yourself is by scoring each on a scale from one to ten, one being complete contentment and ten being extreme discontentment. I suggest that anything over the five line means that you have some work to do. Then you need to determine which of those things scored over five you can actually change for the better, and those you can't. If it's something like being under- or overweight, and you know you can do something to improve, then that's what you need to focus on until you can give it a lower score than five. If it's something like your height, then you just need to acknowledge you can't change that, so you need to thank God for how you are made and look for all the positive things that come with being either short or tall. For example, if you are shorter than most people, you will have no trouble finding pants long enough to fit you, even if you do have to get everything taken up! On the other hand, taller people have no trouble reaching the top shelves at the supermarket, or seeing above a crowd.

The Little Mermaid

The grass always looks greener on the other side of the fence. In my version of the classic fairy-tale *The Little Mermaid*, a story is told of someone wanting something that they didn't have. And in this case, it was a ten out of ten for dissatisfaction to the point where she was prepared to sell her soul to get what she wanted.

There's a whole future life waiting for us when we get comfortable with who we really are and how we are made. If you were born with curves, be grateful for them, because they are truly beautiful. If however, you were born petite, be grateful for that, because you are also truly beautiful. There is true beauty in every body shape, whether big or small, curvy or petite.

The little mermaid lived a life of discontentment, always wishing she was someone else. She aspired to the unobtainable, didn't appreciate what she had, and was prepared to sell her soul in order to gain what she wasn't born with. Her life became full of fear and pain as she sacrificed who she really was to become someone else, someone she was never meant to be. Her whole focus was unhealthy.

Although we sometimes wish to be able to enter the world of another whose life seems much better than ours because of how they look versus how we look, in reality our lives contain the same expansive potential if we just choose to maximise what we have.

Many people today struggle with gross dissatisfaction in how they look and they live in a permanent state of wanting what they don't have. We refuse to listen to other people's affirmation of our beauty, we idolise what is unattainable, and we keep dreaming that the grass is greener on the other side of the fence.

Body Image

Most people think of body image as the picture of the body in the mind's eye. This is only one of four factors that determine our final body image. Body image is the sum total of the visual, emotional, physical and historical aspects of a person and is influenced by their own beliefs and attitudes as well as ideals in society.

In their book *Unloading the Overload*, Dr Cliff Powell and Dr Graham Barker say, 'Self-image is the internal view we have of ourselves, the permanent picture we see inside that dictates most of our actions and responses.'

We will always have some sort of self-image or body image, but that image does not remain the same. Instead, it changes in response to events throughout our life, such as puberty, pregnancy, disability, illness, surgery, menopause, and even different stages in a woman's menstrual cycle. Body image is closely connected to a person's self-esteem. Self-esteem refers to how much a person values or accepts themselves for who and what they are.

We live in a culture that worships thinness. Images of women in the media, advertising and popular culture emphasise beauty, youth and being thin. As some of us don't score highly in one or more of these categories, our body image is often poor. Advertisers speak of 'perfect bodies', suggesting that body flaws should be hidden or even surgically corrected. The diet, exercise, cosmetic surgery and beauty industries are making obscene amounts of money from people's body image misery as we pursue the seemingly ideal body and look.

The problem with the promotion of this kind of ideal is that it does not empower us, rather it undermines our confidence in who we are and how we are made. We do not need to measure up to someone else's idea in order to be truly beautiful and valued.

Not liking something is considered normal human nature; having a 'complex' about yourself, however, will keep you from living free. There are many things that we may not particularly like about ourselves, but there's a big difference between not liking and outright discontentment, which this chapter is about.

There are many things that take part in shaping the feelings we have about our bodies. Here is a look at some common factors.

▶ *The media*: television, movies, MTV, magazines and other media sources give out messages about what the ideal body looks like.

▶ *Family members*: how those closest to us feel about their bodies usually affects the development of our own body image.

▶ *Abuse*: sexual, emotional and physical abuse has a negative impact on body image.

▶ *Diet fads*: unhealthy eating and exercise can cause not only physical damage but also emotional damage, affecting our self-esteem.

▶ *Emotional experiences*: both positive praise and negative criticism received during childhood and adulthood can affect our self-esteem.

▶ *Perfectionism*: an unrealistic desire to be better, fitter, thinner, bigger, prettier or curvier will always end in disappointment.

▶ *Our partners*: the way we are treated by our significant others plays a part in the way we see ourselves. We tend to absorb criticism from those we love.

Body image affects more than our behaviour, it also influences our self-esteem and our identity. Studies indicate that, regardless of actual attractiveness, the better a person feels about his or her body, the higher his or her self-esteem, and vice versa.

It is hard to not be affected by the media bombarding us constantly with the message 'thin is in!' On TV commercials we are told to 'lose weight fast' or 'exercise for five minutes a day' to have a beautiful body; magazines display thin, attractive women to try to convince us that we are not acceptable until we have slim, toned thighs. The overriding message is that we need to change something about ourselves in order to be loved or successful. In particular, if we have thin, fit bodies, we are led to believe that our lives will be perfect.

My experience has demonstrated that this message is not true. In fact the constant striving to be something other than what we are is part of what can keep us dissatisfied with life. The reality is that genetically, we are all born with varying shapes and sizes. A very small percentage of the world's population can expect to achieve the shapes and sizes the media portrays as ideal without endangering their health or resorting to surgery. The media holds this unrealistic goal up to us and suggests that we try to reach it. No wonder so many men and women are struggling with body image dissatisfaction.

The role of body image in the development of eating disorders in adolescent girls is fairly well documented. It is also known that parents have a powerful influence over their children's eating habits. One Melbourne study found that 20 per cent of parents were encouraging their daughters to diet even though in some cases the girls were in the healthy weight range.

There is increasing evidence that boys too are subjected to pressure to attain the 'perfect' body. In extreme cases, this may lead them to use muscle-building steroids.

Model and actress Cameron Diaz, when asked about her body in a magazine interview, replied, 'I'm 175 centimetres tall, weigh 54 kilograms, and I wear a size eight. I'm comfortable with my body. I love it ... I think I have a nice body, I'm happy with it.'

That's great for Cameron, but what about us! Are you comfortable with your body? Could you honestly say that you love it?

Distortion and Dissatisfaction

There are two general types of body image disturbances: distortion and dissatisfaction.

Body image distortion is exactly like the person looking at a wide, narrow, short or tall mirror at a sideshow, and it is characterised by an inaccurate or distorted visual image of the body. Thin people who see themselves as fat experience a body image distortion. Some of them truly believe they are fat and are unable to challenge this thinking. Others can see themselves as thin when looking in a mirror, but nevertheless feel fat.

People struggling with anorexia nervosa experience a body image distortion and as a result, starve themselves. Refeeding the body and retraining the mind are both necessary parts of the treatment for this type of body image distortion.

Body dissatisfaction occurs when a person feels negatively towards his or her body or towards specific parts of his or her body.

There are two components to body dissatisfaction: displeasure with the way you see your body in your own mind, and discontentment with the way you *feel* about your bodily appearance. This dissatisfaction can be felt in varying degrees. Some people experience mild feelings of unattractiveness, while others become obsessed with the way they look, which hinders them dramatically from functioning as a normal human being.

Body image dissatisfaction is so prevalent in our society that it has almost been classified as normal, particularly among teenagers and young adults, both female and male with little distinction between socioeconomic group or ethnicity. So much emphasis has been put on the plight of individual teenage girls battling their own distorted body image that the whole picture is rarely seen. The whole picture is that it affects every one of us.

It seems that some of the most gorgeous models and actresses, who have been voted as having the best bodies in the business, still find reason to complain about certain body parts. Often those women whose body shape is curvy want to be skinny and those who are skinny want more curves. People with darker skin are trying to be fairer and those with fairer skin are sunbaking in order to get darker! Thin lips, fat lips, blonde hair, dark hair, hippy, curvy, thin, busty — the list goes on. Some people can't stand to see photographs or video footage of themselves, or listen to the sound of their voice on tape. There always seems to be something to be unhappy about. People seem to want what they haven't got. Will we ever be happy?

The extent of the dissatisfaction determines the impact it has on a person's life. For example, many people with eating disorders hate their bodies so much they wish they were invisible — many hide in baggy clothes. Some are unable to tolerate loving or affectionate touch and others retreat from social interactions. Many people can be so affected by their dissatisfaction that they choose not to participate in activities that involve wearing revealing attire such as swimming costumes or fitted clothes.

When it comes to body dissatisfaction, picture Michael Jackson and the distortion of his appearance, stemming from his desire to look like someone else. His face is now a different shape and colour and he doesn't even resemble the nice-looking young man he once was. He is the same person inside, however, and no amount of exterior change will ever alter that fact.

We don't need to strive to be something or someone we are not. We each have a personal best to aim towards and it's when we reach our personal best that we are *teleios*, which is an ancient Greek word meaning perfect for now, that is, perfect at one's own particular stage of development.

You can choose either to be on a quest for the ideal of perfection, which is the never happily ever after life, or learn to live in appreciation of who you are.

Beautiful Hollywood actress Jennifer Aniston believes that she has 'a big butt'. In a magazine article Jennifer was quoted as saying, 'I'm not comfortable being heavy. Whenever I gain weight, it goes to my rear.' Jennifer also commented that she wished she had longer legs and not such big hips. If only she could truly see herself!

Change

We all tend to compare ourselves with other people — it's a natural human tendency, but one that usually ends up lowering our body image and self-esteem and heightening our discontentment. Measuring yourself or comparing yourself with someone else is unwise. The mirror of truth is the only place for you to be looking and measuring. The mirror of truth is all about being your personal best, and not about comparing yourself to anyone else.

If you need to change the essence of who you are so someone will accept you, that is wrong. Chasing someone else's looks, life and existence will only rob you of your own. It is not wrong, however, to dream of a better life or even a different life, but to change the essence of you is not the right way to go about it.

Just remember, you can do whatever you want and change whatever you want, but you can't choose the consequences of your choices, or change them later.

You are body, soul and spirit, so changing the way you look doesn't mean you're changing who you really are. You can't escape you!

Having said that, there is nothing wrong at all with wanting to improve yourself; in fact, that's desirable. Wanting to improve what you have does not equal being discontent. Being discontent with unhealthy aspects of your life is a very positive thing, but just remember, trying to be like someone else will only ever make you a poor imitation of the real thing.

Some people simply don't like themselves and they question the reason for their existence because of their poor self-esteem, poor body image and circumstances in life.

'Why was I born?' many have sadly asked.

If you have ever asked that question, I want to encourage you to see your life differently. Instead of asking why you were born, how about asking, 'Why is there breath in my lungs today?' Could it be that you have an incredible purpose and opportunity in your day — in your life?

Questioning your existence implies that you feel there is no purpose or reason for living. On the other hand, asking yourself what opportunities may be in front of you implies that there is a purpose and destiny that you need to fulfil. Changing your perspective will help change your life.

The process of changing your perspective doesn't start with your body, it needs to start with your mind. Change your mind, change your life! Addressing these issues will open a door, beyond which you can start to develop a fondness towards yourself that will see you on your way to improved contentment about who you are and how you are made.

Try the following positive steps to counteract any unhelpful thoughts you've had about yourself:

1. Do not criticise yourself publicly or privately.
2. Do not punish yourself emotionally or physically.
3. Be patient and kind to yourself.
4. Celebrate other people's beauty and success.
5. Look in the mirror and smile at your beauty.
6. Allow others to encourage you.
7. Believe you were born on the 'A' team.
8. Believe you are valuable no matter how you look.
9. Always stand tall in a room full of beautiful people.
10. Be glad you are YOU.

To actively pursue these positive thoughts and a healthier body image, we need to resist any stereotypical attitudes in us or in others that say that only thin is beautiful. If there is any obsession in your life about how much you weigh, it's time to throw out your scales, as your worth cannot be measured by how much you weigh! Ignore the unhealthy message that the media try to bombard you with. Remember, they are just trying to sell you something.

It's important to be healthy but not obsessive with food, as food is not your enemy or your ally, it's simply fuel to live and to be enjoyed. Also, for every negative thought you have about yourself, find a positive counterpart; if you can't think of anything great to say about yourself, don't say anything at all.

Accepting what you can't change and setting a range of short- and long-term goals to change what you can (without compromising who you are), is an important part of the process. Write yourself a list of areas of your life that you want to improve that are beyond your looks. Also, get out and take a positive look at other people. This will help to grow your world view and help you see that people of all different shapes and sizes are beautiful, including you.

Be Content

I have learned to be content, even though it is human to want something that I haven't got. I have straight hair and I wish it were curly like one of my friends, Jules. Jules, on the other hand, doesn't like her hair so she prefers it tied back or straightened. I'm also very tall, nearly 180 centimetres, and for a woman, that's both good and bad. Good for a modelling career, bad for a long haul flight to Europe or New York, and not so great if you're not into basketballer-type guys!

When I began modelling in my late teenage years, I had to learn to be grateful for my body shape and I also had to be prepared to work on aspects that needed improvement. I am curvy and so I was given work that required me to be that way. I was not asked to go to castings as a skinny editorial model because that is not me, and no amount of dieting would help me lose my bone structure. I was able to portray good health and good self-esteem in a sometimes unhealthy environment.

This doesn't mean, however, that I was exempt from criticism. Once I missed out on work because of 'faults' with my looks — I missed a big advertising campaign simply because of a freckle beneath my bottom lip. It was just as easy for the company to book a dark-haired model with no freckle and so that's exactly what they did, and I don't despise my freckle because of what happened.

During my years as a model, the amazing thing was that I got many jobs because of aspects of my body that I had previously not liked and wished I could change. Although it didn't necessarily make me feel better about myself on the inside (again — human nature), I did come to realise that beauty really is in the eye of the beholder.

Acceptance

Be informed, consider the facts and accept the truth, so that you can begin to live in contentment. Here is some information a friend sent me that I think was quite insightful:

▶ There are three billion women who don't look like supermodels and only a few who do.

▶ Marilyn Monroe wore a size fourteen.

▶ If Barbie were a real woman, she'd have to walk on all fours due to her proportions.

▶ The average woman weighs 65 kilograms and wears size twelve to fourteen.

▶ One out of every four 18- to 25-year-old women has an eating disorder.

▶ The models in the magazines are airbrushed and not perfect!

▶ A psychological study in 1995 found that three minutes spent looking at a fashion magazine caused 70 per cent of women to feel depressed, guilty and ashamed.

▶ Models twenty years ago weighed 8 per cent less than the average woman. Today they weigh 23 per cent less than the average woman.

If you feel as though you've tried everything and nothing seems to be working for you, it may be necessary for you to seek professional help. Sometimes someone else leading us towards the mirror of truth is what we need to be set free.

In his book *The Balance of Beauty*, fashion industry hair and make-up artist Gregory Landsman writes, 'The belief in equality of beauty allows us to know that no one is better than who we are, but in the same breath, no one is less. In recognising this truth we can regain the essence of beauty with which we were born.'

In order for you to live a life of true freedom from body discontentment, you need not only to understand how lovely you are inside and out, but you need a deep revelation that won't be shaken — no matter what criticism comes your way. My prayer for you is that this deep revelation will make its way permanently into your heart and mind, so you can live in freedom.

Remember the Truth: contentment starts from within.

Contentment

Oh yes, you shaped me first inside, then out;
you formed me in my mother's womb.
I thank you God. You're breathtaking!
Body and soul, I am marvellously made!
I worship in adoration, what a creation!
You know me inside and out,
you know every bone in my body;
You know exactly how I was made, bit by bit,
how I was sculpted from nothing into something.
Like an open book, you watched me grow from
conception to birth;
all the stages of my life were spread out before you,
the days of my life all prepared
before I'd even lived one day.

PSALM 139:13–16, THE BIBLE

Anna's Story

Dissatisfied. I did not get the attention that I needed. I think I was an attention seeker from the moment I was born. There are countless photos of me playing dress-up, singing into hairbrushes like a rock star, performing for all the family functions, and even setting up a little television studio in the basement of our house where I would proceed to make music videos mimicking Debbie Gibson and Janet Jackson. I was a superstar! But innocently, this is where unhealthy comparisons began.

I can remember my need to be popular even from a young age. I was told I was pretty by all the boys in school and they even chased me during recess to get kisses. It was a fun game, but a game that was showing me my value came from what others thought of me and what others needed from me. I was a people pleaser and needed to be loved by the crowd to know that I was all right.

I began to think of my family as a part of my life that I didn't need. My parents were just the rule makers as far as I was concerned. They wouldn't let me have boyfriends or go to parties, but I did it anyway behind their backs. It made me feel needed, loved and beautiful. I distanced myself from my family, letting my friends dictate my life. What they thought was cool, I thought was cool. Boys and parties and striving towards popularity became my life.

By the time I reached high school, my family had become almost nonexistent in my world. Not by their choice, but by mine. By Year Eleven my popularity was well established at school. I had my hand in nearly every sport, I was involved in almost every school social event, I was part of school government, I stayed fit and I got up at 5 a.m. every morning to get ready just to make sure I looked perfect. I pretty much thought about nothing other than myself. It was an endless task to make sure I always appeared to have the perfect life, but on the inside this constant people pleasing was rotting the real me away.

I left for university with hopes to start afresh in life. I decided to try out for the university's athletics team. I went for it with everything I had, this was my chance! I went to the gym five times a week and worked myself to the bone, looking in the mirror at all times, making sure I looked OK. I made sure the meals I ate were healthy; I didn't want to add an ounce of fat to my body. I was completely driven towards my goal.

Time for the tryouts arrived. I passed the first phase with ease, but during the second phase I broke under the pressure. My name was not called for the team and I was devastated. I walked through the doors of the pavilion and I broke down, I cried uncontrollably and didn't care who saw.

My obsession with the way I looked didn't end here though and I worked even harder. I secretly lived at the gym and the track, punishing myself for not being good enough, and I wasn't about to lose my popularity either, so I partied equally as hard. Maintaining this constant façade of a girl who was accomplishing in life was exhausting. I was so unhappy.

My boyfriend noticed any change in my body even to the slightest degree, and he would voice it so I knew to take care of it. For so long I had made sure that I always kept myself in 'perfect' form ... if there is such a thing. After years of roller-coaster eating habits, skipping meals all through high school and uni and working out like a maniac, I finally tried on several occasions to throw up my meals. I had to look this demon straight in the face.

I am made the way I am for a reason; I needed to stop fighting against who I was or it was going to eat me up. One day I was desperately trying to throw up after a meal and nothing would come out. I stood up and looked in the mirror and just started to laugh at myself through tears streaming down my face. How stupid this all was. There were so many other, better things I could be doing with my life. So I decided, every time I thought of skipping a meal or throwing up, I would look outward and stop being so obsessed with myself. Today I am content with my body. I'm 160 centimetres, 55 kilos and have larger hips than breasts. Let's face it, I have been given this body to take care of and supermodel Kate Moss has her own.

The road to being content with who you are is a constant journey. I won't lie to you and say that I look in the mirror every day and think I am perfect. What I do know is that I have made some choices that have made me content with who I am. I eat in moderation, meaning I have dessert if I want it, but I don't go overboard. I still exercise, but not like a maniac. I go on walks, because they are peaceful, a great time to think, and they get you into good shape.

The turning point in my life was when I realised that I could be either dissatisfied or content forever, but not both at the same time. So I chose contentment. I realised that there has to be a point in your life where you accept you were given the shape and bone structure you have, and it's impossible to change that. And lastly, I am not allowed to compare myself to anyone. If I do, I'll only ever be mediocre. I am who I am, and in that I don't have to prove anything. I can only ever be the greatest, one and only 'me' that has ever been created.

10 Keys to Freedom

from body discontentment

You may want to write out some or all of these keys and stick them to your mirror so you have a daily reminder. Body contentment will never be achieved through knowing how you *should* look; it's about appreciating how you are *now*. Big step? Don't worry — start with one key and you'll soon find yourself well equipped to tackle the rest. FREEDOM is just a thought away!

1. Be grateful for how you were made: no compromise. Look around you instead of above you and appreciate all that you have!
2. Take care of yourself and improve what you have.
3. Accept encouragement and discourage flattery.
4. Look in the mirror every day and tell yourself you are beautiful and intelligent.
5. Stop looking at the lives of other people and wishing you were them.
6. Stop buying magazines that incite you to wish you were famous.
7. Encourage someone every day about their value and beauty.
8. Don't chase and strive for what doesn't belong to you or belong in your life.
9. Choose only the best for your life.
10. Recognise your natural body shape (naturally thin, athletic or curvy) and be content to be the best you can be, with the body shape you were born with.

body soul spirit

ACTION PLAN

body
Showcase your best assets (modestly of course!), and work with problem areas by clever dressing and perhaps choosing darker colours where you don't want to be noticed.

soul
Continually remind yourself that you are beautiful, that nobody is perfect and that you have the right to feel fantastic about yourself.

spirit
Pray for help to do whatever you need to do to feel better about yourself, whether it's losing weight, gaining weight, or simply accepting yourself just the way you are.

My goal is freedom
FROM BODY DISCONTENTMENT

Chapter 4

Under Pressure

freedom from people pleasing

'We spend more, but have less ...
We have multiplied our possessions,
but reduced our values ...'

Pinocchio

Once upon a time, a cobbler named Geppetto who had always wanted a son decided to make himself a little puppet. Geppetto hid a kind heart inside the puppet and named him Pinocchio. He designed the boy to move by the strings attached to him, but in the wrong hands these strings could lead him astray.

Having sold some precious items in order to buy Pinocchio's first school book, Geppetto sent the overjoyed puppet off for his first day at school. On the way, Pinocchio saw a travelling circus and was stopped by one of the performers. Feeling pressured, he sold his school book for entry to the circus. Pinocchio got completely caught up in the crowd; he decided then and there that he wanted to be famous like the circus performers.

The circus manager saw Pinocchio and, thinking he could make some money out of him, put him on show in a cage. Pinocchio cried and begged to be released from the cage, until eventually, the circus manager let him go. He was free at last, and he set out for home without delay.

A beautiful angel, seeing Pinocchio running home, swooped down to ask if he was O.K.

'Tell me what has happened,' she asked. Pinocchio told her his story, leaving out the bit about selling his first reading book. Suddenly, Pinocchio's nose began to grow longer. 'You're not telling the truth, are you?' asked the angel. Blushing with shame, Pinocchio began to weep. Because she felt sorry for him, the angel clapped her hands and his nose shrank to its proper length.

'Now, don't tell any more lies,' the angel warned him. 'Go home straightaway to your father.'

Grateful, he ran towards home. On the way home, Pinocchio came across Carlo, the lazybones of his class. 'Why don't you come to Toyland with me?' said Carlo. 'You can stay as long as you want to and play all day long!' Ignoring his promises to the angel and his conscience, Pinocchio agreed to go. Pinocchio wanted to be just like Carlo — he copied everything Carlo did, hoping Carlo would be his friend. So off they went to Toyland. 'This is the life!' he said to Carlo nervously, hoping that everything would be OK.

Pinocchio and Carlo had been at Toyland a number of days when they awoke to a nasty surprise. They had each sprouted a long pair of hairy donkey ears! The boys had become just like donkeys and were taken swiftly by the Toyland owner to the market to be sold. Separated from his so-called friend, Pinocchio was sold to a farmer who beat him every day. Desperate for help, Pinocchio called out for the angel.

The angel heard Pinocchio's call and saved him, turning him back into a wooden puppet. Then she helped him find his way home. Pinocchio finally realised that following the crowd was only going to harm him and he decided to be honest with himself and his father. This time Pinocchio's heart was genuine and when he looked in the mirror the next morning, he had become a real boy.

Pinocchio went on to become a great leader instead of a weak follower, having learned lessons from his mistakes. Pinocchio no longer lived like a puppet on string, and lived happily ever after.

The End

Fact
Everyone faces peer pressure.

Truth
Confidence allows you to live with 'no strings attached'.

Mirror, mirror on the wall, why is there so much pressure to conform?

What possesses a person to follow another person blindly through life? I believe the answer to this question lies within a person's self-esteem and value. Once we understand who we are and why we were made, we can determine what it is that we are meant to do.

Peer pressure is the most common and often the most powerful tool of conformity. It usually starts at school when friends encourage us to become just like them and to do as they do. This same pressure then continues through to adulthood if we don't take a stand and decide for ourselves who we are meant to be and what we are meant to do.

All of us begin in life like blocks of wood or pieces of clay, and we need shaping and moulding to help us grow and mature. Fighting the shaping process will only keep you in the workshop or on the potter's wheel of life for longer. We can enable that shaping or moulding process by letting people who have experience in life and who are positive role models help us negotiate the twists, turns and challenges of life. Our tendency is always to think we know better. But people who are living positive lives have already done the hard yards and we can learn from them. Parents can be a great example of this.

When I was seventeen I knew everything. That was until I got married and had kids of my own!

Often people can't seem to see or appreciate what they have until they grow up and see for themselves what a great job their parents have actually done. Our human nature tends to always want to know everything and to always be right, even when we may know very little, and are frequently wrong and led away from the truth.

Peer Pressure

Peer pressure means that friends or acquaintances compel you to do something that you may not want to do. They may urge you through negative peer pressure to cheat, steal or say something to someone that you feel uncomfortable about. People who conform to peer pressure are often called 'people pleasers'.

In her book *The Disease to Please*, Dr Harriet Braiker says,

> *People pleasers are not just nice people who go overboard trying to make everyone happy. Those who suffer from the Disease to Please are people who say 'Yes' when they really want to say 'No' — but they can't. They feel the uncontrollable need for the elusive approval of others like an addictive pull. Their debilitating fears of anger and confrontation force them to use 'niceness' and 'people pleasing' as self-defence camouflage.*

Peer pressure is not always a negative force. Powerful, positive peer pressure can shape positive behaviour in people. For example, in some schools with bullying problems, peer pressure has been used to influence bullies to reverse their behaviour. In many primary schools peer groups have joined together to prevent bullying.

Some people give in to negative peer pressure and people pleasing because they want to be liked, to fit in, or because they worry that others may make fun of them if they don't go along with what other people want. Others may conform because they are curious to try something new that they can see others doing. The idea that 'everyone's doing it' may influence some people to leave their better judgment, or their common sense, behind.

'Keeping up with the Joneses' is the adult description of peer pressure. It's the push that adults have from society to own the big house, nice car and all the trimmings. While these things aren't necessarily bad in and of themselves, what it takes to get them might be. If we start sacrificing relationships for material goods, we'll end up missing out on what really matters in life. We should be more concerned about the people in our lives than keeping up with the Joneses.

Too often we race around acquiring more material possessions, responding to social pressure and simply trying to impress people. Then when people respond to the impression we create, this inflates our self-esteem. But for how long and at what cost? Our closets are bursting at the seams, our credit cards are at or over their limit and for some of us, retail therapy is still our chosen form of medication!

The only difference between adulthood and childhood peer pressure is that adults have a little more money and a little more power. When we go shopping, we are influenced in what we buy because we understand that we may be judged on the things that we have and the clothes that we wear.

However, teenagers are identified as those most 'at risk' of negative peer pressure, not because they are necessarily subject to more social pressures than other age groups, but that the type of peer pressure they have to deal with is often extremely difficult to ignore. Since our teenage years are a testing ground for adulthood, it is very common for the peer pressures faced by teenagers to engender behaviour that is anti-social, rebellious or boundary pushing. It's all part of growing up and learning how to make the right choices for ourselves.

Negative peer pressure that isn't dealt with during the teenage years usually surfaces again throughout adulthood. What once was, 'If you don't do this for me, then I won't be your friend any more' will inevitably become, 'If you don't drive a nice car, have an influential job and wear designer clothes, then I won't socialise with you any more.'

The realisation of peer pressure hits home when you are in the company of people you respect, but perhaps disagree with. The power of peer pressure may cause you to say something you don't really mean, in order to win their approval and affirmation. Often we cave into this kind of pressure — to our detriment. There are times of course when you choose to agree with someone in order to bring peace to a situation, when that particular issue doesn't really matter. But what happens when there are times that you are called on to compromise your principles? What do you do?

Peer pressure tries to dictate to us who we should be and what we should do. People who are easily led and not self-confident depend excessively on the approval of others in order to feel good about themselves. Everyone is susceptible to peer pressure and it takes courage to stand, or as the case may be, remain seated, for your convictions.

Pressure brings out what is really inside us. We will all feel pressure, but what we produce is ultimately our own responsibility, security or insecurity.

Pinocchio

In this version of *Pinocchio* we can see the influence of affluence. Pinocchio wanted to follow others to have what they had, at any cost. He didn't have the confidence and self-esteem to reject negative social pressure. He was influenced by affluence and his so-called friend led him astray.

Apart from peer pressure, *Pinocchio* also represents the runaway that is sometimes present in all of us, who wants to depart from any sense of responsibility for the mess we may find ourselves in — whether self-inflicted or otherwise.

Pinocchio was a runaway who wanted to escape to a world that he hoped would make him feel better about himself. Escapism is an outcome of poor self-esteem, and it's not just teenagers who run away. The spirit of the runaway is alive and thriving in many adult lives. People can be present in body yet absent in mind, will and emotion because of poor self-esteem. Running away, or living in denial, is as much a state of mind as it is a physical action.

Affluenza

So, who are the Joneses anyway, and why are we trying to keep up with them? Apparently they started out in 1879 as a snobby family standing apart from the crowd in England. In *Memoirs of a Station Master*, EJ Simmons commented on the way people interacted at a public meeting place — the railway station. He wrote, 'The Joneses, who don't associate with the Robinsons, meet there.'

His observation related to class distinction. One way of dealing with that particular gulf of class difference has been to keep up with the Joneses by buying material possessions that make people look as though they are part of a world that they are not. This is a type of peer pressure called 'affluenza', defined by psychotherapist Jessie H O'Neill as, 'The bloated, sluggish and unfulfilled feeling that results from efforts to keep up with the Joneses'.

It is also an epidemic whose symptoms are stress, overwork, waste and indebtedness caused by a relentless pursuit of the Aussie dream of accumulating 'things'. It is a misguided notion that we can buy our way into who we want to be and it usually ends up with us bankrupt: physically, emotionally and spiritually. Why allow yourself to be reduced to the 'haves' and 'have nots' in life?

Among the symptoms of affluenza which O'Neill has indentified are:

- a loss of personal and professional productivity
- an inability to delay gratification or tolerate frustration
- a false sense of entitlement
- low self-esteem
- low self worth
- loss of self-confidence

- preoccupation with externals
- depression
- self-absorption.

The difference between affluence and influence is huge. Affluence is simply the accumulation of wealth and material objects. Influence is the potential reach of your life and its effect on others.

The relentless pursuit of money has a corrupting influence, if not in a criminal sense, at least in a moral sense of taking our eyes off the things that really matter, like relationships and our own personal wellbeing. What's important is not what we do or don't have, but rather our perspective on material possessions in our life.

Take a good hard look in the mirror and ask why you do what you do, and then assess the impact that the desire for possessions is having on your life. Healthy self-esteem does not come from us acquiring more and more material possessions. Even the poor, who may appear to have no power, no material wealth, no acclaim and no influence, can internally possess all the riches of Heaven itself and a tremendously healthy self-esteem.

All the trappings of wealth and power that we either have and bask in, or wish we had and strive for, are empty in themselves. There is no lasting value to them. If we are caught up in them we lose a sense of personal value. Even as we go about our business, they are fading away. You really can't take any of it with you, and sometimes you can't even keep it while you're here. It's true that we all need material things for day-to-day living, but it is so easy to get caught up in the race of continually getting more and so be snared in a trap of discontentment.

When oil tycoon John D Rockefeller was once asked how much money he thought was enough, he answered, 'Just a little bit more.' This demonstrates that it doesn't matter where you are on the scale of wealth, it's so easy to think, 'If only my circumstances in life could be different.'

When we don't appreciate the life we have, we focus on what we don't have rather than what we do have. We want to have all the stuff everyone else has, and we usually pay dearly for this desire.

If we want to create wealth in our lives in order to be able to help other people, then I believe that is a legitimate reason to work hard and earn lots! To feather our own nest and to neglect the nest of our neighbour is incredibly selfish and damages us. We were born to help others and it's when we learn to share what we have that we tend to become less consumed with materialism and more consumed with helping and contributing to others.

To counter the consumer message, we need to focus on genuine contentment. This comes from love and acceptance and is arguably both the strongest human need and the strongest motivator. Unconditional love is a priceless gift no money can buy.

Our need for acceptance and affirmation by our friends and peers can drive us to do things that we know may hurt us and others. This is an issue that we all must face, as potential pain doesn't seem to stop many of us!

Following are some suggestions to help relieve the pressure of materialism and acceptance, if that is what is weighing you down.

1.   Before you buy, ask yourself: do I really need it?
2.   Consider: how many hours will I have to work to pay for it?
3.   Avoid unnecessary visits to shopping centres.
4.   Splurge consciously, not accidentally.
5.   Create a budget and resolve to get out of debt.

Escapism

Sometimes the need for approval also leads us to want to fabricate parts of our life in order to be accepted. We can tend to live like puppets of other people's opinions if we don't form our own. Negative peer pressure causes people to become like puppets, doing and saying what they think will make them acceptable, whether good or bad, the truth or lies.

People who are prone to succumb to peer pressure usually don't realise a good thing when they have it. They tend to go through life thinking that they don't need character development — just more stuff and more acceptance. This attitude focuses on everything but the real issue. These people become sucked in by so-called friends who promise the earth but only deliver pain.

Pinocchio's story reminds me of another story about a reckless, prodigal son. He was a young man who ran away from a good home where he was loved and decided to follow the course of 'if it feels good, do it' — which caused him to pay a high cost for low living. He eventually saw his mistake and returned home, where he was greeted with grace and forgiveness from his father.

Peer pressure can cause people to do ridiculous, careless and thoughtless things. Running away from home to escape from their problems falls into this category. A person's self-esteem and body image doesn't change by running away. They will only change and grow in a secure environment.

Facing your problems means coming clean with yourself and everyone around you. The truth will set you free. Telling lies always leads to more lies, and there is no way out of the cycle unless you stop. Remember the saying, 'Oh what a tangled web we weave when first we practise to deceive'! When we habitually lie, we become more trapped. A lifestyle of fabrication will do nothing to build your self-esteem; rather, it is guaranteed to destroy it.

I want to encourage you to replace some bad habits:
1. Replace consumerism with contentment.
2. Replace running away with facing your problems.
3. Replace lying with the truth.

Peer pressure can cause us to feel as though we need to be someone else and this negative road inevitably leads to a life of denial and lies. When you decide to be honest and to do what is right by your own conscience and right by your fellow 'man', you will find a positive momentum in your life which will fast-track you upwards. If, however, you decide to be dishonest and to continually transgress your conscience, you will find a negative momentum in your life which will fast-track you downwards. And you cannot fight this kind of gravity!

Remember, if you stand your ground and do what you know is right, you'll never regret it.

It can be hard to walk away from negative peer pressure, but it can be done. Paying attention to your own feelings and beliefs about what is right and wrong can help you determine the right thing to do. Having strong convictions in life helps you stand firm, walk away and resist doing something when you know better.

Insecurity

As social pressure influences you to do that which you don't want to do, insecurity influences you not to do that which you want to do. And insecurity is usually at the root of succumbing to peer pressure. Not being sure of who you are will cause you to want to gain security from what other people say about you.

Insecurity is something that we all face at some time in our lives. Broadly speaking, security is the state of being free from a sense of fear and doubt about who we are.

When we are seeking security, we are seeking a sense of our own value. We believe that our value depends on the work that we do, on our financial status, on our appearance, or on our relationships, but our value is more deeply based than any of this.

Here is a check list for you to see how you measure up.

Insecurity Check list
1. You think someone's not going to like you for no logical reason.
2. You act like someone you're not.
3. You wish you looked different.
4. Insecurity shows in your facial expressions.
5. You live an inward, introspective life, thinking about yourself and your problems.

Security Check list

1. You know who you are and where you're going.
2. You are not afraid to speak up for your convictions.
3. You are often a quiet achiever.
4. You understand that your value is based on who you are and not what people say you are.
5. You live an outward-focused life, caring for the needs of others as well as yourself.

Insecure people live with dreadful anxiety and paranoia about what everyone is thinking about them. What a way to live! Being yourself is much easier, more releasing and freeing.

Insecurity and the need for constant affirmation from others is a trap that will keep us living in an unreal world. We can all be guilty of distorting reality to try to create our own version of reality — one we think will meet our needs — and we sometimes look for people who will tell us what we want to hear.

Many people want to be cool and have the hottest body and the latest stuff to maintain their security. For example, many people have status symbol toys, the latest *everything*, but do they really need them? There's nothing wrong with owning 'things', it's just not healthy to desire to own things in order to establish your identity.

Insecurity is about gaining acceptability. You may feel like you've got to be a style leader, but at what cost, and how will you keep it up? There is a deep longing in each of us to belong and that's normal and understandable, but some people confuse this longing for wanting to be known or famous and they will go to any lengths to see that realised.

An unhealthy desire to be instantly known and accepted robs people of their security, identity, self-esteem and self worth.

In order to gain freedom from insecurity, you must focus on some important foundational keys:

1. Find your value internally, not externally.
2. Don't spend your life savings on things that are 'here today and gone tomorrow'.

3. Don't listen to the crowds around you who just tell you what you want to hear.
4. Find friends who will be honest with you.
5. Be honest with your friends.
6. Don't pretend to be someone you are not.
7. Walk confidently in who you really are.
8. Build balance into your life by improving your body, soul and spirit.
9. Don't be afraid to be transparent.
10. Trust the truth, as it will always set you free.

Confidence

Confidence is attractive and it is essential to a healthy self-esteem. We were all born with confidence, but sometimes life's happenings can knock it out of us. Confidence is often misunderstood. Let's take a look at what confidence is and what confidence is not, and how you can build it into your life, so that the real you can be expressed with a natural confidence and ease.

10 things that confidence is:
1. being sure of who you are
2. boldness
3. assurance
4. intimacy
5. openness
6. security
7. positive and accurate self-talk
8. friendliness
9. graciousness
10. purposefulness.

10 things that confidence is *not*:

1. trying to be someone else
2. arrogance
3. cockiness
4. self-absorbtion
5. self-promotion
6. insecurity
7. negative and inaccurate self-talk
8. attention seeking
9. boasting
10. hiding one's true self.

10 ways to build your confidence:

1. Acknowledge that you are highly valuable.
2. Don't let other people's opinions rule your life.
3. Forgive all the people who have hurt you, and forgive yourself.
4. Always choose with your future in mind. Don't make hasty decisions — think first.
5. Look in the mirror and don't cringe. Learn to accept and be happy with how you are made, and improve what you can without becoming obsessive.
6. Never settle for Mr OK or Ms Average.
7. Always listen to wise people who know better than you.
8. Don't isolate yourself from good friends when life gets tough.
9. Learn to say no, even when you are tempted to compromise.
10. Don't throw away your confidence, because it carries with it a great reward.

Leadership

I can't say that I am the 'easily led' type, but during my lifetime I have definitely done my fair share of leading others who were easily led. At school, most of it was positive, but some of it I am fairly ashamed of today. I was the ringleader and used to get not only myself but a number of my friends into mischief.

Being a leader is a real responsibility. If you are a genuine leader, people will be following you. Once you understand that all of us have people who are looking to us for cues in life, it's important to make sure that where we lead people will cause them to grow rather than fall into the traps and pitfalls of life. We should aim to become cultivators of positive peer pressure.

When we don't have all that we think we should have, we naturally want more. We may not want to be super-rich but we do want to be more comfortable. We become absorbed with getting what we don't have and this is when we need to turn our attention to being grateful for what we do have. There is great power in thankfulness. Take a look at what you do have and be grateful.

The Bible says in Timothy 6:6, 'But godliness with contentment is great gain.' Even godliness needs to have contentment joined to it for us to experience great gain.

I have learned that contentment is a priceless condition and sometimes a hard place to reach and maintain. Envy, that green-eyed monster, can subtly creep into our hearts if we allow it and it will destroy our self-esteem. (There's more on that subject in Chapter 10.)

I value the leadership that is part of my life and I choose to use that gift of leadership to help others develop a healthy self-esteem and identity.

Transparency

Being honest with yourself is essential if you want to live the happily ever after life. Being transparent is neither shameful nor weak. It is in fact a great strength. You need to have a healthy appreciation for who you really are in order to develop healthy, positive relationships. And you can only do this from a position of security.

Go ahead and be you and don't be afraid of the truth. Don't be afraid of constructive observation and criticism and let your image be based on the real you, not on what you think people want to see.

Trying to maintain an image, at any age, can be a real trap. There's nothing wrong with having a positive image, but trying or striving to maintain an image that is not true to who you are will inevitably show. Reputation or credibility is something that has to be built over time and it's based on not just what you do and what you look like, but on who you are.

Mariah Carey is a very beautiful and successful singer–songwriter, but her life has not been without its challenges. Even with all the success in the world, it doesn't matter when you can't see who you really are. She has battled and continues to battle the same insecurities as everyone else.

A *New Weekly* magazine article I read about Mariah discussed her being one of the most successful female singers of all time. Mariah has sold millions of albums and had fifteen number one hits (bettered only by Elvis and The Beatles). She's incredibly wealthy and is the only artist with a number one hit each year in the 1990s — thus was named the Artist of the Decade.

With all the money and fame in the world, even with her great achievements, it still hasn't brought her a sense of belonging or identity. Mariah's parents separated when she was very young and she grew up with little to survive on. Her childhood is more real to her than her fame and fortune. Although she knows she is very blessed, she still feels like the same insecure kid who lived in the worst house in the street, who didn't wear the right clothes or have any of the things other kids did.

Mariah's story goes to show that no matter how much you surround yourself or try to prop yourself up with 'stuff', you still need to decide to like and respect yourself, to truly be content and secure. When we like ourselves and when we are very comfortable with being ourselves, we won't be easily changed or led astray.

When we look at the people who are most respected by their peers, we will usually find people who are confident and who will

stand up for themselves and others and they generally appear to
have strong personal values. And when you value yourself, you are
able to value others in return.

In order for our self-esteem to develop well and flourish, we
have a responsibility to lead wisely and to follow only those who are
going to be a positive influence in our lives.

**Remember the Truth: confidence enables you to decide
for yourself.**

Value

*Life is not defined by what you have,
even when you have a lot.*

LUKE 12:15, THE BIBLE

The Paradox of Our Time in History

The paradox of our time in history is that …
We have taller buildings but shorter tempers,
Wider freeways, but narrower viewpoints.
We spend more, but have less. We buy more, but enjoy less.
We have bigger houses and smaller families,
More conveniences, but less time.
We have more degrees but less sense, more knowledge,
But less judgment, more experts, yet more problems,
More medicine, but less wellness.
We drink too much, smoke too much, spend too recklessly,
Laugh too little, drive too fast, get too angry,
Stay up too late, get up too tired, read too little,
Watch TV too much, and pray too seldom.
We have multiplied our possessions, but reduced our values.
We talk too much, love too seldom, and hate too often.
We've learned how to make a living, but not a life.
We've added years to life, not life to years.
We've been all the way to the moon and back,
But have trouble crossing the street to meet a new neighbour.
We conquered outer space but not inner space
We've done larger things, but not better things.
We've cleaned up the air, but polluted the soul.
We've conquered the atom, but not our prejudice.
We write more, but learn less. We plan more, but accomplish less.
We've learned to rush, but not to wait …
These are the days of two incomes but more divorce
Fancier houses, but broken homes.
These are days of quick trips, disposable nappies,
Throwaway morality, one night stands,
Overweight bodies and pills that do everything from cheer, to
    quiet, to kill.
It is a time where there is much in the showroom window
And nothing in the stockroom
Indeed, truly, these are the times.

BOB MOOREHEAD

Corinne's Story

I was born to a teenage outcast single mother, and I don't know my natural father. I was very independent from a young age, as I had to look after myself and my mother. You could say that I had a dysfunctional childhood. My mother married my stepfather when I was five, and then my sister was born.

Nothing was stable in my life and so my natural tendency was always towards order and overachieving. I was completely insecure.

I felt like I was the one who had to hold the house together and, at the same time, try to help my sister grow up.

I was constantly left alone at home on my own as a child. I was a typical latchkey kid. My whole life became full of fear and anxiety ... all before I had reached the age of seven. Then something happened that changed my life forever. After school I often visited my neighbours for company and it was during those visits that I was taken advantage of — I was repeatedly sexually abused by my neighbours over a period of three years.

In order to cope with the pain, trauma and confusion, I gave myself fully over in every dimension imaginable to superachieving. I had been a shy and insecure mouse of a child, and now I had grown up. By the time I was thirteen years old, I was doing it all — multiple relationships, alcohol and drugs. But it was hidden — the whole time I was overachieving so my parents and teachers thought I was the model child. I was anything but.

At the age of fifteen, I was raped by a stranger at a party. This time, any sense of self-worth that I had pretended to have was completely obliterated. From this time on, my internal life became psychotic. I was achieving straight A-level grades and overperforming in team sports, athletics, music and drama. I had 'achieved' as much as humanly possible, or so I thought. Everything I decided to do, I had to become the absolute number one best at. Needless to say, while I was achieving on the outside, I was completely dying on the inside.

I was always very angry and I continued to live in fear all the time. When it came to relationships, there were no boundaries. Anything went. While my parents and teachers thought I was an angel, my friends and party-pals knew I was crazy and out of control. I had to please everyone.

I did anything to gain approval from my peers and I did anything to numb the reality of the pain I lived with every day. For a time in my life it was as though I had no conscience at all. I had crossed the line too many times.

When I partied, I drank myself under the table and took drugs when and if they were available. My theory was 'feel less, do more'. I often tried to get high before I got to parties — just to make sure I was as numb as possible before doing whatever it took to please people. My aim was to always find someone to be with, at least one person (and hopefully more) in any given night. I enjoyed bragging on Monday morning about how many people I had been with, even though I hated what I'd done. This paradox had become my identity, and it was horrible.

If I had had more money, I would have spent it all; anything to build myself up and away from who I really was. I had tried to create an identity from a false sense of achievement and control because I had nothing else to base my identity on. All the time, at the core of my being I craved real acceptance and love, which I had never known.

Meanwhile, my sister was as bad as I was — I was just smarter. I knew how to live the lie. She continually got caught but I had everyone fooled, including myself. Spending and horrible boyfriends were her weaknesses. Anything to fill her pain and emptiness.

I had managed to disguise my behaviour and my rebellion from anyone I wanted behind a front of superachieving and people pleasing. I found myself convincing people that I really was a nice and good and honest person, even though I knew I was also a total ratbag. My split personality started to take a toll — the extremes of my life were tearing me in two. Although I was a victim of circumstance, I had (albeit unintentionally) milked that circumstance for all it was worth and now I had become a victim of my own doing.

A friend, this time a genuine friend, reached out to me through a letter. She was too scared to talk to me and I was grateful to be able to read her words, as I wouldn't have been prepared to listen to them. Her letter, which I can barely recall now, impacted on me in such a way that I have never been the same since. There was something in her letter that acted as a mirror to my life, which reflected all the pain I was in. I could see the real me, and I so wanted to change what I could see.

But wanting to change and changing are two different things, so I embarked on the journey. As with any journey there were highs and lows and it definitely wasn't always easy! Working through old ways of thinking, all the insecurities I'd lived with and redefining my identity ... it was all hard work, but so worth it to be able to live in the freedom and security on the other side.

Now my self-esteem is no longer based on what I have to hide or what I have to prove. I can live with peace and security instead of my old companions: anger and fear. All the 'bits' of me have been integrated into a whole person. Life has changed for me completely!

The daily challenges of being a thirty-something single woman are more of an adventure than a struggle. It's as though an invisible lid has been lifted off my potential and I am seeing my dreams come true. After being in Sydney for only six months I was offered what has become my dream job, and in the few short years since then, I find myself as a key lecturer, trainer and counsellor to hundreds of students.

I am now leading others on the journey into the freedom and confidence that I've found — it's a dream come true. Only a handful of years ago it looked impossible, but I am able now to say that the very things that happened in my life which were designed to cause a full stop, have now become a comma. My identity is now based on who I truly am and not what I have done.

10 Keys to Freedom

from people pleasing

Expect that applying some of these keys will shake up your relationships. Some may even crumble, but the true and worthwhile relationships will stand the test. It will take concentration and commitment to find the keyhole to unlock the truth — remember, FREEDOM is the goal.

1. Choose your friends wisely. Don't spend time with fools unless you are going to influence them positively. Remember that you can't buy love, friendship, genuine acceptance or happiness; if you relax and be YOU, you will find these.

2. Become a leader and start to set positive trends for others to follow. You are the leader of YOU.

3. Set and keep to a budget.

4. Don't lie or it will catch up with you eventually — what goes around comes around.

5. Always remain true to yourself.

6. Stand for something positive. If you do not stand for something, you will fall for anything.

7. Set standards and values for your own life. Know how you want to be and you will be less likely to become someone you don't want to be.

8. Stand up and speak up for what you believe in — do it feeling afraid if you have to.

9. Set standards and values for your own life.

10. When you honour and respect people they will respect you in return.

body soul spirit

ACTION PLAN

body

Make some decisions for yourself about how you spend your money and what you really need, regardless of pressure you may feel from others. Confidently and securely stand your ground and don't shrink or run away.

soul

Assess regularly whether you are truly living for what you believe in, rather than what everyone else wants for your life. Be committed to your soul flourishing.

spirit

Pray for the ability to discern the influences in your life and to establish what is healthy and unhealthy, and then pray for the strength to draw any necessary lines.

My goal is freedom
FROM PEOPLE PLEASING

Chapter 5

Mind Over Mashed Potatoes

freedom from eating disorders

'Like any addiction, the beginnings of an eating disorder start with a thought and that thought is usually a lie which, if entertained, becomes reality.'

Goldilocks

Once upon a time, three bears lived happily together in a house in the woods. One bear was naturally thin, one was naturally athletic, and the third was naturally curvaceous.

The three bears loved to eat. There was a small bowl for the slim bear, a medium-sized bowl for the medium-sized bear and a larger bowl for the curvy bear. Even though their bowls were different sizes, the three bears ate about the same amount of food.

One day, as they were waiting for their porridge to cool, they decided to take a walk in the woods. While they were away, a young woman called Goldilocks came across their house. Seeing no one home, she let herself in.

Goldilocks didn't like her life at all. She had a lovely figure, similar to that of the curvy bear, but she couldn't see that she was beautiful. She was troubled and had been starving herself for weeks, so now she couldn't resist the porridge that was steaming on the table. Goldilocks tried the first bowl but it was too hot, then she tried the next bowl, but it was too cold. The last bowl was just right, so she gobbled it up. But not being able to stop at just one bowl, Goldilocks devoured the other two bowls too.

Then she headed for the pantry, the refrigerator and then the freezer to see what other food she could find. She found plenty more including bread, cheese, chocolate and ice cream. She ate all of it, and still looked for more. Goldilocks was completely out of control. With so much food in her stomach Goldilocks felt ill, so she made herself throw up. Then she just wanted to lie down and sleep. Trapped in a downward spiral she felt guilty and ashamed, so she sobbed herself to sleep upstairs on one of the bears' beds.

After a while the three bears came home to eat their breakfast, but all they saw were three empty bowls.

'Somebody's been eating our porridge!' they exclaimed.

They began to look around the house. The curvy bear noticed that someone had been in the pantry, because all the food was gone. The athletic bear noticed that someone had been in the bathroom because the bathroom scales were left out.

Then the three bears went upstairs to look in the bedroom. *'There's someone in my bed!'* cried the thin bear.

It was Goldilocks, who awoke with a fright and tried to run away because she knew she had been caught. But the bears stopped her. They gently told Goldilocks not to be afraid and that she was welcome in their home, they wanted to help her.

Goldilocks told the bears how unhappy she was. She felt so sick and so ashamed. Wanting to help her, the kindly bears told her the truth and encouraged her not to hurt herself any more. The bears encouraged Goldilocks as they stood her in front of their mirror until she began to see the truth.

She knew that it would take some time for her to be completely well again, but this moment of revelation had made her really consider what she had been doing.

Day by day, Goldilocks learned to appreciate who she was, to feel better about herself and to begin to live happily ever after.

The End

Fact
Eating disorders can destroy your life.

Truth
Eating disorders can be overcome.

Mirror, mirror on the wall, why can't I stop eating more?

Eating disorders seem to be a socially acceptable way that we can hurt ourselves in the twenty-first century. Drugs, excessive alcohol, smoking — we all know these are unacceptable, but starving yourself or eating and throwing up seems to be acceptable because lots of people do it and most of them not only get away with it, they are sometimes celebrated for it.

When I think about the insidious nature of eating disorders, I get really mad. It all starts with a lie; a lie that says 'you can be in control if you do this', or 'no one will know', or 'you will be so beautiful if you do this'. These lies are all utter nonsense.

Like any addiction, the beginnings of an eating disorder start with a thought and that thought is usually a lie which, if entertained, becomes reality and then expresses itself in physical behaviour. That's why it's so important to challenge your thought processes so you don't just accept everything that you hear or that comes into your head.

Similarly and sadly, many people (especially young women) are driven either to starve themselves or compulsively eat against their own will. This is a result of a number of factors, such as personality type, family dynamics or background. Each of these things plays a significant part and people are affected to differing degrees. Regardless of the reason, our society is faced with a major health issue that has devastating effects, both physical and emotional, and can be fatal.

Many people can relate to not liking who they are or how they look and feeling as though no one understands them. We can sometimes tend to be controlling, yet completely out of control, and all we want is to be free. Every time we look in the mirror, our reflection is distorted in our own eyes and we go to great lengths to change our appearance to try to fit in.

Eating Disorders

The average starting age for females with eating disorders is approximately eleven years of age. Eating disorders are increasing in today's society and not just among teenage girls. The pressure that leads to a person developing an eating disorder doesn't discriminate according to gender or age. More and more women are developing eating disorders in their twenties, thirties, forties and beyond. The onset of anorexia, bulimia and compulsive eating can occur at any time in a person's life.

There are many reasons why eating disorders may develop later in one's life. With the high rate of divorce, many women find themselves back in the dating game in their forties and fifties. They may begin to believe that in order to find another man, they must be thin and look perfect.

Women are constantly being told that they must have a perfect marriage, be a perfect mother and have the perfect career. Women are given the message that in order to obtain all that, they must have the perfect body. Growing older in today's society is very different for women. If a man's body changes or his hair starts to turn grey, he is considered to be distinguished. But if a woman's body changes and her hair starts to turn grey, she is considered to be ageing, or letting herself go.

Eating disorders become a woman's way of escaping the daily pressures of life. We can no longer enjoy food or allow ourselves to provide our bodies with the nutrition it needs and deserves because society and the media make us feel guilty for eating.

Even though the reasons for the development of an eating disorder may vary, the self-perceptions are usually the same: self-hate, worthlessness and low self-esteem. Usually the person believes that thinness equals happiness. Some people may feel that their life is out of control and so they turn to the one area of their life that they feel they can control — their weight. Others may believe that once they attain the perfect body image, then their life will become ideal.

We can become prisoners of foods, the very thing that we try to deny ourselves in order to be thin is the same thing that we use to hurt ourselves. Self-inflicted pain isn't always intentional and a sense of failure continues to feed the disease. This is the roller-coaster of destruction those who suffer from eating disorders are desperate to get off.

In her book *The Monster Within*, Cynthia Rowland McClure describes her life of torment as she struggled with an eating disorder which she refers to in her book as her 'monster'. The book describes a conversation she had with herself about her destructive behaviour. She knew she was hurting herself but she couldn't seem to stop it. The monster of her own mind kept telling her how useless and worthless she was and that she wouldn't ever be able to stop.

The two main forms of eating disorders are anorexia nervosa and bulimia nervosa. Both of these illnesses have similar features, including a preoccupation with weight and food.

Anorexia is thought to affect one or two out of every hundred teenagers. It is twenty times more common in girls than boys. The affected person usually loses at least one-sixth of their body weight and sometimes much more. This happens because they refuse to eat enough food, despite feeling hungry.

A person suffering from anorexia usually has a false impression of their body size, believing that they are fat when others say this is clearly not true. They have an intense fear of becoming fat and may obsessively collect slimming guides, recipe books and other information about food and nutrition. They will often spend a lot of time preparing food for others to eat.

Bulimia usually occurs in slightly older people, from the late teens onwards, and is more common than anorexia nervosa. It is believed that up to one in six tertiary students may experience this problem.

Many people suffering from bulimia will have had previous episodes of anorexia.

People with bulimia go on regular eating 'binges' during which they consume large amounts of high-calorie food, usually in secret and much more rapidly than normal. During the binge they feel out of control and experience a loss of self-respect. To compensate, they make themselves vomit or use laxatives, enemas and diuretics or a combination of these methods to get rid of the weight they may have gained. They may also exercise obsessively. Often they are not underweight and so their problem is not as obvious as that of people with anorexia.

Several factors may be responsible for these illnesses. As talked about earlier in this book, the media and fashion industries tend to portray thin women as the most attractive and teenagers naturally listen to these messages. Other possible factors that can contribute include personal issues such as poor self-image, insecurity, abuse, family problems, the fight for independence and even the pressure to be a high achiever. There are also genetic factors such as chemical imbalance or hormonal changes which can be compounded by stress or trauma, accompanied by a lack of adequate coping skills.

Goldilocks

By applying a new twist to a well-known and loved fairy-tale, we see Goldilocks in a downward spiral, completely miserable with her life. In this adaptation, Goldilocks suffered from an eating disorder and her self-destructive behaviour caused her to live with unbearable guilt and shame.

Sneaky and secretive behaviour meant that she isolated herself and had no way of even being able to gauge the damage she was doing to herself. To support her destructive habits, Goldilocks stole from the three bears. She stole any food that she could get her hands on: porridge, bread, blocks of cheese, tubs of ice cream —

anything that would help feed the habit. And to punish herself for being such a 'bad girl', Goldilocks vomited until she nearly passed out — full of overwhelming discontentment.

Goldilocks's story is one that could be told in countless households around the world. Anorexia, bulimia and binge eating (which is like bulimia except that the person doesn't try to get rid of the food after eating) are disorders that have drained the lives of millions of young people and the incidence of these disorders continues to increase in epidemic proportions.

It wasn't until Goldilocks was brought in front of and faced the mirror of truth that she was able to find true freedom.

Cause and Effect

It is widely understood that teenagers are under a lot of pressure to succeed and fit in. Many spend a great deal of time worrying about what others think and desperately try to conform to an unattainable body image: if they look a certain way, they will be accepted. Since many teenagers regularly buy teen or fashion magazines and watch movies and television shows featuring underweight models and actors, this only reinforces their belief that in order to be happy, successful and accepted, they must be thin.

Research has shown that the family environment can also play a big role in the development of teenage eating disorders. Being part of a family in which emotional, physical or sexual abuse is taking place, a teenager (or any person) may develop an eating disorder to gain a sense of control, to block out painful feelings and emotions or as a way to punish themselves — especially if they blame themselves for the abuse.

Most people with eating disorders will try to avoid conflict at all costs, so they usually don't express negative feelings. Instead, they try to wear a happy face all the time to try to please people. They end up using food as a way to stuff down all those negative feelings and purging usually gives them a sense of relief, almost as if they are releasing the built-up emotions.

Some teenagers are raised in families that are suffocating or don't allow any independence, and they may develop an eating disorder as a way to gain an identity for themselves. While a family that is close and in which people can talk to each other about their problems is great, being too close is not healthy, as teenagers need to develop their own identity within their family.

Being raised in a home where the parents are very weight conscious could lead the teenager to believe that weight and appearance are very important. Many teenage girls learn to diet by watching their mothers. Instead of learning that it is what's on the inside of a person that matters, they learn that appearance and looking good is the most important part of being a woman.

Eating disorders can be very much about control, so if a person feels as though everything around them is out of control, they may develop an eating disorder to regain some sense of control. It is important for families to raise their teenagers to be proud of who they are and not place too much importance on their appearance.

Warning Warning

It wasn't until the 1980s that anorexia nervosa was recognised and diagnosed and since that time, its victims have grown in number and reduced in age.

On 4 February 1983, singer Karen Carpenter died at the age of thirty-two of heart failure caused by chronic anorexia nervosa. Karen's band The Carpenters was one of the most popular groups in history, selling nearly one hundred million records worldwide to date.

Karen had battled with anorexia nervosa for eight years after she was advised to lose a little weight. Six years into her battle she was treated by a psychiatrist, but the damage had apparently already been done. She remained obsessed and trapped by the disease.

Karen's case was extreme and she fought to overcome anorexia throughout the last two years of her life, but she just seemed to run out of time. Her body couldn't take any more. She had been starving herself for seven years using laxatives, drinking water with lemon, taking dozens of thyroid pills daily and even throwing up, and no amount of fame and fortune was enough to save her life.

There is no doubt that both anorexia and bulimia can have serious and even fatal consequences. Inadequate nutrition can cause problems with most parts of the body including kidney failure, muscle cramps and bladder and bowel problems. The recurrent vomiting of people with bulimia may damage the mouth, throat and stomach, and many girls with anorexia find that their periods stop and fine, downy hair may grow on all parts of their body.

Some specific medical problems associated with anorexia nervosa apart from the risk of death are:

▶ heart disease
▶ cholesterol levels
▶ reproductive and hormonal abnormalities
▶ retarded growth in children and adolescents
▶ low birth weights, frequent miscarriages, and birth defects
▶ osteoporosis and other bone loss issues
▶ blood problems, including anaemia
▶ gastrointestinal problems
▶ electrolyte imbalances
▶ bloating and constipation.

As well as physical problems, there may be marked personality changes including withdrawal from friendships, depression and mood swings. The chemical imbalances in the body may make clear thinking difficult, with obvious effects on work or study.

Some specific medical problems associated with bulimia include:
- teeth erosion, cavities and gum problems
- water retention, swelling and abdominal bloating
- loss of fluid
- low potassium levels, which can cause extreme weakness and near paralysis (this can be reversed when potassium is given). Dangerously low levels of potassium can result in lethal heart rhythms.

Help!

If you think you have an eating disorder, tell someone who can assist you in finding help. Do not feel that you are alone. There are people who love and care for you. Contact the eating disorder association in your city, or your local doctor, counsellor, community health centre or pastor. It is vital that if you have an eating disorder, you receive treatment from a qualified health professional.

Eating disorders can be treated and a healthy weight restored. The sooner these disorders are diagnosed and treated, the better the outcomes are likely to be. The first stage in accessing treatment is talking to a doctor. Most cases of anorexia nervosa or bulimia will require referral to a specialist, usually a psychiatrist or psychologist. Most treatments can be carried out as an outpatient, but sometimes it is necessary to go into hospital.

Treatment of anorexia calls for a specific program that involves three main phases:
1. restoring the weight lost
2. treating psychological disturbances such as distortion of body image, low self-esteem and interpersonal conflicts
3. achieving long-term rehabilitation or full recovery.

The primary goal of treatment for bulimia is to reduce or eliminate binge eating and purging behaviour by establishing a pattern of regular, non-binge meals. Attitudes relating to the eating disorder need to be challenged and improved, as well as encouraging healthy but not excessive exercise.

Drug treatments can sometimes be useful in bulimia, but are rarely enough to stop the disorder. Restoring a normal body weight is necessary but not the only thing that will cure the problem. Psychological and physical issues need to be addressed together and this may involve cognitive behavioural therapy or family therapy.

The treatment goals and strategies for binge-eating disorder are similar to those for bulimia.

It is important to realise that people with eating disorders often do not recognise or admit that they are ill. As a result, they may strongly resist getting or staying in treatment, or both. Trust is a big issue. Family members or other trusted individuals can be helpful in ensuring that the person with an eating disorder receives the necessary care and rehabilitation. For some people, treatment may be long term.

Perhaps you have a friend with an eating disorder and you feel you need to help. There is no easy solution. Sometimes any action you take may seem wrong. While it's important for you to be a valuable source of support for your friend, it is also important to encourage them to seek professional help, as eating disorders can have serious medical complications.

On first suspecting that your friend, relative or partner may have this illness, it is important not to alienate the person by reacting too strongly. However, even at this stage it is worth expressing your concern and your willingness to give emotional support. It is important for that person to know that there are people who can help.

Whatever you do, don't panic! Look around for the help you need and don't isolate yourself from those who can help or whom you may be able to help. Join a support group with your friend or relative. The purpose of a support group is to provide a confidential and safe environment where people can share experiences and draw strength from one another.

If you decide to deal with your friend's eating disorder, you should try to remain as understanding, open and compassionate as possible. Be informed about the condition by reading as many helpful books and journals as you can on the subject and when you approach your friend, make sure you do it in a confidential and relaxed setting.

Perhaps your friend is in denial and simply cannot or will not accept that she or he has a problem. They may have no motivation to change and they may see the problem as everyone else's and not their own. Try not to be too judgmental, and tell your friend you'll keep supporting them. Keep in touch even if it feels like they are pushing you away.

Perhaps your friend does accept the possibility that they may have a problem, but isn't ready to address it practically. They have accepted the need for change and treatment but are fearful of taking the next step.

You will know when your friend is ready for action because they have made a decision to get help and have an increased need for your support and the support of others. Taking practical action requires strength from both of you, as it often creates emotional turmoil when the reality of the situation hits home.

Once the eating disorder has been dealt with, maintenance of a new healthy lifestyle is the challenge. Change has taken place and now the challenge is relapse-prevention.

Whatever stage your family member or friend may be at, try to avoid confrontation and try not to overreact to whatever they say. Calm, confident strength is vital. Despite approaching the subject carefully, you may need to accept that your friend may not be ready to tackle the eating disorder. Please don't police or try to rescue them, as you will push your friend further away. Let them know they can come to you if they need help. Be present without being intrusive and help your friend to keep perspective when they're trying to win this war.

It's important that you try not to give too much advice. Be there to listen and encourage your friend to seek professional help but don't try to become a therapist or take responsibility for their problems. You can offer emotional support to your friend but they should also be seeking professional advice.

You may feel as though you simply want to tell your friend to eat more often, but eating disorders aren't just about eating. You need to help your friend take responsibility for themselves. Give them space to express their feelings about eating, but don't tell them what to eat. Avoid getting into major discussions about calories and fat. Instead lead by example, allowing them to see you follow a healthy diet without feeling guilty about what you eat.

If you're very worried about the physical or mental health of your friend, you may feel you need to tell someone. If so, tell your friend what you are going to do and why, and then be prepared for them to feel resentful but know that in the long run, you may be helping them.

Fear Factor

When I was a teenager, it was absolutely normal and acceptable to starve yourself for days or weeks in order to fit into a tiny pair of jeans. At least half the girls in my class used the same method of weight loss. What wasn't discussed or understood was the incredible damage that would be done to oneself physically and emotionally.

I was also very fearful of eating in front of people. I was on a summer camp when I was fourteen and didn't eat for two weeks. That's when I was nicknamed 'Anna' by some of the leaders who didn't know what to do with me. 'Anna-anorexic', they used to say. I don't really even know why I was so fearful and felt so much shame when it came to breakfast, lunch and dinner time. Whatever the reason, it was something that I had to deal with and over time, I have done so.

My metabolism suffered from then until I rectified it with healthy eating and exercise. My body was so used to starving and then eating that it went into starvation mode and used to store fat in order to cope with the famines I was causing. In my early twenties, when I stopped worrying about fitting into my tiny jeans, I piled weight on and so I had to retrain my body's metabolism in order to lose weight and keep it off.

Once I started eating properly and exercising, I won! My body was healthy and felt great and I started working as a model. I had finally worked out how to eat and still be in great shape.

The next time I stacked weight on (40 kilos) was when I was pregnant with my twin boys, and then again (38 kilos) when I was pregnant with my youngest daughter. Apart from pregnancy, I haven't had to worry about my weight like I did when I was a teenager because I've learned the secret of keeping in shape and I've shaken the power of incessant dieting. I am so glad to be able to live free!

Wise Up

The good news is that there are steps that we can take to help prevent the development of an eating disorder:

1. Examine the ways in which your beliefs, attitudes and behaviours about your own body and the bodies of others have been shaped.
2. Look closely at your dreams and goals. Do you overemphasise beauty and body shape?
3. Learn about the dangers of excessive dieting and exercising.
4. Commit to exercise for enjoyment and energy, rather than to just rid your body of excess fat.
5. Don't avoid swimming just because you don't like your body shape.
6. Don't wear clothes that you don't like or that don't fit you properly.
7. Absorb encouragement and reject criticism about how you look.

The good news is that a new start is available to each and every person who has an eating disorder. A correct view in the mirror and modification in behaviour needs to occur so that a new life of freedom and building and growing, rather than tearing down and destruction, can take over.

Food as a comforter must be replaced by authentic relationships and positive patterns of choice. Perhaps you feel that you may be an emotional eater. Here are some steps to freedom from turning to food for comfort:

1. Accept yourself.
2. Give up perfectionism.
3. Establish new boundaries.
4. Don't allow people to walk all over your feelings.
5. Find alternative means of coping.
6. Reward or comfort yourself in new ways.
7. Be open to intimate relationships you can trust.
8. Connect with people from the inside out.
9. Allow yourself to feel your feelings instead of trying to numb them with food.
10. Stop thinking about food and live in freedom!

The need to control everything will need to disappear. Behaviour modification (body) is a necessary beginning to the healing process. Renewing the mind (soul) is the next step and then healing the heart (spirit) is the last and final step. Taking all the necessary steps will see a holistic healing take place.

Remember the Truth: eating disorders can be overcome.

No Fear

For God did not give us a spirit of fear,
but a spirit of power, of love and of self-control.

2 TIMOTHY 1:7, THE BIBLE

Dana's Story

The first time anyone ever told me to lose weight was at ballet class; I was sixteen and weighed 44 kilograms. I felt totally worthless. I became obsessed with my body image and I was so competitive that the recommended weight loss of two kilos, which would make me look 'just fabulous' in a tutu, turned into a full-scale war between myself and my reflection. My eating was so controlled that my weight plummeted. I was impervious to criticism of my efforts. The minuscule size and weight that I attained got me pleasing smiles, competition money and entry into the national ballet school.

I promised myself I wasn't going to let anyone at my new ballet school know how much I struggled with my eating. I was just going to watch what I consumed and not talk about it.

It didn't work. This time I wasn't at home and had no emotional support around me. School was so tough; we would dance all day, surviving on very little to eat. Yet the feeling that I had to lose weight was constant — I weighed just 46 kilograms, but I still felt fat.

In every ballet class I would be thinking about not only how to improve my technique but also how I would feel when I was thinner. The entire wall in a ballet studio is one huge mirror, so it gave me and the other girls plenty of opportunity to pick faults and criticise our appearance. Teachers of course didn't help. I remember the time we were caught smoking and the surprising response we were given: 'Well girls, better smoking than eating'. Each day I left feeling sore, tired, disappointed and always hungry.

Over the next two years things got progressively worse. I was eating less and less and exercising more and more. The only thing I felt I *could* control was my weight and so that's what I did. Glandular fever set in when I was in my second year at the school and this helped me hit a microscopic 41 kilograms. I'd never felt thinner. I was so pleased that my clothes were loose, but not so pleased that I was too sick to dance. When I finally got a little strength back, I returned to school in a skeletal state and was the envy of my peers and the ideal specimen of a ballerina! I had hardly enough strength to walk up a set of stairs but I looked the part and that was all that mattered!

At the beginning of my final year I was small, mentally hazy from lack of nutrients, but I felt very much in control. I didn't mind giving up my alertness as long as I felt good when I was in front of a mirror. I spent gruelling hours in the studio but I was not well, physically or emotionally.

Towards the time of my graduation, puberty had fully arrived and my body rebelled, so I put on a little weight. Teachers felt it was their duty to remind me of my *heaviness*. I was 49 kilograms.

My mind was no longer up for the challenge and in what should have been the best time of my life, I was so depressed about my appearance that nothing else mattered — the opinions of others included. I didn't care what other people thought of my body, it was all about what I saw when I looked in the mirror and how trapped I felt. I hated my physical self so much that I wished I were dead.

Prior to graduation, I passed the auditions for an elite ballet company and yet rather than congratulate myself on what an incredible achievement I'd made, I berated myself for not being 'perfect' — an image that had been solidly ingrained in my mind. I stayed for a year in the company, then decided to stop dancing.

I had no idea how to function outside the tiny insular world I had come to call 'my life' but I stepped out of the ballet world and moved in with my best girlfriend, who was not a dancer. What a relief!

I began to eat, socialise and live properly for the first time in six years. I was having the time of my life on the outside — but it didn't stop me hating myself inside. I kept trying to move forward while defeating myself the whole way. There were so many jobs I wanted to do or audition for but my appearance was totally unsatisfactory as far as I was concerned. Why would anyone want me? I was so fat and ugly. What reinforced the issue for me was that I was having a common show business experience: I was auditioning for musicals and entertainment industry jobs, and missing out every time. The heartbreaking question was, 'But what if I'd been thinner?' This wasn't the reality but my mind kept asking.

I joined an agency and I didn't even have to try and yet I landed dancing jobs and commercials. Nothing, however, changed the way I saw myself. I used to get so annoyed with myself that I would hit myself HARD. This self-harming behaviour was totally upsetting to the man that I had begun dating, but it was uncontrollable. I really hated myself for not being perfect.

I stopped dancing but didn't stop hating myself. Over the next few years I struggled desperately with my self-esteem, believing that I was worthless. I became so paralysed by my dislike for my reflection that everyday life was a massive challenge.

Life finally started to turn around when I allowed myself to be challenged on the inside, rather than focusing solely on the outside of my life. I have found that the most important thing about overcoming an addiction, an eating disorder, or just a bad habit is learning to let it go. I learned that it is a process, but it had to start with the initial decision to let it go and not hold on to it like my life depended on it. To the contrary, my future life depended on me letting it go.

I believe a real breakthrough came when I started to teach classical ballet. One of my little girls told me she was fat. As a ballet teacher, my words have real power to harm or to heal in the lives of my students. I realised that the paralysis inside my own mind was from the power of words spoken over my life; all those years of being told I was 'fat' had completely distorted my own ability to view my reflection accurately.

I still don't view my reflection completely accurately — who does? I'm still learning to let go, eat well and not feel guilty. But I have come to a peaceful place about what I was blessed with in my body. I can honestly say that, as my desire for the 'perfect' reflection gets less and less, I am finding more and more joy in my life.

10 Keys to Freedom

from eating disorders

Professional help and support are important in dealing with eating disorders, but all of these keys will help you to deal with the internal and external triggers that can set off an unhealthy relationship with your body. Seek the truth: truth will always lead to FREEDOM.

1. Remember that food is nourishment for your body and should not be used as a weapon.
2. Starving yourself will eventually make you fat when you start eating properly again, so don't deprive your body of food.
3. Avoid diet pills and laxatives — they are addictive and can cause long-term health problems.
4. Exercise more and diet less.
5. Forgive those who have hurt you. Unforgiveness 'eats' you on the inside and will only make you feel like you need to do something *to* yourself to solve it.
6. Don't allow yourself to dwell on the past and on things you cannot change.
7. Don't punish yourself for what is not your fault. Even if it is, solve it and move on. Mature friends and mentors can be a great help with this.
8. Make yourself look in the mirror each day, and even if you don't like what you see *yet*, tell yourself that you are beautiful because that is the truth.
9. Wear clothes that suit your figure — shop with a friend.
10. Remember that you are the only one who can inflict self-destructive behaviour on you, so take control and don't do it — please!

body soul spirit

ACTION PLAN

body
Commit to not starve, commit to eat healthy food, commit to exercise regularly, and you will feel better about yourself.

soul
Take control of your thoughts and don't allow them to lead you into destructive behaviour. The fight for your freedom starts and ends in your heart and mind.

spirit
Pray daily, hourly, or as often as is necessary to help you stay in control of your eating habits.

My goal is freedom
FROM EATING DISORDERS

Chapter 6

Beware the
Big Bad Wolf

freedom from unhealthy relationships

*'Boundaries define us.
They define what is me and what is not me.'*

Little Red Riding Hood

Once upon a time, there was a young woman who lived in a village near the forest. Whenever she went out, the young woman wore a red riding cloak, so everyone in the village called her Little Red Riding Hood.

One morning, Little Red Riding Hood went to visit her grandmother. 'Remember, go straight to Grandma's house,' her mother cautioned. 'Don't dawdle along the way and please don't talk to strangers! The woods are dangerous.'

But when Little Red Riding Hood noticed some lovely flowers in the woods, she forgot her promise to her mother and she wandered off, not noticing that it was getting late. Suddenly, a young man dressed in a wolf suit appeared beside her.

'What are you doing out here, young lady?' the wolf asked in a devilishly charming voice, his smile revealing large white teeth.

'I'm on my way to see my Grandma, who lives through the forest, near the brook,' Little Red Riding Hood replied trustingly. Little Red Riding Hood had heard about the wolf and his wicked ways, but somehow when she met him she thought that he wasn't really all that bad. Perhaps, she thought, he was just misunderstood.

Then she realised how late she was and quickly excused herself, rushing down the path to her grandma's house. In the meantime, the wolf took a shortcut and arrived at Grandma's house ahead of Little Red, where he stealthily opened the front door and let himself in. He grabbed poor Grandma, gagged her and locked her in a cupboard!

Hurrying to trap his real prey, the wolf rummaged through Grandma's clothes to find a nightgown that would fit him. A few moments later, Red Riding Hood knocked on the door.

When Little Red Riding Hood entered the little cottage, she could barely recognise her grandma.

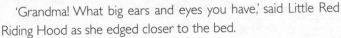

'Grandma! What big ears and eyes you have,' said Little Red Riding Hood as she edged closer to the bed.

'The better to hear and see you with, my dear,' replied the wolf.

'But Grandma! What big teeth you have,' said Little Red Riding Hood, her voice quivering slightly.

'The better to eat you with, my dear,' roared the not-so-innocent wolf and he leapt out of the bed and lunged at Little Red.

Almost too late, Little Red Riding Hood realised that the person in the bed was not her grandma, but the wolf. She ran across the room and through the door, shouting, 'Help! Wolf!' as loudly as she could. A woodsman who was chopping logs nearby heard her cry and ran towards the cottage as fast as he could. He grabbed the wolf and tied him up before rescuing Grandma, who was now rapping on the cupboard door.

'Oh Grandma, I was so scared!' sobbed Little Red Riding Hood. 'I'll never trust a wolf again!'

The woodsman took the wolf outside and carried him deep into the forest, where he wouldn't bother people any longer, and Little Red Riding Hood, her Grandma and mother were happy to never see him again.

The End

Fact
Falling in love is easy.

Truth
Staying in love requires commitment.

Mirror, mirror on the wall, why do I seem to pick them all?

Relationships! Who needs them? Well — we all do! Finding and maintaining meaningful relationships is an important factor in building healthy self-esteem into our lives. When our relationships are healthy, it's easy to feel a great sense of achievement and reward.

What is not easy, of course, is building healthy relationships. It takes commitment and work to produce healthy relationships and the first place we must start is with ourselves. We've often heard it said, or we may have even said it, 'What's a nice girl like her doing with a guy like him?'

A nice girl is with a guy like him perhaps because the nice girl doesn't have a sense of her own worth and value. She's living well below the level that she could be living at and it is more to do with her than the guy. The relationship exists as a result of her poor choice. This is why many nice girls choose guys like him, over and over again. A significant number of people do in fact seem to be attracted to the wrong kind of person for them.

You may feel as though you have a magnet on your forehead that attracts unhealthy relationships. Realising that fact is a great place to start. When you take personal responsibility and shift the blame from the guy to yourself, you are then empowered to break the cycle of unhealthy relationships and begin to assess how valuable you are and who should and can enter your private world.

When it comes to entering any relationship, no matter what happens, it is important to acknowledge that you have something to do with the relationship. It's called 'personal responsibility'.

Unhealthy Relationships

It is easy to get emotional and angry when we see our partner has different values, beliefs or expectations from us. What's important to understand is that there will always be differences in opinions, and how we handle these differences will determine the health of our relationships and how we feel about ourselves.

Some of the issues that have a negative impact on relationships are:

▶ lack of time spent together
▶ lack of communication
▶ lack of understanding of views
▶ different goals or expectations
▶ financial insecurity
▶ bringing up children
▶ inability to resolve conflict
▶ sexual difficulties
▶ different cultural backgrounds
▶ lack of trust
▶ alcohol or drug abuse
▶ affairs
▶ gambling
▶ violence.

Everyone who is in a relationship or cares about their relationships may need assistance at some time to help deal with problems and to learn how to improve them. We also need assistance when a relationship breaks down.

There is conflict in all relationships at times and that is important. Being able to deal with conflict and handle differences in opinion is crucial in building healthy relationships. We cannot eliminate conflict completely, but we can manage it constructively.

Little Red Riding Hood

In my version of *Little Red Riding Hood*, we see that the Big Bad Wolf was ready and waiting to take advantage of Little Red. But just as Little Red had something to do with the predicament she found herself in, we too have to take personal responsibility for our own relationships. For some, the Big Bad Wolf is you! For others, it is a person waiting to jump onto your vulnerability.

Whatever mess you find yourself in as a result of naivety or poor choices, wisdom and wise choices can see you through. When we look at *Little Red Riding Hood*, we see that innocent Little Red thought that she could trust the Big Bad Wolf. She felt sorry for him; after all, he had a bad reputation and she didn't think it was fair. She thought perhaps that she could help him become a better person.

In my version of the story of Little Red Riding Hood, the young woman forgot the promises she made to her mother about going straight to her grandma's house, because in her naivety she did not understand that the boundaries her mother tried to set would help to protect her from contact with the wolf.

Co-dependency

People who tend to be naive about relationships also tend to reflect aspects of co-dependency in their relationships. People who are co-dependent naturally care a lot for people and devote their lives to saving others who are in trouble. They usually try so hard to help and manage someone else's life to save them, but when they fail, their own life tends to fall into a crumpled heap of hopelessness because they lose control.

A co-dependent relationship is one where the partners have difficulty being themselves whilst being in the relationship. In any relationship, people tend to experience the battle between being themselves and being part of a relationship. In a healthy relationship, this can be dealt with openly; as a result, both partners can increasingly feel more secure in the relationship and more intimate as they grow as individuals.

In a co-dependent relationship, these issues are more difficult to deal with. Often they are simply swept under the rug or dealt with in an unhealthy atmosphere of accusations of selfishness, or one partner finds a way to intimidate the other. As a result, there is growing resentment within the relationship.

A co-dependent person may otherwise be known as a 'rescuer' or 'martyr' and they are usually attracted to people who need lots of help, such as alcoholics, drug users, sex addicts, the mentally or physically ill and, perhaps most insidiously, selfish, irresponsible or ambitious people who need someone to support them while they look after their own interests.

Unfortunately, people who have co-dependent personalities usually do not see their own problems, nor do they see the need to take responsibility for them. They are only able to recognise their efforts to help others and they wonder why they are not celebrated or rewarded for them. They simply do not see the choices they have made.

How do you know if you might have a co-dependent type personality? Read through the following check list to see how you rate, and try to be completely honest!

1.   Do you focus solely on wanting others to be happy?
2.   Do you feel responsible for your partner's life?
3.   Do you criticise yourself?
4.   Do you feel excessively guilty and full of shame?
5.   Are you an angry and nagging person?
6.   Do you threaten others?
7.   Do you deny your own problems and need for love?
8.   Do you believe that you can change your partner?
9.   Are you easily depressed?
10.   Do you find it hard to accept what happens to you?

Freedom from co-dependency is achievable. The goals are:
1. You will be able to think and talk about other things besides someone else's problems.
2. You won't feel the need to change other people's behaviour.
3. You will see your role as an encourager, rather than a rescuer.
4. You will know when it's time to get out before it's too late.
5. You will be able to implement tough love, which actually demonstrates the most caring, and has boundaries in place.

Once you understand co-dependency and begin to accept that you aren't responsible for another person's actions and that you can't control the situation and don't hold the cure for the situation, you can then stop supporting someone else's bad habits and get on with developing a healthy life of your own.

Boundaries

When you have identified the key issues and you properly understand your own personal value, it is time to establish some necessary boundaries to protect the health of the relationships in your life. It is vitally important that you don't settle for less than the best for you. This may mean that you have to kiss the harmful and destructive relationships goodbye.

It may be that you will need to detach yourself from the other person and take responsibility for managing only your own life, and in the process, try to be kind to yourself. Detachment or distance from another person does not involve rejecting the actual person, it is simply rejecting the feeling of complete responsibility for them. To become detached from another person requires us to understand who we are. Being able to detach involves having well-defined boundaries.

In their book *Boundaries*, Dr Henry Cloud and Dr John Townsend write:

Boundaries define us. They define what is me and what is not me. A boundary shows me where I end and someone else begins ... Knowing what I am to own and take responsibility for gives me freedom. If I know where my yard begins and ends, I am free to do with it what I like ... if I do not 'own' my life, my choices and options become very limited.

Sometimes we must make a choice that will require a severing of a relationship, if personal boundaries have been transgressed. Having clear boundaries is essential to a healthy, balanced lifestyle. A boundary is a personal property line that marks those things that we are responsible for. When we establish boundaries, we establish who we are and who we are not, where we want to go and where we do not want to go.

Relational naivety and deception can bring pain, and failure to establish adequate boundaries can leave a person feeling deceived, used, abused and afraid. An absence of boundaries allows us to be lulled into a false sense of security which in turn allows us to be led by our feelings and by flattery, which make us susceptible to the advances of someone who is setting out to take advantage of us.

That's where sexual boundaries are so important. Our self-esteem affects our attitudes towards sex. Our behaviour reflects our self-esteem and our self-esteem reflects in our behaviour. A great sex life is experienced when people have identifiable boundaries in place to protect not just their body, but also their soul and spirit.

In *Boundaries* Cloud and Townsend describe boundaries as 'anything that helps to differentiate you from someone else, or that show you where you begin and end'.

Problems will arise when we fail to set good boundaries and maintain them and also when we bond to the wrong kind of people and don't bond to the right kind of people. Outside of relationships, boundaries are easy to see. Fences, walls, signs, or hedges are all physical boundaries. Within relationships, boundaries impact all areas of our lives:

- Physical boundaries help us decide who may touch us and under what circumstances. It is your right to say yes or no.
- Mental boundaries give us the freedom to have our own thoughts and opinions. It's your right to have freedom of speech.
- Emotional boundaries help us to deal with our own emotions, and to deflect the negative and manipulative emotions of others. It's your right to maintain unhindered feelings.

The primary purpose of any wall is for protection. Walls are there to keep vulnerable and valuable things in and harmful things out. However, walls that are built because of fear or negative experiences can isolate and contain you.

Some people learn early on in life that it is unsafe to get too close to others, particularly when someone they love has hurt them. Once this defensive and self-protective belief is instilled, walls are built to protect that belief. The problem is that loneliness and isolation will become an unhealthy by-product.

Other people learn to believe early on in life that in order to be happy, they should have no boundaries at all. The problem with this extremity is that continual heartache and pain will become an unhealthy by-product of this kind of living.

Boundaries assist us to live in balance, providing that the boundaries that we have in place resemble a fence with a gate rather than a brick wall. The fence means that we can see over it and that we can't hide behind it, and the gate enables us to come and go freely and others to come and go as we choose. What you don't want to build into your life is either a brick wall that says 'keep out', or no fence at all that says 'everyone welcome'.

Conflict Management

When it comes to problems, we need to discover our role so that we can be empowered to make necessary changes. That's when we can either turn the situation around by our actions, or we might need to sever the relationship. When we can't see our role in the problem, we lose our power and potentially stay trapped indefinitely.

We've been taught that relationships should be fifty-fifty. In other words, 'You do your part, and I'll do mine.' I have learned, however, that in order to build healthy, strong relationships we need to at least aim to be one hundred–one hundred. The ideal is to aim for a hundred per cent, and even if we fall short, there should be enough juice in the relationship tank to compensate. If we only agree to do what is minimal, we can expect disaster. If we agree and try to give a hundred per cent, we can expect to flourish relationally.

I believe that every person is responsible for the presence or absence of love. In any relationship, each person is constantly reacting to the other and we tend to react according to how we are treated. When you are accepted and appreciated by someone, you usually feel loved and automatically accept and appreciate that person in return. But when you are judged or criticised, you become upset, judgmental and critical in return. When we *react* rather than *respond*, we are not taking responsibility for our own lives. If you are being mistreated, you are still able to respond constructively without becoming a doormat.

In his book *Love is Never Enough*, Dr Aaron T Beck analyses actual dialogue to draw attention to the most common problems experienced by couples, including the power of negative thinking, disillusionment, rigid rules and expectations, and miscommunication. When looking at the issue of miscommunication in conflict, Dr Beck says, 'Rather than seeing that there is a misunderstanding, conflicting partners misattribute the problem to the mate's "meanness" or "selfishness". Unaware that they are misreading their spouses, partners incorrectly ascribe base motives to them.'

We can all get it wrong when we try to second-guess each other's motives and feelings and it's usually just a matter of time before someone gets hurt and upset. We put up walls of protection and resist, attack or withdraw. Then our partner may become upset and do the exact same thing in return and then we become even more upset and react more fiercely, and so the cycle of conflict goes on.

The good news is that to create and maintain this cycle, there must be two people participating. Which means that if you refuse to attack or withdraw or react, then chances are the cycle will be broken and a fresh start can be made. Once you discover your role in the conflict, you can do something about it. You can end the cycle of conflict and restore the love. Conflict management is the practice of identifying and handling conflict in a sensible, fair and efficient manner through effective communicating, problem solving and negotiating.

We need to live on the right side of 'if'. Instead of saying to ourselves, 'If he apologises first, then I will apologise,' how about saying, 'If I apologise, then at least I will have peace of heart and mind.' Make the 'if' relate to your actions, not your partner's. Living on the right side of 'if' empowers us to live in freedom and to take responsibility for our own lives.

To handle conflict constructively, first you will need to make a decision that you will not attack your partner when you get angry. Decide that when there is a conflict between you, you will aim to resolve it as quickly and as constructively as possible.

When conflict arises and you feel angry with your partner, try to follow these steps:

1. Admit that you are angry. Try using 'I' statements to let your partner know how you are feeling, rather that 'You' statements, which will be heard as an attack and lead the other person to be defensive and therefore make the conflict even worse. However, admitting your anger is different from expressing it. Be strong, but don't shout and swear.

2. Ask for time out. This is essential if either you or your partner feels too angry to talk about the problem. Cooling down before discussing the issue is a good idea, but set a limit on it — don't use time out to avoid or ignore the issue indefinitely.

3. Check your feelings. There is nearly always another feeling underlying anger, like sadness, hurt or disappointment. Let your partner know how you feel. The underlying feeling will usually

be a clue to the real issue that you and your partner need to face up to and talk about.

4. Listen to your partner's point of view. There may be an angle on the situation that you haven't considered.

5. Be prepared to acknowledge your part in the problem. Being willing to apologise does not mean that you are accepting all the responsibility.

6. Ask yourself what you can learn from the conflict. This will improve your relationship and lessen the chances of a similar conflict happening again.

7. Be prepared to forgive and make up as soon as possible. Don't make your partner wait as a punishment. Reunion after conflict can lead to a deepening of closeness and intimacy in the relationship.

Although difficulties in any relationship are normal, many relationships do survive such challenges, but healthy relationships are only built with commitment and effort. We can choose to just survive, or we can choose to thrive. It's the difference between existing and living, and it's our choice.

Mr Wrong

At the age of sixteen I had my first 'real' boyfriend. I thought he was the man of my dreams but he turned out to be anything but. I chose not to listen to my parents and he hurt my feelings terribly, and I didn't see it coming.

It seemed that everything I was taught as a child didn't relate to my life as a young woman. My parents hadn't brought me up to be hurt and discarded, they had brought me up in a home of love and respect, but I chose to throw it all away for what I thought was love.

What I shared with this guy was not love. He harassed me constantly about being too fat, even when I was so thin I looked unwell. He often referred to my size and commented whenever I tried to eat anything. So, I wouldn't eat anything. He also reminded me constantly that he wished I was blonde, but I couldn't be thinner or blonde, it just wasn't me.

I eventually saw a glimpse of the future — of what my life should be like, could be like, would be like, if I could only be strong enough to walk away. And that's exactly what I did after years of hanging on. Once I freed myself from this damaging relationship, I could hold my chin up and start feeling remotely human again.

Building Blocks

Acknowledging the existence of an unhealthy relationship is the first step to either restoring or ending it. Taking an inventory of the relationship and identifying the problem areas is the second step, and you may need professional assistance to do this properly.

For some people, the word 'relationship' means security, happiness and peace, and for others it simply means shattered dreams and hell on earth.

Relationships come in all shapes and sizes, and every relationship is unique. The variations are seemingly infinite. If life were easy and predictable, here is how the perfect relationship might go:

- You are on your own and feeling all right with yourself.
- You meet someone you would like to get to know better.
- The two of you decide to go out together.
- You both have a really good time on your first date, when you discover what you have in common.
- You go out again and your friendship and relationship grows.
- After going out together several times you both realise you have found someone special.
- You fall in love and continue to go out regularly.
- You decide to get married.
- You plan the wedding together and await the big day.
- You get married.

❱ You have 2.3 children.
❱ You live happily ever after.

As you probably realise, life is rarely easy or predictable, so it doesn't always work out according to this list. There are lots of reasons why things don't work out this way very often and that is because relationships and people can be very different. Not everyone wants the same type of relationship, nor do they want the same type of person. This sounds obvious, but I think we don't really accept it when the person we love is the one who is not agreeing with us. This conflict within a relationship is not exclusive to those people who don't have it all together — it can happen to the 'I've got it all together' people too. When partners view the relationship differently, it can cause endless inner turmoil and will be a key ingredient in an unhealthy relationship.

The good news is that even if you are in the midst of an unhealthy relationship, within every gram of pain lies a tonne of potential. But this requires action and effort. For every bad choice, a good choice needs to be made. The past needs to be left behind and the future needs to be focused on. Life is full of choices. We are all born with a will, and with that will, we make a way for ourselves. We determine our way, the way in which we lead our lives, by our own choices. Choose to live and love.

As the saying goes, 'You need to be cruel to be kind.' Sometimes you just need to be what may seem cruel to that which is hurting you, and kind to yourself. In order to be truly kind to yourself, you need to cut off destructive relationships, even though it seems like the hardest thing you could do.

It is the only way to free yourself up for your future because at the end of the day, freedom is what you crave and what you need. You deserve to be in a relationship that is totally healthy, totally committed, yet totally free.

For those in destructive relationships, inside the depth of your pain lies the heart of your potential. The potential to rise up and out of a situation you were never created to be in. Whether your pain is your fault or someone else's fault, it's within your power, through your will and your choice, to do something positive about it.

Here are some practical building blocks to help you flourish regardless of your past:

1. Acknowledge that you are valuable.
2. Don't receive criticism and abuse.
3. Think carefully about whom you choose to start a relationship with.
4. Clearly communicate your wishes and respect the wishes of others.
5. Remember that you have the right to start again.

Many people unfortunately go looking for love in all the wrong places. This is all too common a problem. Boy meets girl, boy dumps girl, girl never gets over it!

Life may knock you down to the ground and knock the stuffing out of you, but it's never too late to get back up again. Good people get hurt and age has nothing to do with it. Relationship breakdown can happen at any time.

If you have made unwise decisions that have landed you in trouble, now is the time to do something positive with your future. Don't drag your pain into your future. The past is the past. You can't change it, no one can. Even if you are a victim of someone else's rotten behaviour towards you, you can use it to empower your future. See their behaviour as a lesson in what not to do, rise above the pain they inflicted on you by choosing to love and forgive, and this will make you stronger and in charge of your life. No matter what you've been through, remember, you are not a 'has been', you are a 'will be'!

Determining what a healthy relationship should look like is a great place to start. A healthy relationship is based on respect, when you can have fun together, when you both feel like you can be yourselves, when you can have different opinions and interests and when you listen to each other. Trust is another important factor, as is an absence of jealousy. Then of course there's compromise and the ability to apologise and talk arguments out. Breathing space is also crucial. You don't have to spend all of your spare time together — you can spend time on your own, or with your own friends and family.

Following is a healthy relationship check list for you to see how you measure up:

1. You can both manage conflict and differences without despair or threats.
2. You both protect and nourish the relationship and make it a priority.
3. You both know how to be responsible for your own needs and also for the care of the relationship.
4. You both feel 'special' to the other. Arguments or fights do not lead to abuse or threats.
5. You both communicate wants, needs, feelings and emotional issues with little or no shame.
6. There is unconditional love.
7. The relationship feels and is nurturing, comfortable and fun.
8. You respect each other physically.
9. Both partners are honest.
10. There is no abuse — physical, verbal or emotional.

For a relationship to be healthy and for you to feel good about yourself, be the one to show goodwill by offering to make it work — don't wait for your partner. You may be pleasantly surprised by how much difference taking the first small step can make. Start with you.

Be supportive and don't make judgments when your partner makes mistakes or does things differently from how you would do them. Ask for help when you cannot cope with a situation. Share the domestic load, offering to do what you like to do most, but being prepared to do whatever it takes for the job to be done. Allow yourself the right to put your feet up and relax and make time specifically for you — have a bath, read, listen to music, spend time with friends.

When you are able to express your feelings honestly and show appreciation to your partner for their contribution, when you listen to others and take responsibility for your own life, then you will begin to see healthy relationships develop and flourish in the future.

If you say 'I love him', ask yourself the reasons why. Is he kind, considerate, caring? Is it real love or infatuation? Is it possible that what you think is love, is anything but? Only real love will last and it is not an illusion. Look for someone with the qualities that you respect and admire. Being attracted to someone is important initially, but doesn't mean you will stay attracted to them forever. Wise up and beware the unhealthy relationship traps.

'First-mile love' is primarily about chemistry and feelings, but 'second-mile love' is more about construction, choice and commitment. On that note, I'll leave you with these words from Louis de Bernières's novel *Captain Corelli's Mandolin*: 'Love itself is what is left over when being in love has burned away, and this is both an art and a fortunate accident.'

Remember the Truth: real love takes commitment.

Love

Love is patient, love is kind.
It does not envy, it does not boast, it is not proud.
It is not rude, it is not self-seeking, it is not easily angered,
it keeps no record of wrongs.
Love does not delight in evil but rejoices with the truth.
It always protects, always trusts, always hopes, always
perseveres.
Love never fails.

1 Corinthians 13:4–8, The Bible

Vanessa's Story

Around the age of twenty I would have described myself as fun-loving, full of life, an extrovert who loved people and enjoyed laughing — loudly!

One of my favourite pastimes was nightclubbing. I loved dancing and flirting. One night out, a distinguished-looking gentlemen approached me and took my flirting as a sign that I fancied him. He drove an expensive sports car that gave him extra sex appeal. We dated for a few months. I found him gentle, a little reserved, polite and a man in the true sense of the word.

We continued to fall more in love and one evening he asked if I would consider leaving my friends and family and the small town in which I lived, to live with him in the city.

I had never experienced life away from home before but the bright lights, fun, excitement, nightclubs and casinos seemed to be what I was born for.

My friends and family didn't share my enthusiasm, but within weeks I moved into rented accommodation with my spunky partner.

For my birthday, he bought me an expensive sports car of my own. He told me that we had enough finance to last us for a number of years, so we didn't have to work — we could just enjoy life instead.

My life very quickly took on a routine that revolved around nightclubs and casinos. We partied most evenings and stayed in casinos until closing time at 4 a.m. Within a short period I found myself totally addicted to roulette. I loved the atmosphere of being in the casino, gambling big money, winning vast amounts but then losing everything. It was an incredible thrill.

My new friends included a diversity of personalities. They were very exciting to be around — thieves, ex-prisoners, prostitutes and Hell's Angels.

However, despite my boyfriend's assurances of financial security, eventually we did run out of money. We quickly sold one of the sports cars, which gave us the income to continue visiting the roulette table. But soon even that had vanished. After both cars had been sold, we were broke.

I was then faced with a decision that would change my life forever: either return to the common workplace, or join our friends' initiatives of quick, easy money. With not too much persuasion, I chose the latter and embarked upon a very lucrative job — delivering guns. Soon we once again had enough money to visit the roulette table.

I remember one night when I was sitting at the roulette table, having had a massive fight with my boyfriend. He'd hit me so hard that I had a very painful split lip. I was trapped in this abusive relationship and I was addicted to gambling. My life felt dark and controlled. My heart was in pain and I felt very alone. My self-esteem was below the ground.

My controlling boyfriend devised another plan to bring in some quick money. He spoke about it all the time and made it sound very exciting. He slowly but surely wore me down into thinking that his idea was brilliant. I concluded that I really didn't have much of a choice anyway — if I didn't go along with it and I tried to leave him, he would kill me. So with no real fight left in me, I reluctantly agreed.

The next two and a half years of my life were the most destructive time I have ever experienced — I became a prostitute. I began by visiting businessmen in hotels, then married men with children in their home, and ended up accompanying men in cars for a perverse sexual encounter.

I was no longer the girl at home, innocent and naive, full of life, happiness and laughter. Instead I was dark, hateful, lonely, in incredible pain and had no desire to live.

One night a friend invited me to a businessmen's dinner; she said we should go because the food was free. The dinner was held in a posh hotel so we intended to have a great time. In between the main course and dessert, a guest speaker took the stage. He was a businessman and he spoke about his success in business and his life, which had not always been as good as it now was. I decided to speak to him after the meal. He had changed his life and I wanted to change mine.

This man told me that he had taken a good look at his life and realised that he was not where he wanted to be. The dreams he had when he was younger were far away and he wanted to have his dream back. The man, whose name I don't even know, told me that he began to make decisions based on the future he wanted and not the situation he was in, and his life turned around.

A life of prostitution and gambling had never been in my dreams. When I was younger I dreamt of a great career, a husband and children. That night, instead of going back to the casino to meet my boyfriend, I went home. In the morning my boyfriend said that he had to go out and wouldn't be back until late that afternoon. This was very unusual and I knew I had a chance to escape, so I quickly packed my bags and left. I rang my stepdad and he drove three and a half hours to come and pick me up.

At home I spent six months with my mum and stepdad. It took six months for me to process all I had been through and I rarely came out of my room. My weight dropped to 54 kilograms and my parents didn't know what to do. They just assured me that I could stay as long as I wanted and that they loved me.

For that six months, I sat in my room at night and thought through the stuff I'd done, painful stuff. It was as though I had walked down a path that I shouldn't have gone down. Some do that and they don't ever return, but I had an opportunity to say, 'no, I want to come back.' So that six months I kind of walked all the way back, seeing signposts along the way that said 'forgive yourself' and 'forgive that person', so that way I let it go. Now even though I remember everything, the pain is not there and I am a successful woman with a great future.

The life I have now is absolute proof that it's never too late to turn around.

I met and married the man of my dreams and together we plan to use our experience to help others find the truth of their value and signficance.

10 Keys to Freedom

from unhealthy relationships

Forgiveness can be one of the hardest keys to freedom (see Chapter 9 for concrete suggestions on how to forgive). The following keys are to help you remember that when you find yourself in, or heading towards, a relationship that is unhealthy, you can get FREE!

1. Forgive everyone who's hurt you in a relationship. This may take time, but commitment to the process will set you free.
2. Throw away things that remind you of pain in your past relationships.
3. Don't call or harass a former partner, as it will only damage your self-esteem even further.
4. See yourself as valuable and choose your relationships accordingly — the Prince/Princess is so much better than the Beast.
5. Don't make the same mistake twice — solving a problem fixes a problem, not repeating it.
6. Walk away from an abusive relationship and get help from family or friends.
7. Lift your future standards higher than your past experience. Just because you have had ogres in the past, doesn't mean that is all you deserve to have.
8. Don't replace one dependency for another, such as relationships for drugs or alcohol.
9. Don't allow yourself to be pressured into sex.
10. Do dare to believe that you are someone special, on this earth for something special.

body soul spirit

ACTION PLAN

body
Never allow anyone to violate you physically. Ensure the necessary boundaries are in place so you don't get yourself into a situation where you feel pressured.

soul
Release yourself from people who have hurt you in relationships, forgive quickly and learn to get on with the future without bringing up the past.

spirit
Pray for the right life partner for you and the ability and strength to stay in love, well after the initial phase is over.

My goal is freedom
FROM UNHEALTHY RELATIONSHIPS

Chapter 7

Beneath Skin Deep

freedom from physical and mental challenges

*'We are scarred by operations,
by accidents, by war — by life …
Who turned our bravery into shame?
Who told us scars are ugly?'*

Beauty and the Beast

Once upon a time a hard-working man fell on difficult times. His spoilt children didn't like going without, except for his youngest daughter, Beauty. She was willing and kind hearted.

Thankful for her unselfishness, Beauty's father decided to bring her a beautiful red rose. But while searching for the perfect bloom, he became lost in a blizzard. For hours he stumbled through the freezing forest until he found what seemed to be an old abandoned castle, where he took shelter. As he was leaving, he remembered the rose for Beauty. There were many beautiful red roses in the castle garden, so he picked one. Suddenly there was a loud noise and a man in a dark mask stood in his path.

'I did not,' the angry man roared, 'give you the freedom of my castle! How dare you steal from me. I have a mind to kill you right now!'

Beauty's father begged for mercy and explained who the rose was intended for.

The masked man growled menacingly and said, 'Your life will be saved if Beauty lives here with me. Go and bring her to me!'

Beauty's father left with a heavy heart. When he arrived home, Beauty learned of his experience with the masked man and insisted on going to the castle. When she and her father arrived, the masked man greeted them but Beauty was barely able look at him, not because of his mask, but because of his frightful manner. With many tears, Beauty kissed her father goodbye. Thus began Beauty's life in the castle. Each day she wandered through the many rooms and gardens, but met no one.

Beauty had always shown kindness towards people and she made an effort to befriend the masked man. He was her only hope for a friend and her affection for him began to grow. He earnt his name, 'Beast', because of his frightful temper, but

Beauty discovered the masked man was actually kind and generous. One day he told her about a terrible accident which had caused his face to be disfigured, and she began to understand him. The more she came to know him, the more lovely he became in her sight. But she still missed her family.

The next evening, Beauty decided to ask if she could see her family just once more. The masked man wept, but he loved Beauty so much that he could deny her nothing. He sent her home with four chests of precious jewels, instructing her that she must return to him within two months, otherwise he would die.

When Beauty arrived home she fell into her father's embrace, overwhelmed to be home at last. Two months passed and Beauty remembered that the masked man would die if she didn't return. Immediately she dashed back to the castle. There she found him, lying in the grounds, nearly dead.

'Please wake up! Please don't die! I love you.'

His heart began to beat as her very presence revived him.

'Beauty, have you come back to me?'

Removing his mask, Beauty replied, 'Yes, I love you!' Her heart overflowed with love as she saw beyond his mask and his scars and into his heart. Beauty and the masked man married and enjoyed a lifetime of true love, and they both lived happily ever after.

The End

Fact

Having a special need will require an ability to overcome
extra challenges.

Truth

People who have a special need can have as many joys and
achievements as everybody else and be as beautiful as everyone
else.

Mirror, mirror on the wall, why am I so different from them all?

This chapter is dedicated to some very courageous people
whom I consider champions of self-esteem. These people have
more reason than most to feel not so great about themselves, but
they often surface with a healthier self-esteem and a more secure
identity than many other people who have fewer challenges to
overcome. There is much that we can learn about ourselves from
taking a look at their lives. These people have had to learn how to
live with the challenges of having a disfigurement or special needs,
and with being judged on being different or on what they cannot do
rather than what they can do.

There is no doubt that people who live with disfigurement or
special needs have every opportunity to achieve as much and
sometimes more in life, than those who have few struggles to
overcome. Super-achieving is not unknown territory for these
people who choose to overcome. If someone says 'you can't' then
these tenacious heroes say 'yes I can'.

This type of courage is a wonderful role model to people who
don't have great self-esteem because it is based on overcoming
challenges. I find the lives of others who may be disadvantaged to
be an inspirational mirror, reflecting all that's both good and bad in
life.

The aim of this chapter is to help us focus on seeing beneath
skin-deep, to help you if you have special needs, to see beyond
physical or mental limitations, regardless of whether you were born

with a certain condition or found yourself disabled or disfigured later in life.

Special Needs

Having special needs basically means that a person is not able to do something that other people of their age and community can do, because of a physical or mental condition. It can affect every area of life: social, physical, emotional, mental and spiritual. It can mean extra challenges and sometimes difficulties to overcome, but people who have special needs can also have as many joys and achievements as other people.

Many pictures may enter our mind when we think of the term 'special needs'. We may see the symbol of the stick figure in the wheelchair that shows where people with special needs can have access, or we may see a person with cerebral palsy, or perhaps a blind person with a guide dog. All these pictures do define special needs to a degree, but there are many more people affected by special needs than sometimes meets an able eye.

A special need can mean a number of different things:

▶ an intellectual disability
▶ a neurological or learning disability
▶ a physical disfigurement
▶ a physical disability
▶ the presence in the body of a disease-causing organism (such as HIV)
▶ a psychiatric disability
▶ a sensory disability.

Disability is a loss of physical or mental function, for example, a person who has quadriplegia, a brain injury, epilepsy or a vision or hearing impairment. It also means loss of part of the body, such as in the case of amputation. Then there is malfunction, malformation or disfigurement of a part of a person's body which may be caused by diabetes, asthma, birthmarks or scars.

A person who may learn differently from other people, such as a person suffering from dyslexia, has a disability. Any condition that affects a person's thought process, understanding of reality, emotions or judgment, or which results in disturbed behaviour, for example mental illness, depression, neurosis or personality disorder, is a disability.

We now refer to these as 'special needs' as it more correctly defines them. People with these attributes are not disabled, meaning 'unable', they merely have special requirements in order to achieve what some of us find easier. They are not unable to achieve — they just take another pathway to achieving.

There are obviously particular challenges that people with special needs face in their social lives. They may find it particularly hard to have high self-esteem and to feel good about themselves. This is where good friendships help. Friendships should be a source of emotional support and good friendships should be enriching, involve a sharing of common interests, and be fun. Basically, friends should make life more enjoyable. Good friends are vital and can definitely help with having a healthy self-esteem.

The journey to discovering their value can be long and painful for people with physical needs, and there are several reasons for this. People who are diagnosed as 'special' at birth or early in childhood may have parents who expected that they would be 'normal' and independent in their adult lives and so their rejection can be a significant hindrance to a healthy self-esteem. Parents of special needs children could also be overprotective and thus encourage the child to become co-dependent. These attitudes and behaviours do not help a child with special needs to build a healthy and strong self-esteem and sense of identity.

For people who find themselves with special needs in adulthood, it is often the realisation of their worst nightmare. We all grow up with the stereotype that people with special needs are a burden to their families, they are different and life is just so awkward for them.

We have sat on the other side of the fence and when suddenly you are thrust into the arena of special needs, all those stereotypes come back to haunt you and you may eventually accept them as your reality. Our self-esteem needs to be shaped by our value as people, and not by any special need that we may be living with.

If you have a special need, you may have experienced some of the following things and they may have damaged your self-esteem:

▶ being constantly put down or humiliated at home, work, school or anywhere
▶ being expected to take the blame for things that are not your fault or are out of your control
▶ not having your emotional, social or physical needs met
▶ being abused in some way, for example, physical or emotional abuse
▶ being harassed or discriminated against because of the way you look, walk or talk
▶ being labelled by other people as disabled
▶ being subjected to strong messages from the media or the community about what you are expected to be like.

Living in a culture that gives an unrealistic definition of what is 'perfect' and then expects us to strive towards that perfection, can definitely cause you to question whether or not you fit in, and in turn can affect how you feel about yourself. Definitions are important, but labels are very bad when they are misused, and they are misused in a variety of ways.

Schools can sometimes segregate children with similar special needs in one setting, and adults with special needs are frequently set apart in group homes, sheltered workshops and other settings. This in itself is not necessarily a bad thing, but the reason behind it can be. If these people are being segregated for the purpose of giving them better help and support (although one would assume that they would not be permanently removed from mainstream schooling or society) then this is fine. If, however, the reason is to keep them 'out of the way' and nothing is done to meet their special needs, then it is not good.

In defining a person's special need, it's vitally important that we don't use labels that may dehumanise or devalue or rob dignity from an individual, making the physical or mental condition the focus of their life, rather than the person themselves. If we look beyond our own personal experiences and environments, we'll understand there is not a 'one-size-fits-all' definition of special needs.

Beauty and the Beast

In my version of the story *Beauty and the Beast*, we read that the man regarded as the Beast gained this name not only because of his looks but because of his temper. The Beast had learned to live with his disfigurement hidden behind a mask. He lived marginalised and alienated by others, and he was terribly unhappy. When people are disfigured, some people have difficulty seeing past their outward appearance. This in turn causes people who have already suffered enough to have to put up with people's reaction of revulsion and fear.

Beauty, on the other hand, was beautiful not just because of the way she looked, but because of her kind heart and her willingness to accept and embrace the Beast exactly as he was.

Life isn't simple or perfect. It sometimes throws us curve balls and we need to learn to deal with them. We spend so much energy trying to dodge the curve balls, maybe we should teach ourselves to catch them! That's what I believe people with special needs often do: they don't dodge the curve balls — they learn to catch them.

True Champions

One of Australia's most famous Olympic champions is Louise Sauvage. Louise is a champion in every sense of the word. Louise was born a champion! In her autobiography, Louise says, 'I never thought of myself as being different, or disadvantaged. I'm just me — the way I am. The circumstances of my life put me in a wheelchair, but it has been my own efforts that have taken me around the world, and to the successes I have had.'

Thank God that in the twenty-first century, people like Louise can achieve and succeed just like everyone else. Generations ago, this wasn't the story.

Joseph Merrick, otherwise known as the Elephant Man, was born in England in 1862. Joseph first began to develop tumours on his face before his second birthday. His physical condition worsened as bulbous, cauliflower-like growths developed on his head and body, and his right hand and forearm became a useless club.

Even so, Joseph had a wonderful imagination. Unfortunately, for much of his life his imagination was all he did have. Even though he was highly intelligent (and self-educated), he was never accepted socially because of his appearance. He had to rely mostly upon his imagination.

It was said of Joseph in a letter to *The Times* newspaper in December 1886, 'Women and nervous persons fly in terror from the sight of him, and ... he is debarred from seeking to earn a livelihood in any ordinary way, yet he is superior in intelligence, can read and write, is quiet, gentle, not to say even refined in his mind.'

Later in life, Joseph was unable to get a job; he lived destitute and stripped of all his self worth by the ignorance of the people of the day. He was prepared to take any job that would offer him a living. As a last resort he took a job as a sideshow 'freak'. He died having never known the freedom of life as we know it. He was a prisoner within his disability, because of the ignorance of people who did not know what to do with him.

Seeing the movie *The Elephant Man* as a teenager had a profound impact on me — I have never been the same since. I view all people, regardless of what their physical or mental condition is, as equal — I may be different, but I am not worth less than anyone else. I believe that *The Elephant Man* taught me a lesson in life that I couldn't possibly have learned without hearing this wonderful and courageous story.

Other stories have had a similar impact on me. I have great memories of my kindergarten school days, when I made my first friends. One of them was a boy named Mark and he was very special. Mark was born with no legs and only half an arm but he was a champion soccer player and one of the most popular kids at school. He lived like a champion and inspired everyone around him.

Brett is another wonderful person whom I have had the privilege of getting to know. Brett has cerebral palsy but he is by no means unable to live a wonderful and fulfilled life. When I first met Brett at sixteen he was in a wheelchair, but he soon progressed to walking braces and then very trendy wooden canes. I can remember going on a youth group camping trip with a bunch of young people, Brett included. When it came to chores, Brett was in there with the rest of us. When it came to sleeping on a mattress on the floor of a tent, he was in that too. Brett got his driver's licence and a fantastic job in computing and he was a major contributor to the lives of young people in our youth group. There was no stopping this inspiring young guy. The only things that got in his way, occasionally, were his legs! And he used to get over his legs not working sometimes by cracking jokes about them and making everyone feel at ease. Brett realised that the 'able' folk were having more trouble adjusting than he was. Brett is now happily married and is spending his life helping others build theirs. His attitude and outlook on life are amazing!

The way that we respond to those who have a special need directly reflects our own level of self-esteem. How do you feel when you encounter someone who has a special need or who is disfigured? Are you uncomfortable, embarrassed or unsure? Just remember, if you are overcome with these such feelings, then this is all about you and not them!

Scars of Life

We each have physical and emotional skin to deal with. Our skin is a diary of our experiences, changing as we age. Its layers are a record of our past, of our pain and our joys, and of today as it slides into memory. Scraped knees from fights in the playground, chicken pox scars from the one spot that we just had to scratch. Bruises and scars. Wrinkles from all the smiling and laughing we have done. Every mark is a groove in the record of our life.

We are scarred by operations, by accidents, by war — by life. Women may be scarred by the miracle of birth, and I have my fair share of stretchmarks to prove it! I have chosen to see these scars as 'love tattoos' rather than unsightly and unacceptable marks. I am proud of them as they represent the lives of my beautiful children. These symbols become a rite of passage in life. So why is it then that to many, scars cause feelings of fear instead of being seen as the badges of courage and honour that they truly are? Who turned our bravery into shame? Who told us scars are ugly? And why do so many of us believe it?

The fact is, a person with no special need can have very low self-esteem and someone with a severe special need may have very good self-esteem. Although we all feel better about ourselves if we are 'looking good', true self-esteem is not linked directly to appearance. However, the psychological consequences (or scars) of having a special need or being disfigured are very real.

The great news is that many people with special needs are triumphant over all the bombardment of negativity. They are living lives of fulfilment and are active, contributing members of their communities.

Taking Control

You can't change other people, but what you can do is change the way you see yourself. You can nurture and look after yourself. You also have control over the way you think, feel or behave in your life, regardless of whether you have a special need or not.

There are many ways you can bring healthy self-esteem into your life. Below are some ideas for you to think about. You might use them all or choose the ones you think are best for you.

1. Be kind to yourself! Stop giving yourself a hard time and start appreciating yourself as a unique individual, and don't compare yourself with others.
2. Dream about what you would like for your life.
3. Challenge yourself to become more assertive.
4. Concentrate on your best qualities, then make a list of ways you might use these qualities in the future.
5. Give yourself permission to try and to fail.
6. Get involved in a sporting team or join a community group that will help you give something back to others.
7. Do things that you enjoy and you know you are good at.
8. Help people work out how to respond to you.
9. Smile and accept compliments that come your way.
10. Take control of your life and you will feel better about yourself.

It is vital that you are true to yourself. You will never be able to make everyone happy or meet everyone's expectations about how they think you should be but you can make yourself happy.

If you have a special need, your self-esteem may be positive or negative, but it is not set in concrete. It can always grow and it can always be worked on. If your self-esteem is low, then there are things you can do to boost how you see yourself. When someone has a healthy or more positive self-esteem, they are able to accept themselves. This means acknowledging that we all have strengths and weaknesses, and the weaknesses are absolutely fine, as are the strengths. A healthy or positive self-esteem does not mean that someone has an inflated or self-righteous view of themselves, it is having a balanced view — not over-emphasising the strengths or weaknesses.

It is good to remember that a special need is only one aspect of a person's life. For a person who has a special need, it is important for you to allow yourself to view your need as one component of many in your life — not the only component. Another issue for you may be dealing with discrimination and stereotypes from society. Our society places emphasis on looks, ability and being the same as everyone else. This may make you feel additional pressure to try to meet society's impossible standards. Don't be sucked in by this pressure — whether you have a special need or not, we all feel the pressure to conform to these ideals of perfection and trying to only leaves us feeling less perfect and sometimes less human.

Parents and friends may also have shaped your self-image and therefore affected your identity in ways you wish to change.

There are patterns of thinking that people with lower self-esteem may engage in more than people with higher self-esteem. These thinking patterns often result in a lack of confidence in either one, or many areas. A lack of confidence does not necessarily equal lack of ability. It may just be a false set of beliefs you hold about yourself. For instance, you may believe that you are not very clever, or that you are unable to play certain sports because of your physical attributes. Just because you were told it doesn't mean it is true!

By acknowledging and changing some of these incorrect thinking patterns, you can begin to change how you view yourself. You may feel as though you have had to become an expert at playing on a field that is not level as a result of dealing with your special need and people's attitudes towards it. You need to address not only how you play the game, but the part you play in it. Don't settle for playing the pawn well if you can be the queen or king.

To help you do this, you need to maximise your positive abilities and minimise your limitations, and remember that everyone has limitations, whether they have a special need or not. You should also avoid unrealistic comparisons, and when you are setting goals, make them realistic for your own life.

Another important thing to remember is to try not to overemphasise your special need. There is more that you can do than you probably realise. There is a phenomenal woman — Joni

Eareckson Tada — who was once an outgoing, athletic teenager. One day at a picnic with her friends, she dived into a shallow river and broke her neck, and she is now a quadriplegic. Reading her autobiography and seeing the movie based on her experiences literally changed my life. I realised how precious life is and that what happened to Joni could happen to anyone.

Joni firstly had to acknowledge her limitations but then she learned to focus on her potential, and although she can't move her arms or her legs at all, she is a brilliant artist (having learned to paint using her mouth), a prolific writer and an excellent speaker. Joni is the epitome of 'can do'. Joni said, 'God, if I can't die, then show me how to live.' The trauma of a broken neck and the anguish of a hopeless future grabbed this seventeen-year-old girl's attention and started her on a new journey of learning to appreciate herself all over again.

Since then, she has written a number of books and had a movie made about her amazing capacity to overcome her needs in life. She now travels the world sharing her story and empowering people — special needs or no special needs. Joni learned how to take control of her life and understand who she truly is.

If you have suffered from a tragic accident as Joni did, you must re-learn to appreciate yourself — all of yourself. This means coming to terms with your needs too. There may be times when you feel completely frustrated, but try to focus on the positive aspects of your need. One way to do this is making a list of your strengths including how your need, or your method of dealing with it, is an asset. Think bigger than yourself — it may be something that you use to help others.

My Privilege

I have the wonderful privilege of being stepmum to a beautiful young man called Joshua. Joshua is my husband's son from his previous marriage, and he has special physical and intellectual needs. Joshua was diagnosed with cerebral palsy. Recently his doctors contacted us to say that they thought he may have been wrongly diagnosed, and that he may in fact have been born with a rare genetic condition called Angelman syndrome.

Angelman syndrome has confused the medical community and parents of Angelman children for hundreds of years. Initially presumed to be rare, it's now believed thousands of Angelman syndrome cases have gone undiagnosed or misdiagnosed as cerebral palsy, autism or other childhood disorders. Special needs and confusion sometimes go hand in hand. The need may be confusing to work out, but the people behind the need are special and wonderful and need to be celebrated.

Christmas day at our place is always fun. We have a large family — five children (including Joshua), my parents, my grandmother, my sister and my niece. My beautiful grandmother had a stroke some years ago, and she now has special needs of her own. When it comes to sitting around the dinner table and enjoying Christmas dinner, our small children have learned how to respond to their grandmother who can't feed herself, and to Joshua who not only can't feed himself, but really enjoys flicking food around the place!

Rather than feeling the need to shelter the smaller children from what could be seen as rather anti-social behaviour, I help them see how very special their grandmother and big brother are. They are learning at a young age to not just 'tolerate' those who are different because of a special need, but to genuinely care for, learn from and enjoy the company of these very special family members of ours.

I have often wondered what it would have been like to have actually given birth to Joshua myself. The first question any new parent wants to know is, 'Is my baby OK?' I know that my husband, Jonathan, and Joshua's mother were devastated on learning of his need. My husband has talked to me about sometimes having to fight off feelings of inadequacy, as he faced the fact that he couldn't change Joshua's condition. He came to terms with it and has learned to live way, way above what happened and because of that, is a wonderful father not only to Joshua, but to all of our children. He has determined not to allow what happened to rob his life or the life of his family.

We once took Joshua shopping to buy him some new shoes. He sat down while Jonathan and I went looking for sizes and styles of sneakers and when we returned, Joshua had taken off and we couldn't find him. Jonathan and I went up and down every aisle until we heard an extremely loud and excited shriek! A lady standing next to me jumped with fright. It was Joshua. I just turned to the woman and said, 'I guess some people enjoy shopping more than others!' Sometimes the hardest thing to deal with is helping other people understand that everything's OK.

True Beauty

Some people view their physical appearance, whether beautiful or not, as a limitation or a hindrance. Beautiful Hollywood movie star Audrey Hepburn had every reason to focus on outward appearance, but she chose to focus on a deeper sense of beauty — beauty from witin. On the Christmas before she died, she read to her children a poem by Samuel Levenson called *Time Tested Beauty*. These powerful words resound: 'The beauty of a woman must be seen from in her eyes … and is reflected in her soul.' The real you, the beauty of you, is found in you and will shine through when you discover the truth of these words.

For others, living with a special need is like living trapped in a castle, hoping that someone will discover the hidden treasure of the true you.

Helen Keller once said, 'The best and most beautiful things in the world cannot be seen or even touched. They must be felt with the heart.'

We can learn much about beauty when we look at legends in history who have made a beautiful life from very unpleasant circumstances. People come in all shapes, sizes and colours — and real life cannot be airbrushed! Not all of us walk tall, or walk at all. Not all of us have perfect limbs or even have the use of all four.

Whether you feel that your life relates to the Beast's life or Beauty's life, there is something in this story for everyone to learn from. We need to learn to love unconditionally; we also need to learn to allow ourselves to be loved unconditionally and we need to love ourselves unconditionally.

For those who have eyes to see, your inner beauty can be seen as a diamond. What makes you sparkle as a diamond is much more than your cut, colour, clarity, and carat-weight. It's the combination of all these that give you your uniqueness, which is indefinable and immeasurable. It's what makes you completely unique — one in six billion!

A diamond is a brilliant, precious and very durable stone. Even if you are feeling like a lump of coal, that is the first stage of becoming a diamond. You need to know that at the very core of your being is brilliance, preciousness and durability.

You are a diamond waiting to be liberated, so that your greatness and true beauty can be revealed. We are sometimes placed in circumstances that increase pressures in our lives until we too are changed from a coal into a diamond. When you're going through tough times and tough experiences, just think — this is part of the process of making you shine even brighter.

Never forget that what's inside you is more precious than you could ever imagine. Let your inner beauty shine. And it's only through a healthy self-esteem that this truly happens.

Your self-esteem is a direct reflection of how you feel about yourself, so grow to love who you are. Whether you have a special need or not, your life is what you make of it.

Remember the Truth: people who have a special need can have as many joys and achievements as everybody else and be as beautiful as everyone else.

Time Tested Beauty Tips

For attractive lips, speak words of kindness.

For lovely eyes, seek out the good in people.

For a slim figure, share your food with the hungry.

For beautiful hair, let a child run their fingers through it once
*   a day.*

For poise, move with the knowledge that you'll never walk alone.

People, even more than things, have to be restored, renewed,
*   revived,*

reclaimed and redeemed and redeemed and redeemed.

Never throw out anybody.

Remember, if you ever need a helping hand, you'll find one at the
*   end of your arm.*

As you grow older you will discover that you have two hands.

One for helping yourself, the other for helping others.

The beauty of a woman is not in the clothes she wears, the
*   figure that she carries, or the way she combs her hair.*

The beauty of a woman must be seen from in her eyes, because
*   that is the doorway to her heart, the place where love resides.*

The beauty of a woman is not in a facial mole, but true beauty in
*   a woman is reflected in her soul.*

It is the caring that she lovingly gives, the passion that she knows.

And the beauty of a woman, with passing years only grows!'

SAMUEL LEVENSON

Beauty

God does not look at the things man looks at.
Man looks at the outward appearance,
but God looks into the heart.

1 SAMUEL 16:7, THE BIBLE

Tova's Story

The day I was born I had everything a parent could want in a healthy newborn. I came with a perfect set of ten fingers and toes, some strawberry-blonde fuzz on my head and a set of lungs that could be heard down the hospital hall. The only difference was that I had achondroplasia — a type of dwarfism.

Of the estimated 200 types of dwarfism, achondroplasia is by far the most common, accounting for approximately half of all cases of profound short stature. An average-size torso, short arms and legs, and a slightly enlarged head and prominent forehead characterise achondroplastic dwarfism.

Most achondroplastic dwarfs are born to average-size parents, and account for somewhere between one in 26 000 and one in 40 000 births. Adults, on average, are four feet tall. In many circles of today's society, a midget is the term used for a proportionate dwarf. However, the term has fallen into disfavour and is considered offensive by most people of short stature. The term dates back to 1865, the height of the 'freak show' era, and was generally applied only to short-stature persons who were displayed for public amusement, which is why it is considered so unacceptable today. Such terms as 'dwarf', 'little person', 'LP' and 'person of short stature' are all acceptable, but most people would rather be referred to by their name than by a categorisation!

My dad is also a dwarf, but my mum is not. The day I was born, my father actually went home and cried. He was not sad or even upset that I was born with dwarfism, but overwhelmed with the harsh truths he knew I would have to face in life. Being a dwarf is a big reality in a small package, and one that not many people will understand. He understood with the love of a father. Funnily enough, it has been this commonality between us that to this day has kept us really close.

Life is good when you're small; at least I think it is, and the friends who surround me agree. Being little makes me ... unique.

Dwarfism doesn't define me; it is just the outer shell God has given me. I don't see it as a handicap as others might, but an inconvenience at times ... though I must say, shoes are cheaper! Having a father and little brother that are also LPs (little people) made growing up, in my eyes, normal. I was never treated any differently than any 'average stature' child was. I had the same sharing issues as all the kids do in kindergarten and had to get braces when I was twelve. I went to school, played at recess and did homework like most kids in primary school.

When I reached the age of nine or ten, I went through a period of time when I couldn't stand people staring at me. Though I was comfortable with my dwarfism, I was also very shy because of the insensitivity of people. There would be times when I would have to go with my mum to the store and I wouldn't get out of the car until there was no one around who could taunt me about my size. In stores, kids would literally follow us up and down isles yelling, 'Look, there's a midget!' while pointing and laughing, until their parents would scoop them away, telling them to be quiet.

Other times, my family and I would be on an outing and when parents would see us, and would shuffle their kids away from us as if we were some kind of embarrassment to society. It would always annoy me that parents couldn't just explain to their kids why we were dwarves. There are all different kinds of individuals wherever you go and people, especially parents of young children, need to educate themselves on how to handle situations they might encounter with people who are noticeably different.

As I got older I realised that life doesn't cut the little person many breaks, if any at all. When I was thirteen I went through phases of not wanting to be seen with my parents — especially with my dad. People always thought we were married because I was almost the same height as him! When we had my little brother with us, it was even worse because everyone thought we had the cutest little dwarf family. This was also the age when the friends I grew up with decided they were too cool to be seen with me and I had to resort to hanging with their younger siblings or getting to know the older crowd.

It's harder to get a date too because most men want someone who is closer to their height and has a supermodel-shaped body. That factor in itself could have caused me to have a major complex, I was starting to see myself negatively and feel negatively about myself. I had always known I was different — but what had started out as me thinking it wasn't a bad thing, had me now thinking it was.

With the help of family, friends and the grace of God, I've walked through the rejection and hurt. It's funny because now I don't realise I am different until I see myself in a video or picture — it's just like when someone sings or hears themselves in a recording, that is not how they personally hear themselves. I go shopping with friends and, walking along side of them, I just feel a little shorter, but not different.

I know my true friends, the ones I want in my life, will love and appreciate me. I know that the man I marry will love me for everything I am, looks and all. Because I am confident in this, all my male friendships are great. I don't have to worry about being something I am not to be their friend, for who I know I am is all I can be and it's their choice to take it or leave it.

I am now twenty-two years old and in college. What is different about my attitude today compared to years ago is that I had to choose to either be bitter or better — and I chose better. I had to choose that I would not have pity parties about people not liking me because I was small, but I would be an overcomer and soar in life. I had to choose to smile at people when they would stare and make rude comments. I had to choose to believe the God-given promises like I have a destiny, that I am wonderfully made and the plans He has for my life far too great to fathom. What I have learned is that life is not just hard on a little person; it can be hard on anyone.

My dad always used to tell me when I was growing up that 'it is not the cards you're dealt, but how you play your hand that determines your life'. You might have rounds where your cards are pretty shocking to play with, but know that just because the person next to you might have a better hand in life, doesn't mean they will win. If there is one thing you should know it's that you are a winner and destined for greatness — I know I am!

10 Keys to Freedom

from physical and mental challenges

FREEDOM is a journey as well as a fulfilment of your heart's desire. These keys will help you to practise taking your gaze away from the challenges you face. Start making changes for the better and watch everyone else catch up!

1. Always hold your head up high.
2. Remember, your adversity is also your opportunity.
3. Discover and nurture that which is beautiful in you.
4. Tell yourself and someone else every day that you and they are remarkable.
5. Always say 'thank you' when someone says something positive about you.
6. Spend time each day developing your internal beauty, for at least as long as your external beauty.
7. Appreciate the amazing world in which you live.
8. Help people who may not understand what it is like to be you.
9. Remember that gracious behaviour reflects a loving person, so work on becoming more gracious.
10. As you grow older, remember that true beauty never fades with age, it only increases.

body soul spirit

ACTION PLAN

body
Hold your head up and please don't hide behind a mask. Self-acceptance and others' acceptance will tend to flow more freely as you refuse to allow fear to force you to hide.

soul
You are more than your need. Tell yourself every single day that you are an outstanding human being, full of incredible potential and with the ability to be whoever you put your heart and mind to.

spirit
Pray for healing and at the same time, pray for the ability to accept that which you cannot change and know that this is not what defines who you truly are.

My goal is freedom
FROM PHYSICAL AND MENTAL CHALLENGES

Chapter 8

The Balancing Act
freedom from extreme behaviour

*'An orchestra makes a better sound
when all instruments work together,
and not when each instrument
competes, extreme behaviour will cause
disharmony in your life.'*

The Three Little Pigs

Once upon a time, there were three little pigs. The first little pig was very vain. He dieted and exercised excessively. The second little pig was a slow-moving roly-poly pig, and very lazy. The third little pig was quite sensible and very balanced. He ate well and exercised moderately. All of them wanted to build a house before winter set in.

The first little pig decided to build his house with the finest lightweight straw and he used photographs of himself to line the walls as wallpaper.

The second pig had land that was so littered with old food containers, all he had to do was erect wooden poles and push out the junk on four sides and it formed an entire house around him!

The third pig built his house to withstand the winter weather and the likes of a hungry wolf, so he used strong foundation stones to keep the negative elements out.

Sure enough the day soon came when the wind howled through the forest and large snowflakes drifted down on the little pigs' houses. With winter came a very hungry wolf, who wandered into the little pigs' valley.

At the straw house the hungry wolf huffed and puffed and blew the house down. The wolf grabbed the little pig and was about to eat him, when he decided against it, seeing he would be easily eaten in just one mouthful! The frightened little pig ran as fast as he could to the second little pig's house.

The wolf followed the skinny piggy across to the second pig's house of junk, demanding that the pig come out. Sitting in his armchair watching television, with the first little pig huddled behind him, the second little pig yelled, 'Come back later, I'm busy!' and turned up the volume on his television.

The wolf huffed and puffed and the little pig's house came down. The wolf tried grabbing the roly-poly pig and the skinny little pig, but because he was greedy in wanting both of them, he caught neither as they ran off to the third little pig's house. The wolf yelled after them, 'With a big burp and very bad indigestion, I could eat you two pigs!' More ravenous now than ever, the wolf followed the pigs to the third little pig's house.

At this house, he blew and blew as hard as he could but nothing happened, and the house remained stable. The third little pig, unshaken by the commotion outside, decided to light a fire in the fireplace just as the wolf climbed onto the roof to come down the chimney. The surprised wolf's tail caught on fire. Yelping, he jumped off the roof and ran out of the pig's valley.

Having learned their lessons about their extreme behaviour, the skinny little pig and the roly-poly pig both set about building sturdy brick houses for themselves.

One day the hungry wolf came back again to roam the valley searching for food, but when he saw three brick chimneys, he remembered his burnt tail and ran away for good.

Each of the little pigs learned a healthy appreciation of how they should live, without vanity and gluttony, and the skinny pig and the roly-poly pig learned from the sensible pig how to live happily ever after.

The End

Fact

Obsessive behaviour will never build your life.

Truth

Balance is not one extreme or the other. It is the tension found between the two.

Mirror, mirror on the wall, why am I so unbalanced in it all?

Sitting around on your bottom, ignoring the fact that you may have become a couch potato, isn't going to do much for your self-esteem. Doing two aerobic classes and running for twenty kilometres each day, ignoring the fact that you may have become an obsessive–compulsive exercise junkie who's never satisfied with the way you look, also isn't going to do much for your self-esteem. Both of these are extremes that need balance.

It's great to be able to relax and be comfortable taking it easy, and it's also great to exercise, but there are times when we can become unbalanced and unhealthy in our approach to both these ways of living. Finding balance when it comes to exercise means having to address the issues which may cause us to be either lazy or obsessed with exercise. The root of most obsessive behaviour lies in self-esteem and sense of identity.

If you are naturally and easily relaxed, then you may need to work harder at creating energy and movement in your life. On the other hand, if you are antsy and twitchy, relaxing and taking it easy is something you may need to practise. It is not one rule for all — you have to look at the way you are made up, recognise who you are, and live the best way to flourish in every area of your life.

In order to enjoy a fruitful and happy life, we need to look after our body as well as our soul and spirit. That's why we need to be balanced: because our bodies are the temple of our soul and spirit, so we need to look after our physical wellbeing. It really does matter! Extreme behaviours have adverse effects on the human body.

Our bodies are seen all the time. They are visible and recognisable whether we like it or not. The body is our vehicle, we can't leave home without it. When I am being hugged, my body receives the hug and when I go shopping (and I love shopping), my body receives the clothes. We need to take care of our bodies.

Taking care of our bodies requires activity but it doesn't require extreme behaviour or obsession. We can be extreme about a number of things, such as how we look (see Chapter 3 on body discontentment), or what we eat, or about exercising for hours each day.

Obsession and Laziness

Obsession will convince you to change something using excessive methods and probably for an unreasonable length of time, or it can convince you that you need to change something that does NOT need changing at all. People can become obsessive about exercise or dieting when they feel dissatisfied with the way that they look. Australian research has found that some girls as young as six to eight years of age believe that they should be thinner than they are, and an increasing number of boys are feeling the need to 'bulk up'. In a survey of 438 secondary students and 116 patients already diagnosed with an eating disorder, there was an alarming similarity between the students' behaviour and that of the patients. The percentage of patients trying to lose weight and using excessive exercise was closely matched by the percentage of students doing the same. Seventy-five per cent of students said they felt fat, three-quarters of the students were trying to lose weight, and nearly half the total number of students was restricting their food intake. Between 85 to 89 per cent of students felt that weight, exercise and shape were important to self-esteem.

I am sure that 75 per cent of those students surveyed were not actually fat — they are getting their measuring stick from the wrong place! Fashion magazines and shop mannequins do NOT display the normal or even ideal weight/shape for a person. If women attempted to be the same size as shop mannequins, most would find that their body fat would be so low that they would be unable to menstruate.

Obsessing about the way we look, and about food and exercise, will not only have negative results on our health (as it often leads to such illnesses as anorexia, bulimia and binge eating), but can also have a negative impact on our relationships and even on everyday functions. Wanting to lose weight and exercising is not bad, but obsessing about the two is.

Apart from being obsessed with our bodies, we can also be obsessed with what goes into our bodies by way of food. Striving for 'purity' can actually be unhealthy. Balance is the key to health in body, soul and spirit.

Avoiding obsession can also be used as an excuse for laziness. This is the other end of the spectrum. In the last twenty years, concern has been expressed about the increasing levels of obesity and lack of physical fitness in children and adolescents in Australia. Two studies reported increases in Body Mass Index (BMI, a measure of weight for height) in both Sydney and Melbourne in children from seven to eighteen years, with about 25 per cent of children being overweight. Researchers blame the sedentary lifestyles and diets of children, the low intake of fruit and vegetables and decreasing physical activity throughout adolescence.

The study of the eating and exercise habits of pupils aged five to eighteen showed the weight of those aged ten to fifteen was higher than eight years previously. One-third of the 1800 students surveyed rarely exercised. A decrease in exercise among teenage girls coincided with an increase in dieting.

Young people are getting fatter, despite growing numbers of secondary school children dieting regularly. This sad contradiction was explained by Sydney Children's Hospital dietitian Maggie Aiken as 'teenage girls chasing a slim ideal with the doomed method of skipping meals — often leading to weight gain'.

Maggie went on to say, 'They think dieting means missing a meal, such as breakfast, but that makes them snack more, usually high-calorie food, later in the day. They think they're losing weight, but in fact they're putting it on.'

The Three Little Pigs

In my version of *The Three Little Pigs*, we see what three different lifestyles have to offer: laziness, obsession or balance. Most people can relate to either the obsessive character or the lazy character, and some vacillate between them both. Generally, fewer people are balanced in the area of eating and exercise.

In the story, we read that the wolf saw the first two little pigs as easy game. Because they weren't living a balanced life, he was able to catch them off guard and blow their houses down.

Neither obsession with health and fitness nor neglect is the way to a healthy body image and self-esteem. It won't take much of a storm to shake your self-esteem if you are either obsessive or lazy.

It is usually low self-esteem caused by a poor body image that drives people to be obsessed about the way they look. Although some people might look at an excessively 'healthy' lifestyle and think it is balanced, it is anything but. Being healthy is all about balance, not obsession and striving for perfection. If you are healthy, all areas of your life are functioning well and not just your physical being.

On the other hand, we could sometimes learn a few lessons about getting more active. Couch potatoes aren't always overweight. Lazy people come in all shapes and sizes, and there is nothing noble about their attitude to body image and self-esteem. Some lazy people who neglect their bodies and who are ignorant about healthy eating and exercise will say that they don't care about the way their body looks, and this is as detrimental to their self-esteem as any obsession.

Laziness is a robber of self-esteem and healthy body image. The only way to counteract laziness is to apply discipline. Most people think that those who exercise and eat healthily just like doing it, but it actually boils down to discipline and choice, rather than genetics or disposition.

Fashionable Fads

Health and fitness is not only good for you, but it is also currently fashionable. Perhaps you, or someone you know, may be suffering from a newly identified condition called *orthorexia nervosa*. Symptoms include being obsessed with losing weight and only eating organic food, studying every label on jars, taking every kind of vitamin pill and supplement (orthorexia sufferers would rattle if you shook them!), and fanatical exercise. A sign of orthorexia is that you would rather starve than compromise what you will or won't eat.

Medical professionals don't consider that orthorexia nervosa is an eating disorder. The phrase originally came from author Steven Bratman in his bestselling book *Health Food Junkies: Orthorexia Nervosa*. A spokesman for the UK's Eating Disorders Association says, 'Although the press have descended upon the term orthorexia nervosa as a new eating disorder, it's more of an obsessive–compulsive disorder.'

Former Spice Girl Geri Halliwell is a typical example of this newly identified (but not medically recognised) condition. Known as a binge eater and a regular attendee of Compulsive Eaters Anonymous, Geri has been hailed as the epitome of bodily perfection, because she shed nearly thirteen kilos over eighteen months. Her newly trimmed form has been spread across endless magazines and newspapers as the symbol of what women can do if they hit the gym, give up chocolate, and eat three tiny meals a day!

Geri Halliwell is a natural endomorph, that is, she is naturally curvy. She has dieted and exercised her way to a new body shape, but she has had to work obsessively at it, because it is not her natural body shape. It would also be very difficult for Geri to sustain, and impossible should she start eating normally again. We need balance! Improving ourselves is great, but trying to be someone we are not is simply not sustainable.

We need to understand that perfection is unattainable, because we are human. Celebrities who slim down dramatically have money to hire personal trainers, dietitians, style gurus, the best of everything organic, and state-of-the-art gym equipment. For many of them, it is a full-time job to look a certain way. What is easy for them is a great deal harder for those who don't have all of their resources.

Being a celebrity doesn't necessarily make one automatically healthy. In fact, the so-called 'ideal body' has become increasingly unhealthy and impractical.

Marilyn Monroe was a slim 37–23–36 with 20 per cent body fat, and although she was known to have many unhealthy addictions, she is now regarded as 'voluptuous' and 'curvaceous'. Model–actress Elizabeth Hurley, a slightly slimmer 36–25–35, has even been reported to describe Marilyn Monroe as being fat. While the measurements 37–23–36 may be curvier than most of today's famous beauties, these kind of measurements reflect a fairly healthy body shape.

The current fear of fat doesn't just affect females. In fact, the pressure to trade in beer bellies for six-packs has caused many guys to feel self-conscious about their bodies. Hunky Hollywood actor Brad Pitt underwent a punishing, excessive fitness regime to achieve those rock-hard abs in the cult movie *Fight Club*.

No matter how great these celebrities may look, many of them are exercising too much or eating too little in order to achieve the perfect body image. Long term, that can only lead to poor health.

So rather than believing everything you see on television and in magazines, recognise the images you see in the media for what they are: sometimes constructed, often manipulated, and at times unreal. Even celebrities look like the rest of us, first thing in the morning.

I can remember feeling very shocked and most encouraged when I found out that Jennifer Beals of *Flashdance* fame had body doubles for the famous 'What a Feeling' high-energy dance scene. It was her face and other people's bodies. Unbelievable!

Role Models

If we are going to have great self-esteem and body image, we have to stop comparing ourselves with other people. Be encouraged by positive role models, but don't spend your life conforming to somebody else's ideal. Focus on doing what you can with what you have. Exercise regularly, nourish your body with healthy foods and remember to relax. Challenging and improving your own personal best is a good thing to do.

We need to acknowledge and accept that doing gymwork until we feel faint or starving ourselves to get rid of body fat is not going to help our body image or self-esteem. It will only cause us to be unhealthy, pale, drawn and lethargic. Energy is attractive and desirable, and we won't be able to enjoy the benefits of it if we don't live a balanced, healthy life. You don't gain energy from resting. Resting may rest you, but exercise energises you. You need to sow energy in order to reap energy.

When you feel bombarded by media beauties, take a look around you. We come in all shapes and sizes. There's no right and wrong, just wonderful diversity.

Fortunately there are some famous role models who like to dispel the myth of obsession, and who like to enjoy balance.

▶ Jennifer Lopez: 'I don't believe in beating yourself up.'
▶ Kate Winslet: 'I don't believe in diets, damn it!'
▶ Sandra Bullock: 'I'm never going to be thin and waif-like. I tried. It's sexy to be comfortable in your own skin.'
▶ Catherine Zeta-Jones: 'It's not about starving yourself.'
▶ Portia de Rossi: 'I did lose too much weight before. I got to a weight where I just didn't look good.'
▶ Drew Barrymore: 'I want to eat fun meals and laugh and enjoy myself.'

Although relaxed and confident in their opinions, these women also cannot afford to be lazy and inactive. They have obviously found some balance in their lives.

A Healthy Plan

A great reason for getting in shape and staying in shape is so that we can be an example to other people. The balanced little pig was a true friend in as much as he didn't nag his obsessive and lazy friends; he walked the walk instead of just talking the talk. Telling people that they need to get in shape is not nearly as effective as living the example yourself.

It is a proven fact that regular physical activity is important in the maintenance of good health and prevention of many health conditions. In recent years the Active Australia initiative was launched to help increase and enhance lifelong participation of all Australians in sport, community recreation, fitness, outdoor recreation and other physical activities. Taking care of yourself and living a balanced life will help you eat better, sleep better, work better, feel better and look better.

I believe in people and I believe in the ability of each human being to be all that they were created to be. But you can only do this by addressing the following issues that may be holding you back:

1. **Revelation**
   Understand who you are and why you were created.
2. **Inspiration**
   Choose a role model to help inspire you.
3. **Information**
   Know exactly what you have to do.
4. **Activation**
   Decide then act.
5. **Motivation**
   Find something or someone to help keep you on track.

As tripartite beings, we need to take care of our body, or our physical wellbeing, our soul or our emotions, and our spirit or the condition of our heart and relationships with God and man. All these factors need to work in harmony in order for us to experience healthy balance in our lives, which will then be reflected in a healthy self-esteem. They are ALL important! If one isn't working properly, all suffer and we suffer! Once we properly understand who we are, we can then set goals according to that revelation.

Inspiration will follow when we believe that all things are possible. If you haven't seen that in your own life then find someone who has, and allow them to be a positive role model for you. Some of the things that have helped to inspire me to live a healthy balanced life are:

▶ **Ask the question:** How happy am I with my life right now?
▶ **Picture the end result:** Visualise where you want to be and how you want to look and feel.
▶ **Count the cost:** Weigh up your present life against the potential of your future and think ahead.

When it comes to knowing exactly what we need to do to live a balanced life and to develop a healthy and balanced self-esteem, we were not born with an instruction manual. That is why we each need to properly understand our body, how it works and what makes it tick. If you don't understand it, you will be second-guessing it.

A great telltale sign of second-guessing with regards to getting in shape is when you start on the 'what works for Elle Macpherson' or 'how Cindy Crawford does it' diets, and then you wonder why they don't work on you!

Firstly determine what your body type is.
▶ Ectomorph: naturally very thin with a fast metabolism — example: Kate Moss
▶ Mesomorph: natural athletic tone with a medium metabolism — example: Cindy Crawford
▶ Endomorph: naturally curvy with a slow metabolism — example: Marilyn Monroe

Then work out what to eat and when to eat, how to exercise properly and the best time of the day for you to get moving. The 10 keys to freedom at the end of this chapter give some of the guidelines for eating and exercising that have worked for me.

Expansion and Contraction

I have literally lived through expansions and contractions where my body felt like a concertina file! Having been slim most of my life, I got the shock of my life when I gained 40 kilos when I was pregnant with my twin boys. I expanded east and west and felt like a beached whale. It didn't help that I could hardly move because of a painful physical condition I developed in my pelvic region. Although I wasn't a lazy person, my existence had certainly become one of sitting around, eating and sleeping and not much else.

After the boys were safely delivered, I had a choice to remain as I was or to work hard at losing the weight. I found that the weight did not fall off even though scores of people promised me it would. No, I had to put great effort in but the reward spoke for itself when my first book, *Fat Free Forever!*, was published and became an instant bestseller.

This great contraction back to my size ten figure, however, was followed by another expansion when I became pregnant with my youngest daughter. This time I gained around 38 kilos and I found the weight even harder to lose afterwards. It took me a while longer to get back in shape because of a number of factors, but I did achieve my goal, and released another book, *Back in Shape After Baby*, which is a great book particularly if you need motivation!

The balance I have now found in my life enables me to enjoy what really matters, like spending time with my kids and helping set people free. The cost, of course, is that I don't have four hours a day to train at the gym and some days and weeks I don't even get there, but I live at ease and in balance understanding that there's no point being obsessed about my body.

Whether you are in an expansion or contraction phase, remember that it is effort and consistency that are required to get in shape, not obsession or defeat.

Motivation

Once we understand who we really are, feel inspired to improve, have the information and know what we should be doing, it's time to decide and act. No one can do this except you. Pressure from your partner certainly won't do it, and drifting into something will end with you drifting out of it shortly afterwards. Decide to do it with purpose and focus. Personally I can't stand dieting, so when I decide to do something about my body shape, I generally try to do it the quickest possible way, without cheating. I choose to do it with focus, but not obsession.

The truth is, how you start will usually determine how you finish, so set a realistic short-term goal, working towards your long-term goal. By the way, it takes a special kind of determination for the long haul. I used to be able to lose a size in a few weeks, and now it's very different for me, after three kids. The short-term goals aren't very satisfying, but they definitely make up the end result, so they are important. It's one thing to achieve the first four steps (revelation, inspiration, information and activation), but without the fifth, it's going to be impossible to achieve what you set out to do. Motivation is a major key in the whole body-shape balance dilemma. There are many good eating plans available, which would all work if only people could stick at them long enough. Did you know that the average diet lasts between one to three weeks, max? I believe in addressing the issues of failure and fear of failure and sorting them out up front, once and for all! They are real bodyshaping enemies. I have always told my clients that they can fail as many times as necessary to win.

Famous inventor Thomas Edison actually had 10 000 failed

experiments before successfully inventing the light bulb. He was asked why he bothered continuing after so many failures, and he said, 'I did not fail 10 000 times. Rather, I successfully found 10 000 ways that do not work.'

It's all a matter of perspective and we need to look at our attempts — our glass of effort — as being half full rather than being half empty. If you change your mind you'll change your life, and be able to look at yourself in a more positive way. Release yourself from so much pressure and expectancy. That's what will keep you motivated.

On a very practical note, if you stick to any good eating and exercise plan for the first six to eight weeks or so, the results you receive will automatically become your future motivation. You will learn to motivate yourself and others at the same time, by your success.

In my book *Back in Shape After Baby* you will find a detailed plan to get in shape and stay in shape.

Creating balance in your approach to food and exercise will not only help you maintain harmony in your body, it will also feed your soul and spirit. People generally chase wealth in their earlier years, up to around thirty-five, and then health in later years. The fact is, the body you don't look after while you are young is the body you will have to look after when you are old.

Remember the Truth: balance is not one extreme or the other. It is the tension found between the two.

Balance

*I pray that you may prosper in every way and
that your body may keep well,
even as I know your soul keeps well and prospers.*

3 John 1:2, The Bible

Caitlin's Story

My home life was not happy or stable. In fact, it was so out of control that I wanted to scream some days, so that's exactly what I did to maintain some sanity. I vacillated between being the calm one who brought peace and the crazy one who couldn't cope with the fighting and the drinking and the swearing and the out-of-control home life. My parents hated each other.

No one paid attention to me unless I was actively doing something to fix other people's problems, or actively creating some problems of my own. I became tired of trying to fix everyone else's problems, so I just homed in on me. Life was miserable, and I was so needy — I decided to go on strike until everyone changed around me. I hated my sister, because my mother always compared us. I thought that if I just became a bit skinnier than her, then my mother might approve of me more.

Getting skinny was something that I could control. I just stopped eating, except for half a carrot a day and some water — not too much, in case it tipped the scales. Everything else I imagined was going to destroy my life. Bread, vegetables, chocolate, meat, milk, biscuits would make me fat and unpopular. I exercised day and night to lose weight and tone up. I wanted to be so skinny that everyone would have to sit up and take notice of me.

I was crying out for help, and pushing people away at the same time, and I felt horrible and completely torn inside. I looked great outside though, with slim, sinewy arms, toned legs and a washboard stomach. But I was still the same on the inside, and for me the picture in the mirror didn't change. So I kept going until I just about wasted away. I was so thin and emaciated, weighing just 35 kilograms. I finally had the attention I had always wanted from my family, but I nearly died in the process. I had to get help. No hospital could help me; they just re-fed my body, but they couldn't help my soul. I was craving love and attention and all I got was bowls of fat food to shove down my throat.

It was this near-death experience that caused me to realise that I had gone way too far. I couldn't see myself properly any more anyway, so I decided to listen to the people who were trying to help me. Not my mother though, she was just a hysterical mess as usual. I was finally sent for help to a place that focused on my insides and not just my outsides and it caused me to see who I really was. Eventually I became better, and I started to enjoy eating again. But what I enjoyed most was the attention I received every time I ate and every time I put on another kilo. This was great, I was being recognised and applauded for my achievements.

Slowly over time, though, I lost the plot in the other direction. I had already figured out that it didn't really matter any more if I was skinny or not. It was just too much hard work. People hadn't paid as much attention to me as I had hoped they would, especially my mother, and I nearly died in the process. So, I decided then that I would take it easy for a while and enjoy life a little more.

A while turned into a number of months and I had lost all motivation to look after myself at all. I sat in my room and listened to music and ate all day and all night. My room was a mess and my life was a mess. I slept in until late and just wandered around in my pyjamas all day until I went to bed again at night. I ate and ate and ate, whatever I liked, whenever I liked. I figured that it was an important reward for me suffering for so long, trying to be fit and healthy, after all I had been through with my parents fighting all the time. If I ever felt uncomfortable having overeaten, I would simply throw up and start all over again. I had gone from one extreme to the other. I was a meticulous, skinny and striving overachiever one day and then, it seemed, a fat, lazy, binge-eating slob the next day. All I wanted was some control in my life, but my life was completely out of control, and I didn't know how to stop it. I was so big that I couldn't fit into any clothes in our entire house — even my dad's baggy jeans and sweaters wouldn't fit me. I was huge, weighing 85 kilograms — more than double my previous weight. My poor body. I felt sick, ugly and depressed every waking moment of every single day.

I thought back to the place I had stayed that helped me focus on my insides and I realised that I had done it again, I had nearly destroyed my body and yet still had no peace in my soul. This time I needed to face my demon head-on, if I was ever going to get free. All of this happened to me before my twentieth birthday. Too much too young. I was about to turn twenty, and I knew it was decision time. I had wasted years of my life already, trying to seek other people's attention and approval, and I had nearly killed myself in the process. It was time to stop the insanity.

I am now free, and that decision was the starting point for me — a catalyst for me to get free. It wasn't one decision but a series of them over the past few years that have caused me to maintain my freedom and balance in life. There are consequences from behaviour such as mine, so my body is still recovering, but my heart and soul are free. I have boundaries now that I simply will not cross, and I have thoughts that I will and won't think about myself, and I learned to stop blaming everyone for my life.

I now eat well, and I exercise a couple of times each week, and when I can't, I don't worry about it. It's a real change of life for me, letting go of some of the controls in my life. Things that used to send me over the edge now actually make me laugh. I guess it's part of growing up, but it's also part of being free.

10 Keys to Freedom

from extreme behaviour

These are keys that helped me to develop balance in what I eat and how I exercise. For a more detailed diet and exercise plan, you might find it helpful to talk to your GP.

1. Make a decision to look after your body, but remember, don't become obsessed.
2. Eat a big breakfast, medium-sized lunch and small dinner.
3. Eat a healthy mid-morning and afternoon snack each day.
4. Cut out as many visible fats as possible (fat on meat, oil, margarine, processed food) and include plenty of fresh fruit and vegetables each day.
5. If you need to lose some weight, don't eat too many starchy carbohydrates after 3.00 p.m.
6. The best lean proteins are whey protein concentrate, eggs, fish and chicken breast fillets; lean red meat is good in moderation. These are organised in order of fat content and function (lowest to highest).
7. Drink two large glasses of water before you eat each meal to hydrate yourself and to help curtail your appetite.
8. If you can, walk for forty-five to sixty minutes, three to five days per week.
9. Don't weigh yourself all the time.
10. Have a junk meal once a week and enjoy it!

body soul spirit

ACTION PLAN

body
Identify your body shape and set goals accordingly, but don't allow your life to become 'boxed' by your body shape.

soul
Realign your thinking to ensure that you are balanced. Check regularly that your attitude, as well as your body, remains healthy.

spirit
Pray daily for the ability to be focused and not obsessed. Daily prayer will help to motivate you to keep your life in balance.

My goal is freedom
FROM EXTREME BEHAVIOUR

Chapter 9

Behind Closed Doors

freedom from abuse

*'It takes courage to think forward,
and not back.
Behind you may be pain and bondage,
but in front of you is healing and freedom.'*

Sleeping Beauty

Once upon a time, a king and queen adopted a little baby girl whom they named Princess Annalise. Princess Annalise was very loved.

All the noblemen and noblewomen of the land were invited to come and bless the baby at her christening except one — the king's brother. He had been banished from the royal court because of his wickedness.

One by one, the noblemen and noblewomen blessed Annalise with a life of virtue and beauty. Then the king's uninvited brother appeared. He stood over the cradle and cursed the baby girl with terrible suffering.

There was a stunned silence. The queen fainted. A kind-hearted nobleman came forward and said, 'I cannot undo the curse, the child will be hurt, but instead of death she will sleep for a hundred years, until a prince awakens her.'

Annalise grew up to be as beautiful and good as the noblemen and noblewomen said she would be. On her fifteenth birthday, the king and queen travelled to the city to buy her gifts. Left alone in the palace, the princess went exploring. She came to an old tower and climbed up the winding staircase. Reaching a large wooden door she pushed it gently and it sprang open.

There stood the king's wicked brother and his two evil sons. The young princess remembered with a shudder the things that they had done to her behind closed doors before they were banished. The three men had had their wicked way with her and hurt her terribly many times. In terror she fainted and fell to the ground. The evil men left her for dead. The curse of the king's brother had come to pass and Princess Annalise began to shut down, falling into a deep, deep sleep where she was going to heal.

When she was discovered her parents took her and laid her in a golden bed. In her gown of lace, she looked like an angel asleep. The kind nobleman who had softened the curse came and touched her forehead with his hand and as he did, the entire palace fell into a deep sleep for a hundred years.

After many years, a prince wandered by the forest and was intrigued at the sight of the dark palace, partly hidden by huge thorn bushes. He had heard tales of the sleeping princess in a hidden palace. Could the stories be true?

When the prince came near the thorn hedge, it parted and let him pass unhurt then closed behind him. Upon entering the palace, he saw the court lying asleep in the great hall. He walked deeper into the castle and came to the tower. He opened the door and entered the little room where the beautiful princess was sleeping. There she lay, so beautiful that he could not turn his eyes away, and as he stooped down and gave her a kiss, Princess Annalise opened her eyes.

Suddenly, the palace came alive! The whole court awoke and looked at each other in great astonishment. The fire in the kitchen flared and flickered and the maid, who had been motionless, suddenly finished plucking the fowl.

A great feast was served and the prince and princess took such joy in each other that they decided to be married. With a wonderful new start and in the process of time, they lived happily ever after.

The End

Fact
You may never forget being abused.

Truth
Forgiveness is the key that unlocks the freedom of your future.

Mirror, mirror on the wall, why am I the most used and abused of them all?

Bad things do sometimes happen to good people, and that means that circumstances that are beyond our control can end up controlling us. If you have been subject to abuse of any kind, your memory of it can be so vivid that it drives you to distraction. You may remember every detail of every single thing that ever happened to you, and it may come to mind daily or even hourly. When this happens our will is violated and our self-esteem takes a battering.

Oprah Winfrey's childhood was full of pain and suffering from racial issues, comparisons, poverty, her mother and father's separation and being left alone. She was also subjected to horrific sexual abuse from male relatives. At fourteen she fell pregnant. The child was born prematurely and died shortly after birth.

To cope with the pain and trauma of the abuse that she had suffered, she turned to food. She was able to pick herself up and build an amazing public career, but privately, her heart was still in turmoil.

Oprah is anything but a quitter or a loser. Although she hasn't totally won the victory over her weight, she has certainly made bright inroads and she has definitely settled some of the issues that caused her to board the emotional eating roller-coaster. That takes courage — to face an issue like abuse head-on. As I said in the introduction, the truth is confronting and it can also be painful.

Courage isn't the absence of fear. Courage is continuing on in the face of fear. Anna Eleanor Roosevelt once said, 'You gain strength, courage and confidence by every experience in which you really stop to look fear in the face. You are able to say to yourself, "I lived

through this horror. I can take the next thing that comes along." ...
You must do the thing you think you cannot do.'

Abuse Defined

Abuse is one of the most significant causes of poor self-esteem and poor body image. There are many types of abuse, including emotional, physical, sexual and child abuse.

Emotional (verbal) abuse can include:
▶ teasing
▶ threats
▶ insults
▶ stalking
▶ emotional abandonment (withdrawal)
▶ unreasonable demands
▶ criticising
▶ belittling
▶ rejection
▶ racism.

Physical abuse can include:
▶ hitting
▶ pushing
▶ shoving
▶ burning
▶ shaking
▶ kicking
▶ beatings
▶ tying up
▶ bruising
▶ failing to provide necessities for life.

Sexual abuse can include:

▶ forced sexual touching, fondling, kissing or hugging
▶ forced intercourse (vaginal, oral or anal)
▶ forced masturbation on self or abuser
▶ forced incest
▶ forced to watch other people in sexual behaviour
▶ rape or involuntary penetration
▶ date rape
▶ forced sodomy
▶ forced exhibitionism and sexual exploitation
▶ forced viewing of pornographic material
▶ forced posing for sexual pictures
▶ sexual torture.

Sexual abuse is a serious issue in our society and tragically, it is on the increase, but there is hope for the victims through healing and restoration, and the key is forgiveness. Love and trust also need to find their way back into an impenetrable heart. It may be that you have a broken image of yourself that needs to be restored because abuse of any description can make you feel completely worthless.

Child Abuse

Incest and child sexual assault are sadly becoming more and more common in our society. Sexual assault happens to girls and boys of all ages, from very young children to teenagers. In most cases the offender is a member of the child's immediate family or someone known and trusted by the child. Though child sexual assault happens to both male and female children, more often the victims are girls. Statistics also indicate that the overwhelming majority of, although not all, offenders are male.

Child sexual assault is basically any sexual behaviour imposed on a child. Children are considered to be unable to alter or understand the perpetrator's behaviour due to their early stage of development and powerlessness in the situation. The perpetrator's position of authority and trust enables him or her implicitly or directly to coerce the child into sexual compliance, which is why people who have been abused can suffer from a profound sense of powerlessness.

Child sexual assault involves a range of conduct, including:
▶ fondling of the genital area
▶ masturbation
▶ oral sex
▶ vaginal or anal penetration by a finger, penis or any other object
▶ exhibitionism and suggestive behaviour or comments
▶ exposure to pornography or age-inappropriate nudity.

Any non-accidental physical injury inflicted on a child is considered physical abuse. This may include:
▶ beatings
▶ burns and scalds
▶ fractures
▶ poisoning
▶ bruises or welts
▶ internal injuries
▶ shaking injuries or strangulation.

A constant attitude or behaviour towards a child that is detrimental to or impairs the child's emotional or physical development is regarded as emotional abuse. This may take the form of:
▶ blame
▶ emotional rejection
▶ isolation
▶ continuing verbal abuse
▶ sexual innuendo.

Another form of child abuse is neglect. This is where there is a serious omission or commission by a person that jeopardises or impairs the child's physical, intellectual or emotional development. A child who is neglected may be:

▶ consistently dirty and unwashed
▶ without appropriate supervision for extended periods of time
▶ undernourished.

They therefore may be at risk of:

▶ injury or harm
▶ constant tiredness
▶ hunger
▶ listlessness
▶ medical conditions relating to poor hygiene.

A friend of mine was completely neglected as a child and grew up on the streets of Sydney with her brother. Her parents loved her and weren't intentionally cruel, but they were both alcoholics and abusive of each other, and in order to get some peace in their lives the children fled and lived on the streets.

She suffered so much that it is difficult for her even to talk about everything that happened to her; she says she can't remember many things because it was too painful. As a young teenager she developed a goitre, which is a large lump in her thyroid gland, because she was malnourished.

I am delighted to say that my friend is one of the most remarkable women I know. She has a wonderful marriage and lovely children, she is now a grandmother and she is using her life to help others get over similar hurdles to those she faced growing up.

Facts About Abuse

The problem of abuse is widespread. The Australian Bureau of Statistics, through its Welfare Statistics Branch, has been attempting for many years to ensure that all states and territories collect data that conform to uniform standards. Yet in the case of child abuse, despite agreement in general, national figures are not available. What we do know is that since statistics have been kept by welfare departments, the number of children reported and confirmed as having been abused has increased.

This may be due to a number of factors including growing community awareness, professional education, media reports and TV programs, legal requirements and a change in society's attitude towards breaking the silence surrounding family violence.

While a similar percentage of boys and girls were abused by strangers, percentages varied when comparing abuse at the hands of a family member or a known person. Forty per cent of boys were assaulted by a family member and 56 per cent by a known person, while the percentages for girls is reversed — 56 per cent were assaulted by a family member and 40 per cent by a known person.

Because an allegation of child sexual abuse provokes such strong emotions, and the consequences to both the family and the alleged offender are so serious, it can sometimes be difficult ensuring that a balanced appraisal is made. That is also why it is imperative to seek professional help if you, a friend or a family member has been sexually assaulted.

There is evidence that the immediate effects of severe abuse (physical or sexual) can be catastrophic for children, resulting in mental retardation, brain damage or death. The long-term consequences can also be devastating, leaving physical and emotional scars which result in psychiatric illness, an inability to form meaningful relationships and unusual aggressiveness, which may be turned inward (youth suicide has doubled in the last twenty years) or outward as assault behaviour, with the victims repeating the abuse inflicted upon them.

In a study of sexual offenders, it was found that nearly half of them had been child victims of abuse. Studies of parents who physically abuse or neglect their children have found that most reported extreme violence in their own childhood.

People who inflict abuse are not all the same. What is frightening, however, is that offenders are often considered 'normal' by their friends, families or workmates, until it is discovered that they are inflicting abuse.

Generally speaking, evidence suggests that abusive parents have difficulty controlling their impulses, low self-esteem, a poor capacity for empathy and are socially isolated. Environmental factors, such as poverty, poor housing and chronic illness, are not sufficient causes, but such stresses combined with poor parenting skills and a sense of having little control over one's life are all contributing factors.

Physical abuse or domestic violence is another major issue.

The Women's Safety Survey conducted by the Australian Bureau of Statistics surveyed approximately 6300 Australian women about their experience of actual or threatened physical and sexual violence. Based on the survey results, it was estimated that in the twelve months prior to completing the survey:

▶ 7.1 per cent of the adult female population (490 400 women) experienced violence;

▶ 6.2 per cent of women experienced violence perpetrated by a male, and 1.6 per cent experienced violence perpetrated by a female;

▶ 2.6 per cent of women who were married or in a de facto relationship (or 111 000 women) had experienced violence perpetrated by their current partner;

▶ 4.8 per cent of unmarried women had experienced violence by their previous partner in the last 12 months.

The survey also recorded women's experiences of violence during their lifetime. From the results it was estimated that:

▶ 2.6 million women (or 38 per cent of the adult female population) had experienced one or more incidents of physical or sexual violence since the age of fifteen; 1.2 million had experienced sexual violence and 2.2 million experienced physical violence. For the majority of women (2.5 million women) the violence was perpetrated by a man;

- 8 per cent of women (345 400 women) currently in a marital or de facto relationship had experienced an incident of physical or sexual violence perpetrated by their partner at some time during their relationship;

- Of women who had been in a previous relationship, 42 per cent (1.1 million women) had experienced an incident of physical violence by their previous partner.

Although these statistics are useful, it is widely assumed that most estimates of the incidence of domestic violence are underestimates as large population surveys cannot provide accurate estimates of the extent of domestic violence in Australia.

These underestimates are partly because many victims feel unable to speak out about domestic violence. The pressures of negative community attitudes towards them and feelings of shame and fear of retribution from the perpetrator, contribute to low levels of disclosure of domestic violence and other forms of abuse as well. Also, because domestic violence often occurs in the privacy of the home, there are few outside witnesses. Surveys often require fluency in English, which means that the experience of people from non-English speaking backgrounds may not be adequately represented.

Sleeping Beauty

In my version of the classic fairy-tale *Sleeping Beauty*, what happened to Princess Annalise was one of the most despicable things that can happen to anyone. Sleeping Beauty experienced immeasurable pain as her wicked uncle and his sons sexually abused her. She had come to terms with the fact that she was adopted and wholeheartedly loved by her parents, but her wicked uncle couldn't. She had to deal with the torture of being repeatedly sexually abused. The pain caused the princess to shut down and go to sleep, for a very long time.

You may have read this story and realised that this too is your story, and you can relate all too well to the torment, depression and emotional destruction suffered as a result of sexual abuse. If this has happened to you, it's vital for you to realise that you did absolutely nothing to deserve what happened to you. It is not your fault. It is not your fault. It is not your fault!

If there was ever going to be a time when someone would want to escape reality, a feeling of wanting to just go to sleep and never wake up again, it would be when they are being abused. In her book *Breaking Through*, author Cathy Ann Matthews writes about herself, 'My history will always read ... "abused as a child." But now I have found hope. The control of abuse is broken.'

Cathy Ann went from sleeping to being able to wake up from the nightmare, because the control of the abuse was broken. She recognised the need to break the power of her past from continuing to rule her future. Cathy Ann used a similar method to the 'Chain of Change' mentioned on page 7.

You must face the truth if you have been abused and you need to confront your feelings of self worth. It requires courage for you to make a decision that you will not allow your thinking to revert to your past. This means that every time your thoughts drift backwards, you will need to replace them immediately with thoughts about your future. In time, this will result in positive change and freedom.

Consequences

If you remember being sexually abused, you may have felt or still feel some or all of these feelings:

▶ afraid that you've made it up
▶ angry at him or her for what they did
▶ ashamed at not being able to stop it
▶ betrayed by him or her
▶ scared to tell anyone

- anxious and panicked
- sad because you lost a part of your childhood or adulthood life
- guilty because you think you must have done something to make it happen
- tricked because he or she called it love
- angry because no one protected you
- depressed
- isolated because you couldn't ever tell anyone
- insecure
- worried about what other people will think
- confused about what really happened.

The trauma does not end when the abuse stops, and this is common. Sexual abuse can affect a person's life in many ways.

A victim of abuse may hate their body, be unable to trust people and find intimacy in relationships very difficult; they also may consider sex to be disgusting or humiliating. Then there's the anger. This anger feels the need to destroy. Victims may also 'zone out', trying to escape the pain of how they have been affected, physically and emotionally. They may feel like they are going insane and in order to retain some sense of normality, they may even throw themselves into their career so that they are busy and on the move all the time — anything to try and escape the pain.

Another common behaviour is identified by clinical psychologist John Hodge in Janine Turner's book *Home is Where the Hurt Is*. He says, 'It seems that the more desperate the individual is to escape or avoid the memories of what has happened the more and more difficult to deal with and paradoxically more insistent and more persevering they become. Instead of becoming less distressed over time, for some, distress can seem to grow and overwhelm.'

Displaced guilt is another consequence in the abuse victim's life. There is a powerful scene in the movie *Good Will Hunting* where Robin Williams is counselling Matt Damon in regard to his delinquent behaviour, which was a result of him suffering childhood physical and sexual abuse. In the movie Williams tells Damon over and over again that the sexual and physical abuse that he suffered was not his fault. This continues until Damon breaks down and is finally able to acknowledge that it was not his fault. A friend of mine is a counsellor and she shows this video to people who have been through abuse, as it helps to illustrate the power of putting the blame where it belongs — off the victim and onto the perpetrator.

It may be that the person who was supposed to be a protector in your life became a perpetrator of pain, and this has led to feelings of shame. This shame can cause you to feel like you have to keep secrets and therefore you may not know how to express yourself because of the crippling fear. Perhaps you have had to learn to go to sleep or shut down on the outside, even though your insides are screaming out with pain and longing to be set free.

A helpful book on this subject is *The Wounded Heart*, by Dr Dan B Allender. In this book about hope for adult victims of childhood sexual abuse, Dr Allender recalls the words of a young woman who was facing memories of abuse perpetrated by her father, 'I'd rather be dead than face the truth of the memories.'

This is the tragic reality of countless millions of people today — men and women, boys and girls — who are violated and abused and who simply do not know how to deal with their pain. They are too afraid to talk and as a result, they can feel desperately isolated. As they try to solve the problem alone, feeling trapped and unable to escape and with a strong tendency to shut down to deal with the pain, depression can settle like a blanket over their life. Words such as confusion, betrayal, damaged and hopeless are all too familiar to those who have suffered abuse.

Depression

Although depression is not experienced only by those who have been abused, it is more common among those who have. When depressed, life can seem difficult, meaningless, sad and exhausting. We can go through life feeling like we need to live as everyone expects us to, always cheerful and never tripping over life's problems. There are days when we can feel less than adequate. You are not going 'mad', there is a logical reason for its occurrence and simple steps to dismiss it.

Clinically diagnosed depression is defined as an imbalance of chemicals in the brain and is most commonly brought on as a result of stress. Inside the human brain there are three specific chemicals known as neurotransmitters (serotonin, norepinephrine and dopamine). These three chemicals serve specific functions and it is serotonin that is most often associated with depression. When the level of serotonin drops in the brain, the result is varying degrees of depression and its corresponding symptoms. At some point in life everyone may experience some form of depression. It may last only a short time, but other cases of depression can last much longer when the serotonin level remains low.

We can all probably recount times when we have felt one or more of the following symptoms:

- depressed mood
- lack of interest in almost all activities
- change in appetite or significant weight loss or gain
- unusual sleeping behaviour
- agitation or restlessness
- lack of energy or chronic tiredness
- low self-esteem or self-depreciation
- inability to concentrate or think clearly
- desire to escape (run away, lock oneself away from people, even suicide)
- accelerated thought or worry.

It is important to realise that these symptoms can be a natural response by our bodies to disappointing, unexpected tragic events. Experienced only temporarily, they are nothing to be worried about.

If you can relate to these symptoms, know that you are not alone. Statistics tell us that depression affects one in every four adults to some degree.

Unfortunately for many people, the symptoms listed above do not go away and many or even all of these symptoms can be experienced at the same time. In this case it is important to recognise that what you are experiencing is natural, but these behaviours and feelings are not healthy. In fact, they are indicators that things are not normal, and that the 'emotional pendulum' has swung too far in one direction and needs to be counteracted in order to return the feelings of normality you feel you have lost.

There are two major causes of depression.

Long-term high stress levels
This is a type of depression that can sneak up on you. Through daily life, we can have pressures, deadlines, expectations, responsibilities and stresses that go virtually unnoticed. All these seemingly minor things can compound to create a major imbalance of chemicals within the brain. The end result is, 'I am depressed but don't know why.'

Sudden or severe loss
This type of depression is much more easy to recognise. It stems from a radical change, in which the severity of the change leaves the neurotransmitters unable to maintain balance within the brain. It could be caused by abuse, the loss of a friend or loved one, a job loss, or a similar unexpected or severe loss.

Although depression is a psychological condition, it is linked to our physical health. With this in mind, it is important to understand that the way we treat our physical body is going to affect our mental health.

The good news is that depression is not a genetic defect and therefore it is almost always easily treatable and correctable, once properly diagnosed. Through medication the chemical imbalance within the brain can be restored and with the help of a professional psychologist or counsellor, the junk and the lies we have filled our minds with can be replaced by the truth. The dark glasses through which you may currently view the world can be removed.

If you suffer from ongoing depression from what happened in your past, it is time to break the cycle. In *Home is Where The Hurt Is*, author Janine Turner writes, 'Everyone has to find their trigger points: those times in their life which remind them of an abusive past.' She suggests listing these 'triggers' to give you the ability to recognise when you may be most at risk of falling prey to depressive feelings of guilt, shame, bitterness, fear and despair.

No More Fear

Having experienced physical and emotional abuse myself, I have known what it is to live in the constant grip of fear. It took me a long time to be able to acknowledge that I was not just harmed, but I was abused. I have recollections of bolting out my front door before I could be grabbed and jumping into my car and driving off at high speed. I used to drive fast on purpose because deep down I wished that the police would pull me over so that I could be arrested and rescued. I was never caught. Instead I found myself sleeping on a cold veranda at the local Salvation Army residence. I was too ashamed and afraid to tell anyone what was going on. I loved this person with all of my heart and so I lived with this secret pain for many, many years. I felt worthless and hopeless.

Even though I had been hurt by someone who I loved, I needed to get help, and that's exactly what I did eventually. I was then able to draw a boundary line that meant that I wouldn't allow this to happen to me ever again. Eventually I became strong enough to draw the line and get out of the bin. Sadly many people can't do this and end up in a spiral of depression because they don't know how to stop the pain.

Forgiveness

If you want to deal with the wounds of the past, you will not necessarily feel courageous, nor will you necessarily feel excitement when starting out on a new life journey — the healing process takes time and commitment. You have already lived through the hardest and most painful part — the abuse itself. You have survived and now you can use the strength you have gained to build a future free from the pain of abuse.

If you have been abused, you should seek professional help — also:

- Tell another person who you know you can trust.
- Forgive those who have hurt you; this will release you from bitterness and reliving the pain.
- Believe that it wasn't your fault and stop blaming yourself.
- Feel compassion for yourself, for the person who was frightened and powerless, but don't become self-absorbed.

The only way that we can go forward after being subjected to any form of abuse — whether it is sexual, physical or emotional — is to forgive the person or people who have hurt us. However hard it is to do, however painful the experience may have been, if we want to move forward in life, I believe we must forgive.

Forgiveness starts as a decision and then works its way through your life, as you allow it, by giving it room to take over all the pain and bitterness that may be ruling your existence. Genuine forgiveness opens the door again to trust, so that with adequate boundaries (fences not walls), you will be able to believe again that some people are honest and mean no harm. Some people are safe and reliable and it is OK to believe them, expect from them and even put hope in them.

Forgiveness means we no longer have feelings of anger or resentment towards a person or an action that has caused us harm or upset. We also free someone from their debt towards us. If we don't free them from that debt, it will keep that person connected to us for the rest of our lives. Our forgiveness cuts the cord to the person who has caused us the pain. When we choose to forgive, the past will be the past and not remain the present and the future.

Remember the Truth: forgiveness is the key that unlocks the freedom of your future.

Forgiveness

Keep us forgiven with you, and forgiving others.

Matthew 6:12, The Bible

Caroline's Story

It was sobering to find out I was not who I thought I was. As I phoned my relatives and friends to tell them the 'family secret' was out, I found most of them already knew. I felt so exposed and vulnerable. That day, every fact I thought to be true about my conception, birth, parents and family history turned out to be a lie.

I found myself lying awake at night wondering what my story was. Eventually I contacted the adoption centre and filled in the forms to start the search for my biological mother. Soon afterwards, an envelope arrived. I was a little nervous as I opened it. I pulled out my original birth certificate and hospital records. My biological mother's name was recorded on the form; however, in the box next to father's name was the word 'unknown'. Even more devastating than this was what appeared next to the box where my name should have been: 'unnamed'.

My heart sank. I stood in the kitchen sobbing as I held this piece of paper, feeling so alone, rejected and abandoned. My mind was filled with many thoughts. I wondered why this woman who had carried me in her womb for nine months did not want me. Why did she not even name me?

Not only was I unnamed, but the social worker's report said that my biological mother 'did not appear connected to this child'. In fact she wanted to get it all over and done with as soon as possible and resume work.

My mind began to work overtime. I thought to myself, 'No wonder I was abused for twelve years. I was obviously worth nothing anyway. I was an accident that was never meant to be here. I was never really wanted and a gross inconvenience.'

I had spent all of my teenage years and my early twenties totally imprisoned in my mind with feelings of guilt, fear and shame because of the abuse. I really did not like myself at all, let alone have the ability to love myself.

I was sexually abused by two members of my extended family. Every single week of my life, from when I was just three years of age until I was fourteen, my body was used for their pleasure. It was torture. The sexual abuse only stopped when I was big enough to stop it from happening.

Now I didn't feel sorry for myself at all. Who was I trying to kid, I probably deserved everything I got. It was all my fault.

I know my parents loved me — together they had taken an unnamed two-week-old baby girl and had given me a name. I know that they wanted me, but I found it hard to piece everything together. It wasn't their fault that these men who were supposed to be my family and my protectors chose to abuse me instead, but somehow I didn't feel protected from it.

I continually felt as though nothing good could happen to someone like me. I thought that people like me deserved exactly what they got. I hoped that if I could just endure life, try to be good enough to get people's approval, maybe they would not use or abuse me any more. So I kept trying for another award, another medal, I kept trying to be good enough for people to like me but to stay far enough away from me to never be able to hurt me again. The wall around my heart was so huge and thick. Nothing would ever get in that close to destroy me again.

I came across as hard, driven, focused, lacking compassion and mercy — inside I was dying. My life was spiralling out of control, my emotions were everywhere, my self-esteem was zilch. I kept asking questions: 'Do I belong anywhere? Could anyone just like me for me? Could anyone get deep enough inside me to find the real me? Who is the real me?'

Finally I went for help, and I found it. It's amazing what you can find if you really look with a willing heart. I had to make decisions based on the truth and not just on facts. The truth is that I am fearfully and wonderfully made, even though the fact was that I was treated like a worthless piece of nothing. The way that I saw my past and my future was my choice and I made it, and the truth has set me free.

We are living in a time when almost 15 per cent of the population is in some kind of psychotherapy. Bookshops have entire shelves dedicated to topics such as 'how to heal your soul' or 'caring for your soul'. People are looking for answers as they bear the scars and pain of past abuse, rejection, divorce, poverty and abandonment. We often carry wounds from our past into our families, workplaces and relationships. Regardless of how well we learn to hide them, they will inevitably be revealed.

They often manifest themselves as fear, insecurity, compulsive behaviours, eating disorders, anger or immorality. I came to accept that I needed help. It took months of counselling and the constant application of certain principles like renewing my mind, getting rid of all the rubbish that had made its home in my head and putting good things there in its place.

I chose to leave my past behind. It was a major breakthrough in my life when I was finally able to admit that I had been abused. I chose to forgive those who had hurt me. I remember sobbing and sobbing as I knelt, unable to articulate the words 'I forgive'. When I did, I experienced a release that had been waiting to spring forth for twenty years.

I am now happily married and have a beautiful baby daughter. Seeing her in her little bed sometimes makes me cry happy tears, for all the potential that lies in my little girl. She's a permanent reminder of how wonderful it is to be free to start life over again.

10 Keys to Freedom

from abuse

As you step out from abuse, you will need support from other people. To start with, that may mean a professional counsellor and one trusted friend or relative. Expect that these keys will work best when you involve others.

1. Admit that it happened and do not blame yourself.
2. Be prepared to face the fact that the abuse has damaged you in some way — your image has been broken.
3. Work through past pain with a professional counsellor.
4. Recognise how you see yourself, others and relationships.
5. Explore the habits, attitudes and thought patterns you have developed, and be willing to change them if necessary.
6. Discover the defence mechanisms you have adopted to stop yourself from being hurt, and adopt positive behaviours to help you deal with any future hurt.
7. Learn to re-establish appropriate boundaries (see Chapter 6), with the help of others.
8. Learn to forgive. This is for YOUR benefit and not just for the benefit of the person you are forgiving.
9. Dare to begin to trust and love.
10. Reach out and help someone else. Use your past to give someone else hope for the future.

body soul spirit

ACTION PLAN

body

Allow people you trust to touch you. Allowing hugs from people you trust will help you get over some of the fears associated with being physically violated.

soul

Change the tape in the tape recorder of your mind. Don't listen to past abusive words, and do listen to, believe and live out the wonderful person that you really are.

spirit

Pray for healing and the ability to forgive those who have hurt you, and pray that your story will some day be able to help others.

My goal is freedom
FROM ABUSE

Chapter 10

Stand Tall Poppy

freedom from envy and jealousy

*'A tall poppy culture should be encouraged,
where achievement is celebrated and innovation
and creativity applauded.'*

Snow White

Once upon a time a beautiful royal couple lived in a magnificent palace. One winter day, as the queen sewed beside her window, she accidentally pricked her finger. As she stared at the spots of blood falling on the snow outside her window, she thought of her daughter, with skin as white as snow, lips as red as blood and hair as black as ebony. The queen called her Snow White. Snow White was very close to her mother and when she died suddenly, Snow White was crushed with grief. But time passed and the king married again. The woman he married was attractive, but she was very cold and very jealous of Snow White. The new queen spent hours staring at her mirror, asking, 'Mirror, mirror on the wall, who's the fairest of them all?' The mirror was magic, and it answered her, 'You are the fairest of them all.'

But Snow White was growing up and becoming lovelier. She was beautiful, strong and clever.

One day the queen approached her mirror, and it said, 'Listen, Queen, what I tell you is true, Snow White is far lovelier than you!' The Queen was enraged and she forced a servant to leave Snow White deep in the forest at the mercy of wild beasts. Snow White wandered alone until she came to a tiny cottage. Exhausted, she curled up on one of the seven little beds and fell asleep. When the seven dwarves who lived there arrived home, Snow White awoke and explained how she had come to the forest and all that had happened to her in the palace. The friendly little dwarves encouraged Snow White to stand tall.

The kind men invited her to stay, and the next day they warned Snow White to be very careful of the Queen, because the mirror would surely tell her the truth about her whereabouts:

'You, O Queen, are the fairest here,
but over the hills, in the greenwood shade,
where seven dwarves their house have made,
there Snow White is hiding from you, and she

is far lovelier than you!'

The queen decided to take matters into her own hands. Disguised as an old woman, she walked to the cottage and knocked on the door. Snow White looked up to see an old lady selling apples. 'Try one,' she said. Snow White took a bite from the poisoned apple and immediately collapsed.

'Nothing will save you now!' cried the queen triumphantly. As she ran back into the darkness, it overtook her. She fell down in utter surprise, depression and anguish, not feeling one bit as victorious and free as she thought she would. 'I got rid of her,' she thought. 'I should feel free! Why do I feel worse?' The darkness crowded in around her. 'I refuse to help her! I will not love her!' she screamed into the night. But no one heard her, no one saw her and no one has seen or heard from her since.

When the seven dwarves returned home they found their beautiful friend without breath. Laying her on a bed, they wept for days. They wanted somewhere special for Snow White to rest.

A handsome prince visited the dwarves as they mourned and offered to take the beautiful girl to his palace, where she could lie. As the Prince lifted her limp body, a small piece of apple fell from her mouth, and she awoke. 'Where am I?' she whispered.

'You are safe,' said the prince gently. The Prince took Snow White to his palace, where they fell deeply in love.

Snow White stood with her head held high with the handsome Prince by her side and they returned to the palace where she was reunited with her father and they all lived and reigned in the kingdom, happily ever after.

The End

Fact
Jealousy is an ugly shade of green.

Truth
A blessed life is enviable.

Mirror, mirror on the wall, who's the fairest of them all?

Many people define success in terms of how satisfied they are with their personal and professional relationships. In fact, a great deal of our overall happiness in life can be influenced by achieving success in these personal and professional realms. However, our desire for success can sometimes lead to the harmful emotions of jealousy and envy. Many people who are beautiful, clever and talented are made to feel guilty for it because beauty and brilliance can cause jealousy in others.

The more we shine, the more some people tend to feel threatened and there can be a cruel pressure in life to shrink rather than stand tall.

It is crucial to recognise when people are trying to cut you down to size so that you don't automatically shrink in their presence. Resist the pressure and learn to stand tall and shine, just as you were created to shine. When you maintain a deep sense of knowing that you have been created for a purpose greater than yourself, you simply won't allow yourself to be kept in a box.

On the other hand, you might find yourself falling into the pattern of cutting others down to size, or wanting what they have for your own life. The more you focus on your own gifts and goals, the less you will yearn for what someone else has. This chapter deals with both aspects of jealousy and envy, whether you are receiving it or sending it out.

Jealousy

Most of us have experienced the 'green-eyed monster', jealousy, as described in Shakespeare's famous play *Othello*. At its most intense, it is a horrible, tormenting obsession and often involves power and control, as we want to keep things or people exclusively to ourselves. Yet just as falling in love seems natural and uncontrollable, so too can jealousy. It just comes over us when someone or something threatens what we have.

In order to work out how we should behave in order to maintain a healthy self-esteem for ourselves and others, it's important to understand that jealousy is not always negative. Like hunger and thirst, feelings of jealousy (and envy) are normal symptoms of one or more unfulfilled human needs. Accepting this can help you be free from unwarranted guilt or shame.

One of the first things we need to understand about jealousy is that it is a word used to describe a variety of emotional states that are not all the same. It is confusing when, for example, the same word is used to describe the pain we might feel at learning that our partner has been unfaithful, and the suspiciousness of a person who is constantly seeing signs of infidelity where none in fact exist. One form of jealousy is rational and the other form is irrational.

Unhealthy jealousy and irrational behaviour usually go hand in hand. Sometimes this behaviour results in the destruction of people and possessions, all in the name of not wanting to lose something; as the saying goes, 'If I can't have it, then no one will,' or 'If I can't be with them, then no one will.' So we systematically destroy that which we are so desperate to preserve. All because we aren't secure enough to set people free.

Jealousy that comes from being protective of your relationships is rational, as long as you give the people and relationships in your life freedom to have a life outside you. I personally like the fact that my husband is jealous in a healthy way of our marriage and family; that is, if anyone were to try to interfere with it in a negative way, he would fight to protect it. That kind of concern brings security.

As the famous saying goes, 'If you love someone, set them free. If they come back, they're yours. If they don't, they never were.'

If you want to safeguard your relationships through a healthy self-esteem, then you need to gain security and lose unhealthy jealousy that will only make the person whose relationship you value want to run far away from you.

Jealousy is a very primitive emotion that is displayed at a very young age in each one of us. It is simply the emotion of possessiveness. Young children often display it when they say 'That's mine!' before grabbing something back.

There are two basic sources of jealous feelings. The first is internal and is based upon low self-esteem, a sense of inferiority or preoccupation with loss. The second is external and occurs in response to an actual or perceived loss of attention or caring from someone. Usually there is a blend of both internal and external factors that work together in a self-perpetuating cycle.

Most instances of jealousy arise from insecurity, but sometimes jealousy comes from feelings of scarcity rather than feelings of insecurity in oneself — the fear is that 'there is only so much love to go around'.

Those who suffer from jealousy are usually vigilant and anxiously watchful. They are also apprehensive about the motives of others and they usually have a morbid fear of rivalry in love, career or assets. Suspicion is also an aspect of jealousy. We are jealous when we suspect someone of aiming to deprive us of what we dearly prize.

Basically, the greater the threat, the more intense the jealousy, and, how we perceive the threat influences the jealousy. The following five stages of jealousy reflect what this cycle of emotion can look like:

1. Suspicion

If you are insecure about a situation and you are very dependent on another person, you may be jealous. You may see signs of problems when none are there.

2. Assessment

We may spy on certain situations and lie awake at night worrying and reviewing any evidence we may have. When it comes to relationships, men often see a threat and feel jealous first, then worry that something is wrong with them, whereas women are more concerned with maintaining the relationship. They worry about losing love; they feel inadequate first, then jealous.

3. Emotions
If we decide there is a threat to something we have, we can have a very wide range of responses: clinging dependency, violent rage at the competitor or the partner, fear, obsessive curiosity, self-criticism, depression with suicidal thoughts, hurt, resentment and social embarrassment.

4. Coping
There are two basic choices. The first is to try and do whatever it takes to secure that which is threatened, and the other is to try and protect your feelings when everything's over. The preservation of self-respect is really important when it comes to getting on with the future after losing something or someone has been taken from you.

5. End result
It is important to know whether particular emotional and coping responses are going to help or harm you. Ask yourself whether these responses will build or destroy what may be left of your self-esteem.

Before looking at how to deal with jealousy, it's important to try and understand its causes first. Different theorists have different explanations of jealousy. For example, Freudians say the overwhelming dread and pain of rejection originates in childhood when we discover that we are not our mother or father's favourite person, because our parents are usually that to each other. This insecurity is obviously unconscious.

Sociologists emphasise cultural influences. All societies tell us we should be jealous but in different circumstances; for example, within some cultures men consider it a compliment if a visiting male wants sex with his wife but a visitor wanting to keep the wife would be highly resented. In this instance, jealousy is a learned social reaction, not a natural tendency.

Sociobiologists like Charles Darwin believe that jealousy is inbuilt for genetic survival. Men want exclusive sexual partners so they can pass on their genes, and women want devoted helpers to help with their children.

Therefore jealousy, and also envy, may have different meanings and emotional associations for different people. Being jealous or envious may feel acceptable to some people as a normal, usually harmless human trait, while with others, jealousy may cause them to feel that they are experiencing something wrong.

When our self-esteem is low and when we are unaware of what we are feeling or thinking, we tend to handle negative emotions by becoming uncomfortable in the situation, by blaming someone else; then we react with negative emotions which cause us to feel worse, and so we increase the blame.

Getting beyond the negative emotions that come with the unhealthy jealousy and envy package, we need to stop blaming everyone else and start taking responsibility for why we are feeling what we are feeling and how we are reacting. Otherwise, we will find ourselves stuck in the blame merry-go-round, which is an unhealthy cycle that says 'I am a poor victim'.

The way to deal with this cycle is to assess why you are feeling jealous or envious and then when it comes time to allocate responsibility, recognise right then that you have a part to play in controlling how you are going to react. Once you take control, you are able to dissipate your emotions.

Envy

We sometimes use the terms jealousy and envy interchangeably, but they are two different words with two different meanings. Despite the frequent confusion of these two terms, a clear distinction remains. Envy is defined as 'a feeling of discontent and resentment aroused by and in conjunction with desire for the possessions or qualities of another', while jealousy is being 'fearful or wary of being supplanted, apprehensive of losing affection or position'.

If I want what you have, I am envious of you. If, however, I want to protect something that I have from you, I am jealous of that particular thing.

Deep down, people who are unhealthily jealous do not necessarily want to be rich so much as they want others to be poor. Envy sees that you are rich and wants the same for itself. Here is a clear distinction between jealousy and envy: envy desires the value, but jealousy desires to destroy that value in someone else's life. The jealous reaction to someone or something of value is usually not love, desire and admiration, but the opposite — hate, rejection and disdain.

Unhealthily jealous people usually try to hide their mission to destroy the valuable behind noble causes, or talk about wanting to bring people down to size. Unhealthy envy comes from recognising values and virtues but failing to achieve them personally. These types of people often resent success, happiness, achievement and any good fortune. They rejoice in others' failures.

Because jealousy is more about 'me' and envy more about 'you', the former is often displayed in a much more active and sometimes violent manner than the latter. Yet don't get caught believing that either you or someone else is jealous or envious only if displaying more aggressive emotions, such as anger, as one can feel anxiety as opposed to anger and still be envious or jealous.

Just as with some jealousy, not all feelings of envy need to be seen as negative. For example, it is certainly not wrong to look at a healthy marriage and want a healthy and happy marriage for yourself. We can often look enviously at people who are very blessed in body, soul and spirit, and wish that we could have what they have. They have an enviable life, which means that people are drawn to want the same blessing, and as long as it's for the right reasons, then there is nothing wrong with this type of desire. If you have special feelings of animosity directed toward that person, however, then you are negatively envious of them.

When you experience either jealousy or envy, it doesn't make you a bad person. Learning how to handle them is extremely important for our emotional wellbeing and self-esteem. The main concern is not so much whether we experience jealousy or envy, but what we should do when we have these experiences. If you choose to explore why you feel the way you do, then you have an opportunity to get to the bottom of the emotion. When you understand why you feel jealous or envious, then you can begin to deal with it.

I don't think anyone is immune from either jealousy or envy. As I've said, I don't think people are necessarily wrong to have these feelings, or that they should be suppressed. After all, suppression of anything, and especially emotions, does not make them disappear. And I am most definitely not saying I have never experienced envy or jealousy. However, the occasions have become less and less as I have grown to accept that my focus should be within my own relationships.

When I do feel those twinges of emotion, I view them as signals telling me something. Either my focus is not in the right place, or I have an insecurity or fear which has nothing to do with the other person, and must be dealt with.

Both envy and jealousy, in my opinion, mean self-focus, which is the beginning of the end when it comes to developing a healthy self-esteem. While we must take care of ourselves, we should not be the centre of the universe to ourselves. This is selfish and unhealthy living.

Take your eyes off what you don't have, or what others have got, and turn the scanner within. Find the cause of your envy and jealousy, clear away past negative voices and experiences, then pour some energy into building your personal and emotional security. Then you will be the one others envy, and you can remember the pain and reach out to them.

When unhealthy envy and jealousy are present in your life, they bring discontentment and resentment because of one person's yearning for something possessed by another. This something can be physical or invisible. The longing, and the related relationship stresses, are just the same, and some jealousies are worse than others.

Like all relationship problems, unhealthy envy and jealousy can be seen as either a problem or an opportunity. You have a choice to live with resentment, hurt, anxiety and guilt, or with encouragement, empathy, compassion and constructive internal growth.

Needless to say, the best protection against envy and jealousy is a healthy self-esteem; that is, prevention is better than cure. Envy and jealousy can be reduced by staying active, distracting yourself with friends, doing fun activities, furthering your career, undertaking self-improvement where necessary, and renewing your mind. Before long, the many irrational thoughts and expectations that come with envy and jealousy will be defeated with rational thinking.

Snow White

In the classic story *Snow White*, a young woman was hunted down by someone who was insanely jealous of her beauty. Most people at some time during their lives have either been subjected to, or taken part in, jealous or envious behaviour or both. It is human nature, and jealousy is not just confined to romance. Romantic or relational jealousy is obvious, but other types of jealousy are more subtle and yet can be equally or more destructive.

Snow White became victim to another's jealousy. She became the victim of tall poppy syndrome and was obsessively envied, harassed and hunted down — all because she was fairer than them all. The sad reality is that some people live their lives at a level below their full potential, even though they may be beautiful and bright, simply because they have been subjected to another person's jealousy of them and they have not known how to deal with it. This can cause some people to wish they were small poppies like everyone else.

The wicked queen was a classic small poppy; not just wanting to bring Snow White down to size, but down to a size that was smaller than herself, so she could feel better about who she was.

Despite their size, the seven dwarves were the exact opposite. They nurtured and encouraged Snow White so she grew even taller. They may have been small in physical stature, but by seeing who Snow White really was and not being intimidated by a princess and the 'greatness' that she had within her, they encouraged her to fulfil that greatness, and were therefore giants on the inside.

Tall Poppy Syndrome

The tall poppy is a metaphor for excellence and endeavour. It symbolises outstanding achievement in any field. A tall poppy culture should be encouraged to develop a culture which celebrates achievement rather than cutting down individuals who achieve, and to encourage innovation and creativity.

In Australia we have a tradition of cutting down tall poppies; people who succeed. We tend to back the underdog and make heroes of those who fail if their cause has been noble, because at least they have 'had a go.'

The classic tall poppy is seen to be pretentious, although this is not always the case. People who are threatened by other people's success love to discredit people who take pride in their achievements. If someone appears to be 'too big for their boots' or 'full of themselves', they present themselves as a target to be pulled down, and often very publicly. If successful people commit an act of indiscretion, whether moral, financial or social, the tall poppy syndrome creates a sense that these people flew too high and that they have now been brought down by their own arrogance and folly.

Lady Mary Fairfax once said, 'I hope we'll throw away our secateurs and start watering our tall poppies.'

Although many people take great pleasure in cutting anyone with an overinflated ego down to size, sometimes there are those who we secretly, or publicly, want to cut down to size merely because they are successful, good looking or intelligent. We claim to appreciate modesty and humility, but people who are insecure sometimes don't want others to succeed around them, because they think it will make them appear small. That's when they feel the need to pull out the gardening shears and begin chopping away at them.

We should not be poppy-pluckers or poppy-slashers, so green with envy of those in whose shade we dwell that we'll do anything to trim them down to our level. On the contrary, we should enjoy basking in the fact that they happen to grow around us.

The tall poppy next door should inspire us to grow and provide us with shade. Author Bryce Courtenay once said, 'When you cut down all the tall poppies, all you are left with is the weeds.' To cut the poppies down is to join the throng of those who believe that mediocrity is normal and that colour, vibrancy and dreaming are somehow culpable for the ills of society. That grey, formless world shuns challenge and risk taking. It is no place for us to live. Be happy for someone else's success, and one day you too may enjoy similar success.

You are meant to be tall on the inside. Your shrinking will only prevent you from achieving your potential and keep you living a sub-standard existence. Quit shrinking!

Gifts and Talents

We all have gifts and talents in something. You might not see yours in your 'mirror' because of others' jealousy or envy, or because of your lack of, or excess, self-esteem. But they are there.

Gifts are the abilities we 'just have' and are often called natural abilities. Giftedness means that you have and use untrained and instinctive abilities in at least one field of endeavour. Talent refers to your ability to master steadily developed abilities (or skills) and knowledge in at least one field of human activity at a superior level.

According to Professor Francoys Gagne, who developed a model of giftedness and talent, the outcome of these abilities should place you in the top 15 per cent of your age group if they are to be classed as being a gift or talent. He also states that gifts can progress to talent through systematic learning and training, but not talent to gifts — gifts are the foundation for talent.

Gifts and talents can be progressed or hindered by two types of factors: intrapersonal and environment. Intrapersonally, motivation plays the most crucial role in initiating any move to further develop talent — it guides it and sustains the gift through such things as failure. What is great is that motivation can be developed in us — so we all have the opportunity to grow our gift by increasing our motivation, and not simply leaving it to genetic disposition. Environmentally, influences can be microscopic or macroscopic. Microscopic environmental influences include upbringing and socioeconomic status and macroscopic influences include your geography (where you live) and demography (who else lives there). Again, these things can be changed and therefore your gift increased to talent.

What is also important to note is those things that will hinder your talent development. Peer pressure, the death of a family member or close friend, or being involved in a major accident or incident can all not only hinder self-esteem, but may also keep your talent from finding expression so it remains locked inside you. If you can increase your self-esteem, you increase your chances of unlocking your talent.

Gifts and talents help give us drive and motivation in life — they should therefore be a source of great enjoyment to us. And it is often the recognition of this by others that results in feelings of jealousy and envy, so that they choose to attack that area in your life and try to steal it from you. Don't let it happen! You need to see yourself as valuable and valued and the truth is, there is no one else on earth like you, gifted exactly as you are. You are not dispensable, if you don't want to be you — there will be no other that could be. Take your gifts and talents seriously, find out what they are. And just as poor self-esteem can muddy your seeing what your gift or talent is, so too can an unhealthy enlarging of it.

Sometimes we just won't allow ourselves to see our true gifts and talents because of mind-sets that tell us that the gift and talent that we have is not good enough. This mind-set can come from many areas, often from being rejected before in that area. But don't give up. Gifts and talents can help us realise our dream, so don't let someone stomp on it because it isn't what they have, or because they can't have it or don't want you to have it.

So how do you recognise if you are gifted or talented in something? Firstly you need to ask yourself what it is that you feel you may be gifted or talented at and then read the following statements. If you can strongly agree with the majority of them, it is more than likely that the skill or activity you are wondering about is a gift or a talent in you.

1.   I learn easily and quickly in this area.
2.   After little or no training I have success in this area.
3.   It is a passion of mine.
4.   I get great results in this area.
5.   I have lots of ability in this area.
6.   I recognise it as a talent in myself.
7.   Other people comment on my ability in this area.
8.   I really enjoy doing this and don't get easily bored.

Don't panic if you can't respond to one, or even any, of the above statements — your self-esteem may be quite low but as you build this up (by following the advice set out for you in the previous chapters), you will be amazed at just what you can do! And don't forget about valuable family and friends. Good family and friends can sometimes spot things that we miss and, if you ask them what they think you may be gifted or talented at, it can help you pinpoint it a little more.

Once you have identified a gift or talent, or have a hunch about one, go and get involved with it. If you think it may be music then buy music and an instrument (or borrow or hire one), take lessons, listen to teaching tapes about it, find someone you look up to with that same gift or talent and hang out with them — find out what they do to improve their gift or enjoy it, join a band, organise 'jam sessions' for you and your friends, or just play by yourself if this seems a little too difficult for you to start off with. The idea is to get involved in that area of gifting or talent and equip yourself in it. You have to feed something in order for it to grow, so feed your gift and talent. It will have this wonderful cyclic effect of improving your self-esteem, which will increase your confidence, which will in turn increase your gift or talent, which in turn again will increase your self-esteem. Exercising your gifts and talents creates win–win situations.

Establishing Your Call

Creation is an amazing thing. Have you ever taken the time just to sit amongst it all and just observe? It is great for the body, soul and spirit. What has amazed me over and over again as I observe creation is the way everything moves and connects together. One of those connections is in the way different animals communicate to each other. How does a lamb know its mother from the hundreds of other ewes in the paddock? The mother has a specific call, just for her baby. How does the male seal find his partner amongst the hundreds of identical females that are scattered across the shore? A call. It is meant for only one, and only that one can really answer the call. If another lamb tried to approach the mother ewe, she would reject it — as the bull seal would reject another female.

You and I have a 'call'. It is what you were destined to do and only you can answer or fulfil it — as it is meant only and specifically for you.

Of course, just because you have a call doesn't mean you will answer or fulfil it and just like our gifts and talents, the jealousy and envy that we feel or that others subject us to can hinder or even prevent our call from being realised.

I know what it is like to be envied in an unhealthy way, and I do not like it. I know what it is to have someone want to try and steal my identity. But try as they may, they can't take away who I am, no matter how manipulative and envious they become. This is an example of unhealthy and damaging jealousy and envy, and when an individual tries to do this, it is a sign that their self-esteem is extremely low — otherwise they wouldn't be trying to be someone that they are not.

Regardless of whether you suffer from unhealthy jealousy or envy or both, you need to take charge of your feelings and emotions by thinking about and taking responsibility for your actions. One way of doing this is by looking at your own life and focusing on everything that you are and what you are meant to be doing with your life. As you learn to focus on your own 'lane' in life, you become less concerned with feeling the need to have someone else's life.

Here is an example of how to take a good look at what you are meant to be doing with your life. I have dissected my call as follows.

Me

I am called to be me. That's an important revelation that I must have before I can even begin to focus on what I am meant to be doing with my life. I am also called to ensure that I am healthy in body, soul and spirit. This means that I need to eat well, exercise regularly and get enough sleep! I also need to feed my soul by taking time out for recreational activities. I feed my spirit by reading the Bible, praying and attending church regularly. Looking after 'me' means that I can focus on all the other things I am meant to do with my life.

Mission

Ever since I was a little girl I have wanted to help people. I know that part of my call is to help make a positive difference in people's lives. I have chosen to do this through writing, speaking and pastoring. I work as a pastor, helping people build their spiritual lives, and also as author and speaker, helping people build their natural lives. In my younger years I thought the only way of achieving this desire in my heart was to go and become a missionary in India or Africa, but I have since learned that my mission field is right here in my 'back yard' of Sydney, Australia, and I have much to keep me busy!

Marriage

I am very much in love with my husband and am very happily married. As I mentioned in Chapter 1, my first marriage ended sadly in divorce. Just because it didn't work out the first time, I did not decide all of a sudden that I wasn't called to be married. I believe that marriage is meant to be part of my life, and therefore it forms part of my call. A healthy marriage requires both partners to contribute in a positive and nurturing way, and it requires commitment, selflessness and much unconditional love. With all those vital ingredients (and more), this is a call that is one of the most wonderful things two people in love can do together.

Motherhood

I always dreamed of someday becoming a mummy and now I can honestly say that all of my dreams (and more) have come true. I am head over heels in love with all my babies and I consider my call to motherhood one of the most important roles in my life. And my children help me keep perspective about what is really important! At the end of my life the most important things to me will be my family, and what I have been able to invest into their lives.

Marketplace

Most of us need to work. If we don't we'll starve! I believe our vocational call is incredibly important. We spend most of our lives and waking hours at work, so it's vitally important not to spend all of that time wasting your life away, doing something that you utterly despise. If you look at your vocation as a call it places a different emphasis on it. If what is important to you is job satisfaction, then perhaps taking a pay-cut in order to have that satisfaction fulfilled is what you need to do. However, if working to make money is what you believe you are called to do, then focus on the rewards at the end of the day. Whatever way you decide to look at your vocational call, you should take the time to ask yourself, 'Is this what I'm really meant to be doing with my life?'

When you live out your calling, you move into a fantastic league called the Super Achievers.

Super Achievers

In his book *Secrets of Super Achievers*, Philip Baker writes in praise of tall poppies and the abundance mentality that they should all have.

He says that although there are many people on the ladder of success who believe that in order to get to the top they have to dislodge or remove those above them and tread all over those beneath them, some do not. Success isn't a ladder as much as a journey on a road that has enough room for everyone. The travellers on this road are better off helping those with them than attacking them.

Jealousy doesn't reflect that you have what it takes to be a super achiever; it only reflects your intense needs, your desperation to keep what you want, and unrealistic demands about what the future may hold for you. It wants to say, 'I win, you lose'. Therefore jealousy reflects self-interest and self-love, rather than mutual reciprocal love that not only sets you free, but other people too.

Super achievers do not operate with an 'I win, you lose' mentality, but with an 'I win, you win', attitude to life.

This may surprise you, as stereotypically we envisage super achievers to be ruthless and aggressive — disregarding the cost. When you study the lives of those who qualify as super achievers, this type of attitude is a rarity.

Super achievers understand that individual success does not necessarily mean the failure of others. They have what Baker terms an abundance mentality. They want to succeed, they want to do well, they want to reach their goals and they are not in any way hampered by a feeling of guilt. Guilt only accompanies those who think in terms of 'I win, you lose'.

A genuine super achiever is never threatened by someone else's success. They don't allow jealousy or envy to dominate their thinking processes. We must realise that our own success should help others and not hinder them. When this is understood, we will move out of the fog of self-interest and the destructive style of confrontational competition, into the clear light of freedom and achievement.

Don't get trapped in small-minded, jealous and envious thinking. Life is like an ocean. There is plenty of water for everyone.

Why be jealous or envious of someone when you can still achieve your goal in the future? It is only you who will stop and block what you rightfully deserve. Take some time to dissolve the jealousy and move on. If you saw something you liked but were unable to achieve it then learn from the last experience so that next time it comes along you will be able to achieve it. Previously it might not have been the right time or it was better that the other person receive the reward; it does not matter. Accept and do not dwell on it, move on and concentrate on the next goal and how you will be able to achieve it — and not how you missed out.

If you allow yourself to open your mind and see what you were called to achieve, you can have true love, a good job, and everything positive that your heart desires. You just need to trust and believe in yourself to allow what you deserve to come into your life. Do not limit yourself and try to understand the unseen process of life. There are many factors that you will not see but you just have to accept that it might not have been the right time. When you are ready it will come to you easier than expected because the natural flow of life allows right experiences to come to the right people in the right time.

You can spend as much time as you want thinking about things you have missed out on but it will not change the event that caused the jealousy in the first place. Being jealous will not help but will hinder you in the future. Alexandre Dumas once said, 'Jealousy is the art of injuring ourselves more than others.' Your thoughts should be put into more positive areas by learning from that experience so that you too can achieve more in the future. You must learn to accept and move on and not dwell on the past; recognise that it is the past and you are now in a different time and place, so it is not worth holding on to.

If you find yourself having a jealous thought, make a strong effort to stop. Admit to yourself that this is a jealous thought and that you can control what you think. Remind yourself that you are just as good as the person you are feeling jealous of. Don't allow yourself to go down the jealous thought road. Cut the negative, unhealthy jealous thoughts off and concentrate on your own strengths instead. Stand tall poppy. Your shrinking and jealousy of others serves no purpose.

Remember the Truth: a blessed life is enviable.

Stand

Be prepared. You're up against far more than you can handle on your own. Take all the help you can get … so that when it's all over but the shouting you'll still be on your feet.

EPHESIANS 6:13, THE BIBLE

Stand Tall

Our deepest fear is not that we are inadequate.
Our deepest fear is that we are powerful beyond measure.
It is our light, not our darkness, that most frightens us.
We ask ourselves, 'Who am I to be brilliant?'
Actually, who are you not to be?
You are a child of God.
Your playing small doesn't serve the world.
There's nothing enlightened about shrinking
so that other people won't feel insecure around you.
We were born to make manifest the glory of God that is
*   within us.*
It is not just in some of us; it's in everyone.
And as we let our own light shine,
we unconsciously give other people permission to do the same.
As we are liberated from our own fear,
our presence automatically liberates others.

MARIANNE WILLIAMSON, FROM *A RETURN TO LOVE*

Natalie's Story

At the time of writing, my twin sister Natasha and I are twenty-four years old. We were born in Zambia and spent the first twelve years of our lives in Africa. Our mother is Zambian and our dad is Australian. At the age of seven my parents divorced so we lived with Dad during the week and Mum on weekends.

When my sister and I were thirteen we moved to Australia with Dad and my stepmother. Going to school here was a shock because we had come from an international school, where we had mixed with the children of diplomats, and now we were exposed to a completely different social setting. Our new school was comprised of farm kids and indigenous Australians who were familiar with each other and their setting — but we had no idea about either! We felt very much the odd ones out.

Dad was really focused on us doing well at everything. This included achieving not only academically but also in sports and in the way we presented ourselves. We dressed, walked and talked in a 'presentable' way. He was strict but loving and wanted the best for us. So my sister and I learned to work hard to achieve, and we would always compete with and discipline each other — it meant we were able to accomplish greater things because we spurred each other on. It became a very normal way of life and living for us. However, especially after moving to Australia, I really noticed how different we were and how others found it hard to accept how we did things. It was difficult, but I had my sister and my dad, so I felt I always had people who knew and understood me.

After high school I completed a diploma in Tourism at university and was given the high achievement award for excellence in tourism and hospitality. I had worked hard for this, but some people can make you feel as though you think you are above them for achieving it. I didn't think any of that — I just wanted to do the best I could.

This award led to an eighteen-month international contract which provided great life experiences. I met a lot of successful people, particularly Australians in top executive positions, and have visited twenty countries — living in six. It was such a great learning time for me.

It has been these experiences that highlighted just how other people can misunderstand you, judge you and make you feel. The people I mixed with in this job were successful and they certainly didn't have a problem with achievement, hard work and the desire to reach your potential. They recognised it and understood it. I didn't feel as though I needed to explain why I was the way I was — in fact, I probably would have had to explain why I *wasn't* like this!

After the contract I decided to come back home to Australia to complete a Bachelor of Arts in Tourism Management at university. I found this a real challenge — like most other people and their education. I completed the degree and somehow became the calendar girl and spokesperson for the university. Doing this was just another decision about wanting to fulfil all those desires in my heart — and not necessarily made because I either wanted or needed to prove to everybody else that I was somebody, or wanted to make them feel like they were nobody. The opportunity just came my way and I took it.

After one year of studies my sister joined me. Natasha had just won the Miss World Australia competition for 1999–2000. She also won Miss Photogenic and Miss Congeniality. That was huge! She was the first black Australian to have won the contest. I was so proud of her. We had both been asked by an agent to enter the competition when I had visited her in Darwin. We didn't want both of us in it — it seemed a bit silly as we're identical — so we tossed a coin and she won. It also made sense for her to do it as she had completed her nursing degree and the competition was based where she lived.

Natasha spent a month in London, staying at the Park Hyatt with ninety other girls who were competing for Miss World. She copped a lot of flack for winning the contest. The other girls competing said, 'How can a black person win this?', 'She doesn't deserve it ...' It's so sad, as they had all done so well and it is just what the judges decide on the day that they're personally looking for. I think people can feel so low about themselves that in order to make themselves feel 'bigger', they pull everyone else down around them. My sister and I experienced this a lot — particularly in the world of modelling.

The year 2000 was big in terms of modelling work: we did a number of commercials, worked with Coca-Cola, performed in the opening and closing Olympic ceremonies next to Kylie Minogue and Elle Macpherson, and appeared in music videos. We also modelled for Australian Fashion Week and Melbourne Fashion Week as well as featuring in a few movies. I can almost hear some of you thinking, 'She certainly thinks she is special — name dropping like that!' I just want to tell you how hurtful that can be. I don't think, and know that I am not, any more special than anyone else — I have just taken the great opportunities when they have come my way. Imagine all this happening to you — you would just think, 'Wow, I am so lucky!' That is how I feel. And just to let you know, while practising for the closing ceremony I was asked to step out because I wasn't moving in sync with the choreography. I felt embarrassed as I walked off the platform, with all the other models staring at me, but I held my head up high. I did my best and some could just do better.

The best asset I have learned in life is to always maintain a positive attitude. After a year of modelling I was asked to compete in the Face of Afro Australia competition. There were forty beautiful models of African origin. I was probably the biggest-sized girl there. By what seems to me a miracle, I was honoured to be the first Face of Afro Australia for 2001! As with my sister earlier, there was a lot of gossiping amongst the other models and of course most of it centred around my size. I had to choose not to get hurt and offended, and obviously my size hadn't bothered the judges.

In 2001 I began working with 'Shine', a high school program hosted by Hillsong Church. This is a program that centres on teaching value and self worth. There are Aboriginal Australian girls who attend every week — a group typically recognised as lacking self-esteem and value. I really enjoy this work and particularly the special events we get to organise, such as an indigenous Australian fashion show. This type of event is a great way to build confidence in them.

It has been a challenge to hold on tightly to my dreams amid the criticism of those who tried to pull me down. But facing the opposition has made me stronger in that I've had to decide if I want to really live life feeling regret over opportunities I passed up because of what others thought of me, or take the opportunities and live my life to its fullest. Having a positive attitude through it all helps. Understanding human value and respecting others and myself made the difference in my daily decisions.

Throughout my life's journey I have experienced people who aren't so encouraging of having big dreams and visions. There are very few people I can call true friends, but that's expected when you are always pushing the boundaries of yourself and living outside the 'box'. I have had to learn to stand tall regardless.

10 Keys to Freedom

from jealousy and envy

Some of these keys relate to being jealous or envious of others, while some refer to being the subject of jealousy or envy. Apply what seems most important in your particular situation.

1. Stand tall.
2. Don't deny who you really are and put yourself in positions where you require yourself to be something or someone you are not, but find friends who love you for who you already are and encourage the better 'you' to come out.
3. Bless, or at least ignore, those who curse you, and they will eventually go away.
4. Don't despise your beauty.
5. Stimulate and grow your intelligence.
6. Nurture your virtue.
7. Never pull anyone down to size — that's not your job in life.
8. Water and grow others around you.
9. Recognise that your life has been designed for a purpose greater than you.
10. Decide to use your life to help others grow.

body soul spirit

ACTION PLAN

body
Don't shrink in situations where you feel less than someone else or where you feel like you are standing out too much. Watch your posture. Be you and stand tall, from the inside out.

soul
Desire and work towards attaining the positive qualities you see in others without crossing the line and becoming jealous of them, or obsessed about your own shortfalls.

spirit
Pray to become a person who deflects jealousy, and whose life is one to be positively envied, for all the right reasons.

My goal is freedom
FROM JEALOUSY AND ENVY

Chapter 11

Pit to Prison to Palace

freedom from discouragement

'There's the test of confinement,
when people try to box you into something
that your dream wants to set you free from.
Fight for your freedom.'

Joseph the Dreamer

Once upon a time there was a young boy named Joseph. He was a dreamer and each of his dreams reflected his future, like a mirror. Now, Joseph had ten older brothers who hated him. Of all the boys, Joseph was the favourite son of Jacob, their father. He made Joseph a magnificent coat of many colours and because of it, his brothers despised him even more.

One day Joseph explained to his brothers a dream he'd had that showed him in a position of favour above them. This made their hatred towards him grow stronger. They stripped him of his beautiful coat and threw him into a pit, then sold him to some passing traders. They returned home to their father without him. Thinking that some wild animals had killed Joseph, Jacob wept over the loss of his favourite son.

Joseph was taken to Egypt as a slave where his new owner, Potiphar, favoured Joseph and grew to trust him — putting him in charge of his household. Potiphar's wife was very pleased because she was infatuated with Joseph. She tried to seduce him but Joseph resisted, refusing to put his future on the line.

Offended by Joseph's refusal, Potiphar's wife sought revenge — she lied to her husband, saying that Joseph had tried to seduce her! Potiphar was extremely upset at Joseph's alleged betrayal of him and had him thrown in prison. There, Joseph met two of the king's servants — a butler and a baker. One night these two men each had dreams that they could not fathom and they told Joseph, who interpreted them. The dreams showed that the butler would be released but that the baker would die.

Shortly after, the king reinstated the chief butler but he hanged the chief baker, just as Joseph had predicted. Instead of thanking Joseph, the chief butler forgot him and so Joseph remained in prison.

Years passed and the king himself had dreams that no one could interpret. He was troubled and wanted to know their meaning. Finally, the chief butler remembered Joseph, who was still in prison.

Immediately the king summoned Joseph, who said that his dreams predicted seven years of plenty in the land followed by seven years of famine. He said it would be wise for someone to manage a great storehouse in preparation for the years of lack. The king was pleased and he appointed Joseph to manage the storehouse.

When the great famine struck, Jacob sent his sons to buy grain from the King of Egypt. They came before their brother Joseph, but they did not recognise him.

Joseph gave his brothers grain and asked about their family. They did not understand his questioning, but they answered meekly because of Joseph's position of authority.

When the grain in Jacob's household ran out, the brothers returned once again to Joseph's storehouse. This time, Joseph revealed his identity. They were very afraid because of what they had done to him, but Joseph was not angry or vengeful. He was full of love and forgiveness. He saw that every turn in his life, good and bad, had been used to build the person he had eventually become.

The brothers went home and brought their father and their families to the prosperous land where their brother Joseph now lived. Jacob was overjoyed that his son was alive and they all lived happily ever after.

The End

Fact

Life is a series of expansions and contractions.

Truth

Within every contraction lies the seed of an expansion.

Mirror, mirror on the wall, why can't my dreams come true at all?

One of the most powerful parts of a human being is the mind. It's the directional part of our being which dictates what we believe about ourselves and why. Our heart may be where dreams begin, but our mind is where dreams are formulated and facilitated.

Sigmund Freud's work *The Interpretation of Dreams* caused a stir in the scientific world because of his claim that dreams are not meaningless, idle or purposeless activity of the mind, but that they have a specific purpose and a precise meaning. This was discounted by the scientific community at the time, but many people, including artists, writers, the media and the general population, were fascinated by the idea.

Dreams can cause curiosity, fascination and even terror in people. According to folk wisdom, dreams are the product of the highest and the finest part of the mind and arise from our longings and aspirations. Our dreams guide our thoughts, values and actions, and we live our lives to fulfil our dreams.

Dreams are not limited to our sleeping hours. Dreams are also our hopes and desires for our lives. Everyone has dreams and goals, even if they are hidden. Dreams live in a place deep within that brings you comfort in times of pain, where you can picture how you would like your life to be, the places you want to go, the person you wish to be, the things that you want out of life and what you would like to achieve.

Dreams don't just come true without effort and passion. See if you can relate to some of the following patterns of a dreamer.

A dreamer dreams that their ordinary life will become extraordinary. They dream that their past and present situation will bow down to their future. They dream that their dream will see the light of day and that it will actually come true. They dream that their dream will make a difference to their life and to the world.

A dreamer dreams that they will enjoy a fulfilled and prosperous existence with a healthy body, soul and spirit. They dream of making other people's dreams live. They dream that their dream will live on after they die and that it will become a legacy to the next generation.

Part of the journey to seeing our dreams fulfilled is dealing with self doubt, disappointment and discouragement. All of us at some point in time have to deal with these things. Discouragement is universal; no one is exempt from it. From the richest to the poorest, all have to deal with times of discouragement. I know that all of us would like to think that we are immune to discouragement, but the truth is we're not.

We all experience times of insecurity and uncertainty as to our future and our place in this world. But know that you have a secret treasure chest within, the place that you hold dear to your heart, that only you know. The place where you hold your innermost dreams and desires. They are still there, even if you have spent years trying to ignore and suppress them and pretend that they are not there.

Discouragement

Discouragement is losing the desire and motivation to continue doing something that brings purpose and satisfaction to one's life. To discourage is to dampen or destroy the courage, depress the spirit or lessen self-confidence, to dishearten or deter. We start doing something new, filled with excitement and enthusiasm, and partway through discouragement tends to visit. It is up to us whether we allow it to set in or not.

Discouragement can be contagious. If you are around someone who is deeply discouraged then they can discourage you if you are not prepared to deal with it. We cannot isolate ourselves from those who are discouraged but we can protect ourselves by focusing on our dreams. Contagious does not mean 'incurable'. While we may get discouraged from time to time we must never allow discouragement to become part of who we are. We don't have to stay locked into a lifestyle of discouragement. There is a difference between experiencing discouragement and living discouraged. Sometimes we can look at what we are doing and it may look like we are making little or no progress at all. It may seem the more we work, the less we accomplish. Yet we must never allow ourselves to believe that we are beyond hope.

People may feel discouragement for a number of reasons.

Fatigue

This may be physical, mental, emotional and spiritual. Fatigue and discouragement often hit halfway through a project. We tend to start with loads of energy but after a while the freshness of a new project tends to wear off and boredom, weariness and discouragement can set in. That's why so many people fail to complete what they start. After working hard and long, it can seem that our accomplishments don't match the energy or the effort that we have put in. When we are tired, we tend to see things differently from how they really are. Tiredness blurs our vision and dulls our dreams.

Frustration

The word frustrate means to break, to annul, to do away with, to fail, to render ineffective, to split, divide. We become frustrated when we lose sight of our purpose and goals in life. Frustration sets in when you never quite finish a task. We can all overcome and be effective in what we do, but if we allow ourselves to be overcome by frustration and discouragement we will fail to realise our dream.

Doubt

Doubt is a loss of confidence in something or someone and is a major contributor to discouragement. If we find ourselves doubting our vision, we lose the ability to see how to live a productive life. When we lose our confidence we lose heart. When we lose heart, we lose motivation and when we lose motivation, we become overwhelmed with the empty feeling of not accomplishing what we set out to do. Nothing can be more discouraging than the feeling of being a failure, of not being able to finish something you started. You may have thought you had what it took to succeed, but then you became discouraged along the way and doubt set in. True winners, though, see failures only as temporary setbacks.

Fear

We can sometimes lose our sense of security because of fear. When we allow what other people say to produce fear, this in turn produces insecurity in us. We must be careful who we listen to. Not everyone giving you advice is interested in your wellbeing and success. Fear can make us want to run away, but that's when we should remain immobile and not lose sight of our dreams.

I have been discouraged many times in my life and every time I am faced with a blow to my dreams, I am also faced with a blow to my self-esteem because the two are closely connected. That's when I have to decide to get back up again, dust myself off and try until I succeed (or at least get closure) and that's when my self-esteem grows. As you determine to get up every time you fall down, you are succeeding at something right there!

Joseph the Dreamer

Joseph's dream was tested and so too will yours be. Your dream may suffer the test of familiarity — when people around are so familiar with what you are that they cannot see *who* you are. Don't let it affect you. Your dream may suffer the test of rejection, when people reject you because of your dream. Don't let it affect you. The test of distraction may disable your dream, when people try to pull you off the course of your dream. Don't let them!

There's the test of confinement, when people try to box you into something that your dream wants to set you free from. Fight for your freedom. The test of time — hanging onto your dream for as long as it takes. Be patient. The test of self doubt, when you question what you've actually dreamed. Remember the dream.

Finally, there's the test of grace, where you learn to appreciate the fulfilment of your dream without arrogance or pride, but with grace. Be grateful.

The rewards of being a dreamer can be astronomical! In the story *Joseph the Dreamer*, we see that he reaped the following rewards: influence, impact, prosperity, honour, favour, adventure and longevity. The same could be your rewards for daring to dream.

Joseph wasn't afraid to dream and he wasn't afraid to believe the dream, even when the circumstances were trying to play a different story. Joseph found himself in a pit and in prison before he finally reached the palace. If you are going to dream, you are going to have to take risks — it's all part of the process to seeing your dream fulfilled. You are also going to have to come to terms with the fact that not everyone will want to hear about your dream or see your dream fulfilled, especially if it means that you will have some kind of 'advantage' over them.

Containment

Everyone feels contained at times. Sometimes this happens when we try to finish a task or accomplish something over and over with seemingly no success. Sooner or later we become discouraged and at some point we get so discouraged that we want to quit. This can happen with simple projects, education, and sometimes with a person's life.

A sense of containment can come at any time regardless of what great things we have accomplished already. You may feel as though you've had enough because you've been trying to do something for so long and now you feel that you will never get it done. Abandonment may seem the only option, but abandonment will never see your dreams fulfilled.

Containment will make you think it is not worth it and this thinking affects our bodies, minds and emotions. Sometimes our feelings of containment can be so great that we neglect to do the simple necessities, such as eating properly. Another thing that might be neglected due to containment is taking care of basic everyday responsibilities. When we let things go undone, we wallow in our own self-pity and self-loathing.

The feeling of containment may arise from various causes within ourselves, whether physical, mental and spiritual, or from outside causes such as our circumstances, health, surroundings and associates.

Containment as a result of external factors can sneak up and bite hard. This could include financial loss or want, persecution, false accusations, and many other things that we may not be able to understand and which persist in crowding themselves into our everyday life.

When our dreams seem squashed within us, or taken away from us, that is the time to remember that we do have control of what happens with that dream in the long run. Sometimes the battle is internal and your fight is with your own insecurities, doubts and poor choices, and other times the battle is on the outside from people who want to throw you in a pit to make sure that your dreams never come true. Regardless of the source, it's time to take back control. Your dreams can be successful regardless of what people and circumstances say, and you are the only one who can throw your dreams and self-esteem away.

Former British Prime Minister Sir Winston Churchill once said, 'Never give in — never, never, never, never, in nothing great or small, large or petty, never give in except to convictions of honour and good sense. Never yield to force; never yield to the apparently overwhelming might of the enemy.' Another great quote appears on the headstone of a remarkable woman who had suffered abuse at the hands of a loved one, and who had risen above the circumstances to confront the issue. It reads, 'The greatest success in life is not in never falling, but rising when you fall.'

We will all experience ups and downs, highs and lows, times of feeling elated and times of feeling deflated, as we pursue our dreams. Life is not just one big win, but it is a series of expansions and contractions.

It is good to realise that you are not the only one who has suffered from containment and discouragement. Many people around you have probably already gone through similar circumstances. Seeing our pains and frustrations in the context of the suffering of those around us should help us to deal with our own weaknesses.

One thing that has the potential to hinder the progress of any dream is when we don't relate or work well with other people. We need to work on relating more widely and effectively with people who have different ideas and viewpoints from our own. We need to try to understand what makes other people tick.

Another potential hindrance to seeing your dreams fulfilled is pride. Pride can definitely be part of the problem. When we think that our dream is all that matters and we start bragging to people about what we are going to do and be, we won't necessarily find ourself surrounded with people encouraging us. A person who thinks that they have 'arrived' can see no room in their lives for improvement. They are perfect in their own eyes. They feel and believe that no matter what comes against them they can't be conquered. This is a false sense of security and will lead to unbalanced and unhealthy self-esteem.

It can seem, with your life story, impossible to have or fulfil a dream. In the story *Joseph the Dreamer*, Joseph's life was one big concertina file, expanding and contracting with every dream he dreamed. It seemed that every time he dared to dream, someone or something was waiting to make sure that he would never make it. But he saw the bigger picture — he saw the dream as a future reality.

You need to focus on the bigger picture of your life and aim to put everything you are going to do into some kind of context. If you are unable to do this yourself, get help from someone who can draw some healthy perspective from your life.

Ask yourself if what you are doing is going to take you closer to or further from your dream. A dream isn't a destination, it is a journey that is made up of mostly small choices.

Mistakes

If we choose to dream, sooner or later we will all fail at something. Failure is a universal experience that we risk if we allow ourselves to dream. There are people who have had more failures than successes, but those who are most devastated by their mistakes are those who think and believe that you can live life without ever making a single mistake. We all make mistakes and experience setbacks, defeats and losses in life. We're all human and nobody's perfect. Our failures and defeats can have a devastating effect on our lives if not properly dealt with or handled with the right attitude and frame of mind.

Abraham Lincoln was well versed in failure before he took on his dream role as President of the United States of America:

▶ he failed in business in 1831
▶ he was defeated for legislature in 1832
▶ he failed in business again in 1833
▶ he suffered a nervous breakdown in 1836
▶ he was defeated in his bid for speaker in 1838
▶ he was defeated in his run for elector in 1840
▶ he lost his bid for Congress in 1843
▶ he lost his run for Senate in 1855
▶ he was defeated in running for vice president in 1856
▶ he lost another run for Senate in 1858
▶ he was elected President in 1860.

The rest, as they say is history!

When we feel defeated, we don't have to continue that way. We can conquer feelings of defeat and failure and move on to a brighter future if we learn how to get back up again when we've been knocked down.

In his book *Failing Forward*, bestselling author and motivational speaker on leadership John Maxwell highlights the differentiation between average and achieving people. In his estimation, the major difference comes down to their perception of and response to failure.

Mistakes are a training process that we go through on our way to success. In other words you and I are not going to succeed without making some mistakes along the way. The good news is that our mistakes do not have to be fatal or final. The problem with us is that we stop dreaming because we fear failure, and we cease believing in ourselves.

On a late night television program I once saw actor Harrison Ford being interviewed. He was discussing how he realised early on that success was tied to not giving up. In his experience, most people in the acting business gave up and went on to do other things. Hanging around long enough meant that he was sure to outlast the people who arrived on the bus with him. I for one am glad that he decided to hold onto that dream.

Don't be afraid to keep trying, and don't be afraid to make decisions for your life. If you make a wrong choice, then right the wrong and get on with it! You will never achieve anything you don't even attempt. Any movement forward — shuffle if you have to — is a step in the right direction. In other words, failure is a sure thing if you cease or never have a go.

And don't be a perfectionist. If you want to please everyone along the way, you'll never succeed. It's just not possible to win at people pleasing. Someone, somewhere, in some way, will be disappointed with you and your dream.

Failing at accomplishing something does not make you a failure. What makes a person a failure is their refusal to get up and dream again.

Henry Ford, the inventor of the Ford motor vehicle, once said, 'Failure is merely an opportunity to begin again intelligently.'

World famous basketball player Michael Jordan once said, 'I can accept failure. Everyone fails at something, but I can't accept not trying.'

Down But Not Out

If you have already given up, then it's time to dream again. As long as you have breath, you have the opportunity to dream, and to live your dream. You may have been knocked down but not out. Take one day at a time, and start by working with manageable tasks. Remember that the fulfilment of your dream may also mean the fulfilment of another's dream, so please don't give up. Think about what would happen if you simply couldn't be bothered. When you get discouraged and depressed please don't allow yourself to become inactive and wallow in your own pity. Instead, follow some of the keys to freedom in this chapter, to help you see your dreams come alive.

Following are some suggestions to help you get back up and overcome discouragement in your life.

Rest and relax
Get some rest and relax! Sometimes the best thing to do when you are discouraged is to stop what you are doing and rest your body and mind. Often after a little rest and relaxation you can come back to the same task with a new approach. Eat right, sleep well, exercise and relax. Take some time off and get away from the things that are bringing you discouragement.

Reorganise
Get closure on some tasks. When you are discouraged, often it does not mean you're doing the wrong thing. It simply means maybe

you're doing the right thing but you're doing it in the wrong way. Don't give up on your dream, just reorganise and try a new approach.

Believe

Continue to believe and you will succeed! Make a list of all the things that have been good about life, all the things that have been positive. Count your blessings. Open up your eyes and see everything that you have already achieved. Look forward to the future and see everything you've promised yourself. Listen to the positive voices of people who encourage you to succeed and focus on their belief in you and your belief in yourself to achieve. Stare into the Mirror of Truth and believe in your dream.

Resist

In order to see your dream fulfilled, you need a plan. In order to succeed or accomplish anything we must have a plan. When we don't have a plan to follow we won't know where we are going or how we are going to get there.

Writing down your dreams and goals is an important first step towards achieving them. This will help you visualise your goals and commit to seeing them fulfilled. Although it is wonderful to dream, it is even better to actively commit yourself in both thought and deed.

Record your dreams with as much detail as you can so that you can really visualise them. Do this for as many areas of your life as you can. Your dream could be about physical health, financial security or relational fruitfulness.

List the following:

▶ the area that your dream is associated with (family, work, health)
▶ the specific dream for that area
▶ the steps you are taking to fulfil your dream.

Remember that the best way to make your dreams come true is to wake up! Dreams do not always stay the same, so update your goals as your dreams evolve.

Perhaps you dream to live a long healthy life, or that you want to experience love and stay in love forever. It may be a dream to become a doctor or to return to study so that you can get the degree you have longed for. It could be that you want to start a foundation or charity which helps others who are battling with issues that you have been able to overcome. Maybe you want to write

Remember too that you are never alone. There are always people who have experienced the same thing that you are experiencing at your moment of discouragement. Think about those who push through. Their reward is the satisfaction of seeing their dream fulfilled.

Stand firm and don't run! Don't give into discouragement without a fight. Don't just roll over and give in. Resist it. Resist the discouragement. Remember your dream. Dream for you and dream for others who need to see your dream fulfilled. We are all at war with the negatives of life. You do not have to be discouraged. It is a choice. Don't give in and don't give up.

Never Give Up

Above my office desk is a large white blank canvas. It's intentionally blank, and I'm asked regularly if I intend to paint it sometime soon. The purpose of this lovely white canvas is to inspire me to dream. It reflects the commitment I have to myself to ensure that I flourish personally, even if my circumstances remain the same. I refuse to quit. When I look into the potential of my blank canvas, I can be anyone I want to be and I can do anything I want to do — Heaven is the limit.

I am a dreamer. I have many dreams and aspirations for my own life and for my family, and I was brought up to believe that I could achieve anything I put my heart and mind to. Your goals may be lifelong, or they may be a result of a recent new year's resolution. Whatever the case, you hold the key; it lies within your heart and mind. All it takes is an ordinary person with extraordinary perseverance to see a dream fulfilled.

I finished school after completing my School Certificate, at sixteen years of age. The majority of my year left school at the same time, because only those wanting to go on to do a degree at university would need to stay. Times have now changed, and it has become increasingly important to finish your Higher School Certificate and preferably complete some other kind of formal tertiary education, if you want a good job.

Although I left school early and I don't hold a university degree, I have been able to see my dreams come true. It takes more than information and education to see your dreams come to pass. It takes tenacity and passion and a commitment not to give into discouragement and self-pity, whenever you go through hard times and it seems like you will never reach your goals.

I have some very specific goals, such as:

▶ Enjoying married life, celebrating each year and reaching at least my fiftieth wedding anniversary.
▶ Raising healthy, happy and flourishing children.
▶ Staying in shape for the rest of my life.
▶ Writing a book every year for the rest of my life.
▶ Using my life to help others live in freedom.

Obviously there are more, and these are just a sample of the kinds of things that are in the forefront of my mind when it comes to what I do every day. In order to achieve long-term dreams, we must make choices and take action every single day, in line with our dreams. It's the accumulation of those choices and actions which leads us to see our dreams become reality.

This book could have brought me much discouragement because it has taken me so long to finish it. Trying to find the time and brain space has caused it to take a lot more time and emotional energy than I thought it would. But I refused to allow discouragement to set in. I had you in my sights. I had not only my dreams but also your dreams in mind. Your life and your self-esteem lay within my dream.

My prayer is that your dreams will be released because my dream has been released, and so the cycle of encouragement and fulfilment can go on.

Dare to Dream

Nelson Mandela once said, 'We have laid the foundations for a better life. Things that were unimaginable a few years ago have become everyday reality.'

For the unimaginable to become everyday reality, risks had to be taken. Every time we dream we take a risk. Just about anything that we do in life has some risk associated with it, and nothing of any value is ever accomplished without some kind of risk. This entails setting goals that require time, energy and passion to fulfil. Some people's goal is just to get out of bed in the morning and make it through the day just to go back to bed at night, with absolutely nothing accomplished in between. Where is the long-term life satisfaction in that?

We have to accept responsibility for our own lives. We are responsible for our actions, our words, our attitudes and our reactions toward others and life itself. We can't blame someone else for our shortcomings and downfalls in life, even though it's much easier to blame someone else. It's easy to make excuses as to why we failed or allowed ourselves to be defeated, rather than facing up to the truth.

Great accomplishments only come with great sacrifices. When we start something that requires more work, more energy, more time or more money than we anticipated we should be inspired not to give up before we accomplish what we set out to do.

You can turn any adversity to your advantage if you approach it with the proper attitude and right frame of mind. For every negative experience we have there is a benefit to be had from it.

Oscar Wilde once said, 'For a dreamer is one who can find his way by moonlight and see the dawn before the rest of the world.'

When you look at a seed, you can't see a tree — you can only see a seed. But you know that within that seed is potentially a tree and an entire forest. That's the power of the dream that is within you, waiting to emerge. And within every dream lies another dream, waiting to come true. Dreamers need to stand the test of time. We need to learn that a delay in seeing our dreams fulfilled is not necessarily a denial of our dream happening.

It may appear at times that your dream is lost, but dreams don't ever really go away, unless you choose to throw them away. Choose to allow yourself to see your life as having three walls and a door that will set you free, rather than four walls that say you will never see it happen for you.

Samuel Johnson once said, 'It matters not how a man dies, but how he lives. The act of dying is not of importance, it lasts so short a time.' This great man understood how important dreams are. Your dream is waiting to be birthed. Remember that even if there is a struggle for it to be realised, it does in fact exist, and is waiting for you to wake up and work on it.

Remember the Truth: within every contraction lies the seed for an expansion.

Dream

*For a dream comes with much business
and painful effort.*

ECCLESIASTES 5:3, THE BIBLE

Richard's Story

~ as told by a close friend ~

I met Richard through a mutual friend who was working with troubled young men in the juvenile justice system. From the first time I talked with him I saw the great potential that he had, if only he could escape the world he had found himself in.

Richard was adopted as a baby and raised in Broken Hill. His adoptive mum had already had three children naturally, and when she lost her fourth baby she decided to adopt.

Richard's mum tried to love him as he deserved, but she grieved the loss of another baby, and Richard simply didn't fill the void.

He didn't know anything about his real parents.

Life in Broken Hill was quiet, with not too much to do. Richard found himself bored and restless and becoming involved in things that would get him into trouble. He was arrested for being in a stolen car (he was not driving) and his parents decided to send him to a juvenile justice centre in Sydney. He was just fourteen years old.

This decision did not help Richard deal with the issues in his life. He was a rejected and hurt young man, but instead of being surrounded by a loving, caring family and community, Richard was now amongst criminals worse than himself. These people had more problems than he did and no answers. They took an interest in him and therefore became his mentors and his heroes. This led to a life of crime. He smoked pot and then experimented with the hard stuff — and became addicted. He was in and out of juvenile detention centres for the next four years and prison for the following seven years. During his times out, he stayed with a lovely family who tried so very hard to help him. They would call me often to come and visit him.

I remember one night, really late, I drove up to their place with my Bible in hand — he was wanting to kill himself. Richard and I read together for a little while then I prayed. At a time like that I knew that I could do very little to stop him. I needed God to answer my prayer. I left my favourite Bible with him as I knew he needed it more than I did. He said he felt better after our talk. I kept praying that he would see his potential for a very different life.

He took that Bible with him everywhere he went — it went with him in and out of prison. I never went very long without hearing from him: we sent letters to each other all the time when he was in prison. If time passed and I had not heard from him, I would start to worry. The last time I went without hearing from him I spoke to an old friend of his who said he thought Richard was probably back in prison. More than ever before I felt it was important for me to find him. I had a friend who worked for the Department of Correctional Services and she was able to locate him for me. He was in prison, and so I organised to see him straightaway. He was not in a good way but was pleased to see me.

Richard was involved in a horrific car accident that nearly took his life. He was on life support and nearly didn't make it. I sat by his bedside night after night until I nearly lost my job. He eventually recovered and was awarded a huge amount of money in compensation for his injuries. That's when we lost contact again. He blew the lot of it and wound up back in the same lifestyle he was in before the accident. But his life was saved for a purpose — he needed to know how valuable he was.

The next time I visited Richard in jail I took my mum in and he was really happy to see her. Maybe it was because she had bought him some new shoes (I remember how excited he was and all he would say is when he gets out he is going to repay her and myself for everything we have done), or maybe it was because she always accepted him — no matter what he had done. Richard was finally going to be released and so I organised to pick him up the day he got out, but when I went to meet him he was not there. I thought this was unlike him — he had been so happy that I was going to be waiting for him. But I soon found out why he'd failed to meet me. Although Richard was in jail, he was still able to get drugs and he had been so desperate to get a fix on that day he was released that, as soon as he got out, he headed straight for Kings Cross (our nearest drug 'centre').

After a few weeks, I really felt that I needed to go and find him. I prayed God would help me and headed towards Kings Cross — I had no idea how I would find him, but I did! I still can't believe it, as that place has so many out-of-sight areas for someone to hide in. When I found him he was so badly stoned that I was not sure what to do with him. He had been chased and bashed by the dealers he was working for. I took him home and watched him overnight. The next day I took him to our holiday house and other places along the coast. Over the next few days the drugs started to leave his system, and eventually the Richard I knew appeared. If I had not found him, he would not have reported to his parole officer and then it would have been back to jail. I didn't want that for him, and I knew he didn't want that for himself. He had hepatitis C and he was dying of liver cancer. The only answer I had for him was God and His help.

After a few days we came back to Sydney and I took him to church. He was ready to accept God's help and he experienced something that is difficult for me to describe in words. When he called out to God for help, God really answered him and it brought Richard such peace — peace like I have never seen before. Every day after that he would be found reading his Bible and, incredibly, making plans for the future.

Richard finally saw the light. He seemed to catch a glimpse of what his future could be like. He sat with my sister on the veranda one afternoon talking about all the wonderful things he could do with the rest of his life. It would need to start with proper rehabilitation and he could go anywhere from there. They sat and talked about his dreams for quite some time. She even promised him that she would cover his tuition to go onto college if he wanted to, so that he could help people who had been through what he had in his life.

Richard left inspired. He was ready to take on his future ... he just wanted one last 'hit' before he started over. That was his last hit — it took him out.

I don't have a total recollection of what happened now because it was so traumatic, but I do remember finding Richard dead in bed that morning and calling my mum and the ambulance to come and save him.

It was determined that the cause of death was accidental. Richard finally had a reason to live and not die. I know he didn't mean to end his life — he just wanted to have one last hit to get it out of his system. That's the thing, though, with drugs — one more hit could be the last.

This is a very sad story of a life cut short. Richard's death was not in vain, though, because what happened to him inspired my sister to write a book (this book, in fact) to help people understand their true value and potential. Even though Richard was not able to fulfil the rest of his life's purpose here on earth, I pray that through his death and through this book, many people will see and understand how great human potential and one's future can always be.

10 Keys to Freedom

from discouragement

Freedom from discouragement is best done with encouragement. Enjoy your dreams! Through these keys, the progress towards your goals can become as exciting and as precious as actually seeing your dreams come true.

1. Allow yourself to dream positive dreams.
2. Believe that your dreams will come true. Write down your dreams and a plan for how you might achieve them.
3. Don't be impatient.
4. Don't ever give up.
5. Express your dreams to those you can trust.
6. Allow your dreams to unfold, rather than trying to make them happen through striving.
7. Remain true to your dream and to yourself, and you will see it fulfilled.
8. Don't doubt yourself.
9. Be careful not to miss it when it comes true.
10. Be thankful for the ability to dream and for the fulfilment when your dream comes true.

body soul spirit

ACTION PLAN

body
Keep a record of your dreams, continually adding and updating them as you grow. Work on strategies, with help from others if necessary, to help see your dreams come true.

soul
Cultivate dreams in your heart and continually give yourself permission to dream bigger dreams.

spirit
Pray that you will see your dreams come to pass in your lifetime, and that your dreams will be something to inspire the next generation.

My goal is freedom
FROM DISCOURAGEMENT

Chapter 12

Fully Amazing Grace

freedom from intimidation

*'People do strange things
when they are in pain.'*

The Slave Trader

Once upon a time, there lived a boy whose mother loved him dearly. She taught him about good and evil, warning him to stay on the good path. His mother died when he was just seven years old, leaving his seaman father to care for the lad. By the age of eleven, the boy had accompanied his father on six voyages. When his father retired, the boy was transferred to a military ship where conditions were intolerable.

He fled the service, only to be captured and beaten publicly. After enduring flogging and demotion he volunteered to transfer to a slave trading ship. His mother's words of advice forgotten, he chose this cruel occupation. He was angry at what life had dealt him so far.

The slave trader with whom he worked brought him to his home in Africa to continue trading people for money. There, the trader's wife took pleasure in beating him every day.

His physical appearance changed. His posture and stance became hunched and withdrawn. Distraught, destitute and angry, the young man fled to the shoreline, where he built a fire to attract a passing ship. A ship finally saw the smoke and the skipper came ashore to rescue him.

He lived aboard for a long time. It was not uncommon for as many as 600 natives to be kept in the hold of this ship. One day the young man's temper got him into trouble and he was beaten, thrown down below, and forced to live on rotten vegetables for an unendurable amount of time.

When the skipper brought him above to beat him again, the young man fell overboard. Because he couldn't swim, they harpooned him to pull him back onboard. Bleeding and defeated, he longed to be rescued.

Down below deck, like a ray of light, he remembered the words of his mother. He cried out for help, calling upon grace and mercy to deliver him. He heard murmurs from above, as a gentleman spoke with the captain of the ship. The captain came below the creaky deck and called the young man's name.

'This fine sir just bought you to go and work with him,' said the captain. As they left the ship, the gentleman turned towards the young man and said, 'You're free to go.'

'What?' the young man asked.

'I was once set free and so I promised that I would help another poor wretch like me. Be on your way and remember the freedom you have received today so that one day you will grant freedom to someone else.'

The young man walked away free, aware that he had inflicted much pain on people who didn't deserve it, robbing others of their dignity and freedom through trading in human suffering.

He came to his senses with deep sorrow for what he had done. He wrote about the rich mercy and grace given to him in the famous hymn 'Amazing Grace'. John Newton's life was turned around by grace. Once he had received the grace to start his life over again, he could not help but want to live a life showing grace and mercy towards others. And this became his happily ever after life.

The End

Fact

Hurt people hurt people.

Truth

Grace always overcomes hurt and intimidation.

Mirror, mirror on the wall, who can rescue me from myself?

One of the sad realities of life is that often people who have been hurt end up hurting others. Hurt people hurt people. When we are subject to another person's forceful will on our lives, intimidation can set in.

Everybody hurts somebody at some time or another. Most of us wish that we could avoid hurting others. Yet some people hurt people repetitively, either intentionally or unintentionally, because of unresolved issues in their lives. These people usually lack empathy, healthy assertiveness and decision-making skills. They are also unable to manage their feelings adequately, they generally have a low self-esteem and they rarely feel that they can understand themselves, let alone anyone else.

The presence of good and evil and right and wrong has been on earth for a long time and sometimes in our crazy, mixed-up world, it's difficult to decipher which is which. Something has to win in your life: either good or evil, positive or negative, and no matter what has happened in your life up until now, it is entirely up to you to make the choice to live differently.

Intimidation

Intimidation is no stranger to anyone. Everybody can relate to what it feels like to be intimidated. First day at school or work, friends, peers, bullies. Intimidation is a term I know well. Like many people, I feel it is something that I have come up against time and time again throughout my life, and it's only been in more recent years that I have learned to resist and not succumb to the fear of another person ruling over my life.

To intimidate is defined as 'to make timid or fearful', and fear itself is an intimidator! It happens when someone else threatens to use power or control to get others to do what they want them to do or to prevent them from doing what that individual is about to do. It also happens when someone makes themselves out to be more powerful or forceful than they really are, and when they use coercion or force to get what they want from others, or to cause others to shrink. When people use verbally, physically, sexually or emotionally abusive behaviours to get other people to stay in line, that is considered intimidation. Intimidation can come from people, situations, gatherings and the unknown.

Intimidation occurs when someone acts in such a way that no one would dare question or stand up to them over any of their decisions, opinions or directives, or when they convince others that only they have enough experience, wisdom, intellect and insight to give direction or to have the correct answers to life's problems.

If someone uses physical size, stature and strength to get others to respect and obey them, that is intimidation. Intimidation comes in many forms but it is always ugly.

The primary purpose of intimidation is to keep us 'in line' or 'in a box', and the moment we dare to move outside the line or the box, we are likely to be on the receiving end of anger and more intimidation. Intimidation is definitely one of life's big nasties that seeks primarily to distract, discourage and hurt. It needs identifying and eradicating in order for you to develop a healthy self-esteem.

Intimidators have learned that intimidation works. They do it to feel powerful and in control. There are things you can do to deal with the situation without making things worse. The facts are:

▶ Intimidators keep intimidating as long as it works, and as long as it makes them feel more powerful.

▶ Intimidation takes lots of forms: it can be physical, verbal or emotional, ranging from mild to severe.

▶ Women can be intimidators, although intimidation by women is more likely to be expressed by spreading rumours, leaving people out of social events, or threatening to withdraw friendship, rather than of a physical nature.

Anyone can be the target of intimidation. Most victims often feel less powerful than the person intimidating them, therefore a typical victim is likely to be shy, sensitive and perhaps anxious or insecure. Some people are picked on for physical reasons, such as being overweight or small, wearing different clothing, having a physical disability, or belonging to a different race or religious faith.

Some intimidators are outgoing, aggressive, active and expressive. They get their way by brute force or openly harassing someone. They may even carry a weapon. This type of intimidator rejects rules and regulations and needs to rebel to achieve a feeling of being better than everyone else.

Other intimidators are more reserved and sly and may not want to be seen as harassers or tormentors. They try to control by talking, saying the right thing at the right time, and lying. This type of intimidator gets their power secretively through manipulation and deception.

As different as these types may seem, intimidators do have some characteristics in common:

▶ They focus on their own pleasure.
▶ They want power and control over others.
▶ They are willing to use and abuse other people to get what they want.
▶ They find it difficult to see things from someone else's perspective.

The negative effects of intimidation are many. People who choose to use fear and intimidation to control others will soon find themselves facing emotional barriers in relationships, and they will also risk being seen as emotionally, verbally, physically and even perhaps sexually abusive in their dealings with other people.

I have come to realise first-hand that hurt people hurt people, and therefore if I look deeply at why someone is angry at, hurting and intimidating me, I can see that they themselves, more than likely, have been subject to another person's anger, hurt and intimidation. As a result it becomes a learned art as the intimidator doesn't know any better, and the cycle can continue, or stop, with me. Understanding why people do intimidate doesn't excuse the act, it simply explains it. So don't get dragged into the 'I don't know any better, so it's OK' game.

Intimidation is a twofold issue. There is the intimidator and the person receiving the intimidation. Both people will have suffered a blow to their identity and will need help to develop a healthy self-esteem again. If you have been subject to intimidation, you will have possibly found it difficult reading this chapter so far. Much may seem far too real to you, especially if you are currently in a situation where you are suffering intimidation. While there are varying degrees of intimidation, any of it in any form is wrong and destructive to the human soul.

On the other hand, if you have been able to identify yourself as an intimidator, and you wish to change your behaviour, then you will need to take action.

1. Ask people in your life if they find you intimidating.
2. Find out what it is about you that they find intimidating (your words, your actions, etc).
3. Ask yourself if you can now see these character traits and whether they have been intentional or unintentional.
4. Take a long hard look at the negative consequences of your intimidation, whether intentional or not.
5. Think about the irrational and unhealthy causes for your thinking and beliefs that may have contributed to you intimidating other people.
6. Identify healthy, rational and positive thinking and beliefs that will help to contribute to you ceasing to intimidate in the future.
7. Specify how you will intentionally behave in future.

8. Decide what you can do to lessen any intimidating effects you have on others.
9. Speak up and assure those you've hurt that you no longer intend to intimidate them, and ask them for their continued constructive feedback.

Start acting on your new positive choices and monitor responses from people in your world.

No matter what kind of intimidation and hurt I have been subject to, I refuse to pass that pain on to other people, whether they deserve it or not. That's where I win! I get to choose my future, my friendships, and where my boundaries are set.

The Slave Trader

In *The Slave Trader*, John Newton found it difficult coping with the death of his mother at the tender age of seven. Through intense grief, he ended up making decisions that would steer his destiny away from good, into a life of pain, suffering and loss of self-respect and self-esteem.

John set his life on a path of self-destruction when he ignored his conscience and gave his life over to angry and hurtful living. The more he hurt himself and others, the worse his self-esteem became. When he eventually looked into the mirror of truth, he saw what he really looked like: a wretched man. His self-esteem was as low as it could possibly be, and he dealt with his pain by inflicting pain on others. He treated others with no respect or dignity, because of his own lack of self-respect and dignity.

The slaves aboard John Newton's ship were forcibly and physically enslaved, and you may feel as though that is exactly what your life has become — enslaved by certain circumstances in your life. It doesn't have to stay this way — you do have some control. It may only be a little control at first, but it can grow to a point where you are able to free yourself from the things that you feel intimidate you.

Eventually John Newton saw what a mess his life had become, and he recognised that it was up to him to take personal responsibility for it. Although he was a victim of his circumstances in the beginning of his life, he had now grown up and he needed to stop blaming the world for what had happened to him, in order to start building his life again. He had a reputation for destroying people's lives, when he could have become a builder of people's lives.

People do strange things when they are in pain, and the younger the person, the more challenging it is to negotiate through the haze of pain. Rather than maintaining his life of torment, John cried out for help to get off the roller-coaster of destruction. He finally came to his senses and saw what his life had become, all because he hadn't dealt with his pain in a constructive way.

Yet after inflicting so much more pain on himself and on others, it was going to take a miracle for him ever to be able to forgive himself and have a new start in life. Receiving grace gave John a new approach and a new appearance. He not only was different on the inside, it showed on the outside through his actions and bearing. The life and joy that once was lost in him was found again.

The light that shone through the crack in the ship's deck brought truth and meaning to John's life. Light can either lead us and guide us or blind us; it's up to us to choose.

Anger

Inside the heart of the intimidator is a seed of anger that flares and flourishes if it is fed. Unhealthy anger is the fuel that keeps the cycle of intimidation going. When we look at angry behaviour we can see there are different types of anger and consequences that come with each of them.

Bullying behaviour causes fear and results in intimidation, hurting both the victim and the bully. Bullying is repeated and uncalled-for aggressive behaviour, or quite simply, unprovoked meanness. It's a form of intimidation, designed to threaten, frighten, or get someone to do something they would not ordinarily do.

If a child experiences constant intimidation, they may learn to expect this kind of behaviour from others. They may develop a pattern of giving in to the unfair demands of the intimidator and they may end up identifying with the bully and become a bully themselves — all from a position of fear and intimidation.

We know that the bully or intimidator is also hurt in the process, and if they are allowed to continue the behaviour, it becomes habitual. They become more likely to surround themselves with friends who condone their aggressive behaviour, and they may never truly develop a mature sense of what is right and wrong.

Bullies or intimidators do not go away when school ends. The behaviour continues through high school and even into adulthood. It can lead to serious problems and dangerous situations for both the victim and the aggressor.

Aggressive anger drives one person to hurt another physically, emotionally or psychologically. It is usually expressed by hitting, kicking, harassing, using put-downs and threatening, and sometimes can even result in killing. When someone is aggressively angry they are well aware of that fact, so they try to make someone else responsible by blaming and avoiding responsibility. This type of anger is typical of men who abuse their partners.

Another form of anger is *passive–aggressive*, which is internalising and denying, and is usually expressed by silence, revenge, rumour starting and depression. When bottled up, it will eventually blow up aggressively. The person who is passively angry denies what's going wrong and doesn't want to talk about it.

Assertive anger is expressed in non-threatening ways that do not hurt yourself, another person or property. This form of anger is dealt with by suppression and by acknowledging the feeling and by making the decision to deal with the situation at a more appropriate time in the near future. This kind of self-control speaks of a strong self-esteem and it is the type of anger that is actually considered healthy. An example of this is when we choose to confront an issue that has made us angry, but in a constructive and calm way — without losing it!

People can't *make* you angry. You have the power to choose the feelings you have and power to decide what to do with those feelings in any situation. There is healthy and unhealthy anger, and we can choose to deal with any anger in a way that will either harm or heal and include or reject others.

Besides the physical signs that we sense in our body that tell us we are feeling angry, there are other signs or triggers that we can learn to understand in order to take charge of our anger:

External triggers
These are the things that are done to us.

Internal triggers
These are the messages we tell ourselves that get us all worked up.

When you are feeling angry, recognise why you are angry and try to calm down. Take a deep breath and don't speak. If need be, leave the situation until you can handle it constructively. It's vital that you consider the consequences that come with your response to anger and remember that your response is your choice.

Eleanor Roosevelt once said, 'No one can make you feel inferior without your consent.' And I say, no one can make you angry, intimidated or fearful without your consent.

Control

Intimidation is a control issue because it is the attempt of one person to coerce others into doing what they want them to do, and it usually involves control strategies such as threats, pressure, physical force and power plays. If you don't do what they say, they will try to make you do it or if you don't agree with what they say, they will try to make you agree with it. It's all about their control of you.

If you intimidate another person, it robs them of their free choice and free will, and it makes another person a victim of your control and needs, and this is a violation of their will. It is in no way acceptable to build your own self-esteem by wilfully destroying another's. When you lord it over another person with an angry spirit, you weaken the will in those who feel beaten down, abused and oppressed.

Control comes about through irrational thinking — thoughts like, 'I will use whatever it takes to get my way', or 'No one will ever get away without showing respect for my authority'. Controllers believe that the more they control people, the more they will get out of them. The more 'respect' they receive, the more they will be obeyed. They love to remind others of how much they have done for them, and they think that the only way to get anything done is to whip people until they can take it no more.

Enough is Enough

In order for you to get out from under another person's intimidation, you will need to take some action for yourself, as follows:

1. First you need to recognise if you are being or have been intimidated, which means no more living in denial of the facts.
2. Write down when you were or are being intimidated, and list the people who have in the past or currently do intimidate you.
3. Be specific with what it is they have used to intimidate you.
4. Identify whether the intimidation has been intentional (in their control) or unintentional (possibly outside their control).

5. Identify how long you have been suffering intimidation with each person.
6. List how your being intimidated has affected your relationship with the person.
7. Identify how much of the intimidation you have allowed to affect you because of your own unhealthy beliefs and thoughts about yourself.
8. Change your posture. Stand tall and don't cower.
9. Change your voice. Be calm but firm, and audible.
10. Use eye contact. Don't stare at the ground or the sky. Look people in the eye, remembering that they are human, just like you, and you have nothing to be afraid of.

Allowing yourself to believe you are worth something is the first step in the right direction towards helping you get you out from under intimidation. Following the steps or path out is crucial, as is making a commitment to yourself to accept that there may be unwanted consequences to freeing yourself up from the intentional or unintentional intimidation of this person. This may mean the end of a relationship.

Think practically when it comes to breaking out from under intimidation. Spend time with bigger people, and don't shrink back. Do something that you wouldn't normally do, to challenge fear in your life. Talk to someone whom you would normally try to avoid.

If your circumstances are extreme, you will need to take action to lessen the power of the person who is intimidating you by removing yourself from their presence, if at all possible. Or it may mean more responsibility will be required from you to carry your share of making the relationship healthy.

You will then be ready to behave in a new and less intimidated way. As time passes, you need to continually tell yourself that you are worthwhile. I don't think there's anything wrong with talking to yourself. I do it often! I chat away to God and to myself, and I'd rather chat away to myself and reinforce positive things about myself that I know need to be said, than sitting or sulking in silence waiting to receive affirmation from other people in order to know who I am and how valuable I am.

Tell yourself that you are valuable and deserve better. Remind yourself that we are all equal in the sight of God and therefore you don't need to see others as better than you. As you take more control over and responsibility for your life, you will also become naturally more positively assertive. Once you know better, no one will be able to hold intimidation over you unless you allow them.

Identity

I've been intimidated many times in my life, by bosses, business people and family members, but each time I overcame the intimidation through prayer, faith and choosing to believe that I am worth something. I have learned that it doesn't really matter who or what intimidates you. It could be a shop assistant or a school principal, a work colleague or even your spouse. Even if the cause is external, the solution isn't. It's internal and eternal. Some things we have to work on from within and they may take us all of our lives and into eternity.

I believe that spiritual identity is at the core of self worth and is a major key to overcoming intimidation. When we feel intimidated by another person, internally we're viewing others and ourselves in a kind of pecking order. In other words, we are at the bottom of the food chain, less important, significant or valuable than others.

We can sometimes think 'You're important, therefore I am not,' and 'You are worthwhile, therefore I am not,' and these thoughts become reality if we choose to give them life by thinking about them and believing them. You may think that others are richer, more beautiful, smarter, more important or more popular. The list will be as long as our insecurities are deep. But in all of these scenarios, we are viewing life in only one limited, false dimension. We're adopting an incorrect view of ourselves and others, and we're not seeing the truth.

Having a handle on intimidation doesn't mean that you won't be subjected to anyone's poor behaviour towards you in the future. It just means that you are now aware and skilled in how to deal with their intimidation and your responses. Fears and hurts will still come, but you don't have to live afraid and in pain.

There are many forms of fears, and they are generally categorised into phobias. My natural tendency is towards fear and anxiety. I was a reasonably anxious child, and I internalised most of my fears because I was simply too afraid to express them. When I became an adult, I found that the fears that I didn't deal with when I was younger just grew with me and they then became adult fears. Because of my naturally fearful nature, I succumbed easily to intimidation.

Some of my phobias were fear of spiders (arachnophobia) and flying, and there were many, many more. My grandmother suffered from telephonophobia, or a fear of the telephone! I reckon I had so many fears that I had phobophobia, which is the fear of fear!

Grace to Forgive

Whenever intimidation is present, grace is absent. Grace is the glue that holds together a broken life. But grace must be appropriated, that is, you must first receive it to be able to live it and then, in turn, give it.

In his book *The Grace Awakening*, author Charles R Swindoll says:

We use grace to describe many things in life:
- *a well-coordinated athlete or dancer*
- *good manners and being considerate of others*
- *beautiful, well-chosen words*
- *consideration and care for other people*
- *various expressions of kindness and mercy.*

So, what really is grace? It is truly something that is represented here in the story *Amazing Grace*, and in each of the stories in this book.

Grace is:

▶ the act of showing favour or kindness to someone who doesn't deserve it;

▶ being forgiven for something you've done to hurt someone else;

▶ the act of forgiving someone for something they have done to hurt you;

▶ something that's given and received, not earned.

Without grace, people in trouble cannot pick themselves up off the floor and get on with life, no matter how hard they try. Grace is a gift from above, it doesn't actually come from within, and that's where most people go wrong.

When we feel that we can live life on our own, by ourselves, without anything or anyone to help us, that's when we have made the first big mistake. We need grace to oil our mistakes and our failings and to glue us back together when we fall down.

When someone has been through a tragedy and they can't seem to get over it, whether it has been self-inflicted or inflicted on them by someone else, the absence of grace in their life will prevent them from being free. Grace is active forgiveness, where you choose not to bring up the past against yourself or another person. Grace is absolutely and totally free. You will never be asked to pay it back. No one ever could, even if they tried.

Where someone has a lack of grace, they also usually have:

▶ a lack of love and care for themselves and others;

▶ rationalisation for a life of doing their own thing, regardless of who it hurts;

▶ unwillingness to be accountable to anyone;

▶ resistance to anyone getting close;

▶ disregard for wise advice.

The *Oxford Dictionary* definition of forgiveness is 'to remit, to let somebody off a debt, to cease to resent, pardon, and wipe the slate clean.'

This is what John Newton experienced.

Forgiveness, like love, is a decision. Forgiveness takes courage and determination. No one can make you feel bad. You have the power to choose between becoming bitter or getting better. Take responsibility for your feelings; claim your power. Forgiveness takes practice. Start with small hurts and work your way up to the big ones.

People hurt each other because they are learning and growing. Forgive people for their incompleteness and their humanness. If you find it hard to forgive your parents for their imperfect parenting, remember, they were shaped by the imperfect parenting they received from their parents, and so on.

Forgive yourself for what you regret doing and for what you wish you had done. Forgive yourself for not being fully yourself and for being only yourself. Forgiving yourself cleanses the soul and gives you the power to extend forgiveness to others. Forgiveness is not something you do for someone else; it is something you do for yourself. Give yourself the gift of forgiveness.

Forgiving others is the first *grace key*, and then forgiving yourself and allowing yourself to have a new start is the second grace key in your life. To live a life of grace means that you will be able to:

▶ live without being bound by impulses
▶ be free to make your own choices
▶ not live comparing yourself to others
▶ live a self-controlled existence
▶ fast-track your growth towards greater maturity and freedom, to be the person you were born to be.

The single most powerful thing about grace is when we can accept it for ourselves. You can't give grace unless you have first received it for yourself. That's when you can know a fresh, new start for your life.

My dream and prayer for you is that you come to realise that it is impossible to fall from grace; you have to jump.

Remember the Truth: grace always overcomes hurt and intimidation.

Amazing Grace

Amazing grace, how sweet the sound,
That saved a wretch like me.
I once was lost but now am found,
Was blind, but now I see.
'Twas grace that taught my heart to fear,
And grace, my fears relieved.
How precious did that grace appear
the hour I first believed.
Through many dangers, toils and snares,
we have already come.
'Twas grace that brought us safe thus far,
and grace will lead us home.

JOHN NEWTON, 1725–1807

Grace

When it is sin [anger, intimidation or hurt] versus grace,
grace wins hands down.

ROMANS 5:20, THE BIBLE

Donna's Story

I thought I had this life stuff figured out, but I was like a time bomb waiting to go off. My life was in turmoil!

My friends were drug dealers, kick boxers and thieves. The girls and I could get whatever we wanted and the guys would look out for us in return for favours. They didn't really care about us though, and we never really cared about them. The nightclubs were our lives! We helped dealers get drugs into clubs by putting illegal substances down our bras. Once inside, the boys would give us our drugs and we headed off into the night.

Many times we got ourselves into trouble, and we also enjoyed causing trouble for others. We girls would cause trouble for men by flirting with a guy — we knew full well that his girlfriend was watching. We had to watch out for each other though because our own boyfriends were also in the club. Inflicting pain and humiliation was fun for me.

Fights were just part of our night out. Many unsuspecting girls would get a smack from behind or were even haunted by our group the whole night until they eventually couldn't take it any longer and went home. We made no exceptions and showed no mercy; only if luck was on their side would they escape. I remember smashing a girl down on the dance floor just because she had spoken to my friend's boyfriend. I had to be dragged away by the rest of my group before the bouncers came.

This was my way of life, as crazy as it seems now; it was a lifestyle that came naturally to me. I realise now that I really hurt people. I thought it was exciting and fun but behind the crazy lifestyle and hard girl image, I just longed for my own torment to go away.

On what should have been a normal drunken night out, something happened that pushed me to breaking point: I was raped. You see, it brought back memories, memories I had pushed away, all of which I had kept secret; it was my business, but now I remembered it all.

My pain began as a little girl. My parents were beautiful and I lived with them in a small town, but the town had many hidden secrets, many of which were mine. I remember playing in the street with my friend; we were about eight years old. Two men asked us into the back of their van; there the men did things that were inexplicable to our young minds. My friend got more than I, but I had to watch as they did things to her that no human being should be exposed to, never mind a little girl. My mind is vague about the next eight years of abuse by many different men on different occasions. I suppose I lost my virginity before I knew I had it, and so at a young age I began to sleep around. I began to use people, mostly men, and it was hard to turn back.

Standing in the street one day soon after I was raped, I watched others with resentment and envy; I wanted an opportunity, a break. A girl walked up to me in the street and told me that my life could be different. She told me about hope, something that we all could have. I thought she was talking rubbish and I told her so! She then told me about forgiveness and grace, she told me I had a choice. Again I mouthed off at her, angry at the trash being spoken, and I walked home.

Later, I thought about what she said; her words would not leave me. Forgiveness, grace, hope … I know it sounds cheesy but I thought about it. I saw others it had worked for and wondered if it could work for me. So I made a decision and made some changes. This girl had given me a card with an address on it so I went there to see what it was. I ended up in church! I wanted help, so I wandered in, and the people there were not at all like I thought they would be. They helped me make some practical and spiritual changes to my life.

The changes certainly weren't quick-fix things. I wish I could say that it was easy. It took time and effort but if I didn't resolve these issues they would destroy me and others. I surrounded myself with great people, strong people, people who understood my manipulation and who weren't intimidated by my actions. They spoke truth; they mentored me, challenged me and invested in me and through this I began to choose life.

It came to the point where I had denied reality for so long, I had to make deliberate changes and see the enormity of accepting responsibility for my life and not passing blame onto others.

I began to choose my words carefully, I tried to stop using foul, abusive and aggressive language. Instead of being out of order and out of control I chose to be aware of my issues — it was a choice. I began to see people differently. Before, I was blinded by anger and didn't care what hurt or destruction I would cause. Now I was fully aware of areas like the power of my words. I began to use beautiful and expansive words to build others up and coach them to greatness.

I addressed my body language, and changed it from being forceful and defensive. Even my facial expressions had to change! Now my posture, gestures and appearance were changing. I had to put boundaries into place, I had to change my lifestyle, stop hanging with kick boxers and gangs, and stop watching aggressive movies.

Be honest with yourself, ask for help from others, review and assess your life. Stand tall, dignified and honoured and make your past a distant memory.

Today I am free from my past and I am forgiven for the things I did to others. After all I have done I'm amazed by this grace.

10 Keys to Freedom

from intimidation

These keys are quick to read but may take a long time to implement. Forgiveness in particular is a long-term process, so be patient and press on with it.

1. Ask God to forgive you. Knowing you have a clean slate will help you start afresh.
2. Forgive others. This also helps clear the slate and lets you feel like you have a new start.
3. Forgive yourself. This can be harder than the first two. Just know that you are no different to others — you need forgiveness from yourself too.
4. Be slow to judge and quick to love.
5. Realise that you are powerless to change without grace.
6. Accept grace with open arms.
7. Realise that healthy self-esteem comes from living a *grace life*.
8. Don't dwell on it, but do remember where you came from and the mess your life was once in.
9. Give grace to others.
10. Use your life story to help others.

body soul spirit

ACTION PLAN

body
Count to ten before you open your mouth, and try not to speak through your anger. Wait until you have calmed down enough to communicate constructively.

soul
Don't let the sun go down on your anger. Resolve issues before you go to sleep, for the sake of peace and wellbeing.

spirit
Pray for the ability to remain calm in the midst of turmoil and to deal positively with situations that make you angry or frustrated, and pray quickly for forgiveness — life's too short!

My goal is freedom
FROM INTIMIDATION

Conclusion

An Eternal Perspective

the next level

*'The truth that leads to change
is confronting.'*

The Prince of Peace

Once upon a time the prince of all princes was born. The young prince had a higher purpose in life than just becoming a king. The extraordinary thing about this prince was that he was not born in the palace, where other princes were born, so his identity was hidden from some.

He was on assignment to come and rescue the whole world from injustice and to bring peace into the land — into people's lives. The prince came to show people how valuable they really are.

In those days, people only had highly polished pieces of metal, pools of water or themselves and their own inaccurate views, to rely upon as mirrors of reflection. The prince, however, was very special, because when people looked deep into his eyes, which were like perfect pools of the clearest water, they were able to see themselves, inside and out, with absolute clarity. They saw the truth.

The young prince was very popular, and everywhere he went, many people came to be with him. Everyone in the land was longing to be free. They all came to the prince because they wanted to be happy, healthy and free and they knew that he could help them. The prince was the greatest lover of people and giver of value and esteem that ever lived.

One day, the popularity of the prince came to the attention of the rulers in the land. They did not know that he was born a prince. These men were insanely jealous of him and his kindly heart towards broken and hurting humanity. They wanted to be the only ones that people followed, so they decided that the prince and the truth must be done away with.

Tragically, the prince was betrayed, captured, beaten and killed in the most gruesome and inhumane way. He had done nothing except love and value people and set them free.

But good always overcomes evil in the end, and within a matter of days, the prince came back to life again — much to the shock of even those closest to him. You see, the prince was on assignment, and nothing could stop him from achieving that which he had come to do. He had returned with some freedom fighting business to attend to.

In the meantime, the prince left his friends with instructions that needed to be carried out. He told them that they had much do to on his behalf. He asked them to always love and trust him completely. He also asked them to execute justice on the earth, help to make sick people well, feed the hungry and set the captives free.

Now it was time for the prince to leave, for he had work to do from his new kingdom in Heaven. As the prince left, two angels appeared to his friends saying, 'This same prince who is leaving you now will be back one day soon to take you with him to your happily ever after life.'

And so it was that the prince came, saw, conquered and brought peace to the earth. The prince carried out so many good works that if they were all recorded, one by one in detail, not even the whole world could possibly contain all the books that would be written.

And the people in that land lived in peace and the whole world was given a way to live, happily ever after.

The End

Mirror, mirror on the wall, is God real after all?

In the previous twelve chapters I have endeavoured to tackle some of life's most crippling issues that can lead to a destroyed, or at least damaged, identity. I have written about the problems and then offered some practical solutions. Yes, there is much we can do on our own to change our lives through positive thinking and practical behavioural changes, but the next level in attaining a healthy and most desirable self-esteem is through our spirit being.

I believe that it is this level that will touch the very heart of your innermost need to be loved and to feel valued, and will set you far apart from your problems. This level is knowing your Creator.

Mother Teresa is an amazing example of someone who knew their Creator. With a heart after God and in the most squalid of life's circumstances, she was able to boast of life's great opportunities — a little Heaven on earth. Mother Teresa gave her life to dignifying people and preparing them for eternity, to help them die knowing that they were loved. She did this because she knew her Creator; she therefore knew who she was and understood why she was here. She had an amazing outlook on life. In her own words,

> Life is an opportunity, benefit from it.
> Life is beautiful, admire it.
> Life is bliss, taste it.
> Life is a dream, realise it.
> Life is a challenge, meet it.
> Life is a duty, complete it.
> Life is a game, play it.
> Life is a promise, fulfil it.
> Life is sorrow, overcome it.
> Life is a song, sing it.
> Life is a struggle, accept it.
> Life is a tragedy, confront it.
> Life is an adventure, dare it.
> Life is too precious, do not destroy it.
> Life is life, fight for it.

In this conclusion, I wish to share what I believe will help you ultimately experience this next level in a healthy self-esteem, and what is the secret to my own sense of identity.

I have believed in God and been a practising Christian nearly all of my life. As a small child I was taken every week to Sunday school, then when I was nine years old I was taken with a group of other kids to Randwick Racecourse in Sydney, to hear a man speak. I didn't really know what it was all about, but I can remember this man with very kind eyes, who after he had finished his speech said, 'Come. Come to Jesus.' I may have been only nine years old, but I understood what he was asking and I responded by walking forward to receive Jesus Christ as my Lord and Saviour. My mind may have had trouble comprehending his speech, but my spirit came alive when he talked about how I could have a personal relationship with God. I had been going to Sunday school and learning about Jesus since I was five years old, but I didn't know that I could actually invite Him into my heart and life.

And my life has never been the same again. Turmoil, disappointment, hurt, grief and all kinds of other forms of suffering have come my way, but the difference is that I have a source to tap into for help when I am in despair. No matter what's going on in my life, I am able to live with a peace that surpasses all human understanding. That's God! Peace is not the absence of war, it literally is the presence of God. It is the presence of God in my life that allows me to overcome anxiety and fear, and experience peace and hope.

People are sometimes afraid of God because of how religion has portrayed Him. Some people think He is an intimidating judge, outdated, obsolete, greedy, controlling, powerless — and even that he doesn't exist. That is not the God I know. The God I know is the most loving, caring, freedom-fighting, merciful, generous, kind, thoughtful, powerful person in my life. He knows me even better than I know myself, because He created and loves me. I am who I am today because of Him.

My favourite book and the bestselling book in the world is the Bible. The words within it feed my soul and direct my life. Although many books can help us get to where we want to be, I believe the Bible is the best lifestyle manual available! I can say that I am walking healed and whole in the light of God's Word — the Bible. If you want to get to know your Creator, if you want to really know what God is like and not just know ABOUT Him, then try reading it. It gives the best picture of who He really is and one of the best parts of the Bible that tell us about what our Creator is like, is found in John, chapter 3 verse 16. It says, 'For God so loved the world that he gave his one and only Son, that whoever believes in him shall not perish but have eternal life.' A more modern translation, *The Message*, says, 'This is how much God loved the world: He gave his Son, his one and only Son. And this is why: so that no one need be destroyed; by believing in him, anyone can have a whole and lasting life.'

A controlling, intimidating, powerless or loveless God would not do this. I believe that God is real and Jesus loves you no matter who you are and what you have done. Jesus said that he did not come to judge us, but to save us. Jesus Christ is God's gift to us to rescue us from all the turmoil in our lives, but He doesn't make you choose Him. You can choose to ignore Him and try to cope your way, but His way is so much easier and brings true freedom — all we have to do is turn to Him. It's that easy. The Bible, the mirror of truth in my life, says that if you believe in your heart that Jesus is real and acknowledge Him with your words by telling someone about your decision to follow Him, then you will be saved. Saved!

Being saved not only gives us eternity in Heaven instead of an eternity of darkness and isolation in hell when we die, but it is also about having a free and abundant life while we are here on earth. Being saved is about being able to experience Heaven on earth, as well as Heaven in eternity. It's about being able to go through all the challenges that life brings without being a permanent casualty. Troubles still come, and there will be some scars, but eventually over time they fade, and they don't hurt any more once they are healed. My relationship with God has allowed, and continues to allow, my pain to be healed. You may not have thought about this eternal aspect of your identity. Heaven is the only place that we can experience a true happily ever after life free from pain but I also believe that a genuine relationship with God can grant us elements of Heaven on earth. You can have peace, you can have wholeness, you can have joy, you can have fulfilment, you can enjoy living!

The stories featured at the end of each chapter in this book have been based on real life. These people have not only experienced healing and breakthrough and an improved self-esteem by practical day-to-day decisions and actions, but they also attribute the improvement to their self-esteem and the strength of their identity to their faith in God. They have connected with the reality of the eternity that exists within every human heart.

These people walk in true freedom. They inspire me. Their freedom is enviable and their confidence is real. They are very attractive because they dance like nobody's watching and sing like nobody's listening. They live and love like they've never been hurt — this is true evidence of freedom.

Whenever you are feeling left out, unattractive, stupid, self-conscious, misunderstood, outcast, abused, useless, worthless and forgotten, remember what has been reflected in the Mirror of Truth about you:

> *You are unique*
> *You are beautifully and wonderfully made*
> *You are special*
> *You are priceless*
> *You are valuable*
> *You can be anything you want to be*
> *You are a winner*
> *You are not alone*
> *You are a champion*
> *You are beautiful*
> *You are you!*

Having an eternal perspective, I believe, will help you to make the changes necessary to build a healthy identity because it provides you with the best motivation to do it.

Motivation isn't only about encouraging people to improve for improvement's sake, it's about presenting a powerful reason for immediate action and giving clear responsibility to people for their own life. It is about knowing what is going to move you to action and using that knowledge to create confidence and commitment. Motivation is about painting a vivid and compelling picture of what is possible if you dare to change.

Robert Hriegel and David Brandt in their book *Sacred Cows Make the Best Burgers* give four keys to creating motivation to change things in your life:

1. urgency
2. inspiration
3. ownership
4. rewards.

I have adapted these four keys to self-esteem as follows.

1. Urgency

A sense of urgency can be enough motivation to change something in your life. You can feel bad about yourself and know that you want change, but urgency will give you the motivation to make those changes NOW. Urgency doesn't wait for tomorrow's answers, it doesn't need someone else's permission and its entire energy operates from the thought 'I NEED to do it and I need to do it NOW!' You can help create a sense of urgency by gathering people around you who will motivate you. These people book you into the beauty salon for that facial you have always wanted, the haircut you've always shied away from and they don't listen to you ALWAYS talking about how you are going to change things. They say 'Why wait? Do it now!' They also help you implement a plan to achieve those changes and are mature enough to stop you from becoming unhealthily obsessive about the whole process.

2. Inspiration

Urgency lights the fire. It creates the spark, producing the attitude and atmosphere needed to get you motivated to change. It is urgency that creates an adrenaline burst of action — like when you decided to join the gym perhaps. But this spark will definitely burn out if it is not stoked, and that's where inspiration comes in.

We need a cause, not just a vision for your life. It's not enough for you to feel the need to change, you need direction on where the change is going to take you. You need to aspire to greater heights and go beyond previous limitations. You need passion and enthusiasm for your future. Who do you want to be and how are you going to become that person?

3. Ownership

Ownership is very attractive, as it not only gives you control over your own destiny but you reap all the benefits your life produces. Giving responsibility of your life and self-esteem over to your circumstances is throwing away a great opportunity for you to reap these ownership rewards in your life. You need to be empowered with information and then be responsible with your actions; then you will be personally accountable for the results you receive.

4. Rewards

The best way to motivate you to get excited about your plans to change is by focusing on the rewards. If you sow well, you will reap well. If you sow negatively, you will reap negatively. It's an eternal reward principle. There are different types of rewards — some external, some internal and some eternal.

▶ External: *Body*
  If you eat properly, exercise regularly and take care of your physical appearance, you will reap external rewards, such as great health.

▶ Internal: *Soul*
  If you address areas of your mind (thinking), will (that potentially stubborn side of you) and emotions that may be holding you back from who you are really meant to be, then you will reap internal rewards, such as being in control of your thoughts and emotions.

▶ Eternal: *Spirit*
If you take your spirit, or the condition of your heart, and connect it with eternity, with God, then you will reap eternal rewards, which means eternal life.

The motivation for making these changes should come from within. When you are really ready for change, the sense of urgency should lead to inspiration then personal responsibility (ownership), and it is then that you will reap great rewards.

As I have said before, the truth that leads to change is confronting. You must be prepared to declare war on those things that are enemies to your self-esteem and that are preventing you from living a life of true freedom.

Where there is a lack of freedom, there is usually a lack of self-esteem and the absence of true identity. In war, the sacrifice of life will result in the freedom of people, so too in life is pain almost always the price of freedom and liberty.

You may feel as though your life began downtrodden, without hope of a better future, or you may have grown up in an environment of fear and uncertainty, living in a state of oppression. It is time to stand up, declare war and fight for your freedom.

War is the time to fight and not the time to bow down to the enemy. Your enemy may be an eating disorder, or a battle with the mirror over your body image, or an addiction, bad habit, poverty, or a destructive relationship. Whatever the enemy of your life, you need to fight for freedom. The enemy will not go away — you can choose to ignore it but it will still be there as its eradication does not depend on you choosing not to see it; its death comes in you seeing it and dealing with it — just as in real war. That results in true freedom. Are people who wander around ignoring the enemy in countries that are war torn are truly free? No, true freedom comes from removing the enemy, from dealing with and not ignoring it.

True freedom is also not simply a matter of doing your own thing. True freedom exists within healthy boundaries.

If your freedom is important to you right now, look up at the sky and dream about growing wings to fly. Your freedom is a major key in the healthy development of your self-esteem. It will allow you to feel confident and empowered and to live the life you were created to live.

Remember that a desirable life is one of freedom, not perfection. Take some of these freedom steps and step into a future that you were designed for.

1.   Believe and have faith in your heart that you can and will be free.
2.   Practise positive thinking, seeing and doing.
3.   Don't allow your thinking to be boxed in and confined.
4.   Write a list of what you want freedom from.
5.   Set some healthy boundaries for your life, and don't cross them.
6.   Look up at the sky and see how expansive your world of opportunity is.
7.   Next time you see a bird flying, remind yourself that you can do the same, here on earth.
8.   Be kind to people in your world and allow them to be free in your presence.
9.   Fight for what is good and right, without ever hurting anyone else.
10. Never, ever, ever, ever give up until you are free.

It is my desire that having read this book you will have gained the confidence and tools to shake off self-consciousness, develop a genuine sense of who you really are, and enjoy an inner confidence that will enable you to live out your dreams.

To love ourselves and to love other people properly, we need to be confident. The person with a healthy self-esteem will treat others with respect. To love yourself isn't to be vain or self-indulgent, but rather to have a healthy appreciation for who you are and how you are made.

Stand tall, hold your head up and enjoy your new life of freedom. Know the TRUTH and the TRUTH will set you free.

You are worth it!

Mirror, Mirror

Mirror, mirror on the wall,
Who's the fairest of them all?
You are, of course!
Why can't you see?
Just be the best that you can be.
Discover the truth inside my frame,
And see your worth and value named.
Hope, truth, grace and freedom bound
The true you is set at last to be found.

Action Plan

Creative Journalling

It's my life

For us to like and feel comfortable with ourselves, it is important that we receive constant positive input. Children look to their parents to build their egos and self-esteem, so that they can feel valuable and important. However, sometimes parents become so busy and overwhelmed by life's pressures, they may not say or do the best things to build the self-esteem of their children, and they may well be struggling with their own emotional problems and lack of self-esteem. There is no doubt that lack of positive feedback and reinforcement undermines how we feel about ourselves as we are growing up.

If we are continually corrected and told what is wrong with us and in need of improvement, our sense of identity will not be given the boost we need. Negative reinforcement is fertile ground for low self-esteem, and the reality is we all need encouragement and reassurance. We need to know that we are thought of as valued, capable, worthwhile human beings.

To help log your journey of building your self-esteem, I suggest you keep a journal to start expressing yourself — your successes, achievements, goals, dreams and hopes for your life. As you put pen to paper, I believe you will begin to feel a real sense of ownership for your life and growing self-esteem.

Journals are powerful as they keep account of your life. One of my friends keeps a journal and regularly writes about things that have changed his life. One such time was while he was on a flight from London:

> *Reflection … I've met God today … and I've met myself. On the inside. It's been as if I've been afraid to really meet myself, to look in my eyes. To look IN my eyes. To see my soul. Always when the thought 'Who am I?' came up I ran away from it. But today, when I was in the bathroom on the plane looking at myself in the mirror, I did it — I didn't run away. I just stood there, to face me. The quietness, no one else but me, and God! Because at that moment I felt His presence just come and fill that room. I felt the revelation of who I really am. A man, a spirit and soul, and God has given me this body as a 'shell' while I'm here on earth. He knew me before I was made in my mother's womb.*
>
> *As I stood there I started smiling. All fear disappeared and for the first time in my life I saw Jesus through my own reflection. The light! I just stood there … there was just me and God. Full freedom.*

I know that after this encounter, my friend will never be the same again.

21-Day Creative Journalling

As it generally takes three weeks to break and make a habit, I have devised a 21-day journal for you to follow to increase your self-esteem.

I suggest you begin by starting with just one poor habit that is damaging your self-esteem and work on that habit until the twenty-one days are up. Then, on the twenty-second day, start with the next bad habit and replace it with the opposite, positive action and create for yourself a brand new good habit. You may have many bad habits that have lowered your self-esteem, such as:

◗ negative self-talk
◗ nail biting and lip biting
◗ poor thoughts about yourself
◗ fear of taking risks
◗ presuming the worst.

I have created twenty-one keys for you to follow on the twenty-one days you work at breaking any negative identity cycle you may be living with. Try these suggestions and see what happens. There are many more things that you can do. Let me know how these things work out for you — I would love to hear your story. As you follow each day and keep a journal, your progress — as you challenge yourself and change — will encourage you to continually work towards a healthier self-esteem and identity.

Day 1
All of our efforts are a success if we learn from them.
What effort have you made today towards developing a healthier self-esteem?

Day 2
Courage comes from trying something new.
What new thing have you tried today?

Day 3
You have not because you ask not.
What do you want out of life today, next year and by the time you retire — relationally, emotionally, spiritually, financially? Set some short- and long-term goals.

Day 4
Being able to enjoy your own company is great.
What good things have you learned about yourself when you are on your own?

Day 5

Most people aren't necessarily doing better than you.
Make an honest list of all the people who are genuinely doing better than you and write down why.

Day 6

Accepting yourself the way you are is a great place to start.
List everything that you cannot change about yourself and include a positive comment about each.

Day 7

Opportunities happen all day long, and are nothing to be afraid of.
What were the opportunities you took today?

Day 8

You may feel that you are not as attractive, intelligent and well-off as most people.
List at least three positive qualities you have in relation to your looks, your intellect and your finances.

Day 9

Listen to your inner voice.
What positive things did your inner voice have to say today?

Day 10

If you sow energy, you will reap energy.
Make an exercise plan and make it part of your life, starting from today.

Day 11

A healthy eating plan will help make you feel fantastic.
Find a great eating plan suitable to your lifestyle and make the necessary changes starting from today.

Day 12

We all have reason to be proud of some things in our lives.
What are you proud of?

Day 13
Love and respect thrive when reciprocated.
How did you show love and respect today?

Day 14
Friendliness attracts friends.
What positive thing did you do today to attract a friend?

Day 15
The thoughts that you feed yourself on a regular basis strongly influence your self-esteem.
List the positive thoughts you had about yourself today.

Day 16
You are more successful than you think.
Boost your self-esteem by making a list of your successes.

Day 17
We can all improve who we are.
What did I do today to improve myself?

Day 18
You won the sperm race from around 600 million competitors!
Write down everything that you have won at, including your conception and birth.

Day 19
Everyone's good at something.
List all of your gifts, talents and strengths.

Day 20
Everyone needs encouragement to flourish.
Write down the encouraging comments you received and gave today.

Day 21

Try and try again and don't give up until you have a breakthrough.
Write down everything you have had a breakthrough in, after not giving up.

Your self-esteem journal will prove a useful tool if you are honest, consistent and kind to yourself. In due course, you will reap the benefits of a healthier self-esteem. Now that you have built up a list of positive commentary about your life, read it often. Read it when you are up, and you'll feel even better. Read it when you are down and you'll get a boost (and a kick in the pants for any negativity that may have crept in!). As your healthy self-esteem grows, and it will grow more and more each day, keep writing in your journal and enjoy your new life — you deserve it.

Just as I know that my friend will never be the same again after his 'plane revelation', I know that this can be true for you too as you allow the processes in this book to change your life.

My Identity Creed

I value myself for seeing the positive lessons in what appeared to be a negative situation.

I value myself for doing what was fearful. I did it afraid.

I value myself for getting out of a bad situation by making some difficult decisions.

I value myself for making positive changes in my life.

I value myself for being willing to remove unnecessary walls and to erect safe fences in my life.

I value myself for risking new things.

I value myself for engaging in a healing process.

I value myself for letting go of the past.

I value myself for getting this far on the journey and not giving up.

I value myself because I am fearfully and wonderfully made.

I value God for never giving up on me.

DIANNE WILSON

CONTACT DIANNE VIA

www.diannewilson.com

An Expert Opinion

Beliefs and Behaviour

What the Doctor Says

I met with psychologist Dr Vivienne Riches when researching this book. I found what she had to say very valuable and helpful and so I have included it for your interest.

In her practice Dr Riches uses a method called cognitive behavioural therapy to help people with poor self-esteem and body image issues. Behavioural therapy is a method previously recognised as useful, and more recently a blend of behavioural and cognitive therapy has proven valid.

Original Behavioural Model

Based on the premise that a change in consequences/results leads to a change in behaviour; it does not challenge the beliefs and therefore won't break some cycles.

A	B	C
Antecedent	**Behaviour**	**Result**
E.g. a situation where two kids have one toy	One child hits the other to obtain the toy	The one who hits gets away with it!

Cognitive Behavioural Model

Enables you to change the result, and end the cycle, by challenging the beliefs.

A
Antecedent
E.g. a situation where two kids have one toy

B1
Beliefs
Automatic thought of one child to hit the other.
They believe if they don't hit, they won't get the toy. Their evaluation is based on irrational beliefs: 'If I don't hit, I won't get the toy', or, 'It's OK to hit to get what I want. I want what I want now.'

B2
Feelings
The hitting child is challenged about their auto response, and given 'healthy' options to obtain the toy or even to wait or share a toy.

B3
Behaviour
The hitting child understands it is wrong to hit to get their own way, and so their thinking, feeling and behaviour change.

C
Result
The one who hits doesn't get away with it!

Through cognitive behavioural therapy, repetitive destructive patterns can be found and challenged. This is achieved by firstly understanding that there is a problem, rather than living in denial or ignoring issues, hoping that they will go away, because they won't. The next step is to get in touch with the irrational thoughts and learn how to challenge them.

Dr Riches says that the downside of cognitive behavioural therapy is that it doesn't highlight the human will. She believes that to activate the will is to activate the end solution. In other words, all the therapy in the world, be it behavioural or cognitive behavioural, won't lead anyone into freedom without their will being involved.

To activate a person's will, they must first understand that they can choose to do this. Many people don't understand that they are fully in charge of their will. Where there is a will, there is absolutely a way — to freedom! Once the person's will is activated, a new realm of possibilities is unlocked where previously the destructive and repetitious behaviour would have prevailed.

Exercising the will enables people to overcome habits of negative thinking and behaviour. This cannot be achieved by force, it can only be achieved by the activation of one's will.

For someone who has been engaging in destructive thinking and behaviour for many years, the process of activating their will in a positive sense is usually difficult to establish. The way forward is to start by speaking kindly to oneself and to concentrate on one kind thought and word a day until the will begins to 'kick in'.

In twenty-one years of practice, Dr Riches has spent many thousands of hours counselling patients and she believes wholeheartedly in therapy that covers not only behaviour and thinking, but also the spiritual condition of a person's life. In her practice she has only ever come across two patients who weren't interested in the health of their spiritual condition. She believes that the spiritual condition relates to issues of the heart and relationships, and is at the core of one's belief system.

When asked about how she would take someone with low self-esteem to a healthy self-esteem, Dr Riches mentioned the following three steps:

▶ behavioural
▶ cognitive
▶ spiritual.

Dr Riches usually starts talking to people about their childhood, because most times this is where the belief system is established: through the family of origin and schooling. Then, the process covers understanding how you feel about yourself, the world, and coping with life.

Beliefs are laid down in pain, so conditions such as abuse and eating disorders are at times the most difficult to deal with. The root problem is 'beliefs about who they are and how they think the world works'. People want to be happy, to belong, to be loved, and they also want to be competent in dealing with their lives.

Depression is also an area that Dr Riches deals with on a regular basis. This is addressed by challenging beliefs, because the pain is not necessarily from a person's reality, but from what they believe about their reality. Depression causes chemical imbalance in the brain and this robs people of the ability to choose, and sometimes they choose 'death' by default. It is often misunderstood as sadness, but it's actually a lack of drive or energy and the ability to choose life.

People in the twentieth century often suffered from anxiety, but now in the twenty-first century, people suffer more from stress and depression. People who are perfectionists usually have irrational beliefs about themselves and situations, which therefore result in feelings of worthlessness and shame.

Effective treatment of depression is through these steps:

▶ diagnosis by a GP, psychiatrist or psychologist
▶ medication (usually short-term)
▶ therapy (identifying self destructive patterns and challenging irrational thinking regarding self worth)
▶ positive thinking (personal responsibility).

Further Reading

Nancy Alcorn, *Mercy for Eating Disorders*, Providence House Publishers, Tennessee, 2003.

Dr Dan B Allender, *The Wounded Heart*, Crusade for World Revival (CWR), Surrey, UK, 1991.

The Amplified Bible, The Lockman Foundation, California.

Australian Bureau of Statistics, *Australian Social Trends*, ACT, Australia.

Australian Bureau of Statistics, *Family Characteristics, Australia*, ACT, Australia.

Australian Bureau of Statistics, *Health of Australians*, ACT, Australia.

Australian Bureau of Statistics, *Marriages and Divorces in Australia*, ACT, Australia.

Philip Baker, *Secrets of Super Achievers*, Webb & Partners, Perth, 1997.

Dr Aaron T Beck, *Love is Never Enough*, HarperCollins, New York, 1989.

Eileen Bradbury, *Counselling People with Disfigurement*, British Psychological Society, 1996.

Dr Harriet B Braiker, *The Disease to Please*, McGraw-Hill Books, New York, 2001.

Bob Burns & Tom Whiteman, *The Fresh Start Divorce Recovery Workbook*, Thoms Nelson Publishers, Tennessee, 1992.

Dr Henry Cloud, *Changes That Heal*, Zondervan Publishing House, Michigan, 1993.

Dr Henry Cloud & Dr John Townsend, *Boundaries*, Zondervan Publishing House, Michigan, 1992.

Gary Collins, *Counselling Families After Divorce*, Word Books, Texas, 1994.

Brangien Davis, *What's Real, What's Ideal: Overcoming a Negative Body Image*, The Rosen Publishing Group, New York, 1999.

Dr James Dobson, *Love Must Be Tough*, Word Books, Texas, 1983.

Douglas R Flather, *The Resource Guide for Christian Counsellors*, Baker Books, Michigan, 1995.

Sarah Ford, *Teenagers Growing Up and Out*, Sun-Herald, Sydney, 5 October 1997.

Nancy Friday, *Jealousy*, M Evans & Co. Inc., New York, 1997.

Hillsong Emerge Australia, *Shine Manual*, Hillsong Church, Sydney, 2004.

Tim LaHaye & Bob Philips, *Anger is a Choice*, Zanderras, Michigan, 2002.

Gregory Landsman, *The Balance of Beauty*, Hill of Content Publishing
Company, Melbourne, 1995.

Cathy Ann Matthews, *Breaking Through*, Albatross Books, Sydney, 1990.

Cynthia Rowland McClure, *The Monster Within*, Baker Book House
Company, Michigan, 1984.

Dr Phillip C McGraw, *Self Matters*, Simon & Schuster Source, New York,
2001.

Joyce Meyer, *The Root of Rejection*, Harrison House Publishers,
Oklahoma, 1995.

Mission Australia, *Mission Australia's 2002 Fact Sheet on Youth Suicide*,
Sydney, 2002.

M Gary Neuman & Patricia Romanowski, *Helping Your Kids Cope with
Divorce the Sandcastles Way*, Random House, New York, 1998.

The New International Version Bible, Zondervan Publishing House,
Michigan, 2002.

Merrell Noden, *Oprah Winfrey*, Time Inc., Bishop Books, New York,
1999.

Jessie H. O'Neill, *The Golden Ghetto: The Psychology of Affluence*, The
Affluenza Project, Milwaukee, Hazelden, 1996.

Eugene H. Peterson, *The Message Bible*, NavPress Publishing Group,
Colorado, 2002.

Dr Mary Pipher, *Eating Disorders*, Vermilion Books, London, 1997.

Kay Marie Porterfield, *Violent Voices: 12 Steps to Freedom from Emotional
and Verbal Abuse*, Health Communications, Florida, 1989.

Ayn Rand & Peter Schwartz, *Return of the Primitive: The Anti-Industrial
Resolution*, Plume Books, USA, 1999.

Louise Sauvage, *Louise Sauvage: My Story*, HarperCollins Publishers,
Sydney, 2002.

Serious Issues in School Survey, The Age, Melbourne, 2 July 1999.

Charles R. Swindoll, *The Grace Awakening*, Word Publishing, Texas, 1996.

Joni Eareckson Tada, *Secret Strength*, Multnomah Press, Oregon, 1989.

Doreen Trust, *Overcoming Disfigurement*, Sterling Pub. Co., 1986.

Janine Turner, *Home is Where the Hurt is*, Thorsons Publishing Group,
Northamptonshire, UK, 1989.

Dianne Barker Wilson, *Back in Shape After Baby*, HarperCollins Publishers, Sydney, 2001.

Dianne Barker Wilson, *Fat Free Forever!*, Random House Publishers, Sydney, 1996.

Dianne Barker Wilson, *Easy Exercise for Everyone*, Random House Publishers, Sydney, 1997.

Dianne Barker Wilson, *Fat Free Forever Cookbook*, Random House Publishers, Sydney, 1999.

Dianne Barker Wilson, *Fat Free Forever 101 Tips*, Random House Publishers, Sydney, 1999.

Permissions

Page 146: Extract from *Captain Corelli's Mandolin* by Louis de Bernières published by Vintage (May 1995). Used by permission of The Random House Group Limited.

Page 170: 'Time Tested Beauty Tips' — Reprinted by permission of SLL/Sterling Lord Literistic, Inc. Copyright 1973 by Samuel Levenson.

Page 200: Eleanor Roosevelt quote — Reproduced with the permission of HarperCollins Papers Rare Book and Manuscript Library, Columbia University.

Page 209: Material by Janine Turner — From *Home is Where the Heart Is* © Janine Turner 1989, published by Thorsons Publishers.

Page 213: Material by Janine Turner — From *Home is Where the Heart Is* © Janine Turner 1989, published by Thorsons Publishers.

Page 233: Bryce Courtenay quote — Reproduced with the kind permission of Bryce Courtenay.

Page 242: 'Our deepest fear ... liberates others' from *A Return to Love* by Marianne Williamson. Copyright © 1992 by Marianne Williamson. Reprinted by permission of HarperCollins Publishers, Inc. Portions reprinted from *A Course in Miracles*. Copyright © 1975 by Foundation for Inner Peace, Inc. All chapter openings are from *A Course in Miracles*.

Page 260: Material by John Maxwell — Reprinted by permission of Thomas Nelson Inc., Nashville, TN, from the book entitled *Failing Forward*, © 2000 by Maxwell Motivation Inc. All rights reserved.

Page 261: Michael Jordan quote — Reproduced with the permission of HarperCollins Publishers, Inc. from *I Can't Accept Not Trying* by Michael Jordan and photographs by Sandro Miller. Copyright © 1994 by Rare Air, Ltd. Text © 1994 by Michael Jordan. Photographs © 1994 by Sandro Miller.

Page 287: Material by Charles R Swindoll — Reproduced from *The Grace Awakening* by Charles R Swindoll © 1990, 1996 by Charles R Swindoll, with the permission of Thomas Nelson, Inc.

Page 304: Material by Robert Kriegel and David Brandt — Reproduced from *Sacred Cows Make the Best Burgers* © Robert Kriegel and David Brandt 1996, with the permission of HarperCollins Publishers.

Help

Beyond Blue
National Depression Initiative
50 Burwood Road
PO Box 6100,
Hawthorn VIC 3122
Tel: (03) 9810 6100
Website: www.beyondblue.org.au

Eating Disorders Foundation
PO Box 532
Willoughby NSW 2068
Tel: (02) 9412 4499
Website: www.edf.org.au

Hillsong Health Centre
Suite 5 Mileto House
2–4 Old Castle Hill Road
Castle Hill NSW 2154
Australia
Tel: (02) 9680 4700
Email: healthcentre@hillsong.com
Website: www.hillsong.com

Kids Help Line
PO Box 376
Red Hill QLD 4059
Australia
Tel: (07) 3369 1588
Hotline: 1800 55 1800
Email: admin@kidshelp.com.au
Website: www.kidshelp.com.au

Life Line
Telephone Counselling
24 Hour Hotline: 131 114
Website: www.lifeline.org.au

Mercy Ministries Australia
PO Box 1537
Castle Hill NSW 1765
Australia
Tel: (02) 9659 4180
Toll Free 1800 011 537
Email: info@mercyministries.com.au
Website: www.mercyministries.com.au

Mission Australia
National Office
4–10 Campbell Street
Sydney NSW 2000
Australia
Tel: (02) 9219 2000
24 Hour Hotline: 1300 886 999
Website: www.mission.com.au

Salvation Army
Headquarters
140 Elizabeth Street
Sydney South NSW 2000
Australia
24 Hour Hotline: 1300 36 36 22
www.salvationarmy.org.au
Teen Challenge
40 Hector Street
Chester Hill NSW 2076
Australia
Tel: (02) 9644 7737
Email: info@tcnsw.org
Website: www.tcnsw.org

Relationships Australia
Head Office
15 Napier Close
Deakin ACT 2600
Australia
Tel: (02) 6281 3600
Freecall: 1300 364 277
Website: www.relationships.com.au

HillsongLIFE
188 Young Street
Waterloo
Sydney
Australia
Tel: (02) 8853 5353
Website: www.hillsong.com/hillsonglife